D0142549

SPORT
IN
AMERICA

Recent Titles in
Contributions to the Study of Popular Culture

Tarzan and Tradition: Classical Myth in Popular Literature
Erling B. Holtsmark

Common Culture and the Great Tradition: The Case for Renewal
Marshall W. Fishwick

Concise Histories of American Popular Culture
M. Thomas Inge, editor

Ban Johnson: Czar of Baseball
Eugene C. Murdock

Putting Dell on the Map: A History of the Dell Paperbacks
William H. Lyles

Behold the Mighty Wurlitzer: The History of the Theatre Pipe Organ
John W. Landon

Mighty Casey: All-American
Eugene C. Murdock

The Baker Street Reader: Cornerstone Writings about Sherlock Holmes
Philip A. Shreffler, editor

Dark Cinema: American *Film Noir* in Cultural Perspective
Jon Tuska

Seven Pillars of Popular Culture
Marshall W. Fishwick

The American West in Film: Critical Approaches to the Western
Jon Tuska

SPORT
IN
AMERICA

New Historical
Perspectives

EDITED BY
DONALD SPIVEY

Contributions to the Study of Popular Culture, Number 12

Greenwood Press
Westport, Connecticut · London, England

WITHDRAWN

MOUNT ST. MARY'S
COLLEGE
EMMITSBURG, MARYLAND

Library of Congress Cataloging in Publication Data

Main entry under title:

Sport in America.

(Contributions to the study of popular culture,
ISSN 0198-9871 ; no. 12)
  Bibliography: p.
  Includes index.
  Contents: Horses and gentlemen : the cultural
significance of gambling among the gentry of Virginia /
by T. H. Breen—Leisure time on the southern plantation :
the slaves' respite from constant toil, 1810–1860 /
by David K. Wiggins—Quantification and sport : the
American jockey club, 1866–1867 : a collective bibliography / by Melvin L. Adelman—[etc.]

  1. Sports—United States—History—Addresses, essays,
lectures.   2. Sports—Social aspects—United States—
History—Addresses, essays, lectures.   I. Spivey, Donald.
II. Series.
GV583.S6824   1985   796'.0973   84-25265
ISBN 0-313-24705-6 (lib. bdg.)

OCLC: 11496744

Copyright © 1985 by Donald Spivey

All rights reserved. No portion of this book may be
reproduced, by any process or technique, without the
express written consent of the publisher.

Library of Congress Catalog Card Number: 84-25265
ISBN: 0-313-24705-6
ISSN: 0198-9871

First published in 1985

Greenwood Press
A division of Congressional Information Service, Inc.
88 Post Road West
Westport, Connecticut 06881

Printed in the United States of America

10 9 8 7 6 5 4 3 2 1

Copyright Acknowledgments

Grateful acknowledgment is given for permission to reprint the following articles:

T. H. Breen, "Horses and Gentlemen: The Cultural Significance of Gambling Among
the Gentry of Virginia," *The William and Mary Quarterly,* Vol. XXXIV (April 1977),
pp. 239–57. Reprinted by permission of the author.

Mark Naison, "Lefties and Righties: The Communist Party and Sports During the Great Depression," *Radical America,* Vol. 13, No. 4 (1979), pp. 47–59. © 1979 *Radical America.* Reprinted by permission of the publisher.

Stephanie L. Twin, "Women and Sport," from Stephanie L. Twin, ed., *Out of the Bleachers: Writings on Women and Sport* (Old Westbury, N.Y.: The Feminist Press, 1979), pp. xv–xli. Copyright © 1979 by The Feminist Press. Reprinted by permission of the publisher.

Contents

Preface   ix

I. Horses and Gentlemen: The Cultural Significance of
Gambling Among the Gentry of Virginia   3
T. H. Breen

II. Leisure Time on the Southern Plantation: The Slaves'
Respite from Constant Toil, 1810–1860   25
David K. Wiggins

III. Quantification and Sport: The American Jockey Club,
1866–1867; A Collective Biography   51
Melvin L. Adelman

IV. Baseball in the Small Ohio Community, 1865–1900   77
Carl M. Becker and Richard H. Grigsby

V. In the Ring and Out: Professional Boxing in
New York, 1896–1920   95
Steven A. Riess

VI. Lefties and Righties: The Communist Party and
Sports During the Great Depression   129
Mark Naison

VII. White America Views Jack Johnson, Joe Louis,
and Muhammad Ali   145
Frederic Cople Jaher

VIII. Women and Sport   193
       Stephanie L. Twin

  IX. Sports Violence and Social Crisis   219
       Peter Levine and Peter Vinten-Johansen

   X. Black Consciousness and Olympic Protest
      Movement, 1964–1980   239
       Donald Spivey

      Bibliographical Essay   263

      Index   265

      About the Contributors   281

Preface

Sport is a major force throughout the world. In the United States of America, it is a business enterprise of immense proportions. It is amateurs and professionals, semipros and little leaguers, weekend warriors and occasional joggers, escapism on a Saturday or Sunday afternoon, a happening, and for some the measure of life itself. Why, then, has such an important topic been relegated to second-class citizenship in the scholarly community? For far too long the history of sport was left in the hands of well-intentioned laymen whose conception of sport history was knowing batting averages, points per game, yards gained, and records held; in short, who did what, where, and when in a particular field of athletics. The writing of sport history faired only slightly better. It has been dominated by biographies and autobiographies of former players and has too often been simply anecdotal in approach.

In recent years, however, the study of sport has made important advances. Scholars, serious about the subject, began exploring the many dimensions of sport from political and economic to social and cultural. In 1972, academicians from every discipline banded together to form the North American Society for Sport History, an organization devoted to the inquiry into sport and its impact on society. Further indications that the field is coming of age are the annual meetings of the Organization of American Historians and the American Historical Association over the last ten years, which have routinely included sessions on the history of sport. Despite the general recognition and respect the discipline has received in the past few years, there remain a sizable number of scholars who steadfastly refuse to accept the legitimacy of sport history, who question the quality of the work being done in the field and the importance of the subject altogether. This anthology is recommended for that group of skeptics. I had two primary concerns or criteria for the selection of essays to be included in this volume: Does the essay represent the best in the area of sport history and does it offer fresh insight into the field? Hence, I sought out scholars who were trained in the discipline of history and who were doing stimulating and innovative research on the subject of sport. Most of the essays presented here were written especially for this collection. Several previously published pieces are included because of their pioneering quality and sustained freshness of approach. The collection is not inclusive. I made no effort to cover all sports played in America. My concern was with the significance of sport and with quality, not quantity.

I have organized the essays chronologically because they give insights into American society at various stages in its history. The essays illuminate aspects of the American social structure and cultural value system. T. H. Breen, "Horses and Gentlemen," and Melvin Adelman, "Quantification and Sport," show how sport reinforces and reflects upper-class values, life, and distance from lower classes. Frederic Cople Jaher ("White America Views Jack Johnson, Joe Louis, and Muhammad Ali"), Donald Spivey ("Black Consciousness and Olympic Protest Movement"), David K. Wiggins ("Leisure Time on the Southern Plantation"), and Mark Naison ("Lefties and Righties") discuss race relations and racism in sport. Steven A. Riess, "In the Ring and Out," and Spivey, Jaher, and Naison explore the interaction of sport and politics. Riess shows the role that the profit motive plays in sport, as does Jaher. Big-city and small-town life are examined by Carl M. Becker and Richard H. Grigsby in "Baseball in the Small Ohio Community." Stephanie L. Twin ("Women and Sport") examines sexism and the role of women. Peter Levine and Peter Vinten-Johansen ("Sports Violence and Social Crisis") analyze the impact of American attitudes of violence as they apply to sport and as sport provides a perspective upon American violence.

It is our hope that this collection will help stimulate interest and research in the field of sport history.

SPORT
IN
AMERICA

I

Horses and Gentlemen: The Cultural Significance of Gambling Among the Gentry of Virginia

T. H. Breen

In the fall of 1686 Durand of Dauphiné, a French Huguenot, visited the capital of colonial Virginia. Durand regularly recorded in a journal what he saw and heard, providing one of the few firsthand accounts of late seventeenth-century Virginia society that has survived to the present day. When he arrived in Jamestown the House of Burgesses was in session. "I saw there fine-looking men," he noted, "sitting in judgment booted and with belted sword." But to Durand's surprise, several of these Virginia gentlemen "started gambling" soon after dinner, and it was not until midnight that one of the players noticed the Frenchman patiently waiting for the contest to end. The Virginian—obviously a veteran of long nights at the gaming table—advised Durand to go to bed. "For, said he, 'it is quite possible that we shall be here all night,' and in truth I found them still playing the next morning."[1]

The event Durand witnessed was not unusual. In late seventeenth- and early eighteenth-century Virginia, gentlemen spent a good deal of time gambling. During this period, in fact, competitive gaming involving high stakes became a distinguishing characteristic of gentry culture. Whenever the great planters congregated, someone inevitably produced a deck of cards, a pair of dice, or a backgammon board; and quarter-horse racing was a regular event throughout the colony. Indeed, these men hazarded money and tobacco on almost any proposition in which there was an element of chance. Robert Beverley, a member of one of Virginia's most prominent families, made a wager "with the gentlemen of the country" that if he could produce seven hundred gallons of wine on his own plantation, they would pay him the handsome sum of one thousand guineas. Another leading planter offered six-to-one odds that Alexander Spotswood could not procure a commission as the colony's governor. And in 1671 one disgruntled gentleman asked a court of law to award him his winnings from a bet concerning "a Servant maid." The case of this suspect-sounding wager—unfortunately not described in greater detail—dragged on until the colony's highest court ordered the loser to pay the victor a thousand pounds of tobacco.[2]

The great planters' passion for gambling, especially on quarter-horse racing, coincided with a period of far-reaching social change in Virginia. Before the mid–1680s constant political unrest, servant risings both real and threatened, plant-cutting riots, and even a full-scale civil war had plagued the colony. But by the end of the century Virginia had achieved internal peace. Several elements contributed to the growth of social tranquility. First, by 1700 the ruling gentry were united as they had never been before. The great planters of the seventeenth century had been for the most part aggressive English immigrants. They fought among themselves for political and social dominance, and during Bacon's Rebellion in 1676 various factions within the gentry attempted to settle their differences on the battlefield. By the end of the century, however, a sizable percentage of the Virginia gentry, perhaps a majority, had been born in the colony. The members of this native-born elite—one historian calls them a "creole elite"—cooperated more frequently to unite in resistance against a series of interfering royal governors such as Thomas Lord Culpeper, Francis Nicholson, and Alexander Spotswood. After Bacon's Rebellion the leading planters— the kind of men whom Durand watched gamble the night away—successfully consolidated their control over Virginia's civil, military, and ecclesiastical institutions. They monopolized the most important offices; they patented the best lands.[3]

A second and even more far-reaching element in the creation of this remarkable solidarity among the gentry was the shifting racial composition of the plantation labor force. Before the 1680s the planters had relied on large numbers of white indentured servants to cultivate Virginia's sole export crop, tobacco. These impoverished, often desperate servants disputed their masters' authority and on several occasions resisted colonial rulers with force of arms. In part because of their dissatisfaction with the indenture system, and in part because changes in the international slave trade made it easier and cheaper for Virginians to purchase black laborers, the major planters increasingly turned to Africans. The blacks' cultural disorientation made them less difficult to control than the white servants. Large-scale collective violence such as Bacon's Rebellion and the 1682 plant-cutting riots consequently declined markedly. By the beginning of the eighteenth century Virginia had been transformed into a relatively peaceful, biracial society in which a few planters exercised almost unchallenged hegemony over both their slaves and their poorer white neighbors.[4]

The growth of gambling among the great planters during a period of significant social change raises important questions not only about gentry values but also about the social structure of late seventeenth-century Virginia. Why did gambling, involving high stakes, become so popular among the gentlemen at precisely this time? Did it reflect gentry values or have symbolic connotations for the people living in this society? Did this activity serve a social function, contributing in some manner to the maintenance of group cohesion? Why did quarter-horse racing, in particular, become a gentry sport? And finally, did public displays such as this somehow reinforce the great planters' social and political dominance?

In part, of course, gentlemen laid wagers on women and horses simply because they enjoyed the excitement of competition. Gambling was a recreation, like a good meal among friends or a leisurely hunt in the woods—a pleasant pastime when hard-working planters got together. Another equally acceptable explanation for the gentry's fondness for gambling might be the transplanting of English social mores. Certainly, the upper classes in the mother country loved betting for high stakes, and it is possible that the all-night cardgames and the frequent horse races were staged attempts by a provincial gentry to transform itself into a genuine landed aristocracy. While both views possess merit, neither is entirely satisfactory. The great planters of Virginia presumably could have favored less risky forms of competition. Moreover, even though several planters deliberately emulated English social styles, the widespread popularity of gambling among the gentry indicates that this type of behavior may have had deeper, more complex cultural roots than either of these explanations would suggest.[5]

In many societies competitive gaming is a device by which the par-

ticipants transform abstract cultural values into observable social behavior. In his now-classic analysis of the Balinese cockfight Clifford
Geertz describes contests for extremely high stakes as intense social
dramas. These battles not only involve the honor of important villagers
and their kin groups but also reflect in symbolic form the entire Balinese social structure. Far from being a simple pastime, betting on cocks
turns out to be an expression of the way the Balinese perceive social
reality. The rules of the fight, the patterns of wagering, the reactions
of winners and losers—all these elements help us to understand more
profoundly the totality of Balinese culture.[6]

The Virginia case is analogous to the Balinese. When the great planter
staked his money and tobacco on a favorite horse or spurred a sprinter
to victory, he displayed some of the central elements of gentry culture—its competitiveness, individualism, and materialism. In fact,
competitive gaming was for many gentlemen a means of translating a
particular set of values into action, a mechanism for expressing a loose
but deeply felt bundle of ideas and assumptions about the nature of
society. The quarter-horse races of Virginia were intense contests involving personal honor, elaborate rules, heavy betting, and wide community interest; and just as the cockfight opens up hidden dimensions
of Balinese culture, gentry gambling offers an opportunity to improve
our understanding of the complex interplay between cultural values and
social behavior in Virginia.

Gambling reflected core elements of late seventeenth- and early
eighteenth-century gentry values. From diaries, letters, and travel accounts we discover that despite their occasional cooperation in political affairs, Virginia gentlemen placed extreme emphasis upon personal
independence. This concern may in part have been the product of the
colony's peculiar settlement patterns. The great planters required immense tracts of fresh land for their tobacco. Often thousands of acres
in size, their plantations were scattered over a broad area from the Po-
tomac River to the James. The dispersed planters lived in their ''Great
Houses'' with their families and slaves, and though they saw friends
from time to time, they led for the most part isolated, routine lives.
An English visitor in 1686 noted with obvious disapproval that ''Their
Plantations run over vast Tracts of Ground . . . whereby the Country
is thinly inhabited; the Living solitary and unsociable.'' Some planters
were uncomfortably aware of the problems created by physical isolation. William Fitzhugh, for example, admitted to a correspondent in

the mother country, "Society that is good and ingenious is very scarce, and seldom to be come at except in books."[7]

Yet despite such apparent cultural privation, Fitzhugh and his contemporaries refused to alter their life styles in any way that might compromise their freedom of action. They assumed it their right to give commands, and in the ordering of daily plantation affairs they rarely tolerated outside interference. Some of these planters even saw themselves as lawgivers out of the Old Testament. In 1726 William Byrd II explained that "like one of the Patriarchs, I have my Flocks and my Herds, my Bond-men and Bond-women, and every sort of Trade amongst my own Servants, so that I live in a kind of independence on every one but Providence." Perhaps Byrd exaggerated for literary effect, but forty years earlier Durand had observed, "There are no lords [in Virginia], but each is sovereign on his own plantation." Whatever the origins of this independent spirit, it bred excessive individualism in a wide range of social activities. While these powerful gentlemen sometimes worked together to achieve specific political and economic ends, they bristled at the least hint of constraint. Andrew Burnaby later noted that "the public or political character of the Virginians corresponds with their private one: they are haughty and jealous of their liberties, impatient of restraint, and can scarcely bear the thought of being controlled by any superior power."[8]

The gentry expressed this uncompromising individualism in aggressive competitiveness, engaging in a constant struggle against real and imagined rivals to obtain more lands, additional patronage, and high tobacco prices. Indeed, competition was a major factor shaping the character of face-to-face relationships among the colony's gentlemen, and when the stakes were high the planters were not particular about the methods they employed to gain victory. In large part, the goal of the competition within the gentry group was to improve social position by increasing wealth.[9]

Some gentlemen believed that personal honor was at stake as well. Robert "King" Carter, by all accounts the most successful planter of his generation, expressed his anxiety about losing out to another Virginian in a competitive market situation. "In discourse with Colonel Byrd, Mr. Armistead, and a great many others," he explained, "I understand you [an English merchant] had sold their tobacco in round parcels and at good rates. I cannot allow myself to come behind any of these gentlemen in the planter's trade." Carter's pain arose not so much from the lower price he had received as from the public knowledge that he had been bested by respected peers. He believed he had lost face. This kind of intense competition was sparked, especially among the less affluent members of the gentry, by a dread of slipping into the ranks of what one eighteenth-century Virginia historian called the "common Planters." Gov. Francis Nicholson, an acerbic English placeman, declared that the "ordinary sort of planters" knew full well "from whence these mighty dons derive their originals." The governor touched a nerve; the efforts of "these mighty dons" to outdo one another were almost certainly motivated by a desire to disguise their "originals," to demonstrate anew through competitive encounters that they could legitimately claim gentility.[10]

Another facet of Virginia gentry culture was materialism. This certainly does not mean that the great planters lacked spiritual concerns. Religion played a vital role in the lives of men like Robert Carter and William Byrd II. Nevertheless, piety was largely a private matter. In public these men determined social standing not by a man's religiosity or philosophic knowledge but by his visible estate—his lands, slaves, buildings, even by the quality of his garments. When John Bartram, one of America's first botanists, set off in 1737 to visit two of Virginia's most influential planters, a London friend advised him to purchase a new set of clothes, "for though I should not esteem thee less, to come to me in what dress thou will,—yet these Virginians are a very gentle, well-dressed people—and look, perhaps, more at a man's outside than his inside." This perception of gentry values was accurate. Fitzhugh's desire to maintain outward appearances drove him to collect a stock of monogrammed silver plate and to import at great expense a well-crafted, though not very practical, English carriage. One even finds hints that the difficulty of preserving the image of material success weighed heavily upon some planters. When he described local Indian customs in 1705, Robert Beverley noted that native Americans lived an easy, happy existence "without toiling and perplexing their mind for Riches, which other people often trouble themselves to provide for uncertain and ungrateful Heirs."[11]

The gentry were acutely sensitive to the element of chance in human affairs, and this sensitivity influenced their attitudes toward other men and society. Virginians knew from bitter experience that despite the best-laid plans, nothing in their lives was certain. Slaves suddenly sickened and died. English patrons forgot to help their American friends.

Tobacco prices fell without warning. Cargo ships sank. Storms and droughts ruined the crop. The list was endless. Fitzhugh warned an English correspondent to think twice before allowing a son to become a Virginia planter, for even "if the best husbandry and the greatest forecast and skill were used, yet ill luck at sea, a fall of a Market, or twenty other accidents may ruin and overthrow the best Industry." Other planters, even those who had risen to the top of colonial society, longed for greater security. "I could wish," declared William Byrd I in 1685, "wee had Some more certain Commodity [than tobacco] to rely on but see no hopes of it." However desirable such certainty may have appeared, the planters always put their labor and money into tobacco, hoping for a run of luck. One simply learned to live with chance. In 1710 William Byrd II confided in his secret diary, "I dreamed last night . . . that I won a tun full of money and might win more if I had ventured." [12]

Gaming relationships reflected these strands of gentry culture. In fact, gambling in Virginia was a ritual activity. It was a form of repetitive, patterned behavior that not only corresponded closely to the gentry's values and assumptions but also symbolized the realities of everyday planter life. This congruence between actions and belief, between form and experience, helps to account for the popularity of betting contests. The wager, whether over cards or horses, brought together in a single, focused act the great planters' competitiveness, independence, and materialism, as well as the element of chance. It represented a social agreement in which each individual was free to determine how he would play, and the gentleman who accepted a challenge risked losing his material possessions as well as his personal honor. [13]

The favorite household or tavern contests during this period included cards, backgammon, billiards, nine-pins, and dice. The great planters preferred card games that demanded skill as well as luck. Put, piquet, and whist provided the necessary challenge, and Virginia gentlemen—Durand's hosts, for example—regularly played these games for small sums of money and tobacco. These activities brought men together, stimulated conversation, and furnished a harmless outlet for aggressive drives. They did not, however, become for the gentry a form of intense, symbolic play such as the cockfight in Bali. William Byrd II once cheated his wife in a game of piquet, something he would never have dared to do among his peers at Williamsburg. By and large, he showed little emotional involvement in these types of household gambling. The exception here proves the rule. After an unusually large loss at the gaming tables of Williamsburg, Byrd drew a pointed finger in the margin of his secret diary and swore a "solemn resolution never at once to lose more than 50 shillings and to spend less time in gaming, and I beg the God Almighty to give me grace to keep so good a resolution. . . . " Byrd's reformation was short-lived, for within a few days he dispassionately noted losing another four pounds at piquet.[14]

Horse racing generated far greater interest among the gentry than did the household games. Indeed, for the great planters and the many others who came to watch, these contests were preeminently a social drama. To appreciate the importance of racing in seventeenth-century Virginia, we must understand the cultural significance of horses. By the turn of the century possession of one of these animals had become a social necessity. Without a horse, a planter felt despised, an object of ridicule. Owning even a slow-footed saddle horse made the common planter more of a man in his own eyes as well as in those of his neighbors; he was reluctant to venture forth on foot for fear of making an adverse impression. As the Rev. Hugh Jones explained in 1724, "almost every ordinary Person keeps a horse; and I have known some spend the Morning in ranging several Miles in the Woods to find and catch their Horses only to ride two or three Miles to Church, to the Court-House, or to a Horse-Race, where they generally appoint to meet upon Business." Such behavior seems a waste of time and energy only to one who does not comprehend the symbolic importance which the Virginians attached to their horses. A horse was an extension of its owner; indeed, a man was only as good as his horse. Because of the horse's cultural significance, the gentry attempted to set its horsemanship apart from that of the common planters. Gentlemen took better care of their animals, and, according to John Clayton, who visited Virginia in 1688, they developed a distinctive riding style. "They ride pretty sharply," Clayton reported; "a Planters' Pace is a Proverb, which is a good sharp hand-Gallop." A fast-rising cloud of dust far down a Virginia road probably alerted the common planter that he was about to encounter a social superior.[15]

The contest that generated the greatest interest among the gentry was the quarter-horse race, an all-out sprint by two horses over a quarter-mile dirt track. The great planters dominated these events. In the records of the county courts—our most important source of information about specific races—we find the names of some of the colony's most prominent planter families—Randolph, Eppes, Jefferson, Swan, Kenner, Hardiman, Parker, Cocke, Batte, Harwick (Hardidge), Youle (Yowell), and Washington. Members of the House of Burgesses, including its powerful speaker, William Randolph, were frequently mentioned in the contests that came before the courts. On at least one occasion the Rev. James Blair, Virginia's most eminent clergyman and a founder of the College of William and Mary, gave testimony in a suit arising from a race run between Capt. William Soane and Robert Napier. The tenacity with which the gentry pursued these cases, almost continuations of the race itself, suggests that victory was no less sweet when it was gained in court.[16]

Many elements contributed to the exclusion of lower social groups from these contests. Because of the sheer size of wagers, poor freemen and common planters could not have participated regularly. Certainly, the members of the Accomack County Court were embarrassed to discover that one Thomas Davis, "a very poore Man," had lost 500 pounds of tobacco or a cow and calf in a horse race with an adolescent named Mr. John Andrews. Recognizing that Davis bore "a great charge of wife and Children," the justices withheld final judgment until the governor had an opportunity to rule on the legality of the wager. The Accomack court noted somewhat gratuitously that if the governor declared the action unlawful, it would fine Davis five days' work on a public bridge. In such cases county justices ordinarily made no comment upon a plaintiff's or defendant's financial condition, assuming, no doubt, that most people involved in racing were capable of meeting their gaming obligation.[17]

The gentry actively enforced its exclusive control over quarter-horse racing. When James Bullocke, a York County tailor, challenged Mr. Mathew Slader to a race in 1674, the county court informed Bullocke that it was "contrary to Law for a Labourer to make a race being a Sport for Gentlemen" and fined the presumptuous tailor two hundred pounds of tobacco and cask. Additional evidence of exclusiveness is found in early eighteenth-century Hanover County. In one of the earliest issues of the colony's first newspaper, the *Virginia Gazette*, an advertisement appeared announcing that "some merry-dispos'd gentlemen" in Hanover planned to celebrate St. Andrew's Day with a race for quarter-milers. The Hanover gentlemen explained in a later, fuller description that "all Persons resorting there are desir'd to behave themselves with Decency and Sobriety, the Subscribers being resolv'd to discountenance all Immorality with the utmost Rigour.'' The purpose of these contests was to furnish the county's ''considerable Number of Gentlemen, Merchants, and credible Planters'' an opportunity for ''cultivating Friendship.'' Less affluent persons apparently were welcome to watch the proceedings provided they acted like gentlemen.[18]

In most match races the planter rode his own horse, and the exclusiveness of these contests meant that racing created intensely competitive confrontations. There were two ways to set up a challenge. The first was a regularly scheduled affair usually held on Saturday afternoon. By 1700 there were at least a dozen tracks, important enough to be known by name, scattered through the counties of the Northern Neck and the James River valley. The records are filled with references to contests held at such places as Smith's Field, Coan Race Course, Devil's Field, Yeocomico, and Varina. No doubt, many races also occurred on nameless country roads or convenient pastures. On the appointed day the planter simply appeared at the race track and waited for a likely challenge. We know from a dispute heard before the Westmoreland County Court in 1693 that John Gardner boldly ''Challeng'd all the horses then upon the ground to run with any of them for a thousand pounds of Tobo and twenty shillings in money.'' A second type of contest was a more spontaneous challenge. When gentlemen congregated over a jug of hard cider or peach brandy, the talk frequently turned to horses. The owners presumably bragged about the superior speed of their animals, and if one planter called another's bluff, the men cried out ''Done, and done,'' marched to the nearest field, and there discovered whose horse was in fact the swifter.[19]

Regardless of the outcome, quarter-horse races in Virginia were exciting spectacles. The crowds of onlookers seem often to have been fairly large, as common planters, even servants, flocked to the tracks to watch the gentry challenge one another for what must have seemed immense amounts of money and tobacco. One witness before a Westmoreland County Court reported in 1674 that Mr. Stone and Mr. Youle had run a challenge for 10 pounds sterling ''in sight of many people.'' Attendance at race days was sizable enough to support a brisk trade in cider and brandy. In 1714 the Richmond County Court fined several men for peddling ''by Retaile in the Race Ground.'' Judging from the popularity of horses throughout planter society, it seems probable that the people who attended these events dreamed of one day riding a local champion such as Prince or Smoaker.[20]

The magnitude of gentry betting indicates that racing must have deeply involved the planters' self-esteem. Wagering took place on two levels. The contestants themselves made a wager on the outcome, a main bet usually described in a written statement. In addition, side wagers were sometimes negotiated between spectators or between a contestant and spectator. Of the two, the main bet was far the more significant. From accounts of disputed races reaching the county courts we know that gentlemen frequently risked very large sums. The most extravagant contest of the period was a race run between John Baker and John Haynie in Northumberland County in 1693, in which the two men wagered 4000 pounds of tobacco and 40 shillings sterling on the speed of their sprinters, Prince and Smoaker. Some races involved only twenty or thirty shillings, but a substantial number were run for several pounds sterling and hundreds of pounds of tobacco. While few, if any, of the seventeenth-century gentlemen were what we would call gambling addicts, their betting habits seem irrational even by the more prudential standards of their own day; in conducting normal business transactions, for example, they would never have placed so much money in such jeopardy.[21]

To appreciate the large size of these bets we must interpret them within the context of Virginia's economy. Between 1660 and 1720 a planter could anticipate receiving about ten shillings per hundredweight of tobacco. Since the average grower seldom harvested more than 1500 pounds of tobacco a year per man, he probably never enjoyed an annual income from tobacco in excess of eight pounds sterling. For most Virginians the conversion of tobacco into sterling occurred only in the neat columns of account books. They themselves seldom had coins in their pockets. Specie was extremely scarce, and planters ordinarily paid their taxes and conducted business transactions with tobacco notes—written promises to deliver to the bearer a designated amount of tobacco. The great preponderance of seventeenth-century planters were quite poor, and even the great planters estimated their income in hundreds, not thousands, of pounds sterling. Fitzhugh, one of the wealthier men of his generation, described his financial situation in detail. "Thus I have given you some particulars," he wrote in 1686, "which I thus deduce, the yearly Crops of corn and Tobo. together with the surplusage of meat more than will serve the family's use, will amount annually to 60000 lb. Tobo wch. at 10 shillings per Ct. is 300 pounds annum.'' These facts reveal that the Baker-Haynie bet—to take a notable example—amounted to approximately 22 pounds sterling, more than 7 percent of Fitzhugh's annual cash return. It is therefore not surprising that the common planters seldom took part in quarter-horse racing; this wager alone amounted to approximately three times the income they could expect to receive in a good year. Even a modest wager of a pound or two sterling represented a substantial risk.[22]

Gentlemen sealed these gaming relationships with a formal agreement, either a written statement laying out the terms of the contest or a declaration before a disinterested third party of the nature of the wager. In either case the participants carefully stipulated what rules would be in effect. Sometimes the written agreements were quite elaborate. In 1698, for example, Richard Ward and John Steward, Jr., ''covenanted and agreed'' to race at a quarter-mile track in Henrico County known as Ware. Ward's mount was to enjoy a ten-yard handicap, and if it crossed the finish line within five lengths of Steward's horse, Ward would win five pounds sterling; if Steward's obviously superior animal won by a greater distance, Ward promised to pay six pounds sterling. In another contest William Eppes and Stephen Cocke asked William Randolph to witness an agreement for a ten-shilling race: ''each horse was to keep his path, they not being to crosse unlesse Stephen Cocke could gett the other Riders Path at the start at two or three Jumps.''[23]

Virginia's county courts treated race covenants as binding legal contracts. If a gentleman failed to fulfill the agreement, the other party had legitimate grounds to sue; and the county justices' first consideration during a trial was whether the planters had properly recorded their agreement. The Henrico court summarily dismissed one gambling suit because ''noe Money was stacked down nor Contract in writing made [,] one of wch. in such cases is by the law required.'' Because any race might generate legal proceedings, it was necessary to have a number of people present at the track not only to assist in the running of the contest but also to act as witnesses if anything went wrong. The two riders normally appointed an official starter, several judges, and someone to hold the stakes.[24]

Almost all of the agreements included a promise to ride a fair race. Thus two men in 1698 insisted upon ''fair Rideing''; another pair pledged ''they would run fair horseman's play.'' By such agreements the planters waived their customary right to jostle, whip, or knee an

opponent, or to attempt to unseat him. During the last decades of the
seventeenth century the gentry apparently attempted to substitute riding skill and strategy for physical violence. The demand for "fair
Rideing" also suggests that the earliest races in Virginia were wild,
no-holds-barred affairs that afforded contestants ample opportunity to
vent their aggressions.[25]

The intense desire to win sometimes undermined a gentleman's written
promise to run a fair race. When the stakes were large, emotions ran
high. One man complained in a York County court that an opponent
had interfered with his horse in the middle of the race, "by means
whereof the s[ai]d Plaintiff lost the said Race." Joseph Humphrey told
a Northumberland County court that he would surely have come in first
in a challenge for 1500 pounds of tobacco had not Capt. Rodham Kenner (a future member of the House of Burgesses) "held the defendt
horses bridle in running his race." Other riders testified that they had
been "Josselled" while the race was in progress. An unusual case of
interference grew out of a 1694 race which Rodham Kenner rode against
John Hartly for one pound sterling and 575 pounds of tobacco. In a
Westmoreland County court Hartly explained that after a fair start and
without using "whipp or Spurr" he found himself "a great distance"
in front of Kenner. But as Hartly neared the finish line, Kenner's brother,
Richard, suddenly jumped onto the track and "did hollow and shout
and wave his hat over his head in the plts [plaintiff's] horse's face."
The animal panicked, ran outside the posts marking the finish line, and
lost the race. After a lengthy trial a Westmoreland jury decided that
Richard Kenner "did no foule play in his hollowing and waveing his
hatt." What exactly occurred during this race remains a mystery, but
since no one denied that Richard acted very strangely, it seems likely
that the Kenner brothers were persuasive as well as powerful.[26]

Planters who lost large wagers because an opponent jostled or "hol-
lowed" them off the track were understandably angry. Yet instead of
challenging the other party to a duel or allowing gaming relationships
to degenerate into blood feuds, the disappointed horsemen invariably
took their complaints to the courts. Such behavior indicates not only
that the gentlemen trusted the colony's formal legal system—after all,
members of their group controlled it—but also that they were willing
to place institutional limitations on their own competitiveness. Gentlemen who felt they had been cheated or abused at the track immediately
collected witnesses and brought suit before the nearest county court.

The legal machinery available to the aggrieved gambler was complex; and no matter how unhappy he may have been with the final verdict, he could rarely claim that the system had denied due process.[27]

The plaintiff brought charges before a group of justices of the peace sitting as a county court; if these men found sufficient grounds for a suit, the parties—in the language of seventeenth-century Virginia—could "put themselves upon the country." In other words, they could ask that a jury of twelve substantial freeholders hear the evidence and decide whether the race had in fact been fairly run. If the sums involved were high enough, either party could appeal a local decision to the colony's general court, a body consisting of the governor and his council. Several men who hotly insisted that they had been wronged followed this path. For example, Joseph Humphrey, loser in a race for 1500 pounds of tobacco, stamped out of a Northumberland County court, demanding a stop to "farther proceedings in the Common Law till a hearing in Chancery." Since most of the General Court records for the seventeenth century were destroyed during the Civil War, it is impossible to follow these cases beyond the county level. It is apparent from the existing documents, however, that all the men involved in these race controversies took their responsibilities seriously, and there is no indication that the gentry regarded the resolution of a gambling dispute as less important than proving a will or punishing a criminal. It seems unlikely that the colony's courts would have adopted such an indulgent attitude toward racing had these contests not in some way served a significant social function for the gentry.[28]

Competitive activities such as quarter-horse racing served social as well as symbolic functions. As we have seen, gambling reflected core elements of the culture of late seventeenth-century Virginia. Indeed, if it had not done so, horse racing would not have become so popular among the colony's gentlemen. These contests also helped the gentry to maintain group cohesion during a period of rapid social change. After 1680 the great planters do not appear to have become significantly less competitive, less individualistic, or less materialistic than their predecessors had been. But while the values persisted, the forms in which they were expressed changed. During the last decades of the century unprecedented external pressures, both political and economic, coupled with a major shift in the composition of the colony's labor force, caused the Virginia gentry to communicate these values in ways that would not lead to deadly physical violence or spark an eruption of blood feuding. The members of the native-born elite, anxious to preserve their autonomy over local affairs, sought to avoid the kinds of divisions within their ranks that had contributed to the outbreak of Bacon's Rebellion. They found it increasingly necessary to cooperate against meddling royal governors. Moreover, such earlier unrest among the colony's plantation workers as Bacon's Rebellion and the plant-cutting riots had impressed upon the great planters the need to present a common face to their dependent laborers, especially to the growing number of black slaves who seemed more and more menacing as the years passed.[29]

Gaming relationships were one of several ways by which the planters, no doubt unconsciously, preserved class cohesion. By wagering on cards and horses they openly expressed their extreme competitiveness, winning temporary emblematic victories over their rivals without thereby threatening the social tranquility of Virginia. These non-lethal competitive devices, similar in form to what social anthropologists have termed "joking relationships," were a kind of functional alliance developed by the participants themselves to reduce dangerous, but often inevitable, social tensions.[30]

Without rigid social stratification racing would have lost much of its significance for the gentry. Participation in these contests publicly identified a person as a member of an elite group. Great planters raced against their social peers. They certainly had no interest in competing with social inferiors, for in this kind of relationship victory carried no positive meaning: The winner gained neither honor nor respect. By the same token, a defeat by someone like James Bullocke, the tailor from York, was painful, and to avoid such incidents gentlemen rarely allowed poorer whites to enter their gaming relationships—particularly the heavy betting on quarter horses. The common planters certainly gambled among themselves. Even the slaves may have laid wagers. But when the gentry competed for high stakes, they kept their inferiors at a distance, as spectators but never players.

The exclusiveness of horse racing strengthened the gentry's cultural dominance. By promoting these public displays the great planters legitimized the cultural values which racing symbolized—materialism, individualism, and competitiveness. These colorful, exclusive contests helped persuade subordinate white groups that gentry culture was desirable, something worth emulating; and it is not surprising that people who conceded the superiority of this culture readily accepted the gentry's right to rule. The wild sprint down a dirt track served the interests of Virginia's gentlemen better than they imagined.

NOTES

1. [Durand of Dauphiné], *A Huguenot Exile in Virginia or Voyages of a Frenchman exiled for his Religion with a Description of Virginia and Maryland*, ed. Gilbert Chinard (New York, 1934 [orig. publ. The Hague, 1687]), 148.

2. Rev. James Fontaine, *Memoirs of a Huguenot Family* . . . , ed. Ann Maury (Baltimore, 1967 [orig. publ. 1853]), 265–266; John Mercer, cited in Jane Carson; *Colonial Virginians at Play* (Williamsburg, 1965), 49, n. 1; H. R. McIlwaine, ed., *Minutes of the Council and General Court of Colonial Virginia, 1622–1632, 1670–1676* . . . (Richmond, 1924), 252, 281, 285.

3. Throughout this essay I use the terms gentry, gentlemen, and great planters as synonyms. In each Virginia county a few gentry families dominated civil, ecclesiastical, and military affairs. While the members of these families were substantially wealthier than the great majority of white planters, they were not a class in a narrow economic sense. Their cultural style as well as their financial position set them apart. The great planters and their families probably accounted for less than 2% of the colony's white population. Louis B. Wright, *The First Gentlemen of Virginia; Intellectual Qualities of the Early Colonial Ruling Class* (San Marino, Calif., 1940), 57, estimates their number at "fewer than a hundred families." While entrance into the gentry was not closed to newcomers, upward mobility into that group became increasingly difficult after the 1690s. See Philip A. Bruce, *Social Life of Virginia in the Seventeenth Century* (New York, 1907), 39–100; Aubrey C. Land, "Economic Base and Social Structure: The Northern Chesapeake in the Eighteenth Century," *Journal of Economic History*, XXV (1965), 639–654; Bernard Bailyn, "Politics and Social Structure in Virginia," in James Morton Smith, ed., *Seventeenth-Century America: Essays in Colonial History* (Chapel Hill, N.C., 1959), 90–115; and Jack P. Greene, "Foundations of Political Power in the Virginia House of Burgesses, 1720–1776," *William and Mary Quarterly*, 3d Ser., XVI (1959), 485–506. These disturbances are described in T. H. Breen, "A Changing Labor Force and Race Relations in Virginia 1660–1710," *Journal of Social History*, VII (1973), 3–25. The fullest account of Bacon's Rebellion remains Wilcomb E. Washburn, *The Governor and the Rebel: A History of Bacon's Rebellion in Virginia* (Chapel Hill, N.C., 1957). Several historians have remarked on the unusual political stability of 18th-century Virginia. See, for example, Jack P. Greene, "Changing Interpretations of Early American Politics," in Ray Allen Billington, ed., *The Reinterpretation of Early*

American History: Essays in Honor of John Edwin Pomfret (San Marino, Calif., 1966), 167–168, and Gordon S. Wood, "Rhetoric and Reality in the American Revolution," *WMQ*, 3d Ser., XXIII (1966), 27–30. The phrase "creole elite" comes from Carole Shammas, "English-Born and Creole Elites in Turn-of-the-Century Virginia," in Thad W. Tate and David L. Ammerman, eds., *Essays on the Seventeenth-Century Chesapeake* (Chapel Hill, N.C., forthcoming). See also David W. Jordan, "Political Stability and the Emergence of a Native Elite in Maryland, 1660–1715," *ibid*. The process of forming a native-born elite is also discussed in Bailyn, "Politics and Social Structure," in Smith, ed., *Seventeenth-Century America*, 90–115; John C. Rainbolt, "The Alteration in the Relationship between Leadership and Constituents in Virginia, 1660 to 1720." *WMQ*, 3rd Ser., XXVII (1970), 411–434; and Martin H. Quitt, "Virginia House of Burgesses 1660–1706: The Social, Educational, and Economic Bases of Political Power" (Ph.D. Diss., Washington University, 1970).

4. Breen, "Changing Labor Force," *Jour. Soc. Hist.*, VII (1973) 2–25; Edmund S. Morgan, *American Slavery—American Freedom: The Ordeal of Colonial Virginia* (New York, 1975), 295–362; Rainbolt, "Leadership and Constituents," *WMQ*, 3d Ser., XXVII (1970), 428–429. On the social attitudes of the small planters see David Alan Williams, "Political Alignments in Colonial Virginia, 1698–1750" (Ph.D. Diss., Northwestern University, 1959), chap. I.

5. A sudden growth of gambling for high stakes in pre-Civil War England is discussed in Lawrence Stone, *The Crisis of the Aristocracy, 1558–1641* (Oxford, 1965.) For the later period see Robert W. Malcolmson, *Popular Recreations in English Society, 1700–1850* (Cambridge, 1973); G. E. Mingay, *English Landed Society in the Eighteenth Century* (London, 1963), 151–153, 249–250; and E. D. Cuming, "Sports and Games," in A. S. Turberville, ed., *Johnson's England: An Account of the Life and Manners of his Age, I* (London, 1933), 362–383. It is important to stress here that the Virginia gentry did not simply copy English customs. As I argue in this essay, a specific, patterned form of behavior, such as gambling, does not become popular in a society or among the members of a subgroup of that society unless the activity reflects or expresses values indigenous to that culture. In 17th-century Massachusetts Bay, for example, heavy betting did not develop. A small amount of gambling seems to have occurred among the poor, especially among servants, but I can find no incidence of gambling among the colony's social, political, or religious leaders. See Nathaniel B. Shurtleff, ed., *Records of the Governor and Company of the Massachusetts Bay . . .* (Boston, 1853–1854), II, 180, III, 201, IV, pt. 1, 366; *Records of the Suffolk County Court, 1671–1680* (Colonial Society of Massachusetts, *Publications* [Boston], 1933), XXIX, 131, 259, 263, XXX, 1162; and Joseph H. Smith, ed., *Colonial Justice in Western Massachusetts, 1693–1702: The Pynchon Court Record* (Cambridge, Mass., 1961), 109.

6. Two of Clifford Geertz's essays here helped shape my ideas about Virginia society: "Thick Description: Toward an Interpretive Theory of Culture" and "Deep Play: Notes on the Balinese Cockfight" in Geertz, *The Interpretation of Cultures* (New York, 1973), 3–30, 412–453. Also see Erving Goffman's "Fun in Games" in Goffman, *Encounters: Two Studies in the Sociology of Interaction* (Indianapolis, 1961), 17–81; Raymond Firth, "A Dart Match in Tikopia: A Study in the Sociology of Primitive Sport," *Oceania*, I (1930), 64–96; and H. A. Powell, "Cricket in Kiriwina," *Listener*, XLVIII (1952), 384–385.

7. Philip A. Bruce, *Economic History of Virginia in the Seventeenth Century . . .* , II (New York, 1935 [Orig. publ. 1895]), 1511. "A Letter from Mr. John Clayton Rector of Crofton at Wakefield in Yorkshire, to the Royal Society, May 12, 1688," in Peter Force, ed., *Tracts and Other Papers Relating Principally to the Origin, Settlement and Progress of the Colonies in North America . . .* , III (Washington, D.C., 1844), no. 12, 21. Richard Beale Davis, ed., *William Fitzhugh and His Chesapeake World 1676–1701: The Fitzhugh Letters and Other Documents* (Chapel Hill, N.C., 1963).

8. On the independence of the Virginia gentry see Gerald W. Mullin, *Flight and Rebellion: Slave Resistance in Eighteenth-Century Virginia* (New York, 1972), chap. 1. William Byrd II to Charles, Earl of Orrery, July 5, 1726, in "Virginia Council Journals, 1726–1753," *Virginia Magazine of History and Biography, XXXII* (1924), 27.[Durand], *A Huguenot Exile*, ed. Chinard, 1210. I discuss this theme in greater detail in a paper entitled "Looking Out For Number One: Cultural Values and Social Behavior in Early Seventeenth-Century Virginia" (paper delivered at the Thirty-Second Conference in Early American History, Nov. 1974). Rev. Andrew Burnaby, *Travels through the Middle Settlements in North America, in the Years 1759 and 1760; With Observations Upon the State of the Colonies*, in John Pinkerton, ed., *A General Collection of the Best and Most Interesting Voyages and Travels in All Ports of the World . . .* , XIII (London, 1812), 715.

9. According to John Rainbolt, the gentry's "striving for land, wealth, and position was intense and, at times, ruthless" ("Leadership and Constituents," *WMQ*, 3d Ser., XXVII [1970], 414). See Carole Shammas, "English-Born and Creole Elites," in Tate and Ammerman, eds., *Seventeenth-Century Chesapeake*; Morgan, *American Slavery—American Freedom*, 288–289; and Rhys Isaac, "Evangelical Revolt: The Nature of the Baptists' Challenge to the Traditional Order in Virginia, 1765 to 1775," *WMQ*, 3d Ser., XXXI (1974), 345–353.

10. Louis B. Wright, ed., *Letters of Robert Carter, 1720–1727: The Commercial Interests of a Virginia Gentleman* (San Marino, Calif., 1940), 93–94. Hugh Jones, *The Present State of Virginia Giving a Particular and short Account of the Indian, English, and Negroe Inhabitants of that Colony . . .* (New York, 1865 [Orig. publ. 1724]), 48. Quoted in Thomas Jefferson Werten-

baker, *The Old South: The Founding of American Civilization* (New York, 1942), 19.

11. Peter Collinson to John Bartram, Feb. 17, 1737, *WMQ*, 3d Ser., VI (1926), 304. Davis, ed., *Fitzhugh Letters*, 229, 241–242, 244, 246, 249–250, 257–259. For another example of the concern about outward appearances see the will of Robert Cole (1674), in *WMQ*, 3d Ser., XXXI (1974), 139. Robert Beverley, *The History and Present State of Virginia*, ed., Louis B. Wright (Chapel Hill, N.C., 1947), 226.

12. William Fitzhugh to Oliver Luke, Aug. 15, 1690, in Davis, ed., *Fitzhugh Letters*, 280. The favorite household or tavern contests during this period included William Byrd I to Perry and Lane, July 8, 1686, in "Letters of William Byrd I," *VMHB*, XXV (1917), 132. Louis B. Wright and Marion Tinling, eds., *The Secret Diary of William Byrd of Westover, 1709–1712* (Richmond, Va., 1941), 223–224.

13. Gaming was so popular among the gentry, so much an expression of their culture, that it became a common metaphor in their discussion of colonial politics. For example, an unsigned essay entitled "The History of Bacon's and Ingram's Rebellion, 1676" described the relationship between Nathaniel Bacon and Gov. William Berkeley as a card game. Charles M. Andrews, ed., *Narratives of the Insurrections, 1675–1690* (New York, 1915), 57. In another account of Bacon's Rebellion, written in 1705, Thomas Mathew noted that several members of the House of Burgesses were "not docile enough to Gallop the future Races, that Court see'd dispo'd to Lead'em." *Ibid.*, 32. In May 1697 William Fitzhugh explained to Capt. Roger Jones: "your self will see what a hard game we have to play the contrary party that is our Opposers, having the best Cards and the trumps to boot especially the Honor. Yet would my Lord Fairfax there [in England], take his turn in Shuffling and Dealing the cards and his Lordship with the rest see that we were not cheated in our game, I question not but we should gain the Sett, tho' the game is so far plaid" (Davis, ed., *Fitzhugh Letters*, 352). Rhys Isaac provides a provocative analysis of the relationship between games and gentry culture on the eve of the Revolution in "Evangelical Revolt," *WMQ*, 3d Ser., XXXI (1974), 348–353. See also Mark Anthony deWolfe Howe, ed., "Journal of Josiah Quincy, Junior, 1773," Massachusetts Historical Society, *Proceedings*, XLIX (1915–1916), 467, and William Stith, *The Sinfulness and pernicious Nature of Gaming. A Sermon Preached before the General Assembly of Virginia: At Williamsburg, March 1st 1752* (Williamsburg, 1752), 5–26.

14. The best discussion of these household games is Carson, *Virginians at Play*, 49–89. See also Charles Cotton, *The Compleat Gamester or Instructions How to Play at Billiards, Trucks, Bowls, and Chess . . .* (1674), in Cyril H. Hartmann, ed., *Games and Gamesters of the Restoration: The Compleat Gamester by Charles Cotton, 1674, and Lives of the Gamesters, by Theophilus Lucas, 1714* (London, 1930). After 1750, however, the gentry's attitude

toward household or tavern games seems to have changed. The betting became so heavy that several eminent planters lost fortunes at the gaming tables. A visitor at Williamsburg in 1765 wrote of these men that "they are all professed gamesters, Especially Colonel Burd [William Byrd III], who is never happy but when he has the box and Dices in hand. [T]his Gentleman from a man of the greatest poverty of any in america has reduced himself to that Degree by gameing, that few or nobody will Credit him for Ever so small a sum of money. [H]e was obliged to sel 400 fine Negroes a few Days before my arrival." "Journal of a French Traveller in the Colonies, 1765, I," *American Historical Review*, XXVI (1920–1921), 742. Byrd was not alone. Robert Wormeley Carter and Robert Burwell were excessive gamblers, and as the aging Landon Carter (Robert "King" Carter's son) observed the wagering of the gentry on the eve of the Revolution, he sadly mused, "they play away and play it all away," Jack P. Greene, ed., *The Diary of Colonel Landon Carter of Sabine Hall, 1752–1778*, II (Charlottesville, Va., 1965), 830. On this generation's addiction to gambling see Emory G. Evans, "The Rise and Decline of the Virginia Aristocracy in the Eighteenth Century: The Nelsons," in Darrett B. Rutman, ed., *The Old Dominion: Essays for Thomas Perkins Abernethy* (Charlottesville, Va., 1964), 68–70. Wright and Tinling, eds., *Secret Diary*, 75, 442, 449.

15. Only one mention of cockfighting before 1730 has come to my attention, and that one refers to contests among the "common planters." Jones, *Present State of Virginia*, 48. See Carson, *Virginians at Play*, 151–152. Jones, *Present State of Virginia*, 48. This observation was repeated in other accounts of Virginia society throughout the 18th century. William Byrd II wrote "my Dear Countrymen have so great a Passion for riding, that they will often walk two miles to catch a Horse, in Order to ride One." William K. Boyd, ed., *William Byrd's Histories of the Dividing Line Betwixt Virginia and North Carolina* (Raleigh, N.C., 1928), 258. See also Carson, *Virginians at Play*, 102–105. "A Letter from Clayton," in Force, ed., *Tracts and Other Papers*, no. 12, 35.

16. On the development of racing in Virginia, especially the transition from the quarter-mile straight track to the oval course, see W. G. Stanard, "Racing in Colonial Virginia," *VMHB*, II (1894–1895), 293–305, and Fairfax Harrison, "The Equine F.F.V.'s: A study of the Evidence for the English Horses Imported into Virginia before the Revolution," *Ibid.*, XXXV (1927), 329–370. I suspect that quarter-horse racing was a sport indigenous to Virginia. Besides Randolph, there were John Stone, William Hardidge, Thomas Yowell, John Hardiman, Daniel Sullivant, Thomas Chamberlain, Rodham Kenner, Richard Kenner, William Soan, and Alexander Swan. Aug. 1690, Henrico County, Order Book, 1678–1693, 340. All references to manuscript county records are to the photostat copies at the Virginia State Library, Richmond.

17. Jan. 16, 1666, Accomack Co., Orders, 1666–1670, 9.

18. Sept. 10, 1674, York Co., Deeds, Orders, Wills, 1672–1694, 85. *Virginia Gazette*, Nov. 19–26, 1736, Sept. 30-Oct. 7, 1737.

19. Bruce, *Social Life*, 195–209; Carson, *Virginians at Play*, 108–110. Apr. 7, 1693, Westmoreland Co., Order Book, 1690–1698, 92; "Racing in Virginia in 1700–05," *VMHB*, X (1902–1903), 320. Aug. 1683, Henrico Co. Records [Deeds and Wills], 1677–1692, 254.

20. Oct. 16, 1674, Westmoreland Co., Deeds, Patents, Etc., 1655–1677, 211; Bruce, *Social Life*, 197–198; Carson, *Virginians at Play*, 109. Beverley Fleet, ed., *Richmond County Records, 1704–1724*, Virginia Colonial Abstracts, XVII (Richmond, Va., 1943), 95–96.

21. Carson, *Virginians at Play*, 105. See Aug. 29, 1694, Westmoreland Co., Order Book, 1690–1698, 146. Aug. 22, 1695, Northumberland Co., Order Book, 1678–1698. Pt. 2, 707–708.

22. Morgan, *American Slavery—American Freedom*, 142, 198, 204. Bruce, *Economic History*, II, 495–512. Aubrey Land's analysis of the probate records in a tobacco-producing area in nearby Maryland between 1690 and 1699 reveals that 74.6% of the estates there were worth less that 100 pounds sterling. According to Land, the differences between the social structures of Maryland and Virginia at this time were not "very great." Land, "Economic Base and Social Structure," *Jour. Econ. Hist.*, XXV (1965), 641–644. William Fitzhugh to Dr. Ralph Smith, Apr. 22, 1686, in Davis, ed., *Fitzhugh Letters*, 176.

23. The full covenant is reproduced in Stanard, "Racing in Colonial Virginia," *VMHB*, II (1894–1895), 296–298.

24. Virginia law prohibited fraudulent gaming, certain kinds of side bets, and gambling by persons who had "no visible estate, profession, or calling, to maintain themselves." William Waller Hening, ed., *The Statutes at Large; Being a Collection of all the Laws of Virginia . . .* , IV (Richmond, 1820), 214–218; George Webb, *Office and Authority of a Justice of Peace . . .* (Williamsburg, Va., 1736), 165–167. Wagers made between two gainfully employed colonists were legal agreements and enforceable as contracts. The courts of Virginia, both common law and chancery, apparently followed what they believed to be standard English legal procedure. Whether they were correct is difficult to ascertain. Sir William Holdsworth explains that acts passed by Parliament during the reigns of Charles II and Anne allowed individuals to sue for gaming debts, but he provides no evidence that English courts regularly settled disputed contests such as horse races. Holdsworth, *A History of English Law* (London, 1966), VI, 404, XI, 539–542. Not until the 1750s did Virginians begin to discuss gambling as a social vice. See Stith, *The Sinfulness . . . of Gaming*; R. A. Brock, ed., *The Official Records of Robert Dinwiddie*, I (Richmond, Va., 1883); Samuel Davies, *Virginia's Danger and Remedy. Two Discourses Occasioned by the Severe Drought . . .* (Williamsburg, 1756). Oct. 1690, Henrico Co., Order Book, 1678–1693, 351. See also Aug. 28, 1674, Northampton Co., Order Book No. 9, 1664–1674, 269, and Nov. 4, 1674, *Ibid.*, No. 10, 1674–1679.

25. Stanard, "Racing in Colonial Virginia," *VMHB*, II (1894–1895), 267;

Henrico Co. Records [Deeds and Wills], 1677–1692, 466. Carson, *Virginians at Play*, 109–110.

26. "Some Extracts from the Records of York Co., Virginia," *WMQ*, 1st Ser., IX (1900–1901), 178–179. Jan. 1694, Northumberland Co., Order Book, 1678–1698, Pt. 2, 643. Aug. 29, 1694, Westmoreland Co., Order Book, 1690–1698, 146–146a. Also see Oct. 1689, Henrico Co., Order Book, 1678–1693, 313, and Stanard, "Racing in Virginia," *VMHB*, II (1894–1895), 296.

27. A gentleman could have challenged an opponent to a duel. Seventeenth and early 18th-century Virginians recognized a code of honor of which dueling was a part, but they did everything possible to avoid such potentially lethal combats. I have found only four cases before 1730 in which dueling was even discussed. County courts fined two of the challengers before they could do any harm. ("A Virginian Challenge in the Seventeenth Century," *VMHB*, II [1894–1895], 96–97; *Lower Norfolk County Antiquarian*, IV [1904], 106.) And two comic-opera challenges that only generated blustery rhetoric are described in William Stevens Perry, ed., *Historical Collections Relating to the American Colonial Church*, I (Hartford, Conn., 1870), 25–28, and Bond, ed., *Byrd's Histories of the Dividing Line*, 173–175. On the court system see Philip A. Bruce, *Institutional History of Virginia in the Seventeenth Century . . .* , I (Gloucester, 1910), 484–632, 647–689.

28. Aug. 29, 1694, Westmoreland Co., Order Book, 1690–1698, 146a. Jan. 1694, Northumberland Co., Order Book, 1678–1698, Pt. 2, 643. Sometimes the courts had an extremely difficult time deciding exactly what had occurred at a race. A man testified in 1675 that he had served as the official judge for a contest, and that while he knew which horse had finished first, he was "not able to say much less to Sweare that the Horse did Cary his Rider upon his back over the path." Sept. 16, 1675, Surry County, Deeds, Wills and Orders, 1671–1684, 133. For another complex case see Mar. 5, 1685, Rappahannock Co. Order [no. 1], 1683–1686, 103, 120, 153.

29. For evidence of the persistence of these values among the gentry in the Revolutionary period see Isaac, "Evangelical Revolt," *WMQ*, 3d Ser., XXXI (1974), 348–353.

30. The planters' aggressive hospitality may have served a similar function. Hospitality in Virginia should be analyzed to discover its relationship to gentry culture. Robert Beverley makes some suggestive comments about this custom in his *History and Present State of Virginia*, 312–313. An interesting comparison to the Virginia practice is provided in Michael W. Young, *Fighting with Food: Leadership, Values and Social Control in a Massim Society* (Cambridge, 1971). A. R. Radcliffe-Brown, *Structure and Function in Primitive Society: Essays and Addresses* (New York, 1964), Chaps. 4, 5.

II

Leisure Time on the Southern Plantation: The Slaves' Respite from Constant Toil, 1810–1860

David K. Wiggins

Slaves living on Southern plantations prior to the Civil War never had to worry about having too much leisure time on their hands. In contrast to people in modern industrial civilizations, they were usually more concerned about realizing additional leisure time than about how to utilize periods when not engaged in labor. Oftentimes forced to toil fourteen hours a day for six days a week, the slaves' existence could be extremely varying and oppressive. Even those bondsmen who spent the majority of their lives on only one or two plantations were continually forced to alter their attitudes, perceptions, and behaviors simply to survive the humiliating institution. But to think that slavery was all toil is a misconception and to discuss only its most salient features would be a parody since its reality was far more reaching than this. In order to minimize problems and guarantee a smooth-running plantation, Southern slaveholders found it necessary to requite their bondsmen by granting them brief periods of leisure time. Slaves would have been driven beyond a frightening desperation if they had not been allowed a certain amount of time to do as they pleased.

Surprisingly, an investigation of leisure in the plantation community has never been a topic of special attention. A few historians have written on the subject but in a very superficial manner and only then as part of more general studies dealing with slavery. Most scholars have concentrated on the more apparent aspects of slave life: how harshly they were punished, how long they were worked, how they were taken

LIBRARY OF MOUNT ST. MARY'S COLLEGE EMMITSBURG, MARYLAND

care of during illness, how much food they were given, and so forth. These questions certainly have to be answered before we can have a thorough knowledge of the subject. But to have a clearer understanding of slavery, all aspects of the system must be examined. Therefore, the purpose of this study was to determine the role of leisure on the Southern plantation fifty years prior to the Civil War. More specifically: What specific periods of leisure time were granted the slaves? What types of recreational activities did slaves engage in during their leisure time? What were the planters' motives behind the granting of leisure time? Did leisure time assist the slaves in their fight for survival?[1]

In reality, most Southern planters were neither insensate monsters nor benevolent saints in their dealings with slaves. Whatever their treatment of individual bondsmen, most masters attempted to instill in their slaves a feeling of inferiority and a belief in the innate superiority of whites. In addition to other incentives slaves were accustomed to receiving special periods of leisure time from their master for "appropriate" behavior. Once a pattern of operation had been established on any given plantation, its rules, management, and social code were often enforced through the granting as well as withholding of free time.[2]

The majority of planters did not think it was sound management to have their slaves labor in the fields during inclement weather. Many bondsmen therefore were given an indeterminate amount of free time on cold or rainy days. It did not necessarily mean that their time was their own and that they were excluded from performing other types of work. Masters would often take these opportunities to have their bondsmen cut firewood, shuck corn, clean out their homes, repair machinery, and accomplish a variety of indoor tasks. On the other hand, planters sought shelter from the stormy weather themselves by remaining "snuggly" indoors and were therefore not in the most appropriate position to "keep watch" over their bondsmen. One can safely assume that slaves frequently took advantage of these occasions to nap, gossip, sing, or simply lounge around.[3]

Even though the working day during the summertime would frequently be longer because of the sunup-to-sundown routine followed on most establishments, many planters would requite their field slaves by giving them two hours or more in the middle of the day to rest. Many slaveholders worked their bondsmen only half a day on Saturday. An indeterminate number of the more charitable planters would give their slaves all of Saturday off when not behind with plantation work. It was the usual custom throughout the South to give slaves freedom from labor on Sunday. If planters were behind in their schedule and needed work done on Sunday, they would either give their slaves time off later in the year or pay them for their additional services. In addition to these rest periods, slaves enjoyed extended periods of leisure time during the various holidays that their masters celebrated. Christmas was a particular favorite, but certainly was not the only holiday that slaves were allowed to commemorate with complete earnestness.[4]

Slaves were often able to realize additional leisure time simply by outmaneuvering their "unsuspecting" masters. In contrast to free men, slaves were forced to plot different schemes in order to guarantee themselves periodic rests and the freedom to come and go as they pleased once their regular plantation work was completed. The artful ways in which they were able to outwit the whites insured them a great deal more leisure than their institutionally defined role allowed. Slaves would feign sickness or fatigue in order to get out of work, would forge passes so they could visit friends or loved ones on nearby plantations, would outmaneuver slave patrols by tying ropes or vines across roads to trip up their horses, and would sometimes rub garlic or red onions on their feet to keep dogs off their trail. The Texas slave Tom Hollard said they would "go and fall right in at the door of the quarters at night, so massa and the patterollers thinks we's real tired and let us alone and not watch us. That very night we'd be plannin' to slip off somewheres to see a negro gal or our wife, or go have a big time. . . . "[5]

The house slaves, in contrast to field hands, were sometimes not able to take advantage of these leisure hours. In fact, it was on Sundays and during the various holidays that house servants were often most busily employed—being responsible for serving the guests who visited the plantation on these occasions. They sometimes stayed up all night preparing the holiday barbecue and seeing that the "big house" was in top condition. It was precisely because of this lack of assigned periods of leisure time that slaves often preferred to work in the fields rather than in their master's quarters. House slaves were often "liable to every call, early or late," said the British traveler Basil Hall in 1828. "Everywhere the slaves preferred the field work chiefly, as I could learn from its being definite in amounts which left them a certain portion of the day entirely to themselves. . . . " Quite laudably, the more feeling and sympathetic slaveholders would try to make life more bearable for the domestic servants by compensating them for the leisure time they were denied during the holidays. For example, the Charles Dabney family of Virginia would rotate the field slaves into the "big house" on Sundays to perform chores so the domestic servants could have the day off. The Arkansas slaveholder Mrs. Isaac Hilliard wrote in her diary of 1850: "Attend church—unwilling to deprive carriage driver every Sunday of his holy day, we walk."[6]

In addition to granting certain periods of leisure, Southern slaveholders thought it would contribute to a smooth-running plantation if they occasionally allowed their slaves to have Saturday night parties. On many plantations these parties occurred on a weekly basis, although the planters' material offerings would be minimal in these particular situations. Many masters would furnish a fiddler, a barrel of liquor, and meat for a barbecue, "and left the slaves alone to enjoy themselves." These parties were given in the specific hope of keeping the slaves home during the week. Sometimes the whites of the plantation would attend the Saturday night parties and either enjoy themselves vicariously or actually take part in the festivities. A number of the more arrogant whites would actually arrange and direct these frolics. Slaves obviously could not prevent them from participating in the parties, but they usually resented their presence. If the slaves were not permitted to have a Saturday night party they would either gather at a secluded spot a sufficient distance from the "big house" or with or without a pass travel to a neighborhood plantation that was having one.[7]

As enjoyable as their Saturday night parties were, it was the unauthorized parties held during the week that slaves enjoyed most. Lack of consent meant lack of surveillance and meddling, save the patrollers who might catch wind of a party and break up the evening's festivities. Many planters placed a nine o'clock curfew on their slaves. But the overseers seldom checked the cabins more than once, so the slaves merely played "possum" and slipped out later in the evening. Slaves placed a high value on continuing their parties all night long. A celebration that couldn't be sustained all night was a disgrace to themselves and their plantation community. Many slaves, of course, could afford to party all night considering they had mastered the art of "goldbricking" during the day. Most planters realized that once slaves decided how much work they were going to perform, they renounced working any harder. For example, the prominent Virginia planter William B. Randolph received a letter from his overseer in 1833 complaining of the slaves' not putting in a full day's work.

"I will try to give you a full account of my proceedings," wrote the overseer. "As soon as you left the plantation I had much trouble and vexations with the negroes—with some exceptions—were unruly and wandering about at night and in the day were sleepy. Of course it was almost impossible to make them do anything like a day's work refusing to do any more than they pleased."

Similarly, Frederick Law Olmsted described how many of the slaves on the Virginia plantation he visited would "go through the motions" during the day:

He [slaveholder] afterwords said that his negroes never worked so hard as to tire themselves—always were lively and ready to go off on a frolic at night. He did not think they ever did half a fair days work. They could not be made to work hard. They never would lay out their strength freely, and it was impossible to make them do it. This is just what I have thought when I have seen slaves at work—they seem to go through the motions of labor without putting strength into them. They keep their powers in reserve for their own use at night, perhaps.

It should be noted, however, that many planters made it relatively easy for slaves to perform their daily tasks by setting the standard of labor very low. This way the slaveholders could maintain a semblance of discipline and at the same time improve the morale of his laborers.[8]

If the slaves were forced to hold their parties indoors because of cold or rainy weather, some magical device would be utilized to conceal the laughter of the occasion from reaching the ears of their master. The usual way of absorbing the sound was that of "turning down" the large pots they used for cooking and washing. "In slavery times dey didn't like for us to sing and play loud in de quarters," recalled slave Ruby Tartt of Alabama. "Dey would shut de door so de voice won't get out, an' day would turn de washpot down de door. Dat was to keep de voice inside, dey tol' me." "We had dances in the cabins every once in a while," remembered South Carolina slave soldier Williams. "We dance more in winter time so we could turn a pot down in the door to drown out the noise."[9]

Members of the slave quarter often related humorous tales concerning their illicit parties and social gatherings. Appropriately enough, the figure in most of the stories is the master. For example, Tennessee slave Nancy Jackson related a rather facetious story about one of their dances:

> I remember one big time we done had in slavery. Massa was gone, and then we found out he wasn't gone. He left the house intending to go on a visit and Missy and her children were gone and us Niggers gave a big ball the night they were all gone. The leader of that ball had on Massa's boots, and he sang a song he made up: "Ole Massa's gone to Philiman York and won't be back till July 4th to come; The fact of it I don't know he'll be back at all; Come on you Niggers and join this ball."
>
> The night they gave that ball, Massa had blacked his face and slipped back in the house while they were singing and dancing and he sat by the fireplace all the time.

The aforementioned example helps to illustrate not only the slaves' ability to laugh at themselves, but the pleasure they derived from momentarily assuming a superior but fanciful position to their masters. By temporarily reversing their social roles, slaves were able to briefly relieve any aggressions and hostilities they held toward their owners. The slaves' daily suppressions and inability to express their innermost feelings could be withstood more gracefully if they could occasionally conduct their own "fashionable balls." The slaves' knack for capriciously transcending their masters' authority helped to momentarily liberate them from that pressure and assisted them in coping with the realities of the plantation community. A tremendous feeling of relief resulted from rebelling and "putting one over" on the "Lord of the Manor." [10]

The central feature of slave gatherings was a variety of different dances. Slaves apparently found the "European reels, minuets, and schottishes too sedate and formalized for them," although there are occasional references to these dances in the narratives. The dances in the slave quarters closely resembled African dances in terms of method and style. They were often performed from a flexed, fluid bodily position as opposed to the stiffly erect position of European dancers; they often imitated and portrayed such animals as the buzzard, eagle, crow, and rabbit in realistic detail; they placed great emphasis upon satire, improvisation, and freedom of individual expression; they concentrated on movement outward from the pelvic region which whites found so despicable; and most importantly they were performed to a propulsive, swinging rhythm which animated the whole body. [11]

The animal dances the slaves executed took many forms, but the one mentioned most often was the Buzzard Lope, which was performed on the isolated Sea Island region off the coast of Georgia. Two historians have suggested that it may have been similar to a West African buzzard dance. This explanation is certainly credible. The slaves living on Sea Island cotton plantations had intercourse with few whites except the overseer and his family, and very little contact with slaves from the mainland. Excluded from contact with the outside world, they were unfamiliar with many of the cultural traits of the whites and therefore were more likely to maintain the cultural characteristics of their ancestors.[12]

In addition to their animal dances slaves commonly performed a dance in the quarter called ''Juba.'' It was another dance of African origin and has often been mentioned in connection with the West Indies as a sacred dance. In its original African form the ''Juba'' was primarily a competitive dance of skill. Two men stepped forward into a circle of dancers and began to display their skill at the juba step—a sort of eccentric shuffle. Meanwhile the men in the surrounding circle performed the same step before and after each performance of the two men in the center, in the interim clapping rhythmically and encouraging the competitors with song and verse. In the South it evolved into a dance called ''Patting Juba'' which was characterized by a special routine of slapping the hands, knees, thighs, and body in a rhythmic pattern accompanied by a variety of songs. Slaves attached great importance to improvisation; nowhere is it more evident than in this dance. It was particularly conducive to allowing the performers freedom of individual expression. The emergence of ''Patting'' seems to have been inevitable since most planters, for fear of revolts, forbade their slaves from having drums. Soloman Northup, who toiled for a number of years on a Louisiana plantation, remembered ''Patting Juba'':

. . . A slave dance does not cease with the sound of the fiddle, but in that case they set up a music peculiar to themselves. This is called patting, accompanied with one of those unmeaning songs, composed rather for its adoption to a certain tune of measure, than for the purpose of expressing any distinct idea. The patting is performed by striking the hands on the knees, then striking the hands together, then striking the right shoulder with one hand, the left with the other—all the while keeping time with the feet and singing: Juba dis and juba dat' Juba kill a yaller cat;. Juba up and juba down; Juba running all aroun.[13]

The dance in the slave quarters was often simply a test of physical prowess and a method of winning praise from one's peer group. Slaves took particular pride in their ability to perform arduous movements and vicariously enjoyed the exploits of their fellow dancers. In fact, members of the slave quarter tended to look down upon the whites for the lack of style in their dancing. Slaves normally thought of themselves as being superior and more energetic dancers than the whites and always welcomed the opportunity to display their preeminence. They also utilized their dances to satirize the cultural mannerisms of the whites. Shephard Edmonds recalled how the slaves in Tennessee would perform the cake walk:

It was generally on Sundays, when there was little work, that the slaves both young and old would dress up in hand-me-down finery to do a high-kicking, prancing walk-around. They did a take-off on the high manners of the white folks in the big house, but their masters, who gathered around to watch the fun, missed the point.

The *South Carolina Gazette* of 1810 related an account of a slave dance on the outskirts of Charleston:

The entertainment was opened by the men copying the manners of their masters and the women, those of their mistresses, and relating some highly curious anecdotes, to the inexpressible diversion of that company. Then they danced, betted, gamed, swore, quarrelled, fought and did everything that the most modern accomplished gentlemen are not ashamed of. . . . Whenever or wherever such nocturnal rendezvous are made, may it not be concluded, that their deliberations are never intended for the advantage of the white people?[14]

Several religious denominations of the South, particularly the Methodists, implored their slave congregations to give up the sinful practice of dancing. But for the majority of slaves dancing was too popular to be discontinued. For one thing, many planters encouraged their slaves to dance and certainly did not want them to give it up unless it was voluntary. The slaveholder James H. Hammond, for instance, wrote in his plantation journal of 1857 that "church members are privileged to dance on all holiday occasions and the class leader or deacon who may report them shall be reprimanded or punished at the discretion of the master." The more pious slaves also satisfied their troubled conscience by substituting the "Ring Shout" for their wicked secular dances. They convinced themselves that they did not dance the "Shout," for as everyone knows, you cross your feet when you dance; and since they did not tolerate crossing of feet, they clearly were not dancing. "Us 'longed to de church, all right,'' recalled the Texas slave Wash Wilson, "but dancin' ain't sinful 'ffen de foots ain't crossed. Us danced at de order meetings but us sho didn't have us foots crossed.'' The "Ring Shout" was derived from the African "Circle Dance" and is one of the best-known examples of an African survival in the United States. Several contemporary observers gave brief accounts of how the "Ring Shout" was performed in the praise-houses of the slave quarters. The white Unitarian minister Henry George Spaulding saw the "Ring Shout" performed when he visited Port Royal, South Carolina:

> Three or four, standing still, clapping their hands and beating time with their feet, commence singing in unison one of the peculiar shout melodies, while the others walk around in a ring, in single file, joining also in the song. Soon those in the ring leave off their singing, the others keeping it up the while with increased vigor, and strike into the shout step, observing most accurate time with the music. . . . They will often dance to the same song for twenty or thirty minutes.[15]

When the slaves were not spending their leisure time "cuttin' de steps" on the dance floor, they were often engaged in a hunting or fishing excursion. The men, and less frequently the women, loved to roam the fields and streams of their home plantation in search of their favorite animal or fish. Hunting and fishing was an ideal way for slaves to supplement their diets. Most slaves were not provided with the kinds of food by their masters that would sustain them through their weekly labors. By growing vegetable gardens, picking wild fruits, raising livestock and poultry, and stealing various victuals from their masters and through hunting and fishing the slaves were often able to procure an adequate amount of rations. Silas Jackson, deemed the religious leader of the slaves on his Maryland plantation, remembered that "all of the slaves hunted or those who wanted, hunted rabbits, oppossums or fished. These were our choice food, as we did not get anything special from the overseer."[16]

Very severe laws were passed in the Southern states restricting the slaves' right to hunt, primarily because whites did not want them to possess guns. White dominance could be maintained more easily if the slaves were denied arms. Despite the constraints placed on them, however, many planters were liberal in allowing their slaves the privilege of roaming the fields of the plantation in search of game, especially if they were expected to share a portion of the day's kill with their master. It was not uncommon for slaveholders to permit their older and more trusted slaves to use their guns, as well as their prize dogs, for hunting excursions. In reality the Southern slaveholders were more influential than the law in determining the extent to which the activities of the slaves were abridged. The legislatures attempted to control the type of hunting equipment the slaves used but were usually thwarted by the slaveholders who had ultimate authority. John F. Van Hook, who labored on a large Georgia plantation, recalled that "marse George had a good possum dog that he let his slaves use at night. . . . He was right good about letting his darkies hunt and fish. . . . "[17]

Even without permission from their masters, slaves were too dependent on the meat they procured from hunting to give up the sport very easily. Slave fathers also gained a degree of status by adding delicacies to the family table, as well as finding it gratifying personally. In fact, slave men realized a much-needed feeling of self-worth by adding delicacies to the family table. They continually mentioned the unauthorized nightly hunting excursions they would engage in when they were sure their master was securely snuggled in his bed or out of hearing distance from the baying hounds. Often precluded by their masters from contributing to their families' material welfare, slave men relished the chance to hunt for food. Slave men must have also enjoyed the camaraderie and parity of their fellow sportsmen. There was nothing quite like sitting around a blazing fire relating the tales of the phantom-like raccoon that "got away." Slave men, furthermore, found this activity satisfying partly because it allowed them the opportunity to teach their older children the intricacies involved in hunting. There were not many activities in the plantation community where slave fathers and sons could share in the excitement of common pursuits.[18]

Rarely having the privilege to use guns, slaves were compelled to become experts at trapping rabbits, squirrels, turkeys, and other small animals. There are also occasional references in the narratives of slaves snaring deer and bears. Their favorite type of hunting, however, was the nocturnal raccoon and opossum chases. Of the two animals, the opossum were more numerous and easier to catch without dogs. The slaves also considered it more palatable than the tough and stringy raccoon. Dogs were normally used to hunt both creatures, though very little training was needed to teach them how to "tree" properly.[19]

Members of the slave quarters frequently mentioned different ethereal experiences they had while out opossum hunting. Many slaves were convinced that a spirit world played an integral role in the terrestrial world. In fact, some slaves appeared to believe in a world where physical and spiritual forces grappled for supremacy. There were more than a few slaves who actually felt that ghosts and mysterious spirits held the upper hand. It is very possible that bondsmen utilized their belief in ghosts, witches, and magic as a psychological defense against absolute reliance on and subjection to their slaveholders. Even the planters were feeble individuals compared with the metaphysical world. "Uncle Ben was a great possum hunter, but he died fore I get big enough to go huntin' wid him," remembered John Glover of South Carolina. "He went possum huntin' every night till something went up de tree one night en possum talk to him. . . . " Will Dill, who also toiled on a South Carolina plantation, said he never saw a ghost "unless it was one night when we boys was out with our dogs possum hunting. The dogs treed a possum, so I went up to shake it out, but when I looked down to see what I shook out it got bigger and bigger; I scrambled down the tree right away. . . . "

Besides their hunting trips, slaves thoroughly enjoyed the opportunity to fish in nearby streams or lakes. They utilized a variety of different methods to catch fish, including set hooks, trotline, nets, seines, and baskets. The basket or trap was especially useful, since slaves wasted little time tending them. Trotlines and set hooks could be left untended as well, but most slaves preferred to work them a few hours during the evening to inhibit pillage by alligators. All of these methods were ideal for the slaves, since their maintenance did not interfere with their daily tasks.[20]

Slaves found fishing to be not only a source of simple amusement but a means of obtaining extra spending money. William Hayden, for example, acquired money by fishing on his small plantation in Kentucky. "I applied myself," said Hayden, "during my leisure moments to fishing, at which I was generally successful. These fish I conveyed to market and obtained a considerable sum of spending money." In fact, the slave was so successful in fishing that white commercial fishermen often complained he was monopolizing the fishing holes and putting them out of business. In 1831, for instance, fifty-six petitioners of New Bern, North Carolina, requested the legislature to pass a law that would prevent slaves from fishing unless in the company of a white person. "The petitioners declared themselves to be much injured both in their advocations, and in the management of their farms and negroes, by the large gangs of slaves, who come up from the town of New Bern and the neighborhood thereof, in boats . . . to sell, buy traffic, and fish.[21]

Despite these complaints, however, the majority of planters were not bothered by their bondsmen's receiving money for their angling exploits. As long as it was done during slaves' own time, slaveholders encouraged and occasionally even paid their own slaves for the fish they caught. Frederick Law Olmsted told the story of an overseer who refused to pay a slave for the fish he had caught on the grounds he had garnered his catch during a work day. "The manager sent to him some of the fish for his own use," stated Olmsted, "and justified himself to me for not paying for it on the ground that the slave had undoubtedly taken time which really belonged to his owner to set his baskets. . . . They must do it at night when they were excused from labor for their owner. . . ."[22]

In addition to fishing, slaves were particularly fond of gambling. The more peccant slave men placed bets on everything from dice and card games to local horse races and cockfights. Of course there was frequently the problem of having enough to bet with and the fear that the slaves of the more devout planters would be reprimanded for their gaming. Quite naturally, those slaves who were being converted into particular religious denominations were requested to give up the sinful practice of gambling. By 1830, moreover, a number of strict laws had been passed which forbade slaves from gambling. But no matter the legal restrictions, gambling remained popular among the slaves. The temperament of their masters as well as the economic, social, and political conditions of their community was more important in determining the extent to which slaves were allowed to gamble. And like their other recreational activities, slaves found ways to transcend the various condemnations made against gambling and continued to place bets with a high degree of seriousness. To elude the eyes of their virtuous masters or concerned white community they often had to resort to the woods or some other secluded spot. Not having much money to gamble with, their stakes often consisted of particular objects to which they attached special importance. "De only game I ever played wuz marbles," remembered John Smith of North Carolina. "I played fer watermelons. We didn't hab eny money so we played fer water-melons."[23]

Slaves welcomed the opportunity to engage in very informal and spontaneous boat and horse races. If slave crews happened to pass on the way to coastal markets they would invariably challenge one another to a test of speed. Similarly, slaves were anxious to prove the swiftness of their respective horses by running races on the avenues that led to the quarters. The younger slaves also enjoyed challenging their peer group to impromptu contests that would test their physical prowess. They delighted in seeing who could run the fastest, jump the highest, throw the farthest, swim the longest, and lift the heaviest objects. The ability to perform well in these physical contests usually guaranteed them the respect of their fellow slaves. One of the ways to attain a degree of status and recognized leadership in the slave quarter community was to be successful on the playing field.[24]

One of the significant aspects of the slaves' recreational pursuits is that they spent very little of their leisure time in combative activities. There are frequent references in the narratives to adult slaves wrestling and fighting each other. These contests, however, were usually arranged by and performed solely for the enjoyment of the whites. Confrontations certainly occurred in the slave quarters between people who were trying to settle personal arguments and differences, but the majority of these fights were not decided in a "sporting fashion." It is not suggested here that slaves never engaged in wrestling and boxing matches in a spirit of fun and with the sole purpose of testing physical skills and abilities, but that they occurred very infrequently. It was more common for two feuding slaves to meet behind the quarters and settle their differences—out of the view of the whites. It is even possible that these scuffles were an ideal way for the slaves to vicariously take out their aggressions and frustrations against their master. Not having many opportunities to express their indignation without fear of rebuke from whites, slaves were possibly more inclined to settle disputes with their fists. On the other hand, slaves ran the risk of being banished by their peer group if they unfairly abused other slaves. The thought of ill treating another bondsman was repugnant to most members of the slave quarters.[25]

There were several possible motives behind the slaveholders' granting of leisure time—the most obvious being the seeming concern for the health of their bondsmen. The more sensible planters realized that it was imperative to maintain optimal strength among their slaves if they were to obtain as much work as possible out of them. It was essential, therefore, to allow them certain periods of free time when they could rest and recuperate from their stringent labor.

Many slaves were allowed liberal amounts of leisure time, primarily because of the religious nature of their masters. Southern ministers repeatedly reminded planters of their duties to their bondsmen. Slaveholders were told that it was their responsibility to materially provide for their bondsmen, care for them in old age, demand only a sensible amount of labor from them, and allow them sufficient leisure time. It is important to note, however, that the preachers' discourses did not necessarily guarantee better treatment for the slaves. In fact, a big complaint of many slaves who belonged to "Christian" masters was their inability to do as they pleased with their leisure time. Most bondsmen, for example, looked forward all during the week to Sundays, when they were generally exempted from ordinary plantation labor. They would spend the day participating in their aforementioned recreational activities—in addition to visiting friends and performing personal domestic chores. Some of the more pious slaveholders, however, tried to prohibit their bondsmen from engaging in Sunday amusements. They were not necessarily concerned about the types of leisure activities the slaves engaged in, but only hoped they would utilize their time in more practical or meditative pursuits. In fact, the most devout planters would either arrange for a preacher to visit the plantation, teach Sunday school himself, or attempt to take part in the religious services held in the quarters. In other words, the most appropriate use of leisure time for slaves who belonged to those masters was to spend the day in prayer and reflection—not in unholy amusement. For example, the Mississippi planter, Dr. James Carson "urged his negroes to observe the Sabbath and to refrain from amusement or from work that could be deferred to another day."[26]

Attempts by the planters to guard against their slaves' desecrating the Sabbath were usually not successful. Forced to toil long hours in a six-day work week, many slaves had no other day to enjoy themselves. No matter the kind of restrictions placed on them, they were not about to give up their one day of pleasure very easily. Most planters also did not have a large enough staff to control their slaves' every move. Furthermore, the majority of slaveholders, even if they expressed their disdain for Sunday amusements, ultimately realized they had better allow their slaves to do as they pleased on this day or otherwise confront an insurgent worker. With few exceptions, the more enlightened slaveholders realized that any attempts to limit the slaves' recreational activities were unproductive, unless of course they interfered with the regular plantation work. In the main, if slaves were ready to work when called upon the planters would not concern themselves with the way they utilized their leisure time—unless of course it was detrimental to the safety of the plantation.[27]

Simple custom dictated to many slaveholders how much leisure time they allowed their bondsmen. Once tradition and practice had established how much leisure time was permitted on any given plantation, slaves came to expect nothing less than what was normally given them. Planters very rarely prohibited their slaves from celebrating wanted holidays because it would have enticed the worst kind of indignation, sulking, disobedience, and insubordination. "Tomorrow being Christmas the niggas are anticipating full freedom for the remainder of the week," wrote Mississippi planter Henry Cathell in 1851. "According to old customs I better give it. . . . "[28]

To the Virginia slave Francis Fedric, leisure time and Christmas, in particular, were contrived "to put the seal upon the slaves' own servitude." The planter would supply the slaves with whiskey which kept them in a continual state of intoxication. The bondsmen became so miserable during the holidays, according to Fedric, that they welcomed the return of the normal plantation routine. Likewise, Henry Bibb and his fellow slaves would honestly enjoy Sunday by engaging in some kind of amusement. They would resort to the woods on that day to gamble, fight, get drunk, and break the Sabbath. But these activities were often encouraged by the slaveholders, according to Bibb, for their own selfish purposes. They would make the day miserable for the slaves by forcing them to get drunk, "dance, pat juber, sing and play on the banjo" and then get them to wrestle, fight, jump, run races, and butt each other like sheep.

In the main, there seems to be little truth in the assertions made by Fedric and Bibb that slaveholders gave alcohol to their bondsmen in order to keep them in bondage. It appears to be an abolitionist ploy designed to illustrate the cruelty and barbaric nature of Southern planters. On the other hand, slaves did use liquor more than occasionally— possibly finding it one form of escape from the frustrations, indignities, and loneliness of slavery. They would therefore resort to the woods or some other secluded spot in order to drink unmolested.[29]

The more sagacious slaveholders, induced by feelings of self-interest rather than genuine benignity, realized that life would become too unbearable for their bondsmen if they were not allowed brief periods of leisure time. Planters hoped that "holidays" would tend to procure their slaves' contentment and inhibit any revolutionary impulses to which their bondsmen might pay heed. Recurring periods of leisure time were certainly a small price to pay for a "cheerful" band of servants and a smooth-running plantation. Frederick Douglass, for example, was fully convinced that slaveholders granted leisure time for the purpose of social control. There was no question in his mind that the holidays kept the slaves from revolting. "I believe," said Douglass, "those holidays were among the most effective means in the hands of the slaveholders of keeping down the spirit of insurrection among the slaves." They kept the slaves' minds on such immediate pleasures as singing, dancing, eating, drinking, and playing. But for these, he determined, "the rigors of bondage would have become too severe for endurance, and the slave would have been forced to a dangerous desperation."[30]

For many planters the granting of leisure time was one means of nurturing a paternalistic relationship with their slaves. By allowing their bondsmen some free time the slaveholders enhanced their own vanity and sense of accomplishing selfless service. Besides attempting to instill in their slaves a belief in the benevolence and uprightness of whites, slaveholders endeavored to implant in their bondsmen a sense of loyalty to their masters. An Alabama slaveholder wrote about the "privileges" he granted his bondsmen:

They are much more cheerful and happy when indulged occasionally. I generally give them two or three big dinners as they are termed during the year. That also has a tendency to cheer them and it always contributes largely to my happiness to see others happy, particularly those who are dependent on me. I always give them half of each Saturday, and often the whole day. . . . By pursuing this plan with my servants they perceive that I have an interest in their welfare and they become attached to me, and have respect for my orders.[31]

According to Eugene D. Genovese's interpretation, the planters' granting of leisure time did weaken the slaves' "revolutionary impulses'' but not because they were coerced into pettiness or self-abasement. The slaves' brief periods of leisure time, says Genovese, allowed them to develop a community feeling among fellow bondsmen and to a lesser but yet significant degree ''sense of community with their white folks.'' The holidays, therefore, ''weakened the slave's impulse to challenge the regime frontally, while they contributed to an ability to create a healthy Black community and to guarantee its survival.'' Genovese is correct in thinking that the leisure time afforded the slaves gave them perfect opportunities to foster a healthful black community, but he seems wrong in believing that slaves developed any genuine sense of community with whites. No matter how much slaveholders convinced themselves they had fostered trust and gained a sense of fellowship with their bondsmen through the granting of leisure time, the majority of slaves never felt any kind of group or community spirit with their ''White folks.'' At times individual masters might be viewed with sincere affection because of their attitude about leisure time, but normally the resentment felt toward slaveholders precluded any type of fraternal feelings between the two races.[32]

Even though the slaveholders' granting of leisure time failed to create any sense of genuine community life between themselves and their bondsmen, they apparently felt that the resultant creation of a stimulating black community would indirectly assist them in the management of their plantations. Many planters convinced themselves that the joys of isolation and the developing of an invigorating ''society at home'' cut down on truancy and interplantation partying—in the abstract, a splendid but normally unsuccessful strategy.

''The negro who is accustomed to remain constantly at home,'' remarked an Arkansas planter in 1846, ''is furnished with frequent leisure and all material wants is just as satisfied with the society on the plantation as that which he could find elsewhere.''[33]

There are several possible interpretations as to why slaveholders felt obligated to grant occasional periods of leisure time to their bondsmen. In the final analysis, however, the Southern planters' particular motives for allowing this time was generally aimed at one primary purpose—to make the slaves' lives bearable and at the same time maintain a reasonably efficient and smooth-running plantation. In other words, most planters realized that periodic amounts of leisure time would help countenance slaves in their everyday struggle for survival. They would have been driven beyond a terrifying hopelessness if they had not been allowed some time to do as they pleased. This did not mean that planters never utilized the whip and various other "incentives" to assist them in controlling their laborers. Assuredly, the most self-controlled planters would resort to the lash occasionally if all other methods failed. But most slaveholders felt this kind of treatment could be kept to a minimum and their bondsmen could be more adequately governed if they would dangle the "carrot" as a reward for "proper behavior." Brief periods of leisure time were certainly a small price to pay for a band of merry servants. "I gave my folks a three day Christmas holiday and killed twenty-eight head of beef for their big dinner," remarked an overseer in 1854. "I can do more with them in this way than if all the hides of the cattle were made into lashes."[34]

Leisure time was of significant importance to the slaves because it did help to lighten their burden of hardship and assisted them in coping with the stark realities of their existence. Fond memories of past "holidays" and the anticipation of future celebrations tended to countenance the slaves emotionally in their everyday struggle for survival. The temporary release from the tedious plantation regime was essential in relieving the boredom that invariably pervaded the life of almost every slave. The desolation of most Southern plantations and methodical nature of their labor often combined to make the slaves' lives dreadfully cheerless. The enjoyment of leisure was a natural response to boredom and the want of variety.

Not only did leisure time help relieve slaves of the boredom and monotony of their daily existence, but it furnished ample opportunities for them to engage in such recreational pursuits as dancing, gambling, hunting and fishing, and various athletic events. Many slaves enjoyed these activities simply because they possessed the skills necessary to perform them well. Like most people, slaves realized a great deal of personal satisfaction from being able to execute physical skills with special adroitness. The extremely skilled athletes in the slave quarter were also highly revered and admired by their fellow slaves. They achieved prominence not only for their unique abilities, but because they frequently served as observable role models for slave children and took a leading role in teaching their skills to interested members of the younger generation. It was not, however, the recognition they received from their physical exploits that slaves found most important. Their recreational pursuits were particularly significant because they were often the medium through which they assured themselves of their own self-worth, the means through which they perpetuated their "cultural" past, and the manner in which their individuality was asserted and maintained. Their various diversions, moreover, afforded the slaves an ideal way to vicariously comment on and satirize the peculiarities of their white folk. For example, by temporarily reversing social roles in their numerous dances, slaves were able to briefly relieve any aggressions and hostilities they held toward their owners. Their daily aggressions could be withstood more gracefully if they occasionally had opportunities to "take off" on the high manners of the white folks. This knack for capriciously transcending their masters' authority helped momentarily to liberate them from that pressure and assisted them in coping with the realities of the plantation community.

Obviously, planters attempted to restrict their slaves from participating in leisure-time activities that would threaten the maintenance of the plantation. Every effort was made, for example, to cut down on the slaves' nocturnal activities. Hardly anything bothered the planters more than the weeknight excursions of their slaves. They obviously preferred to have them rest up for the next day's labor, rather than running all over the countryside partying with slaves from neighboring plantations.

Slaveholders were also concerned about the demoralizing effect that neighboring slaves might have on their own. They continually railed against the certain loss of morals and destruction of discipline that would result among their well-regulated slaves if they were allowed to socialize with "strange negroes." "There were certain plantations where we were not permitted to go," remembered Green Willbanks of Georgia. "Certain folks were never allowed on our place. Old boss was particular about how folks behaved on his place; all his slaves had to come up to a certain notch. . . . " Most planters, moreover, prohibited their slaves from engaging in recreational pursuits that required the use of weapons and drums, or necessitated that they leave the plantation for extended periods of time. But slaves were often able to transcend these barriers and realize much more freedom than their institutionally defined role allowed. By plotting various schemes they were often able to outwit their unsuspecting masters and leave the plantation to engage in various pursuits with neighboring slaves. They simply had to be careful not to infuriate their master to the point where he became vengeful and unsympathetic to their basic interests.[35]

For many slaves, reoccurring periods of leisure were significant because it gave them much-needed opportunities to frolic and socialize with fellow bondsmen under comfortable conditions. Even though the planters were incorrect in believing that adequate leisure time would cut down on the slaves' interplantation visiting, they were right in thinking that it would produce an atmosphere conducive to the creation of a spirited black community. In fact, the slaves' zeal for leisure was probably accounted for by the group solidarity and community spirit that it brought forth more than anything else. Leisure-time activities were anxiously looked forward to by members of the slave quarter because it usually gave them a chance to "play" in their own particular fashion free from the surveillance of their white folks. The fellowship attained during these occasions seems especially significant because it furnished individual slaves with a sense of security and a continuity of fraternal feelings that they very seldom experienced under any other circumstances. Moreover, the constant reinforcement, common language, and strong positive sanctions that characterized these events helped to succor the slaves in their fight for survival.

Leisure time not only created an ideal setting promotive of a vibrant black community, it often provided social situations that were particularly conducive to easing the usual formality that existed between them and their master. It is a misconception to think that the relationship between the slave and his master was always one of dependent and superintendent. In many instances sharing the excitement of "holiday" festivities was influential in breaking down the decorum that normally existed between the planter and his slaves. In fact, it was when planter and slave were mutually involved in uninhibited merrymaking that the shackles of bondage were most disguised. The joy and pleasantry of the moment briefly erased the intrinsic differences and antagonisms that existed between them. Susan Dabney Smedes, the daughter of a Virginia slaveholder, said simply that during the Christmas holidays "there was an affectionate throwing off of the reserve and decorum of everyday life."[36]

This does not mean, however, that slaves ever felt any real sense of community with the master and his family. Members of the slave quarter never forgot that it was the planter who enslaved them, whose money chest profited most from their "free" labor and whose authority perpetuated the horrid institution. Mutual enjoyment of leisure-time activities could momentarily ease the discord between them, but it was not influential enough to prevent the slaves from recognizing their master as the ultimate despot. To develop a true feeling of community requires at least a common life-style, common interests and problems, or a common philosophical approach to the world. It would be historically fallacious to say that the sharing of leisure-time activities was responsible for developing these sentiments between master and slave—even for a brief period of time. This is not to argue that mutual participation in leisure-time activities did not temporarily eliminate the usual decorum between the races; it is only that this cultural form was incapable of ever developing a sense of community between two people whose view of this world was so alien.

Slaveholders, like many people in today's world, placed a great deal of importance on and normally evaluated the merit of individuals by the amount of effort they exerted in their work. They considered labor as being both essential for survival and a virtue in its own right. This did not mean that the Protestant work ethic characterized the slaveholders' individual value scheme. In fact, they understood that hard work was inevitable to obtain success, but not if it meant extreme abstinence, indiscriminate acquisition of riches, or an unrealistic attachment of "one's calling." The Southern planters undoubtedly enjoyed "living it up." Their reputation as a fun-loving and sportive society is generally a correct one. Nevertheless, most planters considered leisure-time pursuits as basically trifling in the sense that they were immaterial to "one's being," should be engaged in by gentlemen only in the most organized and refined fashion, and ought to be exclusive in nature and devoid of any frivolous public displays.

Slaves seem to have had a different view of work and leisure than their masters. They certainly did not place the same kind of emphasis on or evaluate the worth of individuals by the successful completion of their regular plantation tasks. "The slaves' sense of accomplishment was identified with the family unit and measured primarily by the successful maintenance of the familial order of the household. They realized the necessity of working long and difficult hours during planting and harvesting seasons, but expected to work considerably less during other seasons. They didn't understand the incessant need for labor and resisted what they felt was senseless work. In other words, work was not generally utilized for determining one's personal integrity. By contrast, leisure time was one area of their life where they could experience a degree of dignity and could assert and maintain their essential being. Considering their subservient position, the slaves' leisure time was vital to their physical and psychological survival. The institution could be withstood much more easily when slaves were allowed periodic respite from constant toil.

NOTES

1. See for example: John W. Blassingame, *The Slave Community: Plantation Life in the Antebellum South* (New York: Oxford University Press, 1972); Eugene D. Genovese, *Roll, Jordan, Roll: The World the Slaves Made* (New York: Vintage Books, 1976); Herbert G. Gutman, *The Black Family in Slavery and Freedom, 1750–1925* (New York: Random House, 1976); Leslie H. Owens, *This Species of Property: Slave Life and Culture in the Old South* (New York: Oxford University Press, 1977).

2. William W. Brown, *Narrative of William W. Brown, A Fugitive Slave, Written by Himself* (Boston: Anti-Slavery Office, 1847), p. 16; Charles Ball, *Slavery in the United States: A Narrative of Charles Ball* (Lewiston, Me.: John Shubert, 1836), pp. 270–271; John Thompson, *The Life of John Thompson, A Fugitive Slave: Containing His History of Twenty-Five Years in Bondage and His Providential Escape: Written by Himself* (Worcester: By the Author), p. 25.

3. Robert Q. Mallard, *Plantation Life Before Emancipation* (Virginia: Wittet and Shepperson, 1892), pp. 42–43; James H. Easterby, *The South Carolina Rice Plantation as Revealed in the Papers of Robert F. W. Allston* (Chicago: University of Chicago Press, 1945), p. 45; Ulrich B. Phillips, ed., *Plantation and Frontier Documents 1649–1863*, 2 vols. (New York: Burt Franklin, 1929), pp. 129–130.

4. Ball, *Slavery in the United States*, pp. 270–271; Daniel R. Hundley, *Social Relations in Our Southern States* (New York: Henry B. Price, 1860), p. 355; P. C. Weston, "Management of a Southern Plantation," *Debows Review*, Vol. XXII (January 1857), p. 40. See for example: W. Conrad Gass, "A Felicitious Life: Lucy Martin Battle, 1805–1874," *North Carolina Historical Review*, 52, No. 4 (1975), p. 376; Hundley, *Social Relations in Our Southern States*, p. 355.

5. William Webb, *History of William Webb, Composed by Himself* (Detroit: E. Hoekstra, 1873), p. 25; also various sections of Ronnie C. Tyler and Lawrence Murphy, eds., *The Slave Narratives of Texas* (Austin: The Encino Press, 1974); George P. Rawick, ed., *The American Slave: A Composite Autobiography*, 19 vols. (Westport, Conn.: Greenwood Press, 1972); Rawick, ed., *The American Slave*, Vol. 4, p. 146.

6. Lewis G. Clarke, *Narrative of the Sufferings of Lewis Clarke* (London: Richter and Sons, 1846), p. 25; also various sections of Rawick, *The American Slave*; Fisk University, *Unwritten History of Slavery: Autobiographical*

Accounts of Negro Ex-Slaves (Nashville, Tenn.: Social Science Institute, Fisk University, 1945); Basil Hall, *Travels in North America in the Years 1827 and 1828*, 3 vols. (Edinburgh: Cadell and Company, 1829), II, p. 216; Susan Dabney Smedes, *Memorials of a Southern Planter* (Baltimore: Cushings and Bailey, 1887), p. 65; Mrs. I. Hilliard Diary, June 9, 1850, Tulane University Library.

7. See for example: Rawick, *The American Slave*, Georgia Narratives, Vol. XII, No. 2, pp. 116–197, South Carolina Narratives, Vol. IV, No. 2, p. 250, Alabama Narratives, Vol. II, No. 1, p. 76, Texas Narratives, Vol. IV, No. 1, p. 135, Alabama Narratives, Vol. VI, No. 1, p. 88.

8. Southern planters developed an intricate patrol system to help prevent insurrectionary plots, keep down interplantation theft, and assist in catching runaways. They usually consisted of four or five men who would roam the countryside checking roads and different slave quarters. For excellent discussions of slave patrols see these secondary sources: Genovese, *Roll, Jordan, Roll*, pp. 618–619; Owens, *This Species of Property*, pp. 71–72, 74–75; Kenneth M. Stampp, *The Peculiar Institution: Slavery in the Antebellum South* (New York: Vintage Books, 1955), pp. 214–215; Weymouth T. Jordan, *Antebellum Alabama Town and Country* (Tallahassee: The Florida State University Press, 1957), p. 54; Joe Gray Taylor, *Negro Slavery in Louisiana* (Baton Rouge: The Louisiana Historical Association, 1963), p. 204; Webb, *History of William Webb*, p. 8; Rawick, *The American Slave*, Texas Narratives, Vol. IV, No. 1, p. 237; Tyler and Murphy, *The Slave Narratives of Texas*, p. 26; Rawick, *The American Slave*, Georgia Narratives, Vol. XII, No. 2, p. 188, Missouri Narratives, Vol. II, No. 7, p. 362; William B. Randolph Papers, September 14, 1833; Frederick Law Olmsted, *A Journey in the Seaboard Slave States* (New York: G. P. Putnam's Sons, 1856), p. 91.

9. Another method of concealing sound was to soak old quilts and rags and then hang them up in the shape of a little room. Rawick, *The American Slave*, Alabama Narratives, Vol. VI, No. 1, p. 27, South Carolina Narratives, Vol. III, No. 4, p. 191.

10. Ibid., Vol. III, No. 2, p. 194.

11. In addition to much testimony in the slave narratives there are many more contemporary as well as secondary sources that discuss the Afro-American dance in America. See for example: Lynn Fauley Emery, *Black Dance: In the United States from 1619 to 1970* (Palo Alto: National Press Books, 1972); Marshall and Jean Stearns, *Jazz Dance: The Story of American Vernacular Dance* (New York: Arno Press, 1968); Henry William Ravenal, "Recollections of Southern Plantation Life," *Yale Review*, Vol. 25 (1936), pp. 748–777; Chadwick Hanson, "Jenny's Toe: Negro Shaking Dances in America," *American Quarterly*, Vol. 19, No. 3 (Fall 1967), pp. 554–563.

12. See for example: Georgia Writers Project, *Drums and Shadows: Survival Studies Among the Georgia Coastal Negroes* (Athens: University of Georgia Press, 1940), pp. 115, 131, 141, 148; Edward C. L. Adams, *Congoree Sketches,*

Scenes from Negro Life in the Swamps of the Congoree and Tales by Tod and Scip of Heaven and Hell with Other Miscellany (Chapel Hill: University of North Carolina Press, 1927), p. 52.

13. Solomon Northup, *Twelve Years a Slave: Narrative of Soloman Northup, A Citizen of New York, Kidnapped in Washington City in 1841 and Rescued in 1853 From a Cotton Plantation Near the Red River in Louisiana* (Buffalo: Derby, Orton, and Mulligan, 1853), p. 219.

14. Rudi Blesha and Harriet Janis, *They All Played Ragtime* (New York: Oak Publications, 1971), p. 96; *South Carolina Gazette*, September 7, 1870; Reprinted in Hennig Cohen, "A Negro Folk Game in Colonial South Carolina," *Southern Folklore*, Vol. XVI, No. 2 (1955), pp. 183–184.

15. See for example: Rawick, *The American Slave*, Oklahoma Narratives, Vol. VII, No. 1, p. 6; Fisk Collection, *Unwritten History of Slavery*, p. 25; *Plantation Book of 1857–1858*, in the James H. Hammond Papers; Rawick, *The American Slave*, Texas Narratives, Vol. VI, No. 4, p. 198; Henry George Spaulding, "Negro Shouts and Shout Songs," in Bernard Kate, ed., *The Social Implications of Early Negro Music in the United States* (New York: Negro Universities Press, 1969), pp. 4–5.

16. Rawick, *The American Slave*, Maryland Narratives, Vol. XVI, No. 3, p. 30.

17. See for example: Guion G. Johnson, *Antebellum North Carolina: A Social History* (Chapel Hill: University of North Carolina Press, 1937), p. 555; Thomas D. Condy, *A Digest of the Laws of the United States and the State of South Carolina* (Charleston: A. E. Miller, 1830), pp. 124–125; Amos Stoddard, *Sketches, Historical and Descriptive of Louisiana* (Philadelphia: Mathew Carey, 1812), p. 335; Rawick, *The American Slave*, North Carolina Narratives, Vol. XIV, No. 1, p. 202; Mary C. Oliphant, ed., *The Letters of William Gilmore Simms*, 5 vols. (Columbia: University of South Carolina Press, 1952), Vol. I, pp. 142–143; Rawick, *The American Slave*, Georgia Narratives, Vol. XIII, No. 4, pp. 75–76.

18. Rawick, *The American Slave*, Georgia Narratives, Vol. XII, No. 1, p. 93, Texas Narratives, Vol. V, No. 3, pp. 210–211, Maryland Narratives, Vol. XVI, No. 4, p. 23.

19. Ibid., Georgia Narratives, Vol. XII, No. 2, pp. 128–129, Alabama Narratives, Vol. IV, No. 2, p. 180, Missouri Narratives, Vol. III, No. 4, p. 175; Elmina Foster Reminiscences, Southern Historical Collection, University of North Carolina, p. 16; Rawick, *The American Slave*, Alabama Narratives, Vol. VII, No. 1, p. 282, Texas Narratives, Vol. V, No. 4, p. 11.

20. Rawick, *The American Slave*, South Carolina Narratives, Vol. III, No. 2, pp. 186–187, Ibid., Vol. II, No. 1, pp. 321–322. See for example: Rawick, *The American Slave*, South Carolina Narratives, Vol. II, No. 1, p. 46; Sub Rosa Paul Ravesies, *Scenes and Settlers of Alabama* (Mobile, 1885), p. 9;

Robert S. Mallard, *Plantation Life Before Emancipation* (Richmond, Va.: Wittet and Shepperson, 1892), p. 26.

21. William Hayden, *Narrative of William Hayden* (Cincinnati, 1846), p. 25; Johnson, *Antebellum North Carolina*, p. 556.

22. Frederick Law Olmsted, *A Journey in the Back Country* (New York: Mason Brothers, 1860), pp. 75–76.

23. See for example: Johnson, *Antebellum North Carolina*, p. 557; Condy, *A Digest of the Laws of the United States and the State of South Carolina*, p. 127; Rawick, *The American Slave*, North Carolina Narratives, Vol. XV, No. 1, p. 273.

24. See for example: Mary Howard Schoolcraft, *Letters on the Condition of the African Race in the United States by a Southern Lady* (Philadelphia: T. K. and P. G. Collins Printers, 1852), pp. 12–13; Olmsted, *A Journey in the Seaboard Slave States*, p. 630; James B. Avirett, *The Old Plantation: How We Lived in Great House and Cabin Before the War* (New York: F. Tennyson Neely Co., 1906), pp. 33–34. See for example: Harvey Wish, *Slavery in the South* (New York: Farrar, Straus, and Company, 1964), p. 29; Erving E. Lowery, *Life on the Old Plantation in Antebellum Days or a Story Based on Facts* (Columbia, S.C.: The State Company Printers, 1911), p. 69; William Wells Brown, *My Southern Home: Or the South and Its People* (New York: Negro Universities Press, 1969), p. 97.

25. It was common for planters to pit individual slaves against each other in wrestling and boxing matches. They frequently took place after corn-shuckings, log-rolling, or other communal gatherings when slaves from all over were gathered at one particular plantation. Slaveholders liked nothing better than placing a wager or two on their favorite combatant.

26. See for example: George W. Freeman, *The Rights and Duties of Slaveholders* (Charleston: Christian Society, 1837), p. 25; H. N. McTyeire et al., *Duties of Masters of Servants; Three Premium Essays* (Charleston: Christian Society, 1837), p. 136. See for example: Charles L. Perdue, Jr., Thomas E. Barden, and Robert K. Phillips, eds., *Weevils in the Wheat: Interview with Virginia Ex-Slaves* (Charlottsville: University Press of Virginia, 1976), pp. 263–264; Rawick, *The American Slave*, South Carolina Narratives, Vol. III, No. 4, p. 63; John Q. Anderson, "Dr. James Green Carson, Antebellum Planter of Mississippi and Louisiana," *Journal of Mississippi History*, Vol. XVIII, No. 4 (October 1956), pp. 256–257.

27. See for example: Elijah P. Marrs, *Life and History of Elijah Marrs* (Worcester, 1893), p. 11; Basil Hall, *Travels in North America in the Years 1827 and 1828*, 3 vols. (Edinburgh: Cadell and Company, 1879), III, p. 180. Some masters, because of distinctive cultural differences, probably felt uncomfortable when their slaves spoke African languages, sang African songs, or performed African dances. But few slaveholders had a managerial staff large

enough or were sufficiently concerned about activities in the quarter to prohibit their bondsmen from engaging in native customs.

28. Henry Cathell Diary, December 24, 1851, Southern Historical Collection, University of North Carolina.

29. Francis Fedric, *Slave Life in Virginia and Kentucky or Fifty Years of Slavery in the Southern States of America* (London: Wertheim, Macintosh, and Hunt, 1863), p. 28; Henry Bibb, *Narrative of the Life and Adventures of Henry Bibb: An American Slave* (New York: Mnerosyne Publishing Company, 1857), p. 29.

30. Frederick Douglass, *My Bondage and My Freedom* (New York: Dover Publications, Inc., 1969), pp. 253–254.

31. Alabama Planter, "Management of Slaves," *Debows Review*, Vol. XII (August 1852), pp. 193–194.

32. Genovese, *Roll, Jordan, Roll*, pp. 579–580.

33. Anonymous, "Management of Slaves," *Southern Cultivator*, Vol. IV (March 1846), p. 44.

34. Quoted in Phillips, ed., *Plantation and Frontier Documents 1649–1863*, pp. 129–130.

35. Rawick, *The American Slave*, Georgia Narratives, Vol. XIII, No. 4, p. 142.

36. Smedes, *Memorials of a Southern Planter*, p. 162.

III

Quantification and Sport: The American Jockey Club, 1866–1867; A Collective Biography

Melvin L. Adelman

During the past two decades, historians have with increased frequency adopted quantification techniques to examine numerous and diverse facets of the human experience. While the application of this methodology to historical investigations has not yielded the often exaggerated benefits articulated by its initial supporters, few challenge any more the contribution this approach can and has made to a better understanding of the past. Virtually untouched by quantification techniques, however, has been the study of sport and clubs.[1]

Ever since Alexis de Tocqueville noted, in the 1830s, that "Americans of all ages, all conditions, and all dispositions constantly form associations," scholars have recognized the significant role voluntary associations played in nineteenth-century America. While historians have offered a variety of explanations for their surging numbers, most have linked this phenomenon to the impact changing demographic, economic, and social conditions had on urban life. Following the lead of sociologist Louis Wirth, they viewed the rise of voluntary associations as a response "to the last of the old patterns of sociability and informal community."[2]

One leading American historian described voluntary associations as "the key to the social system of the nineteenth century city," but little is known about the membership of these organizations. What information does exist comes mainly from what Eric E. Lampard has called "letristic sources." Quantifiable studies are exceedingly scant and have generally focused on "instrumental" rather than "expressive" associations. Only a few pieces on quantifiable data exist on the members of the multitude of urban clubs. Both Edward Pessen and, to a greater extent, E. Digby Baltzell have investigated the relationship between class structure and membership in social clubs. In both these works, however, the focus is on the elite membership, not the total population of the club.[3]

An increasing number of historical studies on sport have also taken place during the past two decades. The overwhelming majority of the new research, however, continues to rely on newspaper accounts and other "traditional" sources. Such data, impressionistic at best and at times inaccurate, has hampered the analysis of sport, particularly as it relates to the class backgrounds of the participants. The few attempts to apply quantification techniques to the study of sport, such as Steven Riess' examination of baseball as a source of social mobility and Stephen Freedman's investigation of the class backgrounds of baseball players in post–Civil War Chicago, have already yielded fruitful insights. However, further quantifiable research, especially on the social class of the members of the voluminous and diverse athletic clubs, is necessary before historians can create more-effective generalizations concerning sport.[4]

The purpose of this study is to create a collective biography of the 862 individuals who made up the American Jockey Club (AJC) of New York during the racing association's first two years, 1866 and 1867. More specifically, the study tries to comprehend these turfmen in terms of five issues: (1) their social characteristics; (2) their family backgrounds, particularly their relationship to New York's antebellum elite; (3) the degree to which these turfmen were occupationally and economically mobile; (4) the affiliation of these men with other prestigious clubs; and (5) to discern whether differences existed between the AJC's governing body—the 50 life members—and the general membership of the association in terms of the four previous areas.[5]

In 1866, a group of wealthy New Yorkers established the American Jockey Club. The formation of the AJC would become a pivotal event in the history of American thoroughbred racing. The new club reestablished racing on a firm basis in New York after the sport had been on the verge of collapse for the previous two decades.

Leonard Jerome was the architect and dominant figure behind the creation of the AJC. The American grandfather of Sir Winston Churchill, Jerome was a prominent Wall Street financier who became a millionaire by selling short during the Panic of 1857. The handsome Jerome gained his greatest notoriety, however, as a leader of the city's social set. A lover of sport, he had been a major backer of racing at Saratoga and was the first vice-president of the jockey club there since its inception in 1863.[6]

The success of racing at Saratoga encouraged Jerome to create a jockey club in New York, as well as build a race course patterned after the elaborate European tracks. Besides providing the initial leadership, Jerome offered up to $25,000 to help defray the cost of the sport, although he embarked on the adventure convinced that the expenses of the track could easily be met. As a result of the overwhelming success of Jerome Park, as the new race course was appropriately named, not a single penny of his generous subsidy was ever required.

While there is little doubt about Jerome's paramount role in the creation of the AJC, the exact process by which the club was formed is unclear. Writing seven years after the establishment of the AJC, Francis G. Fairfield wrote,

First, it was talked up; secondly, it was written up, and this talking up and writing up occupied a period of several months, during which the press teemed with paragraphs dwelling upon the excellent philanthropy of the project for redeeming the turf, and its practical results on popular morals.

Fairfield further noted that Jerome had thrashed out the idea of starting a racing association with Henry Raymond, editor of the *New York Times*, dramatist J. Lester Wallack, August Belmont (whom Jerome handpicked as the AJC's first president) and a host of horsemen from throughout the country.[7]

Fairfield's remembrance, quite possibly romanticism, contains certain flaws. In 1865, *Wilkes' Spirit of the Times* noted that Jerome and his racing partner, Paul S. Forbes, were going to buy a track near Central Park. There was no further newspaper reference to their activities or any discussion concerning the formation of a racing association until the same sporting journal merely reported the formation of the AJC and the club's officers. Fairfield's list of the horsemen that met with Jerome contains the names of horsemen who did not join the club, while excluding many horsemen who did. While Fairfield's version of the events leading to the creation of the AJC is only partially accurate at best, there can be little doubt that horsemen played a paramount role in the formation of the racing association. This is not surprising since they had a vested economic interest in the sport and had been involved in thoroughbred racing prior to the formation of the AJC.[8]

The organizational structure of the AJC indicates the desire of the horsemen to dominate the club. Power was vested in fifty life members, seventeen of whom, not coincidentally, were horsemen. While horsemen constituted only slightly more than a third of the ruling group, they probably handpicked the remaining AJC's decision makers. The nonhorsemen among the life members were generally close associates, often sporting friends and in one case (Lawrence R. Jerome) a brother of a horseman, and were selected in order to provide the club with a solid financial backing and a favorable press.[9]

From the inception of the AJC, few doubted its eventual success. Even prior to the inaugural meeting, one New York newspaper claimed that the AJC was destined to "become the arbiter of [the] sport in this country." Developments during the AJC's first five years did not disappoint the prognosticators. The press unanimously declared that the quality and quantity of thoroughbreds at Jerome Park were outstanding, and that under the sponsorship of the AJC, the turf had achieved a degree of fashion and respectability heretofore unknown in New York. Under the guidance of the AJC, racing had become more than a sporting event; it was a social outing, an arena for the "beautiful" people to see and be seen. By 1870, the *New York Herald* wrote that the AJC had "speedily attained the exalted position of the exemplar of the turf. As a sporting organization it has no superior in the world."[10]

Not surprisingly, AJC members resided overwhelmingly in New York City and vicinity (NYCV). Table 1 indicates that more than 70 percent of the club resided in the city, while another 19.2 percent made their homes in the New York metropolitan region (NYM). The residential patterns of life members showed some variation from the club's regular members. Both groups resided mainly in NYCV, but nearly a 10 percent difference existed between the two types of members. Significant fluctuations also existed in the exent to which these two groups made their homes in the city or the metropolitan region. That roughly a third of the life members were horsemen contributed to the discrepancy in the residential patterns. Of NYCV's eleven horsemen, six resided in the more rural regions of the NYM, where the breeding of horses could take place on their family estate. Similarly, the presence of six Southern horsemen among the life members was responsible for the significant variations in the residential patterns of the two groups in the "rest of the country" category.[11]

The birthplace of AJCers residing in New York did not conform to the city's population in 1870. This development is not surprising since prestigious organizations have never been representative of the population as a whole. Differences in the geographical origins of the club members residing in New York and the city's richest residents in 1856–1857, however, requires some explanation (see Table 2). Several interacting factors contributed to these differences. First, the majority of the two groups among wealthy New Yorkers—foreign and elsewhere—that were disproportionately lower in the jockey club came from regions with limited horse racing traditions. Consequently, rich residents originally from these geographical areas were less likely to have joined the AJC. By comparison, the overrepresented groups came from areas with a rich racing heritage.[12]

Second, wealth lists rely on a single variable, while membership in elite clubs also depended on family and social relations. The wealth list comprised mainly one person per family since it would have been quite rare for both a father and son(s) to have been assessed at least $100,000. Among AJCers, there were at least sixteen father-son(s) and nineteen brother combinations. The family structure of club membership naturally increased the percentage of native New Yorkers. This trend may be illustrated by the fact that three-quarters of the New York–residing AJCers in their twenties were born in the city. Similarly, among the club members were native New Yorkers, such as George Alley, Charles Astor Bristed, and John G. Hecksher, whose wealthy fathers or grandfathers were born outside the city.[13]

Finally, membership in the city's prestigious social clubs was never intended to be restricted solely to the "richest of the rich." As is discussed in greater detail later, "lesser lights" among the city's wealthy inhabitants belonged to all the elite organizations. Among AJCers, native New Yorkers were disproportionately more numerous at the lower income levels. While a certain economic standing was required for membership in New York's elite clubs, it was not the sole criteria. The greater familiarity with the city's social and cultural life made Gotham's clubs more readily open to natives of lesser wealth than those of comparable means originally from outside the city.

The average age of the club members was 42.2, and the median age,

42.5, hardly varied from this figure. The ages of AJCers ranged considerably: from 21 to 78-year-old James A. Hamilton, the son of Alexander Hamilton. More than three-quarters of the membership, however, were middle aged, 30–59. Nevertheless, the ages of the governing group reveal certain different patterns from regular members. The range of their ages was not nearly as extensive, varying from 24 to 60-year-old William J. Minor of Natchez. Consequently, they showed a more clustered pattern; of this group, 85.2 percent were middle aged.

This section focuses on four variables of status—occupation, district of residency, income, and wealth. The occupations of New York turfmen were divided into thirteen categories (see Table 3). Nearly two-thirds of the members engaged in the two economic activities—commerce and finance—associated with wealthy antebellum New Yorkers. In contrast to the dominance of commerce and finance, only slightly more than 10 percent were involved in occupations that have become associated with the increasing industrialization and bureaucratization of the American economy (manufacturing, executives, and transportation). Even these figures overestimate the extent to which AJCers could accurately be described as industrialists. For example, under the category of manufacturing were turfmen engaged in the refining of food, as well as Charles L. Tiffany, the famous jewelry manufacturer. Approximately 5 percent of the club engaged in less prestigious and less lucrative occupations, such as craftsmen, politicians, hotel managers, and clerks.[14]

The majority of life members also engaged in commerce and finance, but only 58.3 percent of the AJC's ruling board were involved in these occupations. Moreover, the breakdown of these two occupational categories reveals differences between the two groups of turfmen. Finance was the most prevalent occupation of life members, while only a quarter of the AJC leaders were merchants, auctioneers, or importers, an appreciable decline from the percentage for the regular members.

Life members were also less often lawyer-judges, manufacturers, and executives. On the other hand, the percentage of the governors engaged in transportation or professionals was nearly twice that of the regular members. Not only did professional life members make up a larger proportion of their group, but, unlike the contrasting group, they were not drawn from diverse occupations. Three out of the four were editors or publishers of newspapers. The presence of these newspapermen in this austere group was hardly coincidental. While James Gordon Bennett, Jr., was among New York's leading sportsmen, Henry J. Raymond and Manton Marble, the other two editors, had little to do with sport in New York. Their selection was part of the club's effort to ensure a positive image. That these newspapermen were among the AJC's governing group did not always ensure that they or their papers supported the policies of the racing club. In fact, the press overwhelmingly opposed the AJC's more exclusive practices. Nevertheless, by propagating the image of the AJC as the redeemers of the sport, the press provided the sanction and justification for those who advocated and supported these elitist policies.[15]

Large variations existed between life and regular members in both the gentlemen and especially the agricultural categories. While only a mere 0.3 percent of the regular members were engaged in agricultural pursuits, 8.3 percent of the life members earned their livelihood from this occupation. In fact, it was the only time in the study when the number of life members exceeded that of the contrasting group. Here the presence of Southern horsemen was once again responsible for the discrepancy. Finally, not a single AJC leader was drawn from the less prestigious occupations.

While occupation and residency differentiated AJCers from the remainder of the city's population, their earnings did so even more. For the purpose of this study, New York's 1863 income tax record was selected. While this source has certain limitations, this published list provides an easy way to assess the earnings of the club members and compare differences between regular and life members. Moreover, the record provides a quick way to demonstrate the superior wealth of these turfmen compared to the population of the city as a whole. At a time when 36 percent of New York's population, or approximately 2 percent of the heads of households, had incomes of at least $3,000, 83.3 percent of the AJC earned this amount.[16]

The average income of AJC members in 1863 was $26,993. The median and mode incomes were considerably smaller; the former was $11,667 and the latter $2,000. Information on life members was limited to only ten individuals, but the data strongly suggest that they were significantly wealthier than regular members. Their mean income, $59,700, was nearly twice that of the contrasting group ($25,000). The median income of life members, $18,500, although considerably smaller than their average, was still larger than the median income of the total membership.

The traditional relationship between occupation, residency, income, and wealth—and the strong relationship between these variables in this study—permits speculation on the economic worth of AJC members within three broad categories: superrich, rich, and well-to-do. Biographical material dealing with the turfmen's personal and family wealth, as well as membership in other prestigious social clubs, was also used to augment the analysis.[17]

Over 60 percent of the AJCers were either rich or superrich, while 38.4 percent were well-to-do (see Table 4). As those turfmen who could not be categorized were more likely to have been drawn from the latter economic group, it is quite possible that nearly a half-and-half division between rich-superrich and well-to-do members existed in the AJC. Given evidence already presented on the differences between life and regular members, it is not surprising that the former were significantly wealthier than the latter.

Differences in the occupations of life and regular members were reflected in the variations in the occupational patterns of their parents. Life member fathers were less frequently engaged in commerce and more often in agriculture when compared to the fathers of regular members. Similar to their sons, the fathers of the governing group were proportionately more often professionals and less frequently lawyer-judges. The percentages of financial and industrialist parents were roughly equal for both groups, although none of the fathers of the AJC leaders were manufacturers. Only one of the select fifty's fathers, Samuel Purdy, the famous jockey and builder by profession, was drawn from the less prestigious occupations.

Exactly half of the members of the racing association were engaged in the same occupation as their fathers. Only 37.9 percent of the lawyers were the sons of attorneys, but approximately half of their parents engaged in either finance or commerce. Similarly, 31.1 percent of AJC members in finance had banker or broker fathers; however, a third had commercial fathers and 7.44 percent were the sons of lawyers. None of the gentlemen were gentlemen's sons. Of their ten fathers, eight were in commerce and another was a lawyer. The only professional parent, Reverend John Bristed, married quite well—the daughter of John Jacob Astor. While one of the six executives was engaged in the same occupation as his father, four others were the sons of either lawyers or financiers.

Occupational mobility was related to age. Only one of the twenty-eight turfmen in their twenties was in a higher-ranked occupation than his father. The figures then rose steadily, ranging from roughly one in six AJCers in their thirties and forties, to about one in four for turfmen fifty and older.

As was the case with their sons, an attempt was made to speculate on the wealth of AJC fathers. The parents were divided into five economic categories—superrich, rich, well-to-do, middle and poor. Comparing Table 6 with Table 4 indicates that the parents were less well off financially than their offspring. Slightly more than half the parents were well-to-do or middle-class, with the remaining being rich or superrich. Only a minute percentage of the club were born poor.

The wealthier life members also had wealthier parents in comparison to the regular members. There were also differences in wealth among parents who lived in the city, the metropolitan region, and outside NYCV (see Table 7). The percentage of rich and superrich fathers was approximately the same for New York and the surrounding area residents. However, 34.9 percent of the city parents were well-to-do in contrast to only one in five from the NYM. Conversely, roughly 10 percent of the New Yorkers were middle class or lower compared to slightly more than a quarter for the metropolitan region. Greater discrepancies in wealth existed between NYCV and non-NYCV parents. Only 20 percent of the parents from outside NYCV were either rich or superrich while 56 percent of them were middle-class financially.[18]

While AJCers experienced only slight occupational mobility, they underwent considerably more financial mobility (see Table 8). Roughly three out of every seven members of the racing association were economically better off than their parents. As only a handful of turfmen had poor parents and less than 20 percent had middle-class fathers, the extent of mobility was small. Two-thirds of the mobile members moved up one economic category from their fathers. Consequently, only one out of seven AJCers showed considerable mobility (advancement of two or more economic categories).

Slight differences existed in terms of the mobility of life members (40 percent) and regular members (43.3 percent). Of the mobile governing group, however, half experienced significant mobility in contrast to less than a third for the regular members. Greater discrepancies in the degree of mobility existed for the different birthplace and age groups. Slightly more than a quarter of the turfmen born in NYCV advanced economically. The percentage was considerably higher for members originally from outside this area, ranging from a low of 50 percent for those born in the rest of the country to a high of 86.7 percent for natives of New England.

Both occupational and economic mobility among AJCers were strongly linked to the geographical movement of the members to the metropolis. None of the turfmen who came to the city conformed to the popular rags-to-riches theme, nor were they, with rare exception, the sons of rich fathers, espècially by New York standards. They were not, however, without what nineteenth-century writers called "advantages." Their parents, whether well-to-do or middle-class, were often prominent and influential residents in smaller towns and cities. Neither self-made men nor men of inherited wealth, AJCers from outside New York moved to the mecca of commerce and finance to improve their economic status.[19]

Economic mobility markedly increased with every succeeding age group with the exception of members sixty years and over, where the decline was slight. Does the evidence indicate that mobility was significantly declining, or are there other explanations? One possible alternative is that the longer life cycle of older members permitted greater opportunity for advancement. A more likely alternative was that the younger members, being born more often in NYCV, were therefore more likely to have wealthier parents, thereby precluding extensive mobility. However, the geographical origins of the members alone cannot be viewed as the sole factor, as the percentage of native New Yorkers who had rich or superrich fathers likewise declined with each succeeding age group. This trend was also present for members outside NYCV. The decline in the rate of mobility was due to the fact that older AJCers (forty and over) were men who more often made their own fortunes, while the younger members were more likely to be men of inherited wealth. Whereas 34.7 percent of the former group had rich or superrich fathers, 73.3 percent of the latter group had parents in this economic category.

To draw definitive conclusions on mobility from this speculative examination of the wealth of AJC members and their parents is obviously impossible. However, the high rate of mobility among AJC turfmen does raise questions of Edward Pessen's contention that mobility among New York's wealthiest residents was quite limited, while supporting Frederic C. Jaher's view that greater fluidity existed among New York's elites during the nineteenth century. On closer scrutiny, moreover, the evidence drawn from AJC members is not in sharp contrast to Pessen's data. In fact, he showed that a quarter of New York's superrich and a third of the rich did not come from the city's wealthy families of a generation earlier. The roughly 10 percent difference between Pessen's mobility figures and the ones here may be explained in a couple of ways. First, elite social organizations, as suggested earlier, always included wealthy individuals who fell below the rich. Possibly, these men contributed to the different rate. Second, changing economic conditions, resulting from the depression of 1857 and the impact of the Civil War, might have provided new opportunities for wealth.[20]

Earlier it was noted that wealth was not the only criterion for club membership, but it was no doubt the major one, especially when it came to dual membership. Slightly less than half of the AJCers in no other club had incomes of $6,000 or less, while only slightly more than a quarter were in the top third. The average income of AJCers in two clubs was 39.1 percent higher than for turfmen in no other club. Moreover, only 22.7 percent of these racing men were in the lowest income bracket, while twice this number were in the top third. Turfmen in three clubs had the highest average income, although their breakdown in the various income groupings followed a similar pattern as two club turfmen. The two AJCers in all the prestigious organizations were in the middle and top income levels. Reversing the process further dramatizes the relationship between earnings and club membership. Over half the turfmen who made less than $6,000 were in no other club. The percentage of middle-income AJCers in no other club dramatically declined from the previous group, while the average number of clubs increased 55.7 percent. From the middle to the highest earning bracket the number of clubs per turfman rose another 11.4 percent even though the percentage in no other club was slightly higher than the previous income group. However, 38.5 percent of the middle-income level were in two or more clubs, while half the turfmen with incomes in excess of $24,000 were in this many organizations.[21]

Membership in the AJC does not appear to have been a stepping-stone to other elite clubs. Only 5.7 percent of the turfmen joined the more prestigious Union Club (UC) after 1866 and the percentage was even less for the other clubs. Of the small group that did become members of these organizations at a later date, most would have been accepted for membership even if they had not affiliated with the AJC. Three factors were probably responsible for the AJC's failure to become a waiting club for entrance into other prestigious associations. The newness of the racing association and the fact that club life in New York, also relatively new, had not yet developed a distinct "pecking order" played a part. A more critical factor was that sporting organizations do not appear to function as a means of club advancement. Since less than half of the AJCers were in another exclusive club, for the majority of the city's turfmen the American Jockey Club was the most prestigious organization to which they belonged.[22]

The 862 individuals who were members of the American Jockey Club during its first two years were, logically enough, very prosperous men. New York's racing association comprised mainly middle-aged residents of New York City and vicinity who were overwhelmingly engaged in the more lucrative and prestigious occupations. Their social backgrounds reflect, however, the diversity of the city's elites in the years surrounding the Civil War. Over half of the members were born outside New York, with the majority coming from the metropolitan area, upstate New York, and New England. Although the turfmen came from "good families," they were by and large first-generation wealth, and inherited wealth among club members was probably still of a recent vintage. As "new men" both economically and geographically, AJCers were generally unconnected with New York's antebellum economic elite.

The social composition of the AJC—the dominance of new wealth and the presence of many men who were only well-to-do—raises questions of our perception of the function of elite organizations. "The history of American clubdom," Cleveland Amory noted, "is the story of Social Security—with capital S's. From the very beginning clubs were formed not primarily to get people in but rather to keep people out." In the sense that the admission fee to the club ($100) and the annual dues ($50) prohibited middle-class involvement, the makeup of the racing association confirms Amory's assertion. However, the basic purpose of prestigious associations had little to do with middle-income people; their exclusion was an accepted fact. Rather, their basic function has been to maintain upper-class hegemony by warding off the challenge of new wealth either by gradually assimilating them or through effective exclusion. Discrepancies between the function and form of New York's clubs has probably always existed. While greater research into this area of New York life is necessary, the city's social organization, in contrast to such urban counterparts as Boston and Philadelphia, have traditionally been more accessible to new wealth. This was especially the case around the mid-nineteenth century when newcomers "easily moved into elite, cultural, social, educational and charitable institutions." Given that slightly more than half of the wealthiest New Yorkers in 1856–1857 were first-generation wealth, this tolerant attitude is not surprising.[23]

The presence of new wealth in the AJC was consistent with other New York clubs, but the presence of so many men of lesser wealth probably was not. In contrast to the UC and the New York Yacht Club (NYYC), the city's racing association was less exclusive. The newness of the racing club and the failure and problems of thoroughbred racing in New York during the previous two decades indirectly contributed to this development. Two interrelated factors were more responsible for the turf association's comparatively more democratic membership. Most important was the club's strong dependency on the money collected from entrance and membership dues to sponsor the sport. Clearly the fiscal problems of horse racing in New York between 1845 and 1865 and the emergence of the more expensive "dash system" made almost anyone who was willing to pay the club's fee welcomed for membership. In addition, the kind and degree of interaction between AJC members differed from traditional urban clubs. Racing meetings were held only two or three times annually, and the size of the racing grounds made the avoidance of other members, if so desired, relatively easy.[24]

That the AJC was open to a broader spectrum of the city's leading citizens indicates that the underlying purpose of all elite clubs was not, as one historian maintained, that they offered "their socially prominent members the twin assurance of exclusiveness and enhanced status." Unlike in the UC, membership in the AJC did not confirm "gentlemen" status, nor did one's absence indicate an inferior social position. In assessing why individuals joined the AJC, it is necessary to begin with the simple explanation that they had a personal interest in the sport. Yet if individual tastes were an important factor in membership, so were social considerations.[25]

"In modern metropolitan America," Baltzell wrote,

the club serves to place the adult member of society and their families within the social hierarchy. These voluntary associations . . . provided an intricate web of primary group milieux which give form and structure to an otherwise impersonal urban society composed of secondary groups.

He further points out that a well-structured club hierarchy exists within urban centers, but within this structure there were significant variations in the types of clubs and the functions they performed. While club life in the 1860s was not as well-developed as in contemporary America, Baltzell provides a framework for understanding AJC membership and its function as an elite club.[26]

Precisely because the racing association was less exclusive, it could act in a manner radically different from the more restrictive clubs, such as the Union Club. While membership in these clubs sought to differentiate among different elite groups, racing, quite possibly more than any other social institution, acted to integrate them. At the two or three annual racing meetings at Jerome Park one could find the greatest mingling among the diverse and broadest segments of New York's elite. While over half the club never joined any of the four other prestigious organizations, membership in the AJC dramatized that they held a certain position within the community.[27]

The differences that existed between the governors of the AJC and the club's general membership was probably typical of most prestigious organizations. In the prevailing pattern, however, one would expect the leaders to have been older, drawn more frequently from the city's established families and wealthier. For the racing association officers, only the latter pattern held true. To what extent the newness of the club played a part in this development is impossible to say precisely. Nevertheless, the problems of the turf in the two decades prior to the formation of the AJC no doubt opened the leadership of horse racing in New York to new men.[28]

In terms of the background characteristics of life and regular members, the similarities outweighed the differences. Both groups were roughly the same age and, with the exception of the Southern contingent among the governors, both revealed similar patterns of residency and birthplace. Although life members had wealthier parents, they, like the more numerous group, were not drawn from old New York families. The difference in the economic backgrounds of the two groups stemmed from the greater proportion of life members with wealthy fathers who lived outside the city.

Significant variations between life and regular members existed for all the status variables. Slightly less evident in terms of occupation and district, the differences were more fully dramatized in terms of membership in other clubs and, most importantly, wealth. The most critical distinguishing characteristic between the governors and not only the general membership, but even the wealthy regular members, was that seventeen of the nineteen horse owners affiliated with the AJC were life members.

This significant difference clarifies our understanding of the organizational structure of the AJC. Unlike other prestigious clubs, the leaders of New York's racing association were men who had a vested and huge economic interest in the club's success. While horsemen made up slightly more than a third of the life members, they had been the major force behind the formation of the AJC and, no doubt, hand-picked the remaining leaders in an effort to provide the new club with a solid financial backing and social respectability. Consequently, while the founders and leaders of the AJC were more than willing to open the club to "lesser lights," the oligarchical structure, with the entire decision-making process resting in the hands of the fifty life members, emanated from the desire of the horsemen and their allies to guarantee their control over the sport.[29]

NOTES

1. For an assessment of the usage of quantification as a historical methodology, see Allan G. Bogue, "Numerical and Formal Analysis in United States History," *Journal of Interdisciplinary History*, 12 (1981), 137–75; Samuel P. Hayes, "Historical Social Research: Concept, Method and Technique," *Journal of Interdisciplinary History*, 5 (1974), 475–82; D. N. Sprague, "A Quantitative Assessment of the Quantification Revolution," *Canadian Journal of History*, 13 (1978), 177–92; J. Morgan Kousser, "Quantitative Social-Scientific History," in Michael Kammen, ed., *The Past Before Us: Contemporary Historical Writing in the United States* (Ithaca, 1980), 433–56.

2. Alexis de Tocqueville, *Democracy in America*, ed. Phillip Bradley, 2 vols. (New York, 1966), 2: 106; Sam Bass Warner, Jr., *The Private City: Philadelphia in Three Periods of Its Growth* (Philadelphia, 1968), 61; Louis Wirth, "Urbanism as a Way of Life," *American Journal of Sociology*, 44 (1938), 1–24.

3. Oscar Handlin, "The Social System," in Lloyd Rodwin, ed., *The Future Metropolis* (New York, 1961), 23; Eric E. Lampard, "Two Cheers for Quantitative History: An Agnostic Foreward," in Leo F. Schnore, ed., *The New Urban History: Quantitative Explorations by American Historians* (Princeton, 1975), 13. For the application of quantification to the study of voluntary associations, see Don H. Doyle, "The Social Function of Voluntary Associations in a Nineteenth-Century American Town," *Social Science History*, 1 (1977), 333–55; Walter Glazer, "Participation and Power: Voluntary Associations and the Functional Organization of Cincinnati in 1840," *Historical Methods Newsletter*, 5 (1972), 151–68; Stuart M. Bluman, *The Urban Threshold: Growth and Change in a Nineteenth-Century American Community* (Chicago, 1976), 166–89. For the differences between "instrumental" and "expressive" associations, see C. Wayne Gordon and Nicholas Babuhuk, "A Typology of Voluntary Associations," *American Sociological Review*, 24 (1959), 22–29. Edward Pessen distinguished between voluntary associations concerned with public issues and problems, and social clubs. See his *Riches, Class and Power Before the Civil War* (Lexington, 1973), 222–23. Pessen, *Riches*, 222–30; E. Digby Baltzell, *Philadelphia Gentlemen: The Making of a National Upper Class* (New York, 1958), 335–63.

4. Steven A. Riess, *Touching Base: Professional Baseball and American Culture* (Westport, Conn., 1980), 151–219; Stephan Freedman, "The Baseball Fad in Chicago, 1865–1870: An Exploration of the Role of Sport in the Nineteenth Century City," *Journal of Sport History*, 5 (1978), 42–68. Also see Richard G. Wettan and Joe D. Willis, "Social Stratification in the New York Athletic Club: A Preliminary Analysis of the Impact of the Club on Amateur Sport in Late Nineteenth Century America," *Canadian Journal of History of Sport and Physical Education*, 7 (1976), 49–53; Melvin L. Adelman, "The Development of Modern Athletics: Sport in New York City, 1820–1870" (Ph.D. diss., University of Illinois, 1980), 298–301, 330–33, 356–64, 397–403, 437–39, 443–57.

5. For members of the AJC in 1866–1867, see American Jockey Club, *Officers of the Club*, 2 vols. (New York, 1866–1867). Identification of AJC members presented certain problems. Club records merely differentiated between members who resided or worked in New York State from those who lived outside the Empire State. Although AJCers listed as "New York" could theoretically live anywhere in the state, the study worked under the assumption that they were residents of, or at least worked in, New York City. Of the New Yorkers, 590 were listed in *Trow's New York City Directory* from 1865 through 1868. Other AJCers were identified through obituaries, biographies (individual and collective), histories of racing, and genealogical records. However, 21.1 percent of the turfmen could not be identified either because no information could be found or because there were too many individuals in

the directories with the same name. The major sources used were Lyman Weeks, *Prominent Families of New York* (New York, 1897); Charles Morris, ed., *The Makers of New York* (Philadelphia, 1895); Margherita A. Hamm, *Famous Families of New York*, 2 vols. (New York, 1902); and William T. Bonner, *New York: The World's Metropolis, 1623–1624—1923–1924* (New York, 1924). Also helpful were Walter Barrett (Joseph Scoville), *The Old Merchants of New York*, 5 vols. (New York, 1885); Pessen, *Riches*, esp. 92–108; Robert C. Albion, "Commercial Fortunes in New York: A Study in the History of the Port of New York about 1850," *New York History*, 16 (1935), 158–68; Brian J. Danforth, "The Influence of Socioeconomic Factors in Political Behavior: A Quantitative Look at New York City Merchants, 1828–1844" (Ph.D. diss., New York University, 1974); George T. Strong, *The Diary of George Templeton Strong*, ed. Allan Nevins and Milton H. Thomas, 4 vols. (New York, 1952); Allan Nevins, ed., *The Diary of Phillip Hone, 1828–1851* (New York, 1970). Works on horse racing consulted were John Hervey, *Racing in America, 1665–1865*, 2 vols. (New York, 1944); Dan Bowmar III, *The Giants of the Turf: The Alexanders, the Belmonts, James R. Keene, The Whitneys* (Lexington, 1960); William S. Vosburgh, *Racing in America, 1866–1921* (New York, 1922). Numerous biographies were examined. Some examples are Wayne Andrews, *The Vanderbilt Legend: The Story of the Vanderbilt Family, 1794–1940* (New York, 1941), and Henry Clews, *Fifty Years on Wall Street* (New York, 1915). Finally, national encyclopedias such as *The Dictionary of American Biography* and *Appleton's Encyclopedia of American Biography* were consulted. Information was also gathered from the volumes of the *New York Genealogical and Biographical Record*.

6. Anita Leslie, *The Remarkable Mr. Jerome* (New York, 1964); Allen Churchill, *The Upper Crust: An Informal History of New York's Highest Society* (Englewood Cliffs, 1970), 56–57; Ralph G. Martin, *Jennie: The Life of Lady Randolph Churchill, The Romantic Years, 1854–1895* (Englewood Cliffs, 1969), 14–28; *Wilkes' Spirit of the Times* 8 (August 22, 1863): 393; *New York Times* 5 March 1891. For the development of racing at Saratoga, see Hugh Bradley, *Such Was Saratoga* (New York, 1950), 142–45; William H. P. Robertson, *The History of Thoroughbred Racing in America* (Englewood Cliffs, 1964), 102–3; Adelman, "Modern Athletics," 149.

7. Francis G. Fairfield, *Clubs of New York* (New York, 1873), 168.

8. *Wilkes' Spirit* 12 (August 12, 1865): 376; 13 (February 24, 1866): 408. In this paper, I distinguish between "horsemen" and "turfmen." The former category refers, obviously, to the owners of thoroughbreds. The latter category refers to all the members of the racing association.

9. During the AJC's first five years, the oligarchical structure of the club came under constant criticism. For discussion of this theme, see Adelman, "Modern Athletics," 163–65.

10. *New York Herald*, 6 October 1870, 16 September, 22 April 1866. Also see *New York Times*, 12 October 1867, 11 October 1868; *Wilkes' Spirit*, 17 (September 7, 1867): 51 (October 12, 1867): 151, 21 (January 22, 1870): 364.

11. NYCV encompasses New York City and the New York metropolitan region. For this study, the NYM included the current boroughs of Brooklyn, Queens, the Bronx, and Staten Island, along with the remainder of Long Island and Westchester counties. On the New Jersey side, NYM included what is currently Hudson, Essex, Bergen, Morris, Middlesex, and Monmouth counties. The presence of six Southern horsemen among AJC leaders illustrates the changing conditions of thoroughbred racing in the immediate post-Civil War years. With the destruction of Southern racing during the Civil War, Southern breeders became increasingly dependent on Northern tracks to race their horses.

12. Ira Rosenwaike, *Population History of New York City* (Syracuse, 1972), 63. The differences in the geographical origins of AJCers and New York's wealthiest residents in 1856–1857, I believe, can hardly be explained in terms of the passage of ten years. While future research would probably reveal some change in the geographical origins of New York's wealthiest in 1866 from that which existed a decade earlier, the difference would probably be minor. The wealthiest New Yorkers in 1856–1857 were defined as those assessed at $100,000.

13. Jaher did not list the wealthiest New Yorkers in 1856–1857. It is possible that two or three father-son combinations existed. It would have required an elderly father and an already middle-aged son. For example, John Jacob Astor and his son, William B., were among the wealthiest New Yorkers in 1845. (See Pessen, *Riches*, 323.) At this date, John Jacob was already eighty-two, while William B. was fifty-three years old. Since no other studies of prestigious New York clubs exist, it is impossible to say whether the geographical origins of AJCers were representative of other prominent social organizations.

14. An examination was made of a variety of occupational classification systems used by recent historians in their studies of nineteenth-century cities. Since these works often dealt with a larger and more diverse occupational universe, they provided only useful insights. For examples of these studies, see Michael Katz, "Occupational Classification in History," *Journal of Interdisciplinary History*, 3 (1972), 63–68; Clyde Griffen, "Occupational Mobility in Nineteenth-Century America: Problems and Possibilities," *Journal of Social History*, 5 (1972), 310–30; and Theodore Hershberg et al., "Occupation and Ethnicity in Five Nineteenth-Century Cities: A Collaborative Inquiry," *Historical Methods Newsletter*, 7 (1974), 174–216. Pessen has correctly noted that rich men engaged in a variety of economic activities (*Riches*, 49). While true, I am concerned with the turfmen's primary occupation.

15. Adelman, "Modern Athletics," 152–53.

16. *The Income Record, A List Giving the Taxable Income for the Year 1863,*

of the Residence of New York (City) (New York, 1865). As a source, the 1863 tax record had two limitations. First, it only measured the individual's earnings for one year. The question of this year's being representative of the turfmen's annual income was complicated by the influence of the Civil War. In addition, certain sources of income went untaxed. One major benefit of this list is that it provided an accurate assessment of the earnings of these wealthy turfmen. While tax rolls are notorious in underassessing the earnings of the rich, the willingness of the wealthy to pay their fair share during the war years makes the list a more accurate one. See Rufus S. Tucker, "The Distribution of Income Among Taxpayers in the United States, 1863–1935," *Quarterly Journal of Economics*, 52 (1938), 561–69.

17. No particular formula was established to categorize the turfmen, but general guidelines were created. For example, men with incomes of $100,000 or more were classified as superrich and those earning $10,000 tended to be placed in the rich category unless the other variables and biographical material suggested the contrary.

18. Throughout the study, the more information that could be found on an individual turfman the greater was the likelihood that he was rich. In terms of the wealth of non-NYCV fathers, significant differences existed between regular and life members. Whereas only 10 percent of the latter group were rich or superrich, 60 percent of the former group fell into this economic category. This difference was largely responsible for the fact that life members had wealthier parents than did the general membership.

19. The AJC members from outside New York did not come from other urban centers. Only seven came from Boston, three from Baltimore, and one from Cincinnati and Charleston. None came from Philadelphia.

20. Pessen, *Riches*, 77–163. For criticism of Pessen's conclusions, see Frederic C. Jaher, "Elites and Equality in Antebellum America," *Reviews in American History*, 2 (1974), 86–87; Whitman Ridgway, "Measuring Wealth and Power in Antebellum America; A Review Essay," *Historical Methods Newsletter*, 8 (1975). For Jaher's view of the social backgrounds and social fluidity among wealthy New Yorkers in the pre-Civil War period, see his "Nineteenth-Century Elites in Boston and New York," *Journal of Social History*, 6 (Fall 1972), 34–58.

21. For the connection between club membership and more broadly conceived income levels, see Adelman, "Modern Athletics," 231–33.

22. Of the twenty-seven AJCers who joined the UC after 1867, eight (29.6 percent) were in their twenties, suggesting that they came from inherited wealth. The prestigious Racquet Club in Philadelphia, Baltzell wrote, "is only in a limited sense a 'waiting club' for inclusion in one of two exclusive men's club. . . . In fact, many Racquet Club members only reluctantly joined the Philadelphia Club in later years because of its usefulness in business, especially at the upper eschelons." See his *Philadelphia Gentlemen*, 353–54.

23. The average income of AJC members on whom data were available for all the variables examined in this study ($41,100) was almost twice the average income of the turfmen for whom only partial information could be found ($21,200). Cleveland Amory, *Who Killed Society?* (New York, 1960), 196. For the relationship between social clubs and the upper class, see Baltzell, *Philadelphia Gentlemen*, 335–63; Pessen, *Riches*, 222–30; Jaher, "Nineteenth-Century Elites," 60–66; Cleveland Amory, *The Proper Bostonian* (New York, 1947), 201–310; and Jaher, "Nineteenth-Century Elites," 37, 63.

24. For the economic problems of thoroughbred racing in New York, see Adelman, "Modern Athletics," 58–60, 147.

25. Pessen, *Riches*, 225.

26. Baltzell, *Philadelphia Gentlemen*, 335–54. A major problem with Pessen's analysis of the relationship between clubs and class in antebellum New York was his failure to differentiate significantly between the types of clubs. This is not surprising given Pessen's attitude that "no matter what formal purposes were adopted by these societies . . . , it is clear that one of their most significant objectives was to provide men of wealth and distinction a social outlet largely confined to others of similar standing." Although no prosopography of other clubs has been made, the evidence drawn from this study suggests that the composition of the UC, a purely social club, differed from the Century Club, a literary society. Fairfield pointed out that literature was scarcely represented in the UC. Pessen did note that the CC was composed of luminaries from the world of art and letters and the world of commerce and finance, but in his brief treatment of the club he paid no attention to the fact that these were divergent elite groups. See Fairfield, *Clubs of New York*, 66; Pessen, *Riches*, 225–29.

27. "The circulation of elites in America and the assimilation of new men of power and influence into the upper class," Baltzell writes, "takes place primarily through the medium of urban clubdom." See *Philadelphia Gentlemen*, 340. There are critical differences, however, between the integrative function of the AJC and the assimilation function of such exclusive clubs as the UC. The latter obviously takes place within a more narrow and select group. More important, the assimilation process of the leading social clubs gives testimony (at least theoretically) to a greater degree of equality among its members. In the sense that all AJCers had the same privileges and access to facilities, the racing club produced certain equality among its members. But the parity created by the ritualistic involvement with thoroughbred racing was only temporal and occurred rarely throughout the year. The AJC was not constructed nor was the membership perceived as creating permanent equality among its members.

28. In his examination of voluntary associations in Jacksonville, Illinois, Doyle based his conclusions upon association officers and prominent members, believing that "these men were not significantly unrepresentative of the

membership at large." See his "Social Function," 336. While this conclusion may be true for a frontier town, I doubt that in most cases officers would be representative of the club as a whole. For a view that officers and members were different, see Adelman, "Modern Athletics," 357–60, 399–401, 445–49.

29. In the NYYC, voting privileges were restricted to yacht owners despite the fact that they composed only a small fraction of the club members.

Table 1
Residency of AJC Members

Group	Regular Members No.	Regular Members Pct.	Life Members No.	Life Members Pct.	Total Membership No.	Total Membership Pct.
New York City	409	71.5	21	51.2	430	70.1
New York Metropolitan Region	106	18.5	12	29.3	118	19.2
New York State	13	2.3	0	0.0	13	2.1
New England	21	3.7	2	4.9	23	3.8
Rest of the Country	18	3.1	6	14.6	24	3.9
Foreign Countries	5	0.9	0	0.0	5	0.8
Total	572 =	93.3	41 =	6.7	613 =	100.0*

Source: Study data; Frederic C. Jaher, ''Nineteenth-Century Elites in Boston and New York,'' *Journal of Social History,* 6 (Fall 1972): 49.

*Total may not equal 100 percent due to rounding.

Table 2
Percentage of the Birthplaces of AJC Members Living in New York City and New York's Wealthiest Residents in 1856–1857

Group	1856–1857 Wealthiest	AJC Members
New York City	37.5	58.2
New York State	6.2	14.3
Elsewhere	33.8	19.9
Foreign	22.5	7.7

Source: Study data; Frederic C. Jaher, ''Nineteenth-Century Elites in Boston and New York,'' *Journal of Social History,* 6 (Fall 1972): 49.

Table 3
Occupations of AJC Members

Group	Regular Members No.	Regular Members Pct.	Life Members No.	Life Members Pct.	Total Membership No.	Total Membership Pct.
Gentlemen	12	2.0	2	5.6	14	2.2
Lawyer-Judges	54	9.1	2	5.6	56	8.9
Professionals	33	5.6	4	11.1	37	5.9
Finance	152	25.7	12	33.3	164	26.1
Commerce	245	41.4	9	25.0	254	40.4
Skilled Craftsmen	13	2.2	0	0.0	13	2.1
Politicians	9	1.5	0	0.0	9	1.4
Hotel Managers	8	1.4	0	0.0	8	1.3
Agriculture	2	0.3	3	8.3	5	0.8
Clerks	2	0.3	0	0.0	2	0.3
Manufacturing	21	3.5	1	2.8	22	3.5
Transportation	17	2.9	2	5.6	19	3.0
Executives	24	4.1	1	2.8	25	4.0
Total	592 = 94.3		36 = 5.7		628 = 100.0*	

*Total may not equal 100 percent due to rounding.

Table 4
Estimated Wealth of AJC Members

Group	Regular Members No.	Regular Members Pct.	Life Members No.	Life Members Pct.	Total Membership No.	Total Membership Pct.
Superrich	15	4.1	5	14.3	20	5.0
Rich	200	55.1	25	71.4	225	56.5
Well-to-Do	148	40.8	5	14.3	153	38.4
Total	363 = 91.2		35 = 8.8		398 = 100.0*	

*Total may not equal 100 percent due to rounding.

Table 5

Occupational Mobility Among AJC Members by Birthplace and Age

Birthplace	No. That Were Better Off Than Their Fathers		No. of Fathers		Pct. of Mobility
New York City	5		111		4.5
New York Metropolitan Region	2		13		15.4
New York State	6		22		27.3
New England	4		16		25.0
Rest of the Country	4		13		30.8
Foreign Countries	3		10		30.0
Total	24	of	185	=	13.0
Age category					
20–29	1		28		3.6
30–39	6		36		16.7
40–49	8		50		16.0
50–59	6		26		23.1
60 and over	2		8		25.0
Total	23	of	148	=	15.5

Table 6

Estimated Wealth of AJC Fathers

Group	Regular Members		Life Members		Total Membership	
	No.	Pct.	No.	Pct.	No.	Pct.
Superrich	15	8.1	2	8.7	17	8.2
Rich	68	36.8	12	52.2	80	38.5
Well-to-Do	59	31.9	5	21.7	64	30.8
Middle-Class	39	21.0	4	17.4	43	20.7
Poor	4	2.2	0	0.0	4	1.9
Total	185 =	88.9	23 =	11.1	208 =	100.0*

*Total may not equal 100 percent due to rounding.

Table 7

Estimated Wealth of AJC Fathers by Their Place of Residency

	Superrich		Rich		Well-to-Do		Middle Class		Poor		Total	
	No.	Pct.	No.	Pct.	No.	Pct.	No.	Pct.	No.	Pct.	No.	Pct.
New York City	15	10.6	64	44.8	50	34.9	11	7.7	3	2.1	143	68.8
New York Metropolitan Region	0	0.0	8	53.3	3	20.0	4	26.7	0	0.0	15	7.2
Non-NYCV*	2	4.0	8	16.0	11	22.0	28	56.0	1	2.0	50	24.0
Total	17 =	8.2	80 =	38.5	64 =	30.8	43 =	20.7	4 =	1.9	208 =	100.0

*Non-New York City vicinity.

Table 8

Estimated Wealth of AJC Members by the Estimated Wealth of Their Fathers

	Superrich		Rich		Well-to-Do		Middle Class		Poor		Total	
	No.	Pct.	No.	Pct.	No.	Pct.	No.	Pct.	No.	Pct.	No.	Pct.
Superrich	4	30.8	3	23.1	4	30.8	2	15.4	0	0.0	13	8.7
Rich	11	9.3	62	52.5	28	23.7	14	11.9	3	2.6	118	70.8
Well-to-Do	0	0.0	1	3.0	17	51.5	14	42.4	1	3.0	33	20.5
Total	15 =	9.1	66 =	40.2	49 =	29.9	30 =	18.3	4 =	2.4	164 =	100.0

LIBRARY
OF
MOUNT ST. MARY'S
COLLEGE
EMMITSBURG, MARYLAND

IV

Baseball in the Small Ohio Community, 1865–1900

Carl M. Becker and Richard H. Grigsby

In Ohio villages and towns of the late nineteenth century—from about 1865 to 1900—baseball was one of "those healthful sports that graced the peaceful scene." Indeed, often it flourished and became well-integrated into the life of a village or town. It could draw together local players and spectators reliving and celebrating vicariously a hard-earned victory—"The time you won your town the race/We chaired you through the market-place;/Man and boy stood cheering by. . . ." Especially a small, homogeneous community, with all its informality and neighborliness, was a congenial setting for the game.

People cheering, if not chairing, local heroes lived in communities of this sort in the villages of Germantown, Miamisburg, West Liberty, and Spring Valley and in the towns of Xenia, Troy, and Findlay, Ohio. Strung up and down the Miami Valley, all were similar to one another. Among the villages only Miamisburg experienced noticeable growth from 1870 to 1900, its population rising from 1,425 to 3,941. Germantown had only a nominal increase in the same period—from 1,440 to 1,702. At West Liberty the population rose from 741 to 1,236, at Spring Valley from 290 to 522. The town of Xenia enjoyed only modest growth in the three decades after 1870—from 6,377 to 8,696. Growing more rapidly was Troy, with its 1870 population of 3,005 rising to 5,881 by 1900. Findlay, though seeing its population rise rapidly from 4,633 in 1880 to 18,553 in 1890 as a direct result of an oil boom in the area, was still a small town when baseball took root there in the 1870s. In these communities, with one exception, the people were essentially native to the nation—in fact, to the state. Even Germantown, despite its name's implying settlement by Pennsylvania Germans, could count only 6 percent of its residents as foreign-born in 1880. In 1880 only Miamisburg, with about a quarter of its population natives of German states, had a significant number of immigrants. Only in Troy was there more than a handful of blacks.[1]

Economic life did not vary greatly from village to village. Residentiary trade characterized activity at Germantown, West Liberty, and Spring Valley. A few small factories in Miamisburg were producing buggies, wheels, and twine. Xenia and Troy were the commercial and political centers of their counties. Once a small trading center, Findlay became the focus of oil drilling and oil refining in northwestern Ohio after 1880.

By and large, economic activity, since it was not particularly variegated and was not changing rapidly, did not create substantial social differentiation in these villages and towns. Additionally, ethnic uniformity and stability were conditions giving rise to personal relationships characterized by informality and openness.

Historians of American sport have often looked at the late nineteenth century as the "takeoff" stage of organized sport in the nation. Typically, they have given primary attention to professional sport or mass spectator sport in American life. They have tied the rise of sport to the massive urbanization of society after the Civil War. And they have, of course, seen baseball largely in an urban and commercial context.[2]

At one level, material in nature, they have noted that the density of urban population, improved transportation in cities, mass communications, and the increase in leisure time, among other elements, supported the development of baseball for the masses. They have attributed the rise of the game as the "national pastime," especially in its professional aspect, to urban conditions. At a social level, historians of American sport have portrayed baseball as particularly suited to an urban order that, while undergirding efficiency, objectivity, and statistical complexity, needed "play" to reduce the force of impersonality and heterogeneity. The game brought to the city, they have suggested, images of a more pastoral, individualistic, and informal way of life identified with a rural past.

Whether baseball in the city evoked rural images or not, historians

usually have worked with the sport in its urban and professional setting. They have accorded only passing attention to the structure of the
game in the village and small town. As a consequence, they have left
relatively untouched old portraits of baseball as a medium through which
the localism and parochialism of small communities found expression.
Umpires who were "homers," players who were "ringers," home
crowds that intimidated visiting teams, and teams that failed to appear
for scheduled games all have remained staples in American folklore.

Down through the years, popular writers often depicted scenes of
such disarray in small communities. In *The Shortstop*, a novel for juveniles describing at one point a game between two Ohio villages at
the turn of the century, Zane Grey recounted traditional accounts of
inequity. The umpire, a "homer," rigged the rules in favor of Jacktown against the visiting Brownsville team. When Brownsville, nonetheless, appeared to have the game won, he suspended play and gave
the game to Jacktown because the visitor's pitcher was throwing a
"crooked ball." Worse yet, the local fans then chased the Brownsville
players from the field, threatening them with violence.[3]

Though surely the localism of a Jacktown was not wholly fictional,
it did not represent the realities of baseball in a small coherent community. There, beneath the veneer of parochialism, the game could
become internalized in personalism, informality, and spontaneity. Depending as it might on support from the whole community, it could
thrive in such a social environment.

Organization of a baseball team in a small community exemplified
various informal and institutional patterns of life. At Germantown
spontaneity and equality seemed to underlay efforts to play. When the
mania for the game first struck there in 1869, evidently a group of young
men meeting randomly in different settings—in churches, social clubs,
and even saloons—decided to organize a team. After "drilling to meet
and vanquish their neighboring brethren of the bat and ball," they
conducted a "test" of all the players to sort out the best nine. Two
captains chose sides that played a game ending in a score of eighty-
six to seventy. Presumably the leading hitters and fielders then became
the nine of a team denominated the "Essayons."[4]

Probably spontaneity was an element in the willingness of men in a
small community to take up a game about which they knew little. At
Troy, in 1866, though none had ever played baseball, men organized
the Troy Baseball Club and then asked a man from outside the com-

munity to instruct players and the manager in the sport. Nearby in Piqua in the same year two Presbyterian ministers who apparently had learned the game as students at an Eastern college found young men ready to join them in forming a club. Obviously pride, an aspect of personalism in a community, might give rise to a baseball team. No doubt it had play in Cedarville, a village near Xenia. An "enterprising little town," Cedarville was "bound to have" baseball and go "full length" at it. Men there, proud and envious of the Reds in Cincinnati, organized a team in 1875 known as the "Yam" club. They thought that they could play any amateur team and lay them out "to dry."[5]

Teams sprang naturally, though usually only momentarily, from the everyday life of small communities. In Miamisburg in 1873 workers at a paper mill and cutlery factory formed a team to play employees of a sash and blind factory, with both teams disbanding after meeting in one "match" game. More than a decade later, men working in two paper mills in the same community were regularly playing "friendly contests." At Xenia in 1889 the "boys" in a railroad office put together a team to challenge young businessmen there. There could be enough sectional differentiation in a village, however coherent its everyday life, to support the creation of rival nines. In Germantown, the Main Street Nine and the Plum Street Nine confronted one another in 1882. Sectional rivalry was at play in Miamisburg in 1886 when the "Up-town" and "Down-town" clubs contested "match" games. So-called picked nines, teams temporarily organized to play but a game or two against an established nine, frequently appeared in small towns. Seeing their elders at play, juveniles often formed teams. As soon as the Essayons in Germantown were playing, smaller boys there took to the field as the "Locust Roots." The Young Americans at Miamisburg were boys who "waxed" opponents one summer in 1878.[6]

Rhythmic-like, year-in, year-out, men and boys acting out of various motives organized baseball teams in small Ohio communities. But no matter what their derivation was, seldom did teams retain their identity for more than a year. It was unusual, for example, when the Buckeyes of Findlay remained in existence for three consecutive years in the 1880s. Nonetheless, because players from extinct teams often joined newly organized clubs, continuity of play developed early in most towns. The very frequency with which teams appeared testified, moreover, to the growing roots of the game.

Teams employed a variety of names reflecting local and national interests and values. Sometimes names implied presumptions defining the character of a community. At Germantown, the first baseball club denominated itself the Essayons; the local editor thought the name quite appropriately called attention to the determination of the "whole village." Players in Springboro were to be Actives in their games. Obviously, the Stonewalls of Findlay saw themselves as strong and unyielding. Teams often took names of Indian tribes, but not necessarily of those that had been inhabitants of Ohio. The Mohawks of Xenia and the Senecas of Troy memorialized Eastern tribes. When early in the 1870s the Modoc Indians of Oregon took up arms to protect their land, clubs in Miamisburg and Springfield seemed to sympathize by calling themselves the Modocs. Probably the proximity and repute of the Cincinnati Red Stockings accounted for the repeated use of Reds and Red Stockings. But local interest and pride could dictate the naming of teams. In 1870, at the news that railroad promoters in Germantown were proposing to build a line to Mackinaw in Michigan, players in Germantown decided to call their club the Mackinaw Base Ball Club. A team might turn to use of the nickname of its community, as did the Star City Club of Miamisburg. Identifying with the state of Ohio, more than one team became the Buckeyes. Geography called forth names; players of the Twin Valley Club in Germantown lived in a twin valley. Especially pick-up nines adopted fanciful or amusing names; in Miamisburg one summer the Qui-nines met the Agues. Among others, the Shamrocks, the Uticas, the Atlantics, the Grangers, the Nine Spots, and the Pastimes all were playing for villages and towns in Ohio in the 1870s and 1880s.

Obviously, men organizing teams intended to play other teams. Certainly there were few problems in arranging games when workers at a paper mill or young businessmen formed a team to play another team in the community. But scheduling games outside a village required more effort. Frequently teams challenged squads in other villages and towns, and usually they were then able to arrange games. Teams often simply announced that they were open to games and then awaited offers. Following a typical procedure, the Spring Valley Grays announced by "dodgers" and in the local newspaper that it would play opponents at home on any day except Monday and would play away on any day except Saturday. The Grays asked for 40 percent or 60 percent of admission fees depending on when the game was played.[7]

Teams scheduled nearly all their games in June, July, August, and

September. (Of eighty-two games reported in local newspapers from 1865 to 1900, seventy-six were played in these months.) Seldom did they take up formal play before summer. The game was hardly an act in the rites of spring. Spring brought too much rainfall for clubs to work out a fixed routine of practice, and moreover it was a season of considerable work in small communities, permitting limited time for play. Only after Decoration Day did teams begin to play regularly. If baseball bespoke a pastoral image, it did so on green fields turning brown under a solstitial sun.

Sometimes problems did attend the scheduling of games. In 1879 the Nine Spots of Findlay had scheduled two home games with the Hop Bitters of Lima, one for a Thursday, the other for Friday. After his team played on Thursday, the manager of the Bitters refused to play on Friday unless the Nine Spots made a promised payment of money before the game. At West Liberty on Decoration Day in 1891 a large crowd gathered to see a game between teams from Urbana and Bellefontaine; neither team appeared, Urbana expecting to play at Bellefontaine, Bellefontaine at Urbana. Challenges could take on the aspect of a comic opera, too. According to a report circulating in Spring Valley in 1890, a club in Millidgeville, a nearby village, had sent a "sassy" challenge to the team in Spring Valley: "Spring Valley boys can you play ball? If you think so come up to Millidgeville and win or lose $10, or if you haven't got the money we will play you for free." As it turned out, though, Millidgeville denied issuing the call for a game, declaring, nonetheless, that it was willing to play Spring Valley.[8]

Once a team agreed to play a game away from home, it had to find transportation. Means of transport varied, of course, from community to community, especially in respect to railroads. When the Essayons of Germantown had to go fifteen miles to Springboro in 1869, they took a horse-drawn omnibus that took about three hours to reach its destination. It was a jolting but direct ride. But the club at West Liberty faced a circuitous journey that was not unusual even two decades later. Scheduled to play at Plain City about forty miles due east, the players rode by wagon ten miles south to Urbana and there caught the "cars" for Plain City. Their ride to New Carlisle one weekend surely was tiresome. Taking two "sample" wagons from West Liberty at 3:00 A.M. on Saturday, they drove to Springfield, there to catch a train to New Carlisle. They arrived there at 8:00 A.M. and, feeling "dead" when they took the field, played poorly in losing. But a trip to the opponent's field could be festive. On a Saturday, a team from Spring Valley, shouting "all aboard," jumped onto a picnic wagon and rode merrily but bumpily to New Burlington, there to enjoy an easy victory. For all their discomfort, at least wagons, unlike trains with scheduled departures, did not dictate the length of a game.[9]

More than the planning of transportation, the selection of fields for play could be impromptu or could involve makeshift arrangements. Probably the first permanent fields available to village teams were those marked off at county fairgrounds. They were not, however, always easily accessible to players and spectators. Within or near a town or village, players "laid out" diamonds on whatever grounds they could find. A level pasture obviously was an inviting site. The West Liberty club found an open site near a railroad bridge that evidently offered some topographical barriers to smooth play. But at Findlay, the private grounds of Judge Whitley were "excellent," indeed were the "finest" in northwest Ohio.[10]

Unlike fields of play, players' uniforms could be a source of pride for a community. Typically, teams resorted to various means to obtain suitable attire. Sometimes players bore the expenses, sometimes they used admission fees to defray costs, and sometimes they solicited support from a local businessman. In any event, the community could glory in the splendor of new uniforms. When the Essayons of Germantown played their first game, the local editor declared that they were "beautifully uniformed." They wore, he noted in detail, blue knee breeches with red cord running down each leg, white cotton hose, white shoes, white caps with red stars on the crowns, and black patent leather belts. Each uniform had painted on it in golden letters the name of the team and the player wearing it. At Xenia, "our boys" made a fine appearance in dark blue shirts and knee breeches, scarlet hose, and white caps with sky blue binding. Evidently sponsored by a local merchant, the Rosenthals of Findlay wore new gray shirts and pantaloons in 1887. Their stockings were red, their caps were gray and trimmed in red, and their belts were white with "Rosenthals" embossed on them. Supposedly their shoes were the "best that money could buy." Unfortunately, no matter how attractive, uniforms could become quite mundane and impermanent; after a team in Spring Valley discontinued play for the year, the players used them as underwear through a cold winter and threw them into the ragbag.[11]

Once on the field and ready to play, teams had to perform and comport themselves in a manner to the credit of their community. For as much as any discrete group, they seemed to represent the virtues and values of a village or town that saw itself as a unique community. The editor of a Germantown newspaper asserted that the players of the local team were "thoroughly men of Germantown, carrying its banner through the valley to victory and to good repute for our good village." Editors of local newspapers, the quintessential boosters of the community, often noted play of individuals and teams in grandiose language. "Parker," wrote the editor of the *Weekly Jeffersonian*, "was great on first base." Becker was a "dandy base runner." At Spring Valley, Tom Aspenwall made "magnificent" catches. The catcher at West Liberty could "freeze" onto the balls that the pitcher "sent . . . home like cannon balls." Players on the Germantown team would have lost had they not "handled the stick" in a "clever manner." [12]

Seeing players as men who held the good name of the community in balance, editors could not help but point out deficiencies in their play, sometimes rather sarcastically. Theirs was a commentary characteristic of personalism in a village or town. "Evans," proclaimed one writer inclined to metaphor, "should have had a fence-board for a bat." Viewing the ineffective pitching of one Jim Little, an editor declared that evidently he "had been practicing with chunks of coal." A reporter at Xenia, evaluating the play of the local team, found that Smith was "nervous" and that Fields and Gilmore required practice on fly balls hit over their heads. Drawing a cartoon showing a balloon tied to a base, the editor of the *West Liberty Banner* then employed doggerel to make clear his point.

Captain McCune couldn't hit a balloon
And fell in a swoon,
And they carried him off the field.

Even though he could report a victory for Germantown over Eaton, a Germantown editor complained that the local team played inexcusably in muffing fly balls and making wild throws. Though editors often presumed to speak for a community when they called on a team to improve its performance, mayors and councils might also sound words of admonition and encouragement. The mayor of Zanesfield instructed the local team on "how to win"—but to no avail. At Germantown, the village council urged players to perform with greater zeal.[13]

If boosters critically evaluated the performance of fielders and batters, they also scrutinized their deportment on the field. They expected players to be sportsmen, win or lose. When opponents were not "gentlemen," they thus heightened the exemplary conduct of the local heroes; if the home champions fell short of the mark, they brought shame to their community and lessened its integrity. As an editor at West Liberty saw it, "Our players must remember that their behavior is the behavior of West Liberty. Let them think of that when they take up 'kicking' against the umpire."[14]

By and large, though, visiting and home players won praise for their conduct. Indeed, reporters often called special attention to their commendable behavior. Players from Xenia and Wilmington were "exceptionally respectful" to one another and to the umpire. At West Liberty the visiting and home teams completely foreswore swearing and "kicking" at the umpire. Despite losing, the visiting "boys" from Franklin were a "gentlemanly lot." The Stonewalls from West Liberty, playing and losing to a team in Findlay, were a "good-looking set of boys [who] behaved in a manner becoming of gentlemen." Coming to Findlay seemingly were only gentlemen: "There never was a more gentlemanly set of ball players visiting [Findlay] than the Lima boys, who are a credit to the town they hail from." An editor in Miamisburg seemed delighted to report on a game where there was no "rag-chewing" that was evident among some players.[15]

Following a game, even one in which tempers flared, the good will and neighborliness of a village could become quite evident. Even though the players from Zanesfield did not conduct themselves as gentlemen in a game that they lost, the West Liberty team treated them to a supper after the game. Women of the Christian Church furnished an "elegant supper" to the West Liberty and Woodstock teams following a hotly contested game. In Miamisburg the host team gave "hospitable entertainment" to the losing visitors. A generous merchant in West Liberty gave all players "good cigars" at the conclusion of the game.[16]

Players did, of course, break the mold of decorum on occasion. By word and deed, they might abuse the crowd, the umpire, or opposing players. The profanity of visiting players at West Liberty was terribly "offensive" to the ladies among the spectators. Besides calling the umpire "vile names," a team from the village of DeGraff openly insulted women at West Liberty by their disgraceful language. Editors did not single out visitors alone for censure. It was not creditable to their community, lamented an editor from Xenia, that the players from his town had indulged in "ugly kicking" at the umpire's decisions. Sometimes unseemly conduct was more than a matter of language. One McAdams, appropriately a member of a team from Urbana that continually "kicked" at umpires' calls, was a dirty player who deliberately ran over West Liberty basemen. The atmosphere already poisoned by an insulting letter sent anonymously from Germantown to players at West Alexandria, the game at West Alexandria between the villages ended in a dispute over the score, and allegations that Germantown had bribed the umpires; to escape the wrath of the crowd, the team from Germantown finally locked themselves in a hotel room.[17]

The village or town usually saw a team as an intrinsic element of the community. Therein might lay a dilemma. On the one hand, all the players had to be residents of a Germantown or West Liberty to make their team at one with the community. On the other hand, the team and its supporters wanted to win and to that end might use "ringers" of one sort or another. Not surprisingly, local newspapers were particularly argus-eyed in discovering the status of opposing players (were they really "amateurs" and residents of the community that they represented?) but much less so in identifying the origins of players from the home town. It was not inconvenient to raise complaints about ringers. If a team lost to a club accused of using ringers, the losing players had explanations ready at hand; if their team won against such a club, they found victory all the sweeter.

Reports of ringers were commonplace. A team of West Carollton defeated one from Miamisburg even though the latter team had imported three "scientific" players from Kentucky. The Banners from West Liberty won against teams from Antioch College and Mount Victory loaded with players from the Ohio State University. When Quincy attempted to "run in" three of DeGraff's "best" players against West Liberty, West Liberty would not permit their use. Players on a Germantown nine complained that they had been tricked into playing a team of "stars" recruited from two communities. Similarly, the Star City Club of Miamisburg saw deceit in the use of a "combined" nine by Lebanon. Expecting to play a team of amateurs from Dayton, the Brown Stockings of Miamisburg lost to "old" and "experienced" players—virtually "professionals"; it was tantamount, the editor from Miamisburg argued, to boys playing men. DeGraff blamed a loss to West Liberty on the "salaried" men employed by the winners.[18]

As they did with players, people in small communities looked for faults in the performance of umpires. In fact, umpires, as one would expect where informality prevailed, took on the character of essential participants in the game. Editors, spectators, and players all could readily discover in an umpire deliberate partiality or absolute fairness. A party to a relatively unsophisticated game in unsophisticated settings, an umpire was an easy target for winners and losers alike.

Allegations of improper or unfair calls derived from all kinds of circumstances. In Miamisburg, though the home team won, "the umpire was so partial," insisted a reporter, "as to call down sharp rebuke from spectators." At London, Ohio, an umpire caused a near riot when he refused to award first base to a London player purportedly struck by a ball while batting. A team in Spring Valley lost a game because the umpire supposedly had called a long foul a fair ball. In a game between nines from West Liberty and Springfield, West Liberty consented to accept an umpire from Springfield but then after repeatedly "kicking" at his calls apparently insisted on removing him in the sixth inning and replacing him with an umpire from a neutral town; but then the Springfield players refused to take the field after he made what they deemed to be an unfair decision at home plate. An editor in Germantown suggested that an umpire making questionable calls had bet money on the winning team and thus had been "controlled by umpire motives."[19]

All was not kicking, though. Though receiving anathemas from both sides at Xenia, Cal Crain seemed to make "fair" calls. Teams and spectators in Miamisburg commended Con Riley for his "fair rulings." Except for two decisions at first base, the umpire at a game in Williamstown rendered "unexceptionable" calls. At Findlay an umpire in a spirited game made "unbiased decisions."[20]

As many editorialists saw it, the size and conduct of a crowd said something about the worth of a community. Especially they discerned in the "good order" of spectators testimony to stability of a village or town. One observer was certain that a "courteous" crowd spoke to the capacity of his village to accept good or ill fortune with equanimity and intelligence. Another editor lamented the "boisterousness" of spectators as a manifestation of social disintegration in his community.

A crowd might take on various characteristics, none of which defined very specifically life in a village. Ladies and gentlemen at a game in Miamisburg were fairly quiet, more curious than enthusiastic about the play before them. There could be among the spectators many "rattlers" or hecklers whose principal sin was a desire to root their team on to victory. Boys and girls in a crowd occasionally taunted players—but players of both sides. As important as the conduct of the crowd was its classless unity. Like the commemorative celebrations of a village—an Independence Day, for instance—a baseball game drew together all people in a community. It was no accident that the sport often occupied a central place in the festivities of a holiday in small communities; it was not surprising that spectators might then even march with a band to the field of play. At Miamisburg following the local team's victory, the crowd formed a procession and, led by a band, marched to the town hall and then broke ranks in "good humor."[21]

The size of a crowd might depend on many factors—the reputations of teams, the rivalries of teams, the size of population in a community, admission fees, and so on. Admission ran ten or fifteen cents for men, nothing for women and children. Usually played in the afternoon, infrequently in the morning, and virtually on any day of the week, a game might attract a "large" or "respectable" crowd, half of which might be women. More specifically, a crowd might number 100, but more likely would be 400 or 500. But even in a small village like West Liberty as many as 1,000 people, most of them women, attended games. At least on one occasion, more than 500 people from that community traveled to Bellefontaine for a game. Attendance at games could be sufficiently large to send rippling effects through a village. At Germantown in 1870 baseball emptied church pews on the Sabbath; but later it supposedly did more to close saloons on Sunday than all ordinances had done.[22]

Crowds, whatever their size or conduct, were not necessarily a measure of the general interest in baseball in a small community. The game and interest in it might spread in multiple ways through a village or town. Literally it might become the talk of a town. "Findlay," noted an observer in 1879, "is gone on baseball. Every man, woman and child in that town thinks the 'Nine Spots' are the noblest work of God." In Miamisburg when workers of two paper mills organized teams, baseball became "all the rage." At Germantown at one time the game was the "staple" of the community. Conversation about it entered all avocations and engrossed conversation and thought.[23]

When baseball reached beyond organized teams, chaos could result. The practice of playing on the streets of Miamisburg in the 1880s became "so common and dangerous" to persons and property that people were calling for the council to enact stringent measures to control it. An editor demanded an ironclad ordinance against indiscriminate play. Reportedly boys playing ball frightened horses and broke windows. A baby "wheeled in a cab" by her mother narrowly escaped "having her brains dashed out by a ball diverted in its course." Apparently, though, nothing came of the calls for legislation, and the council was still discussing the issue a decade later.[24]

At another, less direct level, baseball asserted itself in villages and towns. People in the 1880s were becoming increasingly interested in compiling statistics on the game, particularly those of the home team. Their local newspaper was the principal source of information. Whereas newspapers in the 1870s might publish only the score of a game or at most the score by innings, by the 1880s often they were running box scores, which, of course, lent themselves to the compilation of records. Editors might even develop cumulative records. Reviewing the scores of the Findlay Nine Spots in July 1880, the *Weekly Jeffersonian* ran a column noting that the team had outscored its opponents forty-six to forty in the month, in earned runs seven to four. "Those fond of figures," advised the editor, "should clip it out and paste it in their hats." The compiling of statistical data brought to a small community a touch of modernity and objectivity that gave it kinship with urban life. Baseball was thus becoming at least a gentle wave pulling people from the old moorings of informality.

Newspapers in villages found local readers also seeking information about nationally known teams. Especially in the 1880s they began reporting scores and standings of clubs in such leagues as the Eastern League and the American Association. Additionally, they were running syndicated columns on the origins and development of baseball in the nation. Articles such as "Gossip of the Diamond" also were regularly appearing in newspapers of small communities—in the *West Liberty Banner*, for example.[25]

As organized, played, and perceived in a Germantown or Spring Valley in the late nineteenth century, baseball was a game attuned to the essential qualities of a coherent small community, a game tied to the order of real community. At its organization, it emanated from informal, neighborly circles of men and boys at work and at leisure. In its play, far from becoming a persistent carrier of localism, it aspired to fairness and friendliness. Through its followers, it spoke for the equality, the classless unity, of the small community.

No other sport in a village was as bound up in social processes or was as closely related to a sense of communal pride as was baseball. Even though bicycling was popular in the small communities of Ohio, especially in the 1890s, it did not take on the coloration of a sport integrated into everyday life. Germantown, West Liberty, Miamisburg, and the other communities noted here all regularly saw the organization of baseball clubs; but few, if any at all, had the bicycle club which, according to a historian of American creation, appeared in "every sizable community." Fundamentally, at least in the village, bicycling was an individuated, private activity. At Germantown when Hugh Oblinger mounted his "splendid" bicycle one Sunday morning in 1893 and began pedaling a hundred miles to Indianapolis, few spectators came out to cheer him on his way. Learning of his exploit, the local editor saw no reason to identify or celebrate it as a triumph of the community. Despite their large number, the bicyclists of Germantown did not compose an interest sufficiently strong to stay the enactment of local ordinances prohibiting their use of sidewalks and restricting their speed.[26]

More nearly a sport of the small community was the walking or running race. Sporadic in appearance, such a race momentarily might create considerable interest. At Findlay in 1879, a newspaper man believed that "pedomania" was ruling the day. But not unusually, the sport there was revolving around an individual. Elsa Von Blumen became the cynosure of all eyes when she successfully tried to walk one hundred miles in under twenty-seven hours. Similarly at Miamisburg in 1886, an individual, one Fred Volkes, appropriated much of the interest in running. A short-distance runner from England, he challenged any local sprinters to run against him. Clearly he was attempting to exploit the gambling that, apparently much more than in baseball, attended running and walking matches. When three men in Miamisburg walked against one another in 1873, they wagered $10 on the outcome, the winner then offering to walk for any amount against anyone else. Some racing, though, did take place merely "for fun." "Fat men" in Findlay staged special matches for the entertainment of their fellow citizens. Occasionally, too, walkers or runners would compete in the name of their village or town against men from another community. On the whole, nonetheless, competition in walking and running did not sustain continuity over many years, nor did it involve many segments of a small community; and rarely, if ever, did it represent for people the elemental value of their communal life.[27]

Other sports—croquet, horseshoes, and so on—had a place in the life of small Ohio communities. Unlike other games, croquet brought young women and young men to play together. It became so fashionable in Germantown for a moment in the 1880s that it was *de rigueur* for young women to try their hand with the mallet. Much less delicate was horseshoe pitching. Chewing tobacco and spitting its juice indiscriminately, swearing, and exchanging ribald remarks on the sexual connotations of throwing ringers, young and old men alike might while away the evening hours in Miamisburg at the horseshoe pits. But croquet and horseshoes were too sporadic or too often principally vehicles of social interchange to occupy a central place in the athletic life of a village or town.

Pedaling a bicycle, striking a croquet ball, pitching a horseshoe— none could contest the dominion of baseball as the essential game of a village or town. Whatever it might become in an urban order, whatever it might come to mean to the urban masses, baseball was attuned to the social realities of the small community.

NOTES

1. Compiled from published census returns of 1870, 1880, 1890, and 1900.

2. To a greater or lesser degree, the following titles, among others, set forth the urban dimensions of baseball: John Richards Betts, *America's Sporting Heritage: 1850–1950* (Reading, Mass., 1974); Christian K. Messenger, *Sport and the Spirit of Play in American Fiction: Hawthorne to Faulkner* (New York, 1981); Steven Riess, *Touching Base: Professional Baseball and American Culture in the Progressive Era* (Westport, Conn., 1980); Arthur Meier Schlesinger, *The Rise of the City, 1878–1898* (New York, 1933); Harold Seymour, *Baseball: The Early Years* (New York, 1960); and Dale A. Somers, *The Rise of Sports in New Orleans, 1850–1950* (Baton Rouge, 1972). For a view of baseball in its pastoral image and as a sport particularly susceptible to the modern needs for quantification, see Allen Guttmann, *From Ritual to Record: The Nature of Modern Sports* (New York, 1978), 91ff.

3. Zane Grey, *The Shortstop* (New York, 1909), 14ff. Probably the story

derived from an actual incident involving Zane Grey. In 1890, then using his given name of Pearl, he was traveling through small towns in central Ohio extracting teeth, a skill that he had learned from his father, a dentist. He had already pitched for a semiprofessional team in Columbus, evidently learning how to throw a curveball, then a fairly new pitch. One Saturday he found himself in Baltimore, Ohio, where the local team was scheduled to play the nine from nearby Jacktown that afternoon. Believing that small-town players knew little about the curveball, he asked the manager of Baltimore to let him pitch against Jacktown. The manager accepted the offer but did not use Grey's real name for fear that someone from Jacktown would recognize Grey as a ringer. The game was played at Baltimore; but Grey, perhaps wishing to emphasize the unfair behavior of the Jacktown players, depicted Jacktown as the home team in *The Shortstop*. Though the umpire did in fact call the game in Jacktown's favor because Grey threw a "crooked ball," he also noted that Grey was a ringer. In his novel Grey did not have the umpire point out the deception. The Jacktown players had some reason to complain in both the novel and reality. See Frank Gruber, *Zane Grey* (New York, 1970), 22–25.

4. *Dollar Times* (Germantown, Ohio), August 20, 1869; September 3, September 10, 1869 (hereafter cited as *DT*).

5. Thomas B. Wheeler, *Troy: The Nineteenth Century* (Troy, Ohio, 1970), 108; John A. Rayner, *The First Century of Piqua, Ohio* (Piqua, Ohio, 1916), 198; *Xenia Torchlight*, September 8, 1875 (hereafter cited as *XT*).

6. *Miamisburg Bulletin*, August 1, 1873 (hereafter cited as *MB*); July 8, 1884, July 2, 1886; *Xenia Gazette*, June 18, 1889 (hereafter cited as *XG*); *Germantown Press*, August 30, 1882 (hereafter cited as *GP*); *MB*, July 2, 1886. See, for example, *MB*, September 24, 1875; *XB*, July 27, August 13, 1886; *DT*, October 1, 1869; *MB*, October 11, 1878.

7. *Spring Valley Blade*, June 15, 1895 (hereafter cited as *SVB*).

8. "Hop Bitters vs. Nine Spots," *Weekly Jeffersonian* (Findlay, Ohio), September 12, 1879 (hereafter cited as *WJ*); "Base Ball," *West Liberty Banner*, June 4, 1891 (hereafter cited as *WLB*); "A 'Sassy' Challenge," *SVB*, June 28, July 19, 1890.

9. *DT*, September 24, 1869; *WLB*, September 13, 1894, August 22, 1895; "Slide," *SVB*, August 31, 1895.

10. *WLB*, July 26, 1894; *WJ*, June 25, 1880.

11. "Baseball," *DT*, September 24, 1868; *XT*, August 18, 1883; "Base Ball Notes," *WJ*, June 22, 1887; *SVB*, July 12, 1890.

12. *GP*, August 10, 1883; "Base Ball Notes," *WJ*, June 2, 1887; *WLB*, August 9, 1883, May 27, 1886; "Again Victorious," *GP*, June 25, 1890.

13. "The Ball Game," *WLB*, May 27, 1886; *XT*, August 18, 1883; *XG*, July 12, 1889; "Buckeyes Beaten," *WLB*, June 6, 1895; "Again Victorious," *GP*, June 25, 1890; "West Liberty Won," *WLB*, May 17, 1894.

14. *WLB*, June 11, 1884.

15. *XG*, August 6, 1889; *WLB*, June 4, 1891; *GP*, June 25, 1896; *WJ*, August 7, 1884; *MB*, September 22, 1898.

16. "Base Ball," *WLB*, September 20, 1889; *Miamisburg News*, September 22, 1898; "Base Ball," *WLB*, August 20, 1895.

17. *WLB*, July 18, August 15, 1895; *XG*, July 26, 1889; *WLB*, August 1, 1895; "On the Muscle," *GP*, August 20, 1890.

18. *MB*, June 6, 1890; *WLB*, August 1, September 26, 1985; July 26, 1894; "Base Ball," *DT*, November 11, 1870; *MB*, August 21, 1885, September 3, 1875; *WLB*, June 13, 1895.

19. *MB*, August 9, 1889; "Base Ball," *XG*, July 19, 1889; "Base Ball," *SVB*, June 6, 1894; "Had Them Down," *WLB*, August 8, 1895; "Base Ball," *DT*, October 8, 1869.

20. *XT*, August 18, 1883; "Baseball," *MB*, July 27, 1888; "Scooped," *WJ*, August 21, 1884, July 26, 1883.

21. *GP*, August 10, 1884; *WLB*, August 16, 1883; *MB*, July 11, 1884; *WLB*, June 4, 1896.

22. See, for example, "Lima Licked," *WJ*, September 14, 1882; *MB*, August 9, 1889; *XG*, June 18, 1889; "Had Them Down," *WLB*, August 8, 1895; *WLB*, June 6, 1895; *DT*, September 23, 1870; *GP*, August 1, 1883.

23. *WJ*, August 8, 1879; *MB*, July 4, 1884; "Baseball," *DT*, September 23, 1870.

24. *MB*, August 1, 1884, April 10, 1891; *WJ*, August 6, 1880.

25. See, for example, "The National Game," *WLB*, July 10, 1884; *XG*, August 17, 1886.

26. Foster Rhea Dulles, *A History of Recreation: America Learns to Play*, 2d ed. (Englewood Cliffs, N.J., 1965), 265; *GP*, June 1, 1893.

27. "Pedomania," *WJ*, October 24, 1886; "The Fat Men's Match," *WJ*, October 31, 1879; *MB*, August 7, 1885, July 20, 1894.

V

In the Ring and Out: Professional Boxing in New York, 1896–1920

Steven A. Riess

The history of boxing has been largely neglected by historians, perhaps due to the distasteful character of the sport. But it is the very seamy nature of professional boxing that makes it an important subject for historical inquiry. The purpose of this essay is to examine the development of prizefighting in New York City from 1896, when it was first legalized, until 1920, when the sport secured permanent legitimacy. New York at this time was the sporting capital of America, and competed with San Francisco as the mecca of prizefighting. New York was the first state to legalize boxing by statute, and New York City was the site of many important bouts, the home of more fighters than anywhere else, and the center of the boxing publishing business. The primary focus of this essay is the process of legitimization of boxing and the nature of governmental regulation of the sport.[1]

The boxing heritage of New York dates back to the antebellum era when it was influenced by the massive Irish migration and the development of professional politics. In a recent exhaustive study of New York sport during the mid-nineteenth century, Melvin Adelman points out that by the 1820s boxing was taught in local gymnasiums to gentlemen seeking to copy their English counterparts in learning the "manly art of self-defense." In the 1830s there were a handful of contests regulated by rules, and the number of matches increased in the next decade. Four championship fights between heavyweights occurred between 1849 and 1860, culminating in the first international heavyweight championship match in England between their native son Tom Sayers and the American James Heenan. This event drew more attention than any sporting event of that era. The early professional fighters were maily lower- and lower middle-class Irishmen and Irish Americans, who were seeking fame, prestige, and social mobility. Many first gained a reputation by participating in a criminal gang in New York such as Captain Isaiah Rynder's Empire Club. These gangs were often in politics, usually working for Tammany Hall or nativist parties. The job of these "shoulder hitters" was to intimidate voters to select the "right" candidate. The most famous of these shoulder hitters was John Morrissey, the American heavyweight champion from 1853 to 1858, who subsequently became a Tammany state senator, U.S. congressman, and the leading gambler at Saratoga Springs.[2]

The press of the day universally condemned the sport, chastising it for its brutality, its association with gambling, and the social character of its sponsors, participants, and spectators. Nevertheless, they covered the major contests, albeit begrudgingly, because of competition with other newspapers for a mass readership. The press did find some positive things to write about the sport, for instance, that it fostered courage, physical fitness, self-confidence, and temperance for men in training. As Adelman notes,

the rigorous discipline and training required of a fighter and the courage and confidence that emerged from the ability to defend oneself appealed even to opponents of pugilism and pugilists. Despite their disapproval, none could point to any other sport which accomplished this to the same degree as boxing.

He attributed this to the increased concern for the health of urban folk and the cult of manliness.[3]

After the Civil War, boxing remained relatively unorganized. Politicians continued to associate with boxers, but with Tammany ensconced firmly in power, it had no need for the shoulder hitters. Matches were fought with bare knuckles, usually in out-of-the-way places to evade the law. These places included barns, barges, and the back room of a saloon. Some important bouts were fought in New York during the 1880s at Madison Square Garden, an imposing edifice built by William K. Vanderbilt in 1879. The main drawing card in the early 1880s was heavyweight champion John L. Sullivan, who fought a number of four-round matches. Sullivan's most famous match in New

York occurred on May 14, 1883, when middleweight Charley Mitchell from England knocked him down in the first round in front of what was described as a democratic and elegant crowd. The police stopped the match in the third round. A year later, the police stopped another Sullivan fight, this time with Alf Greenfield, "for tending to corrupt public morals." Early in 1885, when Sullivan was matched before 10,000 spectators with the previous champion, Paddy Ryan, the police stopped the fight in the first round. That marked the end of the Garden as a center for boxing. The local press covered these contests and other major matches extensively. The enormously popular *World*, for example, had eighteen front-page stories on boxing between the middle of 1883 and January 1885. Their headlines conveyed a sense of great excitement rather than disapproval. Yet even the *World* called for the police to suppress these "gatherings of a disorderly character which attract the worst ruffians and criminals in the city." Although the professionalized version of the sport drew heated criticism, amateur boxing, which promoted "manliness," took place at the well-to-do athletic clubs such as the New York Athletic Club, the Manhattan AC, and the Pastime AC, where fighters scrapped for gold medals and belts.[4]

By this time, Coney Island had become the major site for professional boxing in the New York metropolitan area. Popularly known as "McKane's Sodom-by-the-Sea," Coney Island was a wide-open resort in the town of Gravesend, located just north of the city of Brooklyn, in Kings County. It was an area of low-life activity that had become a major sporting center, complete with several race tracks, a cycle track, and boxing clubs. Political power there was completely concentrated in the hands of John Y. McKane, who was concurrently president of the town board, chief of police, and head of the health and water boards. He had also served several terms as president of the Board of Supervisors of Kings County. Only 8,000 people lived in Gravesend, yet as many as 6,000 ballots were cast during elections. McKane used his very substantial power to prevent big boxing matches from occurring at Coney Island unless he had a piece of the action. There were well over a dozen boxing clubs in Kings County by 1890. The most important was the Coney Island Athletic Club (CIAC), established in 1892 in a building owned by McKane. The CIAC was completely controlled by the local Democratic politicians. McKane provided protection from political interference, Magistrate James T. Tighe ran the financial affairs (he was a prominent figure in local amateur athletics), and Police Justice Dick Newton arranged the matches. Among the other principal investors were Justice of the Peace Kenneth Sutherland and his brother, Fire Chief Bob Sutherland.[5]

By all accounts, the CIAC was very profitable. From the time it was organized in May 1892 until the end of September 1893, sixteen bouts were staged there. The purses and other expenses for these contests amounted to $74,400, while the CIAC took in $222,300 at the gate. The most ambitious bout it planned was a heavyweight championship fight between James J. Corbett and Charley Mitchell, the Englishman who had put Sullivan down on the canvas in 1883. The purse was announced as $40,000 plus a $10,000 side bet. An unexpected ground swell of opposition to the match developed, largely promoted by newspapers such as the *Sun*, the *Times*, and the *Tribune*. They succeeded in mobilizing clerics and other opinion makers to put pressure on political leaders to stop the fight. The bout was canceled because Democrats in Brooklyn and Albany were afraid that this issue could cause their defeat in the fall elections.[6]

The other boxing clubs had a great deal of political clout. In Brooklyn, for example, the Atlantic AC president was Justice of the Peace Edward C. Murphy. The Seaside AC at Coney Island was backed by some of the county's leading Democratic politicians, including Police Justice James Tighe, John H. O'Rourke, T. F. Carney, Michael J. Dady, and Stryker Williamson, a friend of John Y. McKane. The Seaside had a lot of trouble from Republican Mayor Charles Schieren, who refused to give them a license because they were allegedly staging prizefights. It took an injunction from Judge William Gaynor to compel the mayor to grant the necessary permits.[7]

Boxing matches were held in Queens County at athletic clubs that had a lot of political influence. The Empire AC held matches in New Town at a site about a mile outside the city line on the property of a former highway commissioner. Its directors included Police Justice James T. Tighe, formerly with the Coney Island AC, and James C. Kennedy, a prominent sportsman who had owned the Brooklyn franchise in the American Association in 1890.[8]

Boxing matches were also staged in Long Island City, located across the East River from New York, where gambling and other vices flourished. Mayor Patrick G. Gleason owned a part of the lot where the New Puritan Boxing Club was located. His associates in the club included noted fight manager Tom O'Rourke, the manager of world featherweight champion George Dixon, former Judge Dick Newton, recently released from a prison sentence arising out of corruption during the 1893 election, and Big Tim "Dry Dollar" Sullivan, the boss of the Bowery and the Lower East Side. Sullivan was second only to Richard Croker, and later Charles Francis Murphy, as a power in Tammany Hall. Beginning in 1886 when Sullivan was elected to the State Assembly, he spent most of his career in Albany, except for one term in the U.S. Congress. A lot of his early support came from infamous gangsters such as Monk Eastman, Kid Twist, and Paul Kelly, who provided him with intimidators and repeaters at election time. However, he was also renowned as a friend of the poor, who could always be counted on to provide jobs, presents, relief, or any other assistance that his constituents needed. Besides monopolizing boxing in the Croker era, Sullivan raced horses, gambled heavily, and controlled the pool room business in New York. One student of New York politics claimed that no one dared open a pool room without first clearing it with Big Tim.[9]

In 1895, legislation to legalize boxing was introduced for the first time in Albany. Senator George Horton's bill was supposedly aimed at curtailing boxing, but actually the goal was to promote the sport by permitting sparring at athletic clubs. While the measure failed in its initial try, the upstate legislator reintroduced his bill in 1896, claiming his purpose was to prevent irresponsible clubs from holding prizefights. Prizefights were regarded as contests in which the winner received money or other valuable compensation. These matches were characterized as unscientific brutal fights, where the object was to smash the opponent into submission. Horton's new measure called for the legalization of sparring with five-ounce gloves for a maximum of twenty rounds in buildings owned by incorporated athletic associations. Big Tim Sullivan was the main figure behind the movement that got the bill passed. The Horton Act meant that New York was the only state that permitted boxing and, in effect, permitted prizefighting. The *Police Gazette* was an ardent supporter of this new law, hoping that it would put out of business those clubs that had flimflammed the public, while opening the sport to legitimate sporting clubs. The *New York Sun* also supported the Horton Act as a means to promote virile interest in boxing.[10]

Despite the Horton Act, fight clubs could not operate with impunity. They needed to be licensed by the mayor and the police board. At times, clubs could not get a license or might lose their license because they lacked sufficient political clout, or the mayor might be opposed to prize-fighting. The latter was the situation in Brooklyn where Republican Mayor Fred Wurster was a vigorous foe of boxing at Coney Island. In December 1896, he succeeded in preventing the staging of a heavy-weight championship bout at Coney Island between Jim Corbett and the Australian Bob Fitzsimmons.[11]

Another problem for the boxing clubs was that the police were usu-ally in attendance with orders to stop the matches if they degenerated into brutal bouts. Sporting clubs whose fights were stopped faced the threat of losing their license. One important contest that the police broke up was a fight between Peter Maher and Sailor Tom Sharkey, a bud-ding contender for the heavyweight crown. The match was held on June 9, 1897, at the Palace AC in front of 7,000 spectators. Sharkey lost his head in the seventh round of a scheduled twenty-five–round match, slugging Maher and his second after the bell had rung. The police en-tered the ring and arrested the principals, their seconds, and the ref-eree. The judge lauded the police for their action, but ruled no viola-tion of the law had occurred and released all the prisoners. The affair gave the *Times* an opportunity to lambast prizefighting and the "sport-ing fancy" that supported it.[12]

The political connections of Tammany sportsmen were very useful in their dealings with the police department. The police chief at the turn of the century was Bill Devery, a prominent Tammanyite and sportsman who, after his political demise in 1903, became co-owner of the New York Yankees with the notorious gambler Frank Farrell. Devery became a policeman in 1878 and used his political patrons, Richard Croker and Tim Sullivan, to advance in the department. Cap-tain Devery was fired in 1894 following criminal charges emanating out of the Lexow Investigation of police corruption. However, he was reinstated after winning an acquittal on technical reasons. By 1898 he was police chief. His tenure as chief was replete with corruption, doc-umented by the Mazet Investigation of 1899. His position was abol-ished by the legislature in 1901, but the action was circumvented when the new police commissioner appointed Devery as his deputy and left the department in his charge.[13]

Devery rarely interfered with New York City boxing during his ten-ure. Perhaps the most important bout during his tenure was the heavy-weight championship match staged on June 9, 1899, at the Coney Island AC between Bob Fitzsimmons, the conqueror of Gentleman Jim Corbett, and James J. Jeffries. The Coney Island club was owned by theatrical and sporting promoter William Brady, the manager of Jim Corbett, and Martin Julian, brother-in-law and manager of Fitzsimmons. The Tammany-controlled Lenox AC wanted this big contest and did all it could to thwart its Brooklyn rival. Its management had led the fight to secure the Horton Act and was spending money to prevent legislation that would repeal it. The Board of Police Commissioners would not grant the CIAC a license until powerful political forces were marshalled behind the Brooklyn club. Brady and Julian's partner was politician Alexander Brown, who got the county Democratic boss, Hugh McLaughlin, to work on their behalf for a permit. The *Police Gazette* thought that the political conflicts this fight was stirring were putting the city government on the verge of disruption. However, the rival Democratic machines patched up their differences and the Coney Island club got the match. By the end of the summer, an agreement would be reached to divide up all major bouts in the future between the CIAC and the two principal Tammany clubs in Manhattan, the Lenox AC and the Broadway AC.[14]

The big match was castigated by the *Times* as "the City's Disgrace." New York was invidiously compared to less civilized parts of the country where governors, sheriffs, and other public officials did their duty and prevented prizefights. The pugilists were described as gorillas and bears. The paper was especially critical of Chief Devery, who had disgraced himself and his uniform by doing nothing while brutal blows were being struck. The *Times* recommended that he be fired, although they recognized that he was just a cog in a venal political machine:

Who knows how far we can go in blaming this man Devery, who is a more irresponsible unit in a vast controlling aggregate of political and civic turpitude? Can we doubt that he had his orders from the superior authority and that he obeyed them faithfully . . . ? He behaved as they all behave . . . , like a man without scruple, without honor, slavishly willing to break his word and ignore his duty. . . . The commands of law and duty have no weight with a Tammany office holder as the orders of the high men of the organization.[15]

Late in January 1900, Republican Assemblyman M. E. Lewis resubmitted a bill he had previously introduced a year before to repeal the Horton Act. In hearings held before the Codes Committee, advocates of reform pointed out that the Horton Law had opened the door to prizefighting. Reverend Dr. Hite, an Albany Episcopalian, claimed that the overwhelming sentiment in the state favored repeal. Assemblyman Lewis pointed out that the sport was prohibited in forty-four states because it was so dangerous. (Nine men had died from boxing in 1899.) Supporters of the Horton Act decried the critics as narrow-minded clergymen. Charles Feldman, the attorney for several Buffalo clubs, argued that the finest people attended boxing matches. He said that it was no worse than football, and if boxing were to be abolished, so should football. There were also spokesmen present on behalf of the Amateur Athletic Union (AAU) who opposed repeal for fear that amateur as well as professional boxing would be forbidden.[16]

Senator Tim Sullivan led the fight against repeal. This political conflict was watched by boxing fans from all over the country who were concerned about the future of the sport. A leading Chicago boxing writer pointed out, "Were this law to be repealed, there is not the slightest doubt that boxing all over the country would receive a setback from which the sport would not recover for years." Efforts elsewhere to legitimize boxing depended on its being permitted in the nation's largest state. The *Police Gazette* warned of lost revenue from a decline in the tourist trade of visiting sportsmen. The *Gazette* blamed the government for poor inspection which allowed abuses to creep in. The *Times* gave a similar perspective on the Horton Act. The legislation had not been inherently bad, but it was impossible to enforce "because the sympathies of the high controlling police officials were altogether with the criminal classes who made large sums of money by violating it." Not only did the police give a liberal interpretation to the Horton Law, but they permitted prizefighting to go on "with their express sanction and under their approval."[17]

The Horton Act was repealed in mid-April. It was reportedly the first time in Tim Sullivan's career that a measure that he was deeply interested in was turned down by his Senate colleagues. Passage of the Lewis bill had required a special message from the governor, who had offered a convincing argument against professional boxing (noting the various abuses that had crept in), substantial public pressure, and a Republican party caucus in the Senate where the bill had passed by a narrow 26 to 22 vote. The support Governor Theodore Roosevelt gave to a measure to end boxing in New York probably surprised most pugilism fans, since he had been a boxer in college and had previously supported boxing as "a sport which should be encouraged among boys and young men generally." He believed that boxing was "a vigorous manly pastime, one of those pastimes which have a distinct moral and physical value, because they encourage such essential virtues as courage, hardihood, endurance, and self-control." Furthermore, as president of the Police Board, he had been a frequent visitor to the bouts at the Broadway AC. He had established the principle that knockout contests were all right if the police commissioners had granted a license to an athletic club whose members were free to invite their friends to see the matches and also contribute money toward a purse for the fighters.[18]

Once the Lewis bill had been passed and signed by the governor, it meant that as of September 1, it would be a misdemeanor to aid, instigate, or engage in a fight for prizes where admission was charged. The police commissioners wanted to stop boxing in New York City immediately and not wait until the end of the summer. They indicated that if an act was illegal in four months, why wasn't it illegal immediately? The commissioners decided not to renew any licenses after May 1, which was when licenses traditionally expired. There was considerable confusion at first, but as a result of a test case, a Manhattan magistrate ruled that a license was completely unnecessary since the Horton Act had been repealed. The result, predictably, was that cheap clubs rapidly sprang up all over the city. Sam Austin, the principal boxing expert for the *Police Gazette*, expected that after the repeal of the Horton Act:

Swell club men and the better element of businessmen with a fondness for fistic sport, dodging the minions of the law, will be an almost nightly spectacle. . . . The now comfortable surroundings will be replaced by cold, cheerless barns or cellars, dimly lighted by candles or stinking oil lamps, and into which the favored ones who get the tip will crawl as secretly as if they were on some evil mission. Instead of contestants carefully trained and in the pink of condition, we shall see a lot of rum-sodden bums who fight nightly because that occupation affords them an easier way of getting booze than any other. In the absence of any moral protection, there will be free fights and riots, and perhaps murder. There will be jobs, robberies, and all kinds of crooked things happen through the incompetency and dishonesty of referees. . . . [19]

Certain fights that had been scheduled before the Horton repeal were staged along with bouts at new cheap clubs. Early in May, veteran Jim Corbett fought the young heavyweight champion Jim Jeffries. The match drew the biggest gate of the Horton era, $60,000. However, to many fans the outcome was a foregone conclusion, and there was very little wagering. To everyone's surprise, Corbett put on an outstanding fight. In fact, he had the better of it for most of the contest, but eventually tired and was knocked out in the twenty-third round.[20]

The *Times* blamed the continued boxing violations on Mayor Van Wyck, President York of the Police Board, and Chief Devery. Prizefights were just another example of what the *Times* claimed was Tammany's chief business, selling permits to allow violations of the law. New York City was chastised as the only metropolis whose government was completely "in the hands of a venal organization that is an attractive place for the lovers of brutality and gambling all over the country." The boxing business was in the hands of a political trust that promoted the fights and had a monopoly of protection for those events.[21]

The major boxing clubs tried to hold as many big bouts as possible as the day for the end of legal boxing approached. The last match was the fight between Kid McCoy, one of the cleverest fighters of the day, and Jim Corbett on August 30 at Madison Square Garden. Corbett, who outweighed his 170-pound opponent by 20 pounds, was the 10 to 6 favorite. Three weeks before the fight, rumors had spread that the fight was fixed. It was said that the combatants had secretly agreed to divide the fighters' share of the gate evenly instead of the contracted 75–25 percent division. Another factor was that Mrs. McCoy (who was involved in marital problems) had revealed some of her husband's deceptive tactics in the ring, such as faking weariness to fool his opponent. This created an impression that he had fixed some earlier matches. Consequently, the twenty-five–round fight, which drew 8,000, had a disappointing gate of $50,000, just two-thirds of the anticipated take.[22]

To everyone's surprise, the match was not the crafty contest the experts had predicted, but a ferocious brawl. McCoy was knocked down and out in the fifth round. This outcome convinced the *Times* of the integrity of the bout. However, other observers were more dubious, especially when McCoy jumped to his feet soon after he had been counted out. A few days later, Corbett secretly left for England, running away with Marguerite Corneille, a beautiful vaudeville singer. His distraught wife went to the *New York World* and told them her husband had left to avoid the consequences of a fraudulent fight. She claimed an agreement had been made that McCoy was to win, but then Corbett had double-crossed him. A few days later, she sued for divorce.[23]

On September 1, after approximately 3,350 fights, the Horton Act was no longer in effect. Boxing rapidly went on the skids. Only a small number of bouts were held in 1901, usually in private. Fights to a finish were secretly staged in the city on barges, in the back of saloons, or at old clubs like the Lenox AC, which held stags that included boxing in its entertainment. Other matches were held on the outskirts of the metropolitan area, in barns or comparable sites, on Long Island, Coney Island, or New Jersey. The purses ranged from ten to fifty dollars, although the take could be increased by side bets. The *Police Gazette* reported that for one dollar spectators saw poorly managed, brutal fights, which were said to be as unfair and rough as either hockey matches or football games. Nearly all the old boxing clubs went out of business. Some became dance halls, while the Lenox became a theater. The only important site that remained in 1903 was Madison Square Garden, but it had always been used for much more than just boxing. The number of matches by this time had probably increased but were still being arranged in secret. Fans were told to gather at a certain spot, usually a saloon, and then were taken to a series of other sites in order to evade the authorities. The crowds were generally small, but side bets made up the bulk of the rewards. The money was supplied by the fighters' backers, who usually included gamblers and saloonkeepers.[24]

After repeal, efforts started almost immediately to get new legislation passed to permit boxing in some form. However, with the Republicans in control of the state legislature, the prospects were not good. Assemblyman Charles F. Brooks of Buffalo was among those in the forefront of this effort. The former boxing promoter submitted one bill that would have permitted boxing in Buffalo under a state commission for the duration of the Pan-American Exposition. He also presented another scheme that would have permitted the AAU to hold fifteen-minute amateur bouts. Both proposals were defeated as entering wedges for the resumption of prizefighting.[25]

One year later, Assemblyman John T. Dooling, an officer of the Metropolitan AAU, sponsored legislation to permit amateurs to spar for fifteen minutes for nonmonetary prizes under the supervision of a legally incorporated amateur athletic association. He had the support of the AAU but was opposed by the *Times*. While the bill was favorably reported out of committee, it failed to pass. A more ambitious bill, introduced by Republican Assemblyman Manee, a Brooklyn plumber, also failed. Manee wanted the governor to appoint a boxing commission to a five-year term to establish rules and regulations for boxing exhibitions and to supervise the sport. Matches would have been held at sporting clubs licensed for $2,500. In 1903, leadership of the effort to secure boxing fell to Senator James J. Frawley. The Harlem legislator was the president of the Knickerbocker AC and an official of the Metropolitan AAU, as well as a personal friend of boxing expert Sam Austin. Eventually, legislation bearing his name would be passed legalizing boxing in the state.[26]

In 1904, Frawley proposed two bills to permit amateur and professional boxing, but opposition to the resumption of professional fighting was so great that both bills failed. A year later he focused his efforts on securing amateur contests under AAU supervision. A number of his Democratic colleagues were unhappy with this measure since the professionals were being frozen out. They saw this as an example of class legislation that discriminated against the boxer who wanted to earn a living in the ring. Boxing promoters decried the Frawley legislation because it would deprive them of an opportunity to promote boxing exhibitions. The measure sailed through the Senate and the Assembly but was vetoed by Republican Governor Frank Higgins.[27]

Although professional boxing was still outlawed by statute, bouts were held nearly nightly and people who were interested had no trouble finding out about them. Approximately a dozen private clubs such as the Avonia AC, the Polo AC, or St. Bartholomew AC regularly held three-round matches. Spectators were on a regular membership list of these small clubs and the police did not interfere. The membership dodge was based on a ruling some years before by Judge Tighe, who had decided that it was not against the law for incorporated athletic clubs to hold boxing matches if no admission charges were levied. Some clubs permitted "applications to be made at the door where the board of governors goes through the formality of electing an applicant to membership." Upon payment of the "membership fee," the boxing fan was admitted into the club to see the scheduled matches. The *Police Gazette* compared this evasion of the law to the efforts of the Brooklyn Dodgers to circumvent the Sunday blue laws in 1905 by admitting purchasers of scorecards into Washington Park since it was illegal to sell tickets to a Sunday ball game. Accounts of the better fights were reported in the daily papers the next day. Some commentators, like Sam Austin, feared overexposure. Things seemed to be getting out of hand as get-rich-quick schemes led to the renting of private gardens, riding academies, and even old churches as sites for pugilistic contests. Austin was also worried that some greedy promoters did not bother giving physical examinations to the combatants and that novices were sometimes mismatched with more experienced boxers.[28]

Although some smaller clubs suffered severely from overcompetition, interest in the sport had increased sufficiently by 1906 to encourage a revival of boxing at Madison Square Garden. A chartered athletic club was organized to run the contests. Revenue came from the one dollar initiation fee that was charged to new "members." This seemed to augur well for the future of fighting in New York and rumors started that major bouts were going to be arranged for Coney Island. New York City promoters were receiving a lot of support from local magistrates in their efforts to sustain boxing. While there had been 131 arrests for violations related to prizefighting during the first five months of 1906, there had been very few convictions. The reform Police Commissioner Thomas Bingham blamed the low rate of convictions on the interpretations of the law made by the lower courts.[29]

Governor Frank Higgins surprised most boxing patrons by issuing a directive at the end of May to Sheriff Nicholas Hayes, ordering him to stop all prizefights in Manhattan. Higgins was an acknowledged foe of boxing and had recently refused to sign a bill that would have permitted amateur boxing. The sheriff announced that he would send his deputies to all future boxing contests to make sure that no violations were occurring. The immediate reaction was that the important Long Acre AC cancelled its weekly contests, and other clubs followed. When subsequent efforts to secure injunctions against the sheriff failed, the clubs suspended their operations. The *Times* vigorously applauded the governor's actions, asserting that "the time has gone by for prize fights in this great city. To permit it would be to put a stain upon its name." The blame for the recent revival in boxing was placed on the yellow press which seemed to believe "that its readers demand the exhibition in its columns about thrice weekly of the repulsive features of these brutes and bruisers. The low tastes of these persons are catered to and their primal human or inhuman instincts are developed and stimulated by such newspapers.''[30]

Sam Austin blamed the boxing promoters for Governor Higgins' intervention. He believed that as long as bouts had been limited to three- and six-rounders, the prevailing feeling had been that no great harm was being done. However, once a major organization such as Madison Square Garden moved back into the sport to make a big, quick profit, trouble resulted. The promoters, Harry Pollack and Patrick Powers, president of the Easter Baseball League, knew that to fill the Garden they needed name fighters who would engage in full-scale fights. They made a match between two internationally renowned fighters, Jimmy Britt and Terry McGovern. The fight drew too much public attention and, consequently, the governor had stepped in.[31]

At the 1907 session of the state legislature, Senator James Frawley resubmitted a measure that Governor Higgins had pocket vetoed a year before. There was considerable sentiment in favor of amateur boxing, which had once been very prominent in New York. Until the repeal of the Horton Act the AAU national boxing championships were usually held in New York City, often at the Metropolitan Opera House. Some opposition during debate came from Tammany men such as Marty McCue of New York, himself a former professional boxer. He declared that the bill would create a monopoly for the AAU and would prevent fighters from getting compensated for their ring work. Once the bill passed the legislature, the AAU sent a delegation to Governor Charles Evans Hughes to urge him to sign the bill. Hughes also received telegrams from sportsmen such as Gustavus Kirby of Columbia, and Barton S. Weeks of the New York Athletic Club urging his approval of the Frawley Act. In fact, when the governor held a hearing on the amateur bill, there was virtually no opposition at all. Nevertheless, the progressive governor felt this bill was a step in the wrong direction and vetoed it. He felt the state should prevent the excesses that would surely result if the sport was overly stimulated by permitting paying exhibitions at amateur boxing shows. During his governorship, Hughes not only was an opponent of boxing, but was against Sunday baseball and vigorously fought a successful fight to outlaw horse racing.[32]

Despite the legal problems, boxing under the membership system continued in New York. The sport was still dominated by politically influential clubs known as the "boxing trust." An exclusive Tammany-dominated club was the National Sporting Club which was restricted to 300 members when it was established in 1907. It was controlled by gambler Frank Farrell, the owner of the Yankees, and James Gaffney, a political associate of Boss Charles F. Murphy, who later owned the Boston Braves. When the club opened on April 1, the crowd included such notables as Diamond Jim Brady, Jesse Lewisohn, and Florenz Ziegfeld. The most prestigious club in the city was the National AC, which was dominated by Tim Sullivan and his associates. Its membership list was said to number well over 3,000 who saw boxing matches in a "plush-lined" club. Although the National denied it, they were said to sell tickets (''memberships'') to anyone on a fight night. Another major club with powerful political protection from Tammany was the Fairmount AC in the Bronx. Its main figure was Billy Gibson, a politically astute manager and promoter. Among the fighters he managed during his career were Benny Leonard and Gene Tunney.[33]

By October 1908, boxing had revived to such an extent that approximately sixteen clubs held weekly matches in Manhattan and Brooklyn. However, few were as audacious as the Fairmount, which late in the month staged a major bout between two great lightweights, the fighting dentist Lave Cross, the idol of local Jewish fight fans, and Packey McFarland, the brilliant Chicagoan. Over 3,500 attended the fight at the 137th Street arena. The overt public nature of these obvious prizefights drew the attention of boxing critics, including the police commissioner. Bingham ordered that all prizefights be stopped. With the police on the alert, many clubs briefly suspended operations. The promoters instituted a couple of test cases to determine how the law was being interpreted by the courts. In the principal case, Justice Samuel Seabury of the State Supreme Court agreed with the officers of the Fairmont AC that they had the right to restrain the police by an injunction from interfering with private sparring and boxing bouts that were conducted for the amusement of club members. Thereafter, most clubs were able to operate once they had gotten an injunction forbidding the police from unwarranted interference.[34]

By 1911, boxing activity in New York had grown to the point that about thirty athletic clubs were holding weekly bouts. Little had been done to seriously upset the membership plan which circumvented the law. As long as promoters were not too greedy and did not book championship-caliber matches, the system was permitted to operate. Since September 1909, policemen had been under direct orders to collect evidence at club room fights which could be used in court to convict alleged violators of the statutes prohibiting prizefighting. This was difficult to do since uniformed officers were not legally entitled to enter private property without a warrant, and club managers would not give them tickets to get in. Detectives watched for payments that were direct charges of admission, but no manager was foolish enough to sell tickets. When plainclothesmen arrested perpetrators, they had a difficult time convincing magistrates that a violation had occurred. Judges wanted evidence that heavy blows had been struck, that the fighters were seeking to knock out their opponents, and that knockouts had actually occurred. Sometimes officers brought newsclippings with them when they went to court to prove that the alleged prizefighting had taken place, but such evidence was not always accepted.[35]

Another means of trying to put pressure on athletic clubs was through the fire department. Clubs were threatened with closing if they did not comply with the fire codes. The problem of fire in crowded places was very serious at this time. In 1903, the ferryboat *Slocum* burned with the loss of 1,030 lives and eight years later 150 girls were killed at the Triangle Shirtwaist Factory fire. As Tunney pointed out, the sporting clubs were firetraps, often lacking fire escapes, sufficient exits, and adequate fire appliances. Only the Fairmont AC and the Twentieth Century AC were free of code violations. The other arenas were at times under pressure to comply with the building codes or get closed up. This situation undoubtedly made them more vulnerable to local politicians who wanted a piece of the action or wanted to close the club because it was competing with a boxing club under their protection.[36]

The fight that probably generated the greatest general interest among New Yorkers since the repeal of the Horton Act occurred on March 3, 1911, when K. O. Brown won a popular decision over Ad Wolgast, the reigning world lightweight champion. The crowd of over 2,000, which included nearly all the leading sportsmen of the day as well as many notable professional people, paid $20,000 to see the fight. Thousands more crowded outside the *Times* bulletin board for round-by-round reports. Opponents of prizefighting had been sending many complaints to Governor Hughes regarding nonenforcement of the penal codes, and after this well-publicized fight, the governor wanted some action by the police commissioner. A number of policemen were called on the carpet for not properly attending to their duties. A few officers were reprimanded, and two were fined a week's pay.[37]

When the legislators convened in Albany that spring, conditions were propitious for Senator Frawley to again seek passage of legislation legalizing boxing. There was a new governor, John A. Dix, who was a Tammany-backed Democrat. In addition, for the first time in decades, the party had captured both houses of the legislature. In the middle of April, Frawley introduced a bill to establish a state athletic commission to run boxing. The three commissioners would be appointed by the governor and serve without compensation, leaving the day-to-day work to a paid secretary. Boxing would only be allowed at licensed associations or clubs that had a year's lease on a suitable facility and had posted a $10,000 bond to guarantee honest bouts. Fighters had to be licensed and their fitness certified by a commission-approved physician. Contests were limited to fifteen rounds (amended down to ten) and gloves had to weigh a minimum of eight ounces. The bill prohibited the sale of alcoholic beverages on the premises of any sparring contest and required clubs to pay the state 5 percent of their gross profits.[38]

The *Times* was very suspicious of this bill which it saw as a device to indirectly secure legislation to permit a miserable business to operate which the public would surely reject if directly and honestly appealed to. The paper continued to believe that the sport was a useful, innocent exercise that taught self-defense. However, as a business it was evil. The *Times* argued that real athletic clubs, including those that emphasized boxing, were already adequately conducting themselves under the law. It felt that "only clubs of a very different sort . . . want and need immunity from general laws . . . ," and there was no reason to accommodate them. The editors felt that legitimizing the vicious and demoralizing money-making clubs would be a public calamity.[39]

The Frawley bill made its way through the state legislature with a minimum of problems. On June 7, the Senate approved the measure with some minor amendments by a wide margin, 37 to 7. The *Times* reported the news glumly, pointing out that the fight club managers who were behind the measure would henceforth be free from occasional police harassment. Two weeks later, the bill easily passed the Assembly, and shortly thereafter Governor Dix affixed his signature, thereby legalizing boxing.[40]

By the start of 1913, there were 89 boxing clubs in the state, including 49 in New York City. However, there was very little stability. In 1912 alone, 40 new clubs were organized, and many did not survive the year. By the end of 1914, there were 58 clubs in the state, although a total of 132 clubs had been licensed since the Frawley law went into effect. Smaller clubs had a particularly hard time surviving. The competition from organizations such as Madison Square Garden was hard to bear. Sportswriters felt that part of their problem were the guarantees promoters gave fighters to sign for a bout. They felt the fighters should take a percentage of the gate, thereby sharing in the risks and gambling on their own drawing power. The bigger clubs could afford to give a guarantee because they had more regular fans and a greater seating capacity. Some of the smaller clubs required their fighters to hustle tickets and paid them on the basis of the number of tickets each pugilist had sold. The financial costs to the state of regulating the sport were more than paid by its share of the gate. In 1912, nearly $1 million was grossed by the boxing clubs, and the state's share was over $49,000. Boxing did not do as well in 1914, when the receipts amounted to $650,000, and the state's take was about $32,000.[41]

The Democratic domination of the state government ended with the November 1914 elections that returned control of the legislature to the Republicans and awarded the governorship to Charles S. Whitman, the former district attorney of New York County. Speculation began about the future of boxing in the state. Whitman was not an opponent of boxing per se, but he did seem determined at least to revamp the State Athletic Commission, whose term was to expire in a year. Sheriff Harburger and others had previously suggested making the job a paid position to attract better people who would make it a full-time job.[42]

In April, the new legislature reorganized the athletic commission. The Republicans gained new patronage slots by establishing a three-man commission, each of whom was to get paid $3,000. They also reduced the secretary's salary to $3,000 and raised the tax on gross receipts to 7.5 percent to help meet the new expenses. The bill also called for the establishment of headquarters in Albany, ostensibly to save money. This was not wise, since nearly all of the commission's work involved boxing in New York City.[43]

The reorganization of the SAC came at a time when the sport had never been as clean as it was then. The commission's work had become routinized, and most of it was rather mundane. One of the health problems the commission tried to alleviate was smoking at the prize-fights. They wanted to stop smoking because it was bad for the fighters and because the smoke often got so dense it was impossible for spectators to see the ring. However, the public strongly opposed the edict forbidding smoking. When manager Jimmy Johnston of Madison Square Garden imposed the no-smoking ban, he was swamped with letters decrying that deprivation. A good cigar was part of the ambiance of attending a boxing match. It was ''a pleasure that fits in better at a boxing show than any other place.'' Consequently Johnston decided on his own to permit smoking at the Garden. The SAC recognized the public demand and also acceded.[44]

A more serious infraction was the use of children as fighters. This matter came to light mainly through the efforts of the Brooklyn Society for the Prevention of Cruelty to Children which sought to prevent the exploitation of children for money-making purposes. The most notable case involved the Broadway Sporting Club which had boys battling at its weekly Monday matinees. No action was taken against the club in 1915, and when the problem recurred a year later, the club was only briefly suspended. John Weismantel had introduced the non-holiday matinees in January, using alleged amateurs, although the bouts were not sanctioned by the AAU. One of his goals was to attract women spectators. Women at this time were virtually never seen at prize-fights. He advertised that women would be charged only fifty cents or one dollar. Over 1,000 men showed up for the first matinee, but just one woman. Weismantel then announced he would give triple trading stamps to all women attending his matinees as an inducement to ''flee pink tea and sewing circles for masculine sports.'' Two women appeared at the next match.[45]

Until 1915, legal bouts had only been held indoors because the Frawley Act was interpreted to permit contests held inside buildings. But after the state attorney general ruled that bona fide athletic clubs could hold matches out of doors, the commission agreed to permit it. That was important because the summer was normally a relatively slack season for boxing because of the absence of adequate ventilation at most clubs. The first out-of-doors bout was held at Ebbets Field on May 31, attracting a crowd estimated at 15,000. The ring was pitched near home plate, and it was illuminated with arc lights. Among the spectators were some "highly excited women in spring millinery," and on their behalf, the announcer requested that the males present refrain from vulgarity. At a second outdoor bout there, attended by 10,000, the *Herald* reported that about 500 women were present.[46]

The biggest outdoor fight of the season was held on September 11 at the Brighton Beach Motordrome, promoted by the site's owner, William C. Marshall. The main event matched Packy McFarland, coming out of retirement, and Mike Gibbons of St. Paul. The original press reports estimated the crowd at over 60,000, but the official count was later adjusted down to 26,092. The promoter charged "popular prices." About 5 percent of the crowd got in on complimentary passes. The official gate was $58,069, of which $17,500 went to McFarland and $15,000 to Gibbons. Marshall was so disappointed with the financial returns that he decided to return to businesses he knew something about. The entire affair was chaotic, and disorder reigned. Many reserved-seat holders could not get to their seats. The spectators broke down a wire partition separating the $3 seats from the cheaper sections. The private guards could do little to keep order and even during the fight the aisles were crowded by fans who had left their cheaper seats for a better look. What they saw was a boring match, with two fighters waltzing around the ring, unwilling to trade blows.[47]

In the fall, Governor Whitman removed the three members of the old State Athletic Commission and replaced them with his own men. Whitman made the changes a few months early because of rumors that the Show Corporation, which promoted boxing at Madison Square Garden, was the object of extortion threats. The management was allegedly threatened that their license would not be granted unless certain favors were given to particular individuals. There was a lot of jockeying for the choice commission appointments. The new chairman was Fred A. Wenck, a local sportswriter and editor. Wenck was a graduate of City College of New York and had been a highly successful all-around athlete at Yale Law School. Boxing was one of his sports, and as a senior law student he took an American college boxing team to England to participate in the King's Coronation Tournament. He had been a member of the NYAC and was twice the champion swimmer of North America. His colleagues on the SAC were Frank Dwyer of Geneva, the former manager of the Detroit Tigers, and John Franey of Albany, a former county clerk. The new secretary was William F. Mathewson, a former Republican assemblyman from Brooklyn, whose brother had been Bronx borough president.[48]

One of the first things the new SAC had to deal with in 1916 was the use of local regimental armories for boxing matches. A Washington Heights ministers' association discovered that the Twenty-second Regimental Armory at 168th Street was going to be used for boxing, and they complained to their congressman and the governor. Governor Whitman advised Adjutant General Louis W. Stotesbury not to permit boxing in his facilities, and the general complied. Army officials in the city supported holding the bouts at armories to encourage enlistments. Major R. S. Cooke of the Twenty-third Infantry pointed out:

> The installation of bowling alleys, billiard tables, and so forth is made to make military service as attractive as possible to young men. If regimental activities were strictly confined to drill and other military work, the various organizations would find it impossible to fill their ranks.

It was reasoning along these lines that had led to the establishment of the Military Athletic League (MAL) several years earlier. The goal of the MAL was to promote all branches of athletics among National Guardsmen to improve their fitness, and to help in recruiting.[49]

The *Times* and the *Police Gazette* felt that boxing in New York was on the decline at this time, as evidenced by alarm among the promoters, who had cut the number of bouts by half. They agreed with Commissioner Wenck, who felt that the fans had tired of the same boxers and the same matches. The sporting public wanted to see new blood as they were accustomed to on the vaudeville circuit. The *Gazette* felt that the smaller clubs were suffering the most. Many that once had weekly bouts now only had a match every three weeks.[50]

Wenck had a number of proposals to increase interest. As previously discussed, he wanted to restore mixed bouts. The chairman wanted referees to be empowered to render a decision at the end of a contest. He also recommended that the state establish its own championships, which each titleholder would have to defend every two months. However, Commissioners Dwyer and Franey voted down all these proposals.[51]

The future of boxing in New York was becoming increasingly tenuous. Its condition became very bleak at the start of 1917, when formal charges were filed by three leading New York City promoters with the governor's office against SAC chairman Fred Wenck. The complainants were former Alderman John J. White, Patrick Powers, and Harry Pollok. They were all affiliated with the new Madison National Amusement Company, which in November 1916 had sought a license to stage bouts in Madison Square Garden. The Garden's owners had gone broke and the facility had been put into receivership. White was the president of the promotional concern and Pollok was scheduled to be his matchmaker. They charged Wenck with discrimination and misconduct in his refusal to grant them a license.[52]

These were serious charges, and Governor Whitman agreed that they should be investigated. He assigned his legal advisor, Franklin B. Lord, to listen to testimony on these allegations. Emil Fuchs, the counsel for the promoters, protested his selection, because Lord was a close friend of Wenck, but to no avail. When the hearings began on January 29, Powers and Pollok testified that they had tried to get a license to promote boxing at Madison Square Garden but were denied on the grounds that their lease was not legal. They subsequently drew up a new lease with the approval of the deputy attorney general but were still refused a license. Pollok remembered that Wenck had told him that he did not like some of the people associated in the Madison National Show Company, which was the firm seeking a license. In addition, the chairman wanted a $1,000 bribe before he would grant a license. Pollok said he gave Wenck a check for $100 but stopped payment on it. A few days later they had a fistfight in Grand Central Station. Pollok's testimony was completely corroborated by Pat Powers. Powers claimed the chairman had told him, "A lot of people are making money from this boxing game and I am going to get mine."[53]

Wenck testified on his own behalf and sought to prove his innocence of any malfeasance. The commissioner admitted that Pollok and Powers had come to him seeking a license, even though their lease was phony. They told him that if he did not go along with them, he would be framed. Wenck told his visitors that it had been their associates in the Show Corporation, John H. White, Billy Long, and the notorious gambler Frank Farrell, who had "ruined boxing in the days of the Horton Law, get[ting] hold of the biggest boxing clubs in the city." Wenck indicated that after having refused the revised license, Fuchs and he had almost come to blows, and that President White had threatened him. Wenck admitted getting a check from Pollok, but claimed that it was a partial payment of $300 owed him for publicity work done before becoming commissioner.[54]

When Wenck was cross-examined by Fuchs, his testimony did not hold up. He was tripped up on his story of the alleged frame-up. The commissioner was forced to acknowledge various financial deals with fight managers and promoters. Wenck admitted that in June 1916, he had granted Pollok a license to stage fights at Brooklyn's Washington Park, the former playing field of the Dodgers. After the fight, Pollok paid him $100. Wenck also admitted that he had gotten money from Jack Curley, Jesse McMahon (he claimed this was for repayment of an old debt), and Dan McKettrick, all well-known promoters. Fuchs further accused the commissioner of himself promoting a fight between heavyweight Fred Fulton and Al Reich while he was a member of the SAC. Wenck indicated that he had written up the document, but claimed this was done solely as a favor for a friend, without any thought of sharing in the profits.[55]

No indictments were returned against Wenck after these hearings, but his credibility, and that of the Athletic Commission, was destroyed. He had become an embarrassment for Governor Whitman, who fired Wenck in late March for incompetence. Sam Austin welcomed that action, asserting that "it would be difficult, indeed, to find anywhere outside of a jail a more detested lot of scamps." Austin felt that if the sport would be temporarily banned so it could be cleansed and reformed, nobody would be sorry.[56]

The Wenck investigation and the death on January 31 of a fighter named Young McDonald in a match that was attended by commissioners Dwyer and Franey hardened the determination of the governor to repeal the Frawley law. Whitman's political advisors told him that the commission would bring discredit to his administration by fostering brutal exhibitions under fly-by-night promoters. They expected that a fight against boxing would be supported by the protemperance and antitrack betting people who made up the heart of the Republican party. Whitman decided abolition was the only course, since no law could be produced that would guarantee boxing exhibitions before an admission-paying audience that would be within the bounds of propriety and decorum.[57]

The *Times* supported the political effort to eliminate the prizefight promoters. It was the promoters, the editors argued, that were to blame for the situation in boxing. Too many were out for easy money. Rather than real promoters, they were:

typical parasites of the boxing game, men preferring the subterranean to the open; men with no objection to a fixed fight, provided the public squeal was not too loud; men who would promise an enterprising card of lively bouts, and put on the tamest—and cheapest—of unskilled boxers; men who cared not a whit whether the purchaser of a seat got that seat; men, in a word, disgracing the name of sportsmen, and with ears attuned only to the tinkle of gold. They, with some unscrupulous boxers and considerable numbers of rowdy fans brought boxing to this situation.

But the *Times* was worried that if the Frawley law was repealed, it might also mean the end of amateur boxing, which it did not want. Amateur boxing had been superbly conducted since the Frawley Act had gone into effect. The AAU had been instrumental in securing its passage, and amateur athletic officials had been active in running the SAC during its first five years.[58]

Whitman's goal of repealing the Frawley Act had rough sledding in the state legislature. The Davis bill to repeal the boxing law was twice defeated in the Assembly by a coalition of Democrats and about twenty Republicans. The identical Slater bill did not even get favorably reported out of committee in the Senate once the Assembly had gone on record opposing the elimination of pugilism. The governor then sent a strong message to the state legislators, accusing them of shirking their responsibility. Whitman's pressure forced the legislature to accept his will. In the waning hours of the session, the Assembly repealed the Frawley Act as a party measure by a vote of 94 to 42. All but one Republican voted with the governor while only two Democrats supported him. In the Senate, where no Democrat voted for repeal, the margin was much closer, 26 to 20. Among the Democrats voting to keep professional boxing was Senator Jimmy Walker, who said, "The trouble with the Legislature is that it is run by long-haired men and short-haired women. If we enact many measures like this, next year they will elect some he-men to take our places in the legislature."[59]

The repeal of the Frawley Act seriously damaged boxing in America. Although the sport was permitted in twenty-three states, prize-fighting was still severely restricted in the major markets, if not illegal, as in New York and Chicago. In San Francisco, where there had been more title bouts than anywhere else, matches only went four rounds, with no decision, due to a three-year-old law that had ended twenty-round bouts. Since 1914, most of the principal prizefights in America had occurred in New York City, including the first heavyweight championship match in the East since 1900. But opportunities for prizefighters in New York substantially declined after the end of the Frawley Act, although they did not completely disappear, since there was a return to the old membership system as a means of dodging the law. However, after November when the new law went into effect, no one dared stage a major promotion, and the police were probably more vigilant in curtailing pugilism, even in smaller clubs, than they ever had been.[60]

Beginning in 1918, vigorous efforts were made to restore boxing, and the movement would succeed in 1920. One of the most active people in seeking the restoration of the sport was Brooklyn Assemblyman Marty McCue. When the state legislature convened for the 1918 session, McCue was very active in trying to restore boxing to good graces. In cooperation with many leading promoters such as Billy Gibson of the Fairmont AC, Charles Doesserick of the Pioneer AC, Jim Buckley of the Atlantic AA, and Charles Harvey, the former secretary of the SAC, McCue developed plans to legalize boxing. He recommended the creation of a new athletic commission with a single director and a deputy for each county where boxing clubs were organized. McCue wanted to license no more than twelve clubs—seven in New York, three in Buffalo, and two for the rest of the state. Twenty percent of the total gate would be spent for athletic equipment for military camps.[61]

The outlook for legalized boxing in the Empire State was bright. One reason was that the prestige of the sport was improving because it was being used to help train soldiers. Another reason was that in March boxing was legalized in New Jersey. Its governor approved the Hurley bill, which called for eight-round, no-decision fights with eight-ounce gloves. It had been modeled on the boxing bill that Assemblyman McCue had introduced in Albany. Local fans were excited by the prospect of seeing important bouts in nearby cities such as Jersey City, and they hoped the example of New Jersey would be emulated by their own legislature.[62]

In 1919, legislative efforts to permit boxing were increased, and observers expected little opposition to legalization. This optimism was partly due to the improved stature of the sport because of its use by

the military during the war, and because the new Democratic governor, Tammanyite Al Smith, had indicated that he would sign a sound
bill. Senator Leonard Gibbs, a Republican from Buffalo, presented the
first of several bills submitted during the session to permit prizefighting. Gibbs wanted ten-round decision bouts only at clubs that were used
exclusively for boxing. The sport would be supervised by a single-
member athletic commission to be appointed by the governor. His restrictions on the types of clubs to be licensed was mainly aimed at those
promoters out to make a quick profit and at Madison Square Garden,
which exhibited a broad variety of sports and entertainments. Marty
McCue supported this legislation, arguing that decision contests were
the only way that the sport could gain acceptance in New York. Under
the Frawley days, decision bouts were regarded as bad because they
promoted wagering on the outcome. However, most observers now
believed that an official decision would encourage fighters to do their
best and would forestall the risk of fake fights.[63]

The Gibbs bill was favorably reported out of committee and was approved on April 10 by the Senate, 27 to 18. There had been some rough
sledding for a time, since Democrats hesitated to support Gibbs, who
had voted against Sunday movies and Sunday baseball. The glee of
boxing supporters was tempered by the realization that the bill was not
going to be reported out of the Assembly's Rules Committee. As one
ranking Republican pointed out:

We can't afford to be too liberal. I am inclined to think that the fellows
from the cities who voted for the baseball and movies bill will seize the chance
given them to show conservatism and vote against the boxing bill. Of course
there will be change in the voting of the rural members, who were recorded
against baseball and movies, and who can be counted upon to be recorded.

Urban assemblymen who had voted to liberalize Sunday blue laws were
given a chance to hedge by turning down the boxing bill.[64]

A week after passing the Gibbs bill, the Senate also passed a second
boxing bill which had been introduced by Jimmy Walker. The minority leader was acting on behalf of William Gavin, the manager of the
prestigious National Sports Club of London, and the Army, Navy and
Civilian Board of Control (ANCBC). Gavin had come to America in
1918 and started an organization patterned after his London club. He
drew up a set of rules which became the basis for Walker's bill. The

ANCBC had been organized in January to run athletics for the military, the Knights of Columbus, and the YMCA. It was an ardent supporter of boxing, mainly because the military had used it as an integral part of training. The president of its Boxing Board of Control was the patrician Major Anthony J. Drexel Biddle of Philadelphia, a famous amateur boxer in his youth. Walker's legislation called for the establishment of a five-man athletic commission to supervise boxing. The responsibility for licensing all participants and clubs would be given to the Boxing Board of Control. Fights were to last a maximum of twelve rounds, and two judges would render a decision if the match went its full length. The Board planned to regulate the affairs of fight managers, including keeping them out of the promoting side of the business and restricting their share of their fighters' purses. However, these plans went for nought, because the Walker bill was stymied in the Assembly and never made it out of committee.[65]

One year later, Senator Walker reintroduced his boxing bill. There was far more support for boxing than ever before, mainly because of the improved status of boxing which had resulted from its use during the war to train soldiers. Even the *Times*, a traditional opponent of boxing, could no longer see why New Yorkers should be denied a privilege that neighboring states enjoyed. The editors believed that the supervision of the sport by the Board of Boxing Control, along with the establishment of the prestigious International Sporting Club by William Gavin, was an important guarantee of proper conduct for the sport. Some opposition still existed on the grounds of brutality and corruption, and there was mounting concern that wartime slackers might be licensed to fight. However, nearly all of the sport's critics were reduced mainly to chastising the commercialization of the ring, focusing on the assumption that the bill had been mainly introduced to get the Dempsey-Carpentier championship fight for New York.[66]

The Walker bill called for a three-man commission, each to be paid $5,000 along with an unpaid three-man license commission. Clubs were to be bonded and had to either own or have a one-year lease on their facility. They could not own a share in any fighter appearing in their arena. Military armories were to be approved as sites for matches. The bill established a moderate license fee for clubs—$500 in New York and other major cities, less in smaller towns. Spectators under sixteen were not permitted. Fighters and all other participants had to be licensed. Gloves had to be six ounces for lightweights and heavier fighters and five ounces for lighter pugilists. Tickets were required to have the purchase price clearly printed on them as a means to thwart scalpers.[67]

The Walker bill passed the Senate on March 24 by a 31 to 19 vote. All the Democrats voting supported the bill and a sufficient number of Republicans joined them to pass the bill. It had been criticized as a patronage grab, but Walker assured his colleagues that Governor Smith would only hire men "who will not serve for salary, but because they are high-grade lovers of the sport." The measure passed the Assembly on April 24 by an even wider margin, 91 to 46, despite the stronger and more organized opposition than existed in the upper chamber. There had been some talk among the ex-servicemen in the Assembly of fighting any bill that would permit slackers to box. However, nearly all the veterans voted in favor of passage.[68]

According to journalist Gene Fowler, the managing editor of the *American*, Governor Smith was not disposed to signing Walker's bill. Smith aspired to the presidency and was afraid that signing a boxing bill would harm his public image. Fowler claimed that the governor personally resented the close relationship between prominent Tammany men and the low-life types who ran boxing. Smith held a public hearing on the fight bill on May 20, nearly a month after it had passed the Assembly. An overwhelming expression of favorable sentiment came from distinguished military leaders—men of distinction in private life—and various religious leaders. The opposition was led by Canon W. S. Chase, a long-time opponent of professional boxing and Sunday baseball, and Mrs. Francis W. Graham, who led a delegation of the Women's Christian Temperance Union. Chase revived familiar arguments that the bill would legalize brutality, demoralize amateurs, and advance the interests of the underworld by increasing graft, encouraging gambling, and developing gangsters. Mrs. Graham focused on the Dempsey-Willard championship fight scheduled for July 4, calling it a national disgrace.[69]

On the following day, which was a Friday, Walker personally pleaded his case before the governor but could not convince Smith to sign the bill. However, Smith told Walker that if over the weekend he could get one hundred Protestant clergymen to send him messages of support, then he would sign the bill. This was a difficult task since it was the Protestant clergy who had constituted the strongest foes of boxing. Smith employed such a stipulation because he knew that Walker could easily get the signatures of Catholic priests who were boxing fans or rabbis who identified with lightweight champion Benny Leonard.[70]

Walker turned to Anthony Biddle for assistance. Biddle had recently given a half million dollars to his Bible society and he requested their New York office to inform the state membership about the value of the Walker boxing bill. The result was that 600 telegrams and letters were sent to Governor Smith. Smith fulfilled his bargain with Walker and signed the boxing bill. He explained his reasons:

> The stress of the times demands healthy and wholesome amusement for the men of the State, and when an amusement can be afforded under such rigid restrictions and control by the State itself as this bill provides, no possible harm can, and on the other hand, a great amount of good will results from its enactment.

He saw it as a superior piece of legislation that would aid the state both economically and morally.[71]

On August 12 Al Smith appointed the members of the boxing and licensing commissions, placing two Democrats and one Republican on each board. The new chairman of the Boxing Commission was Joseph H. Johnson, the secretary-treasurer of the Encyclopaedia Brittanica Corporation and a former fire commissioner under Mayor Gaynor. The chairman of the Licensing Commission was Lawrence McGuire, an attorney who had been the president of the Real Estate Board of Trade and had served Al Smith as a member of a factory investigating committee. He had been a director of Madison Square Garden and was the former chairman of the New York Athletic Club's boxing committee. None of the six appointees (with the possible exception of McGuire) had any identification with professional boxing, but they were all regarded as sound selections who would work to keep the sport clean.[72]

With the implementation of the Walker law, New York quickly regained its position as the national center of boxing. The first legal matches in three years were held on September 17 at Madison Square Garden when a crowd of 12,000 saw Chicago lightweight Joe Wiling defeat Johnny Dundee in a fifteen-round match. It was the first decision fight in New York in twenty years. Three months later, on December 14, the Garden was the site of a heavyweight championship match between Jack Dempsey and Bill Brennan. Fourteen thousand surprised fans saw Brennan carry the fight. The challenger appeared on his way to victory when Dempsey knocked him out in the twelfth round. Under the leadership of Tex Rickard, Madison Square Garden quickly established itself as the mecca of American boxing. Rickard had originally intended to become the matchmaker at William Gavin's International Sporting Club. Rickard knew that whoever controlled the biggest arena would be in a position to control New York boxing for years, and consequently he sought control of the Garden. His chief rival for the facility was Joe Humphries, the most famous ring announcer of the day. Humphries was a Tammany man who was backed in his efforts by the boss, Charles F. Murphy. But Rickard also had powerful backers, including Al Smith, who interceded on his behalf with the owners of the Garden. Smith felt that only Rickard had enough exciting ideas and promotional techniques to successfully operate the Garden. Rickard managed to get a ten-year lease for $400,000 a year. His financial backing came from John Ringling, who would use the arena for his famous circus.[73]

Rickard rapidly achieved his goal of making boxing into a respectable sport. According to a leading historian of pugilism, Rickard accomplished this in one year. During the 1920s important boxing matches at Madison Square Garden were attended by people of all social origins—not just the rowdy blue-collar workers in the gallery or the rich politicians, gangsters, businessmen, and blue bloods who made up the sporting fraternity who sat ringside, but also the respectable middle classes. In addition, while the Garden was still primarily a center of the male bachelor subculture, it was increasingly becoming a place for upright women to be seen. In the 1920s, boxing at facilities such as Madison Square Garden became eminently respectable and profitable. And its heroes, particularly Jack Dempsey, were as prominent as any other sporting heroes during the Golden Age of Sports.

NOTES

1. Two recent biographies are Al-Tony Gilmore, *Bad Nigger! The National Impact of Jack Johnson* (Port Washington, N.Y., 1975), and Randy Roberts, *Jack Dempsey: The Manassa Mauler* (Baton Rouge, 1979). For a recent study of prizefighting in one city, see Thomas M. Croak, "The Professionalization of Prize-Fighting: Pittsburgh at the Turn of the Century," *Western Pennsylvania History Magazine* 62 (October 1979): 333–43. We need an in-depth study of boxing in San Francisco for the late nineteenth and early twentieth centuries.

2. Melvin Adelman, "The Development of Modern Athletics: Sport in New York City, 1820–1870" (Ph.D diss., University of Illinois, 1980), pp. 560–73; Gustavus Myers, *History of Tammany Hall* (New York, 1901), p. 189; Alfred H. Lewis, *Richard Croker* (New York, 1901), pp. 42–44.

3. Adelman, "Development of Modern Athletics," pp. 575–78.

4. Joseph Durso, *Madison Square Garden: 100 Years of History* (New York, 1980), pp. 58–59; P. F. Dibble, *John L. Sullivan: An Intimate Narrative* (Boston, 1925), pp. 38, 40–41, 64–67; George Juergens, *Joseph Pulitzer and the New York World* (Princeton, 1966), pp. 124–27.

5. On Coney Island, see John F. Kasson, *Amusing the Million: Coney Island at the Turn of the Century* (New York, 1978). On McKane, see Raymond A. Schroth, *The Eagle and Brooklyn* (Westport, Conn., 1974), p. 100; Henry I. Hazleton, *The Boroughs of Brooklyn and Queens and the Counties of Nassau and Suffolk, 1609–1924* (New York, 1925), pp. 1083–85; *Chicago Daily News*, 16 September, 1886; *New York Times*, 24–26 September 1893; "Arthur Lumley, Veteran Sportswriter, Manger and Promoter," *Ring* 6 (May 1927): 23.

6. *New York Times*, 21–25, 27, 28 September, 1, 2 October 1893; *National Police Gazette*, 14 October 1893, p. 2, 4 November 1893, p. 10. McKane was caught that fall engaging in certain serious election abuses. He and Judge Dick Newton were both sent to prison. See Mortimer Smith, *William J. Gaynor: Mayor of New York* (Chicago, 1951), pp. 31–34; and Lately Thomas, *The Mayor Who Mastered New York: The Life and Opinions of William J. Gaynor* (New York, 1969), p. 74.

7. *National Police Gazette*, 22 September 1894, p. 10, 16 March, 25 May 1895, p. 10, 6 July 1895, p. 11; *Brooklyn Eagle*, 11–13 June 1895; *New York Times*, 14, 15, 18 June 1895.

8. *Brooklyn Eagle*, 6, 15, 25 August 1895; *National Police Gazette*, 31 August 1895, p. 4, 14 September, 22 November 1895, p. 11.

9. *National Police Gazette*, 13 December 1890, p. 6, 16 February 1895, p. 10, 25 January 1896, p. 11; *New York Clipper*, 14 February 1891, p. 778; *Brooklyn Eagle*, 26 January 1895, 15 March, 14 April, 23 December 1896; *New York Times*, 29 May 1896. On Tim Sullivan, see M. R. Werner, *Tammany Hall* (Garden City, L.I., 1928), pp. 344, 438–40; Roy Crandall, "Tim Sullivan's Power," *Harper's Weekly* 58 (18 October 1913): 14–15; Theodore A. Bingham, "The Organized Criminals of New York," *McClure's* 34 (November 1909): 62–63; George K. Turner, "Tammany's Control of New York by Professional Criminals," ibid., 33 (June 1909): 117–34; Thomas M. Henderson, *Tammany Hall and the New Immigrants: The Progressive Years* (New York, 1976), pp. 1–15.

10. *National Police Gazette*, 18 May 1895, p. 11, 1 June 1895, p. 10, 8 February, 5 December 1896, p. 11; *Brooklyn Eagle*, 24 October 1896.

11. Mayor Worster throughout his administration was a foe of prizefighting. See, for example, *New York Times*, 22, 24 July 1896; *New York Clipper*,

25 July 1896, p. 329, 9 January 1897, p. 720; *Brooklyn Eagle*, 31 December 1896; *National Police Gazette*, 16 January 1897, p. 11. In New York City, Mayor Strong also used his discretion not to license certain fight clubs. See *New York Clipper*, 27 November 1897, p. 649. When Nevada passed legislation to permit boxing, it was with the understanding that a heavyweight championship match would soon be staged there. See *National Police Gazette*, 13 February 1897, p. 11. The match occurred on March 17, with Fitzsimmons winning in the fourteenth round when he knocked out Corbett with a blow to the solar plexus. This contest had been anticipated with great relish. The mass-oriented press covered all the preliminary preparations for about a month. *New York Times*, 18 March 1897.

12. *New York Times*, 10, 11, 17 June 1897; *New York Clipper*, 19 June 1897, p. 259; *National Police Gazette*, 25 February 1899, p. 7.

13. Steven A. Riess, *Touching Base: Professional Baseball and American Culture in the Progressive Era* (Westport, Conn., 1980), pp. 71–73; Richard J. Butler and Joseph Driscoll, *Dock Walloper: The Story of "Big Dick" Butler* (New York, 1928), pp. 487–91.

14. William A. Brady, *The Fighting Man* (Indianapolis, 1916), p. 9; *New York Sun*, 7, 8 February, 24 March, 14 May, 10 June 1899; *National Police Gazette*, 1, 22, 29 April, 20, 27 May, 3 June 1899, p. 11; *Sporting News*, 8 April 1899, p. 8. On the establishment of a boxing trust, see *New York Sun*, 7 March, 15 October 1899; *Brooklyn Eagle*, 9 September 1899; *National Police Gazette*, 21 October 1899, p. 11.

15. *New York Times*, 11 June 1899.

16. *National Police Gazette*, 18 February 1899, p. 11; *New York Times*, 25 January, 8 February 1900.

17. *National Police Gazette*, 17 February, 21 April 1900, p. 11; *New York Times*, 16 February 1900.

18. *National Police Gazette*, 21 April 1900, p. 11; Theodore Roosevelt, "The Recent Prize Fight," *Outlook 95* (16 July 1910): 550.

19. *National Police Gazette*, 28 April 1900, p. 10, 5, 12, 19 May 1900, p. 11; *Brooklyn Eagle*, 3, 4 May 1900. One interpretation was that the anti-licensing stand of the Police Board was due to the efforts of Tim Sullivan and O'Rourke to gobble up Brooklyn boxing by taking over the Seaside AC. This did not please Brooklyn politicians, who used their power to hold up the licensing procedure until Sullivan and O'Rourke withdrew to Manhattan. However, the *Eagle* thought the cause was internal squabbling among the former partners of the Lenox AC who had fought over the choice of Charley White as the house referee. *Brooklyn Eagle*, 4 May 1900; *National Police Gazette*, 28 April 1900, p. 10.

20. *National Police Gazette*, 12 May 1800, p. 2.

21. *New York Times*, 18, 25 July 1900.

22. Robert Cantwell, *Real McCoy: The Life and Times of Norman Selby* (Princeton, 1971), p. 70.

23. *New York Times*, 31 August 1900; *Brooklyn Eagle*, 11, 12 September 1900; Cantwell, *Real McCoy*, pp. 70–75.

24. *National Police Gazette*, 16 March 1901, p. 10, 2 August, 4 October 1902, p. 10, 6 June 1903, p. 3, 9 September 1903, p. 10.

25. Ibid., 2 January 1901, p. 10, 13, 27 April 1901, p. 10, 11 May 1901, p. 10. Amateur fighters would get medals for their efforts. They could then make a few dollars by selling them back or pawning them.

26. *New York Times*, 16, 25, 30 January, 1, 28 February, 6 March 1902; *National Police Gazette*, 17 January, 21 February, 4 April 1903, p. 10.

27. *National Police Gazette*, 28 January, 25 March, 1 April 1905, p. 10.

28. Ibid., 13 May 1905, p. 6, 2 September 1905, p. 10, 3, 10 February 1906, p. 10; *New York Times*, 16 November 1905.

29. *National Police Gazette*, 28 April, 19, 26 May 1906, p. 10; *New York Times*, 1 June 1906.

30. *New York Times*, 1 June 1906.

31. *National Police Gazette*, 17 June 1906, p. 10.

32. *New York Times*, 17, 26, 28, 30 April 1907.

33. Ibid., 2 April 1907, 2 November, 18 December 1908; Scrapbooks on Boxing, vol. 1, pp. 87, 93, Chicago Historical Society, Chicago, Ill.; *New York Call*, 26 October 1908.

34. *New York Call*, 26 October, 2, 4 December 1908; *New York Times*, 2 November 1908, 1, 5, 7, 12 January 1909.

35. Nat Loubet, "In the Days of Injunctions," *Ring* 38 (January 1960): 49; *New York Times*, 12, 13, 17–19, 22–24 March, 7 April 1911.

36. Gene Tunney, *A Man Must Fight* (Boston, 1932), p. 33; *New York Times*, 19 May, 30 August, 7 September 1911.

37. *New York Times*, 4, 12, 16, 17 March 1911.

38. Ibid., 13 April 1911.

39. Ibid., 4, 5 May 1911.

40. Ibid., 8, 9, 22 June 1911.

41. Ibid., 15, 29 February, 3 March 1912, 26 April 1913, 4 January 1915.

42. Ibid., 5 February 1915, 9 November 1912.

43. Ibid., 31 March, 23, 27 April 1915.

44. Ibid., 10, 23, April 1915; *New York Herald*, 5 February 1915.

45. *New York Times*, 21 January 1912, 19, 20 January, 3 March 1915; *New York World*, 21 April, 3, 4, 9, May 1916; *National Police Gazette*, 6 May 1916. The attendance of boys at matches did not seem to be a problem, although the Brooklyn Society for the Prevention of Cruelty to Children had been concerned with that in the past. *Brooklyn Eagle*, 15 August 1898. On female fans see *New York Times*, 19, 20, 26 January 1915.

46. *New York Times*, 12 November 1914, 17 March 1915; *New York Herald*, 1, 19 June 1915. Under the cloak of charity, there was a three-round contest between Fitzsimmons and Sharkey at the American League Park in 1904. *National Police Gazette*, 16 July 1904, p. 10.

47. *New York Times*, 13, 18 September 1915.

48. Ibid., 5, 9 October 1915; *New York Herald*, 30 November 1915.

49. *New York Times*, 3, 11 January 1916; *New York World*, 7, 12 January 1916.

50. *New York Times*, 30 January 1916; *National Police Gazette*, 19 February 1916.

51. *New York Times*, 18 February 1916; *York World*, 15, 17 July 1916.

52. *New York Times*, 4, 25, 28 November, 6, 30 December 1916; *National Police Gazette*, 9 December 1916, p. 10.

53. *New York Times*, 30 January 1917.

54. Ibid., 31 January 1917.

55. Ibid., 31 January, 6 February 1917.

56. *National Police Gazette*, 31 March, 7 April 1917, p. 10.

57. *New York Times*, 1–3 February 1917; *National Police Gazette*, 17 February 1917, p. 10.

58. *New York Times*, 5 February 1917.

59. Ibid., 24, 26 April, 8, 11 May 1917.

60. *National Police Gazette*, 9 June, 24 November 1917; *New York Times*, 19, 24, 28 November 1917.

61. *New York Times*, 24 January, 10 February 1918.

62. Ibid., 28 February 1918.

63. Ibid., 4, 18, 27 February 1919; *National Police Gazette*, 18 January 1919, p. 11, 22 February 1919, p. 3.

64. Ibid., 10, 11 April 1919.

65. Ibid., 20 March, 17 April 1919.

66. Ibid., 24 November 1919, 18, 23 February 1920. On the International Sporting Club, see ibid., 14 December 1919.

67. Ibid., 25 April 1920.

68. Ibid., 25 March, 2, 25 April 1920.

69. Gene Fowler, *Beau James: The Life & Times of Jimmy Walker* (New York, 1949), p. 100; Roberts, *Jack Dempsey*, p. 94; *New York Times*, 21 May 1900.

70. Fowler, *Beau James*, pp. 100–102. In Roberts' account, he wrote that the meeting occurred on Friday, May 22. However, Friday was actually May 21. Roberts, *Jack Dempsey*, p. 94.

71. Fowler, *Beau James*, pp. 102–3: *New York Times*, 25 May 1920.

72. *New York Times*, 13, 16 August 1920.

73. Ibid., 18 September 1920; Roberts, *Jack Dempsey*, pp. 95–99. On Rickard and his involvement with Madison Square Garden, see Butler, *Dock Walloper*, p. 264; Mrs. Tex Rickard, *Everything Happened to Him: The Story of Tex Rickard* (New York, 1936), pp. 274–75.

VI

Lefties and Righties: The Communist Party and Sports During the Great Depression

Mark Naison

One of the most important and long-lasting legacies of the New Left has been the regeneration of popular insurgency in American sports. The Civil Rights movement, and the rebirth of feminism inspired broad based efforts by blacks and women to win equal access to athletic resources, while the anti-corporate agitation of the student movement helped set the stage for sports action groups like FANS and Sports for the People. Sports activism has persisted and even expanded throughout the seventies, as feminists have carried the battle for equal athletic funding into schools throughout the nation, campaigns have arisen to prevent sports franchises from squandering public funds in Minneapolis, Syracuse, and New York, and protests to end sports contacts with South Africa have achieved many of their objectives.

Most of those involved in these protests, and their critics, have regarded sports activism in the United States as something unique to the '60s and '70s. But thirty years before, under the aegis of the Communist Party, a very different movement arose to reshape American sports. From the late twenties through the mid-forties, Communist youth, fraternal and trade union organizations sponsored independent sports leagues in cities throughout the country, participated in two Olympic boycott movements, sponsored numerous track meets and benefit games for political prisoners, and waged a thoroughgoing effort to end the exclusion of blacks from major league baseball. Although sports organizing was rarely mentioned in party theoretical journals and party resolutions (except those of the Young Communist League), it represented a major theme in organs directed at the party rank and file. From 1928 to 1935, the *Young Worker*, the Young Communist League newspaper, devoted far more attention to sports than to any other cultural activity, and from 1936 on the *Daily Worker*, the party's national newspaper, sponsored a sports page that took up fully one-eighth of the paper's space.[1]

An examination of this activity promises to contribute to the growing debate on the possibilities of American radicalism during the Depression years. Some New Left scholars, notably James Weinstein and Staughton Lynd, have argued that the Communist Party's reluctance to espouse explicitly socialist objectives during the late Depression years prevented the emergence of a strong socialist movement—minimally a labor party on the British model—as a permanent feature of the American scene. They imply that the American working class was receptive to socialist perspectives and that the Communist Party's adoption of New Deal liberalism as the American version of "antifascism" undercut the growth of radical forces. The usual focus of this discussion is the party's trade union work and electoral activity, but a look at party sports organizing suggest these critics may have significantly overestimated both the breadth of working class radicalism, and the party's ability to shape working class attitudes.[2]

In the early 1930's Communists tried to organize a workers sports movement with an explicitly socialist orientation. They confidently posed this activity as an alternative to professional and collegiate sports, to YMCA and AAU recreation programs, and to company and church sponsored sports leagues, but failed to attract participants beyond a tiny immigrant constituency. Only as Communists gradually embraced existing patterns of working class spectatorship and participation—from enthusiasm for prize fights and pennant races, to involvement in YMCA and church sponsored leagues—did Communist sports activities reach a sizable audience. Moreover, the most effective Communist efforts to influence the shape of American sports—the campaign against Jim Crow in baseball and the effort to create trade union sports leagues as an adjunct of the organizing campaign of the CIO—made "democracy" rather than socialism their rallying symbols. This experience—even when interpreted cautiously—suggests that working class receptivity to socialism was less than overwhelming, and that the Communist Party's movement toward liberalism and practical reform may have been the price it had to pay to attract an American-born constituency and acquire a modicum of influence in the mainstream of American life.[3]

During the 1920's, Socialist and Communist parties throughout Europe organized workers sports movements that attained impressive size and strength. Designed to encourage class consciousness among workers and to insulate them from "bourgeois" sports organizations that had military and nationalist overtones, these organizations became a distinctive aspect of sporting life throughout central Europe. The German organization grew to a membership of 1.4 million by the early thirties, the Austrian to 250,000 and the Czech to 200,000, with smaller but significant movements arising in Switzerland, Belgium, Finland and France. The largest of these organizations were affiliated with the Socialist International, but Communists were also quite active, and both parties took the initiative in sponsoring international workers sports festivals as alternatives to the Olympics.[4]

The American Communist Party tried to found a workers sports movement in the United States, but its effort in this direction assumed a very peculiar shape because of the immigrant character of the party. When the Communist Party was founded in 1922, no more than 10% of its membership spoke English as its first language. After an intensive Americanization program, the percentage rose to over 40% by 1929, but the organization was still overwhelmingly composed of the foreign-born, the largest groups of which were Finns, Jews, and South Slavs (in that order). Some of these immigrant Communists had strong networks of sports clubs, providing a sound initial basis for a workers sports organization, but the sports which they emphasized—soccer, gymnastics, and track and field—were ones which had little attraction for native Americans or even second generation immigrants. From the very first, Communist sports strategists faced a contradiction between their desire to insulate their existing following (which consisted of fewer than 10,000 Party members) from "bourgeois" influences in sport—the mass media, the AAU, and church and corporate organized sports clubs—and their desire to build a left wing sports movement that attracted American born workers.[5]

The CPUSA's sports organizing began in 1927. In January of that year, representatives of Finnish athletic clubs in the Detroit area, aided by some English-speaking Communists and Detroit labor officials, founded an organization called the Labor Sports Union whose purpose was "to encourage athletic activities by workers and win them away from the bosses who utilize the Amateur Athletic Union and similar bodies to spread anti-union propaganda.'' The Young Communist League assumed the task of spreading this organization nationwide and started a regular sports page in its monthly newspaper, the *Young Worker*.[6]

During its first year of operation, the Labor Sports Union held track and field and gymnastic competitions in New York, Detroit, Chicago and several smaller cities. Its national track meeting, in Chicago, attracted 300 participants, including three world class runners (2 Finns and a Filipino) and several thousand spectators. In the fall of 1927, the New York chapter of the LSU founded a Metropolitan Workers Soccer League that grew to 28 teams and 400 participants by February of 1928, and the Detroit LSU formed a soccer league shortly thereafter.[7]

These activities had an extremely narrow social base. "The bulk of the participants" in the LSU national meet were Finnish, the *Young Worker* complained, and the soccer leagues drew exclusively from the memberships of foreign workers clubs—Czechs, Germans, Hungarians, Finns, Estonians, Spaniards and Jews. "It is the American workers who are mostly the victims of bourgeois sport," the *Young Worker* editorialized, "commercialism, professionalism, and corruption, and among them must the work be carried on."[8]

To advance the Americanization of the movement, editors of the *Young Worker* began to examine popular American sports like baseball, boxing, and football, and to analyze working class patterns of recreation. Their evaluation of what they saw was uniformly hostile. In the eyes of *Young Worker* sportswriters all "bourgeois" sports organizations, whether amateur or professional, represented conscious efforts to insure working class loyalty to capitalism and to inspire individualist and escapist fantasies that prevented workers from dealing with their problems. Although the vision that underlay their writing was constricted and sectarian, some of their analysis was shrewd. As the *Young Worker* charged, many large corporations whose workers were not unionized (among them General Motors, Westinghouse, U.S. Steel, Standard Oil, Metropolitan Life, and General Electric) had set up large sports programs for their employees during the twenties, and management consultants openly advocated such activities as a way of saving workers from "street corner agitators . . . painting fancied wrongs." In addition, the huge sports programs sponsored by the American Legion, the YMCA's and religious organizations often explicitly inculcated values hostile to radicalism, and *Young Worker* writers erred only slightly when they argued that wealthy businessmen supported such programs in order to "deaden class feeling . . . and break class solidarity." In an extraordinarily heavy-handed manner (a typical headline was "American Legion and Public School Athletic League Poison Minds of Children"), *Young Worker* writers did raise the issue of business domination of American sports programs, and presented arguments why trade unions and the left should sponsor sports programs of their own.[9]

However, in dealing with mass spectator sports, *Young Worker* writers presented the far more questionable position that popular enthusiasm for sports, particularly identification with professional teams and athletes, represents the outcome of a capitalist plot to render the working class politically passive. The political impact of spectator sports is a continuing subject of debate among radicals, but the *Young Worker* presented the most extreme formulation of an argument which portrays "rooting" as *merely* the quest in fantasy for the power one lacks in real life, and something which invariably diverts energy from political struggle. In an article on the 1929 World Series, Walter Burke argued that:

Thru the means of this professional capitalist "sport", the capitalists were able to hoodwink the greater part of the American workers to eat, sleep and talk nothing . . . but baseball for a week. . . . Baseball is still a method used in detracting . . . the American workers from their miserable conditions.[10]

The May 1930 issue of the *Young Worker* printed pictures of heavyweight boxers Max Schmeling, Jack Sharkey and Gene Tunney under the heading "Three Dope Peddlers," and denounced them as "tools of the bosses in doping the workers to forget the class struggle." College football players, another *Young Worker* writer declared, are given under the table payoffs and soft jobs in order to "feed the young workers an opium that beclouds their minds and draws them into an ocean of patriotism and faith in the robbers of their bread and butter." The paper occasionally accompanied this critique with discussions of real abuses in big-time athletics—professionalism in college sports, discrimination against blacks, fixed boxing and wrestling matches, the class based distribution of facilities, the abandonment of athletes after they passed their prime—but the only solution they proposed for these ills was for athletes to join the Labor Sports Union, which they claimed, was preparing "one mighty on-slaught which will send this corrupt professionalism to its grave." [11]

During the spring and summer of 1930, YCL leaders launched an effort to Americanize the Labor Sports Union, to transform it from a "small unknown, sectarian and isolated sports organization," in a "mass workers sports organization composed of young American workers." Leaders of the group were urged to shift their emphasis from sports popular with immigrants, particularly soccer and gymnastics, to American games like baseball, boxing and basketball, and to actively recruit American-born workers into the organization. [12]

Labor Sports Union organizers tried to follow these directives. They founded basketball and baseball leagues in some of the cities in which they were active and tried to broaden the publicity for the track and field meets which they sponsored. During 1931 and 1932, the LSU took responsibility for organizing an International Workers Olympics in Chicago in protest against the official Olympic movement, and sponsored "Free Tom Monney" street runs in cities throughout the country that attracted thousands of onlookers. The LSU actually banned its members from participating and brought a small number of black athletes into its activities for the first time. In addition, the LSU used the Counter-Olympics as a basis for a campaign to demand free gymnasium space for worker-athletes, and won some confrontations on this issue in New York, Cleveland and Chicago. The final outcome of this activity, the International Workers Athletic Meet, was an impressive spectacle, attracting 400 athletes (100 of them black) and 5000 fans. Women athletes were included in the competition, participating in seven of the thirty-four events. [13]

But the campaign for the Counter-Olympics fell far short of the ambitious objectives that the YCL had set for it. The LSU did grow—by the summer of 1932 it had some 5,000 members, with centers of activity in New York, Philadelphia, Pittsburgh, Cleveland, Chicago, Minnesota, and New England. But the hoped-for influx of American workers never materialized. Although basketball and baseball leagues arose under LSU auspices in certain areas, reflecting the growing popularity of American sports within the immigrant milieu, the most popular LSU activity remained the old immigrant standby, soccer. Probably the most impressive sustained achievement of the LSU was the founding of the Metropolitan Workers Soccer League in New York, which incorporated 45 teams in four divisions (two of them were West Indian teams from Harlem) and drew crowds of up to 6,000 for its championship matches. While activities such as this flourished, the English language publication of the organization, *Sport and Play*, failed to attract more than a few hundred readers for any of its issues.[14]

The weakness of the Labor Sports Union in the early thirties is striking, not only when compared to workers sports organizations in Germany or Austria or Czechoslovakia, but when compared to another American sports organizations founded roughly in the same period, the CYO grew to a membership of millions of young people by the end of the 1930's. The mass enthusiasm which it generated, in contrast to the LSU, reflected both the size and influence of the American Catholic subculture (churches, schools, and parish organizations) and the limited appeal, at least in the United States, of an effort to organize working class leisure around revolutionary socialist objectives. Workers in the United States, if the LSU's experience is indicative, did not respond positively to sports programs that tried to segregate them by class and undermine their interest in professional sports. The openness of professional sports, their seeming transcendence of class barriers, constituted one of the major components of their appeal, and Communists assured their marginality by dismissing them as "opiates."[15]

During the spring of 1933, the Young Communist League began to recognize the limits of the Labor Sports Union, and indeed, its whole approach to sports. Like all aspects of party activity, sports organizing was deeply affected by a new Comintern line promulgated after Hitler's rise to power, which encouraged Communists to break out of their isolation and make limited alliances with trade unions and Socialist groups. YCL leaders, in applying this line to sports, called upon the Labor Sports Union to develop a new approach to "Y's, Community Centers, Boys Clubs, etc." where working class youth were concentrated and try to draw such groups into its activities rather than agitate against them. In addition, the YCL suggested that Communist organizers, inside the Labor Sports Union and out, should shift the focus of sports organizing from the neighborhood to the factory and concentrate their efforts on building factory and trade union sports leagues.[16]

Along with this strategy came a whole new approach to professional sports. In the fall of 1933, the *Young Worker* began covering major league baseball in a manner virtually indistinguishable from the daily press, predicting pennant races, and analyzing teams and players, in a breezy, journalistic style. Although no theoretical pronouncement accompanied this change, it seemed to imply a belief that big league baseball represented a legitimate focus of working class enthusiasm, and that covering baseball in a lively manner in party publications would make Communists more acceptable to workers they hoped to organize.[17]

The paper still continued to give extensive coverage to sports leagues organized by the LSU, the YCL, and other party-affiliated organizations and to publicize campaigns such as Olympic boycotts and struggles for free gyms. But the sports page as a whole projected a far more relaxed attitude toward the American sports scene, a sense that even professional athletes could play a progressive role if approached in the right way. In 1934, one of the most publicized sports events under left auspices was a benefit game for the Scottsboro boys in Harlem, pitting the Renaissance Five, a black professional basketball team which possessed an 88 game win streak, against an all-star team of white pros.[18]

In the spring of 1935, the Communist Party's approach to sports underwent yet another shift in emphasis that led to the virtual abandonment of the Labor Sports Union. The Party's movement in this direction was tremendously accelerated by the Seventh World Congress of the Communist International, which called upon Communists to make alliances with Socialists and liberals to stop the rise of fascism, and to become defenders of the democratic traditions of their respective countries. The International Program prompted American Communists to begin identifying their movement with egalitarian trends in American history and popular culture, no matter how little they embodied "class struggle" themes or explicitly socialist ideals and objectives.[19]

The new line had a particularly dramatic impact on the Party's Olympic boycott strategy. Throughout the summer and fall of 1935 American Communists worked to unite a broad coalition of organizations in opposition to American participation in the 1936 Berlin Olympics. Anti-fascism, not workers sports, served as the party's credo; it chose the American Youth Congress and the American League Against War and Fascism (both large organizations with many non-Communist members) as its mobilizing vehicles for the campaign, and defined the goal of the movement as a demonstration of American solidarity with anti-fascist forces in Germany. Communist organizers, who in 1932 had used the Olympic issue as a springboard to attack the AAU for pursuing anti-labor policies, now praised the president of that organization, Jeremiah Mahoney, for requesting the Olympics' removal from Germany. They spoke approvingly of the breadth of the anti-Olympic coalition, which included leaders of the AFL, many Congressmen and state officials, and prominent Catholic, Protestant and Jewish clergymen.[20]

A labor sports emphasis remained central to the party's program, but it was distinctly subordinated to other political objectives. In February of 1935, Communists called for the merger of the Labor Sports Union with Socialist athletic clubs in the United States (admitting that both parties' sports clubs were "small, weak and isolated from the mass of American sportsmen") and Communist counter-Olympic propaganda rarely mentioned it by name. After the AAU approved American entry into the Olympics, Communists joined with Judge Mahoney and liberal and Socialist leaders in planning a "People's Olympiad" in Barcelona, Spain. When the Spanish Civil War forced cancellation of this event, its organizers sponsored a "World Labor Athletic Carnival" at Randalls Island which included participants from amateur athletic clubs and trade union sports programs, and attracted 25,000 spectators. The event had a mildly anti-capitalist flavor (what came as much from Socialist trade unionists as from Communists) but its literature emphasized that trade unions, rather than party-affiliated sports organizations, should be the focus of labor sports activity.[21]

The party's movement away from the cultivation of an oppositional subculture of workers sports was also symbolized by the introduction of daily sports coverage in the Party's national newspaper, the *Daily Worker*. The manner in which the paper justified this step bespoke a powerful impulse among American-born party cadres, unleashed by the Popular Front, to lead the Party out of the immigrant milieu in which most of its activities had been confined and make it acceptable to the population at large. "When you run the news of a strike alongside the news of a baseball game," Mike Gold wrote, "you are making American workers feel at home. It gives them the feeling that Communism is nothing strange and foreign, but is as real as baseball. . . . Let's loosen up. Let's begin to prove that one can be a human being as well as a Communist. It isn't a little special sect of bookworms and soapboxers."[22]

From 1936 on the *Daily Worker* sports page represented an amalgam of previously antagonistic themes, combining "apolitical" coverage of baseball, basketball and boxing (the sports most popular with

"Daily" readers) with stories on trade union and left-organized sports programs. Criticism of the professional sports scene, whether for corruption, discrimination, or unfair pay scales, rarely blamed the athlete. Communist journalists took pride in the working class origins of star athletes and regarded their success, especially when achieved "cleanly," as a symbol of working class fortitude and strength. Like the major dailies, the *Worker* regarded athletes as heroes, particularly when they lent their support to anti-fascist causes or drives for union recognition.[23]

Nevertheless, the *Daily Worker* sports page did have a critical edge. Communist sports writers may have taken pride in their press passes and ability to interview major league players, but on two issues, they did assume the role of "crusaders": the advocacy of trade union sports, and the demand for the integration of major league baseball.

Daily Worker writers took great pride in the rise of trade union athletic programs that accompanied the meteoric growth of CIO unions. Industrial unions, particularly those organized by Socialists or Communists, developed a wide range of recreational activities for their members, and sometimes consciously tried to draw them out of their employer-sponsored programs. In New York, a coalition of trade unions, led by Communist-organized unions such as the furriers, transit workers, and electrical workers, formed a Trade Union Athletic Association in 1937 and began sponsoring baseball, basketball and soccer leagues on a city wide basis. By 1940, it had grown to include 55 Union locals. Inter-union leagues also took hold in Chicago, Detroit, Philadelphia and Cleveland, while large unions such as the United Autoworkers Union and International Ladies Garment Workers Union organized elaborate sports programs catering only to their own membership. By the end of the Depression, according to the one historian who has made a survey of this activity, unions had begun to pose a strong challenge to the corporate monopoly on employee recreation.[24]

In addition, the Young Communist League and the International Workers Order (the party's fraternal and insurance society) organized sports leagues and tournaments, many of which involved non-Communist athletes and organizations (Joe Dimaggio threw out the first ball in a New York IWO softball tournament in 1938). The IWO leagues—which, like trade union sports, deserve much more detailed examination—helped keep alive the athletic traditions of the immigrant constituencies which identified with the Party while providing the youth of those groups with the opportunity to "Americanize" their athletic tastes within a left Milieu. They reflected some of the dynamism of the Communist subculture, despite its small size, during the Popular Front era and the organizing drive of the CIO.[25]

Nevertheless, *Daily Worker* writers did not describe these programs as signs of an embryonic socialist sports culture which would uproot capitalist sport. Indeed, the word socialist only appeared when describing sports in the Soviet Union. The political message of the sports page rarely extended beyond visceral appeals to labor solidarity or hatred of fascism. *Worker* sports writers, though critical of team owners as employers, rarely presented an analysis of how private ownership corrupted sports, or evoked a vision of what sports would look like in a Socialist America. They had little to say about women in sports, or how competition could be reconciled with socialist values. With a caution and practicality that had come to characterize their whole party, they declined to discuss objectives that would strike the "average American worker" as abstract or utopian.

The party's acceptance of many traditional perspectives on sport emerged most dramatically in the campaign waged by the *Daily Worker* sports staff for the integration of major league baseball. From the first day sports became a daily feature, *Daily Worker* sports writers gave enormous space to the exploits of black athletes and tried to arouse public sentiment to end racial discrimination in sports. On an almost daily basis, articles appeared describing exhibition contests between black and white teams (in which blacks more than held their own), quoting major league players, managers, and sports writers who favored integration, and providing colorful portraits of black athletes in every major sport. Although sports writers in the white dailies spoke out occasionally against baseball *Jim Crow*, and black papers hammered away at the issue, *Worker* writers made a real contribution: they got Joe Dimaggio to declare that Satchell Paige was the best pitcher he had ever faced, National League President Ford Frick to proclaim there was "no written ban against Negro stars," and Satchell Paige to pose a public challenge to play the winners of the World Series to determine his fitness for the major leagues.[26]

After three years of agitation in print, more practical measures followed. The Young Communist League, in 1939, began circulating petitions supporting an end to baseball's color bar at major league ball parks. Communist city councilmen in New York proposed resolutions banning discrimination in baseball, and Communists endorsed anti-discrimination bills in the New York State Legislature offered by Harlem representatives. In 1942, the *Daily Worker* editor arranged a tryout for Roy Campanella with the Pittsburgh Pirates, and in 1945, the *Daily Worker* and the Harlem *People's Voice* jointly sponsored a tryout for two black players with the Brooklyn Dodgers. That same year, Communists picketed the Yankees' home opener to press that club to hire black players. Though integration of the sport would eventually have come without Communist activity, the Party's agitation probably accelerated the process. Virtually every book on the subject mentions the Party's contribution. *Daily Worker* sports editor Lester Rodney recalls that when the Dodger publicity man read the announcement that Jackie Robinson would be brought up to the Dodgers, two writers from the other papers came over to him and said, "you guys can be proud of this."[27]

In waging this campaign, Communists presented themselves as defenders of the American democratic heritage. *Daily Worker* writers hailed baseball as a great American tradition "with roots . . . deep in the heart of the American people" and claimed (with a certain amount of wishful thinking) that owners rather than players and fans posed the opposition to integration. "Abner Doubleday . . . did a job to be proud of," one article declared. "The one flaw in the American baseball setup is the discrimination against Negro ball players by the major league magnates, but the campaign to banish Jim Crow from the diamond . . . is making good progress." *Daily Worker* sports editor Lester Rodney, equally confident of victory on the issue, claimed that the values inculcated on the playing field were incompatible with racial prejudice: "American sportsmanship can no more be denied than American democracy. They go together and grow together."[28]

Though silent on the crucial question of women's exclusion from sports, this vision of a "democratic impulse" within American sports had a certain resonance with events. During the mid- and late 1930's New Deal construction programs vastly expanded the amount of recreational facilities in the U.S. and promoted a boom in sports participation as well as in hiking, camping and vacationing. In addition black athletes, notably Jesse Owens and Joe Louis, emerged as national sports heroes with white followings, suggesting that egalitarian attitudes on race had begun to spread, in a somewhat muted form, beyond an elite of white intellectuals. Such developments gave Communists active in sports work the feeling that they were only the cutting edge of a broad democratic tendency in the society, and that the pragmatic militancy they espoused offered no barrier to social acceptance.[29]

No set of events reinforced this world view more than the huge popular celebrations in black communities that followed Joe Louis' victories. "Millions of Negroes," Richard Wright wrote in the *Daily Worker*:

are looking upon Joe Louis to uphold the honor of his race. Because boxing is simple, and the desire to knock out a man is easy to understand, millions are pinning their submerged racial and social hopes upon two men in a ring whaling away at each other. . . . Many people will deplore the wild elation of millions over a prizefight, but against the background of deadening cynicism, indifference, and money-grabbing, such wholesome enthusiasm is bracing. It signified . . . that there lies in the simple heart of the masses of people for loyalty, devotion and exultation, all of which can be channelized toward meaningful and historic ends.

When whites participated, Communists waxed even more enthusiastic. Benjamin Davis Jr. proclaimed that the huge interracial demonstrations in Harlem that followed Louis' victory over Schmeling "expressed the sentiment of . . . all who treasure the American traditions of liberty and clean sportsmanship. . . . Nothing is more indicative of the power of Negro and White unity for progress and democracy— once it hits full stride."[30]

Such sentiments, written by black Communists, showed how far the Party had changed from the days when it looked contemptuously on American sports from its vantage point in the immigrant ghettoes. The Americanization of the Communist movement, so dramatically displayed in its sport writing and sports organizing, coincided with a period of rapid party growth. From a rather insular and sectarian body with less than ten thousand members (most of whom spoke little English) the party had swelled by 1938 to include over 50,000 members and had begun to exert significant influence in the labor movement, among intellectuals, and in black protest activity.[31]

Nevertheless, the evolution of Communist sports activism offers a telling commentary on the weakness of working class radicalism in the United States and the marginality of the left. Communists did some creative and important sports organizing in the late Depression years.

Their work in building trade union sports programs, along with the sports activities of their fraternal groups, represented a modest beginning in detaching workplace and community sports from business sponsorship and control. (Why this initiative lost momentum is an important subject for further study.) They made discrimination against blacks in sports a major political issue and initiated a campaign of protest and education aimed at integrating major league baseball. But in doing so, they abandoned all efforts to develop a socialist critique of sports, to root concepts of labor solidarity and racial equality in a larger socialist vision.

In their sports organizing, Communists proved unable to find a language that could simultaneously express socialist goals and resonate with the values and world view of the mass of American workers. In the late '20s and early '30s, they tried to organize an opposition sports movement among American workers, antagonistic to professional sports, but reached only foreign-born workers who already identified with the left. American-born workers proved deeply resistant to politicizing their habits of sports spectatorship and participation; they responded to trade union sports programs as an adjunct of unionization, but not to workers sports leagues that sought to undercut their interest in big league baseball, football and boxing. Communist sports activists who shared some of the tastes and enthusiasms of the people they tried to organize could not remain immune to the response to their activity. Once released from the "workers sports" strategy by the Popular Frontline, they found themselves pulled inexorably into a romantic identification with the openness of American Sports, their ability to give talented people from the working class an outlet for creative energies. But in doing so, they were drawn into a vision which was more liberal than Communist, which defined the good society in terms of equal opportunity rather than a working class seizure of power.

Some have defined this shift as a lost opportunity, a failure to develop a popular socialist politics in a period of great political upheaval. But if sports policy is an indication, it represented a concession to popular sentiment that was the price of the most minimal political influence. American society, even after ten years of Depression, did not represent fertile soil for revolutionary upheaval, and Communists found their metier as an exponent of democratic reforms, which, while compatible with a socialist program did not inevitably lead in that direction.

NOTES

1. On Communist and left strategy in "the arts," see Daniel Aaron, *Writers on the Left* (New York: Harcourt, Brace, World, 1961); James Gilbert, *Writers and Partisans* (New York: John Wiley and Sons, 1968); Morgan Himmelstein, *Drama Was a Weapon: The Leftwing Theatre in New York* (New Brunswick: Rutgers University Press, 1963); Richard Wright, *American Hunger* (New York: Harper and Row, 1976); Richard Pells, *Radical Visions and American Dreams* (New York: Harper and Row, 1973).

2. James Weinstein, *Ambiguous Legacy, The Left in American Politics* (New York: Franklin Watts, 1975), pp. 57–86; Staughton Lynd, "The United Front in America: A Note," *Radical America*, Vol. 8, No. 4 (July-August, 1974), pp. 35–36; and the debate between Max Gordon and James Weinstein in *Socialist Revolution*, No. 27 (January-March, 1976).

3. E. P. Thompson, *The Making of the English Working Class* (New York: Pantheon, 1963); Herbert Gutman, *Work, Culture and Society in Industrializing America* (New York: Alfred Knopf, 1976).

4. On workers sports movements, see Robert F. Wheeler, "Organized Sports and Organized Labour," and David A. Steinber, "The Workers Sport Internationals, 1920–1928," *Journal of Contemporary History*, Vol. 13, No. 2 (April, 1978).

5. Theodore Draper, *American Communism and Soviet Russia* (New York: Viking Press, 1960), pp. 17–27; Nathan Glazer, *The Social Basis of American Communism* (New York: Harcourt, Brace, World, 1961).

6. Si Gerson, "Six Years of Workers Sports in America," *International Press Correspondence*, Vol. 13, No. 3 (19 January, 1933); *Young Worker*, January 1, 1927 and January 15, 1927.

7. *Young Worker*, August 1, 1927, November 1, 1927, and February 15, 1928.

8. *Young Worker*, August 1, 1927, and April 1, 1928. *Young Worker*, August 1, 1927.

9. John R. Betts, *America's Sporting Heritage* (Reading, Mass: Addison-Wesley, 1974), pp. 314–316; Wheeler, "Organized Sport and Organized Labour," pp. 194–195; *Young Worker*, August, 1928 and December, 1929. Wheeler, p. 164; Cary Goodman "(Re) Creating Americans at the Educational Alliance," *Journal of Ethnic Studies*, Vol. 6, No. 4 (Winter, 1978); *Young Worker*, August, 1928, August 15, 1929; December 1929; July 7, 1930.

10. *Young Worker*, October, 1928.

11. *Young Worker*, May 19, 1930. *Young Worker*, October 21, 1930, *Young Worker*, April, 1930.

12. *Young Worker*, July 7, 1930, October 21, 1930, and November 17, 1930.

13. Gerson, "Six Years of Workers Sports in America"; *New York Amsterdam News*, April 20, 1932; *Negro Liberator*, August 1, 1932; *Young Worker*,

November 19, 1931, December 28, 1931, February 29, 1932, April 11, 1932, April 18, 1932, August 22, 1932, September 5, 1932.

14. *Young Worker*, August 22, 1932, May 30, 1933, October 20, 1933, December 19, 1933, February 13, 1934.

15. Betts, *America's Sporting Heritage*, p. 281.

16. *Young Worker*, May 30, 1933.

17. *Young Worker*, September 15, 1933, October 15, 1933.

18. *Young Worker*, November 7, 1933, March 27, 1934; *Daily Worker*, March 31, 1934.

19. On the "People's Front," see Weinstein, *Ambiguous Legacy*, pp. 57–86; Al Richmond, *A Long View from the Left* (Boston: Houghton Mifflin Company, 1972), p. 254; George Charney, *A Long Journey* (New York: Quadrangle, 1968), p. 60.

20. Leo Thompson, "The Movement Against the Nazi Olympic Games," *International Press Correspondence*, Vol. 15, No. 70 (21 December, 1935). *Daily Worker*, August 21, 1935, October 24, 1935. On the breadth of the anti-Olympic coalition in the U.S., see Betts, pp. 302–303, Richard Mandell, *The Nazi Olympics*, (New York: Macmillan, 1971), pp. 69–81.

21. *Young Worker*, February 12, 1935. Betts, p. 317; Mandell, p. 81; *Daily Worker*, November 27, 1937.

22. *Daily Worker*, August 31, 1935.

23. *Daily Worker*, June 15, 1937, November 25, 1937, January 30, 1938, December 10, 1938.

24. Betts, pp. 316–319; *Daily Worker*, January 21, 1937, September 16, 1937, December 27, 1937, May 25, 1938, March 6, 1940.

25. *Daily Worker*, June 15, and September 16, 1937, February 28 and May 9, 1938, and March 26, May 1, and May 21, 1939.

26. "Sports for the Daily Worker; An Interview with Lester Rodney," *In These Times*, October 12–18, 1977; *Daily Worker*, September 27, 1936; June 23, 1937, September 13, 1937, September 16, 1937, December 27, 1937.

27. Betts, p. 341; Robert Petersen, *Only the Ball Was White* (New York: Prentice Hall, 1970), pp. 177–185; Dick Young, *Roy Campanella* (New York: A. S. Barnes, 1951), p. 36; "Interview with Lester Rodney," *Daily Worker*, May 31, 1939, July 15, 1939, July 21, 1939, July 25, 1939, August 16, 1939, March 6, 1940, June 9, 1940, July 25, 1940.

28. *Daily Worker*, June 14, 1939. *Daily Worker*, July 19, 1939.

29. Betts, pp. 276–287.

30. *Daily Worker*, June 22, 1938. *Daily Worker*, June 23, 1938.

31. Glazer, *The Social Basis of American Communism*, p. 91; Sidney Lens, *Radicalism in America* (New York: Thomas Crowell, 1969), pp. 317–325.

VII

White America Views Jack Johnson, Joe Louis, and Muhammad Ali

Frederic Cople Jaher

The heavyweight champion may be the world's supremely admired athlete. In Europe and America and, since the advent of Muhammad Ali, increasingly in the Third World, he is the ultimate symbol of male prowess. If blessed with exceptional talent and charisma or skilled publicists, the titleholder may become *the* sports celebrity of his time. If his reign embraces social forces outside the ring he may become a legend.

Although the crown has been won by an Englishman, a Canadian, a German, an Italian, a Swede, and a South African and has been sought by challengers from Latin America and other European countries, like many other claims on power, riches, and glamor, it usually remains in the United States. From John L. Sullivan (1882–1892), the first to defend the championship under Marquis of Queensbury rules until today American fighters have ruled the heavyweight division for all but nine years. As a result of this dominion, we have long regarded the championship with proprietary patriotism and its holder usually with respect and sometimes with reverence.

Success in a man's world is the fundamental value of the national creed. Few achievements are as compellingly masculine as winning the heavyweight crown or seem as likely to fulfill American "macho"

The author wishes to thank his friends and colleagues Blair B. Kling and Thomas A. Krueger for their helpful comments on an earlier draft of this essay.

fantasies of instant riches, indomitable manhood, awesome status, and the conquest of beautiful women. Hence many American males, imbued with the success cult yet fearing (or knowing) that they lack wealth, prestige, virility, or sex appeal, identify with the champion. Idolizing him as an archetypal American gives average men a share of the action otherwise denied them by their own lack of exploits and abilities. This vicarious and precarious hold on "the good things in life" also inclined Americans to reject aspirants to the throne who do not look or act like genuine national heroes. The strong, the patriotic, the modest, the grateful, and above all the white, deserve the fair, the money, and the title. But the public coddles its heroes. Minor sins are often forgiven, especially if the champion is Caucasian. Sullivan drank and bragged and Jack Dempsey stayed out of uniform in World War I, yet they were revered.

White Americans historically considered black Americans as the most negative outgroup. Prior to Joe Louis (1937–1949) only Jack Johnson (Little Arthur) (1908–1915) had crossed the color line drawn by Sullivan and every succeeding heavyweight titleholder or his manager or promoter. In the early days of boxing, blacks were permitted to contend for championship in the lighter weights (before Johnson, five blacks held such crowns), but since 1937 the situation has been reversed and only three whites (for a total of six years) ruled the heavyweight division. Until the "Brown Bomber" legitimized for whites the reality of a black heavyweight king most Americans looked upon the prospect of an Afro-American titleholder as an intrusion of a despised group into an exalted realm of American masculinity and sport. Fantasies nurtured through identification with Sullivan, Dempsey, and other Caucasian champions were turned into nightmares by the triumphs of insurgent black titleholders Johnson and Ali (1964–1967, 1974–1978, 1978–1979). White America uneasily adjusted to black heavyweight kings and the relationship between the former and the latter has not been primarily determined by what occurred in the ring. National and international events and forces and the interplay of deeply rooted and changing cultural values shaped—in triumph and in tragedy—the lives of the foremost black heavyweight champions.[1]

Louis had the longest reign in the history of the division, Ali the third longest (his exile from the ring between 1967 and 1970 prevented him from surpassing Louis), and Johnson the fifth longest (it would have been longer if white titleholders had not avoided fights with him until he was thirty). Each fighter exemplified his era: Johnson was a stormy symbol of the Progressive Period, Louis was a hero of the New Deal and World War II, and Ali personified the turbulence of the 1960s and early 1970s. Signifying social forces and movements, the three champions obsessed the American consciousness. Emblems of their times and historic figures, they assumed mythic properties analogous to the heroic or demonic repute of Al Capone, Charles Lindbergh, Martin Luther King, Jr., Theodore Roosevelt, and the Kennedy brothers.

Students of the life and times of Jack Johnson must often wonder if they are in the realm of fact or comtemplating an extravagance of the Romantic imagination or the allegorical vision of a twentieth-century American Jonathan Swift. Johnson won the most precious prize in sports while blacks were rigorously excluded from athletic competition outside the ring. His 1910 defeat of Jim Jeffries provoked the first national race riot in the United States. "Little Arthur" married three white women, flaunted his liaisons with others, and opened an integrated cafe in Chicago during a period of extensive racial exclusion and oppression and amid an antivice crusade in that city. He was arraigned for abducting a Caucasian damsel, but she refused to testify against him and wedded the defendant shortly after the trial. Again under attack for sullying white womanhood, he was convicted of transporting a white female across state lines for immoral purposes. The Mann Act violater then fled the country to avoid a prison term. Despite these distractions Johnson retained the championship until 1915, when he was defeated in a fight that he may have thrown for money and a promise of amnesty and immediate return to this country. This deal, if true, fell through and he came back to the United States in 1920 and spent a year in the penitentiary. Now no longer the *bête noire* of white America, Johnson lived uneventfully but not unhappily until his death in 1946.

The significance of the original black heavyweight champion, however, lies less in the pyrotechnics than in the representational meaning of his career. This is equally true of Louis and Ali, also major players in the drama of American race relations. During Johnson's reign the blacks experienced their worst treatment since the Civil War. After Reconstruction, which ended the year before Johnson was born, court decisions, legislative and executive actions, informal arrangements, publicly and privately sanctioned terrorism, the "findings" of biologists and social scientists, and the metaphors of writers and movie makers denied blacks economic opportunities, separated them from whites in all but servile interactions, and stigmatized them as childlike brutes genetically incapable of participating in civilized society.[2]

Athletics inevitably mirrored this situation. Blacks were prohibited or severely restricted even in such déclassé sporting roles as professional baseball players, jockeys, and boxers. They were barred from major and minor league baseball in the 1880s and the color line gradually advanced into horse racing. Fourteen of the fifteen riders in the 1875 Kentucky Derby were black, but after 1911 Negroes could not appear in that race and virtually vanished from other tracks. In boxing, widely considered the lowest form of professional sport, blacks were not permitted to contend for the heavyweight title, although they could still win crowns in other divisions.[3]

Given the racial situation in American sport and society, how did Johnson manage to capture the heavyweight title? The so-called golden age of boxing ended when the 1905 retirement of Jim Jeffries terminated an era in which Sullivan, Jim Corbett, Bob Fitzsimmons, and Jeffries—superb fighters and attractive public personalities—consecutively ruled the heavyweight division. These titleholders refused to fight black challengers, but Tommy Burns—a comparatively colorless and mediocre champion—reluctantly rescinded this ban because the current white heavyweights drew little more than yawns when they fought. Desperately seeking a lucrative bout and under pressure to prove himself, he defended the title against Johnson. Since white America did not regard blacks as part of the national community, that is, as legitimate citizens, and since Burns was a Canadian and the fight took place in Australia, racial and territorial imperatives that ordinarily would have created an outrage over a heavyweight bout between a Caucasian champion and a black challenger did not surface in this match. The relatively calm reception of the prospective contest prompted Theodore Roosevelt and the *New York Sun*, the *St. Louis Post-Dispatch*, and other newspapers to argue that Johnson, clearly the ranking contender, merited a fight with Burns. If the absence of a territorial imperative made the contest possible it also meant that white Americans did not take pride in the fact that Johnson returned the title to this country. Novelist Jack London, who covered the fight for the *New York Herald*, asserted that he "was with Burns all the way. He is a white man, and so am I. Naturally I wanted to see the white man win." For most Americans race took precedence over nationality. This order of priority was reinforced when reports of the fight emphasized that Johnson taunted Burns and mastered the champion physically, mentally, and emotionally. Although ex-champion Corbett found the outcome "a bitter pill for the American people to swallow," the majority did not seethe over the result. Newspapers in Omaha, Nebraska, were resigned, if not happy; London conceded that the best man won in a fair fight; the *New York Times* declared that Johnson disproved the contention that he had a yellow streak and the *New York Morning Telegraph* and the *Philadelphia Enquirer* daringly criticized the color line in boxing as an injustice to black fighters.[4]

Grudging acceptance of the 1908 match unfortunately was the high point of white America's reaction to Jack Johnson. Immediately after his triumph began the search for a "white hope." London concluded his articles on the fight with a plea to Jeffries to come out of retirement and restore the title to white America. The 1910 Johnson-Jeffries battle provoked more intense racial conflict than did "Little Arthur's" previous bouts. Unlike Burns, Jeffries was American-born and an extremely popular champion. Johnson defeated five white hopes in 1909 and Jeffries, as London put it, became "the chosen representative of the white race." Moreover, the fight took place in the United States, a factor that exacerbated the territorial imperative implicit in white America's racist perspective on the heavyweight title. With rare exceptions the press viewed the upcoming match as a contest for racial supremacy and treated its readers to an orgy of cartoons depicting Johnson as a gorilla or a watermelon-eating, dialect-speaking black brute, and to articles portraying Jeffries as a superman and his opponent as a subhuman creature whose dim wits, cowardly spirit, and genetic inferiority doomed him to deserved defeat. The pulpit vigorously participated in the outcry for race pride and "justice." Reverend John H. Trumball of Paterson, New Jersey, compared the champion to an ape, a Baltimore minister warned that a Johnson victory would make it unsafe for white women and children to walk the streets, and an Omaha clergyman told his congregation that he hoped "every man with red blood in his veins should see Jim Jeffries regain the heavyweight championship. . . . " According to Johnson biographer Robert H. McCoy, William Jennings Bryan telegraphed Jeffries, "God will forgive everything Jeffries does to that nigger in this fight. . . . Jeff, God is with you." Boxing experts, including ex-heavyweight champions and other famous fighters and sportswriters, expressing the stereotypical vision of Negro inferiority, picked the challenger to win. This judgment was shared by the sporting crowd and Jeffries was a 10 to 7 betting favorite.[5]

Reno, Nevada, July 4, 1910, was the scene of this unprecedentedly publicized and important boxing event. The fight, according to the *New York Times*, was "a foremost topic of conversation among all sorts and conditions of men—and women." An estimated 18,000 to 20,000 attended the fight, and another 30,000 stood outside the *New York Times* building to follow the action via the newspaper's wire service. Howard Gould, William K. Vanderbilt, Jr., and other socially prominent millionaires received the *Times* bulletin in the splendored privacy of the Edgemere (Long Island) Country Club. Famous novelists Jack London and Rex Beach headed a press corps of 600, including Corbett, Sullivan, and a female reporter to cover the "woman's angle" of the struggle. The Jeffries-Johnson bout, with its media "hype," "big-name" writers, huge purse, celebrity presence, and large female attendance, ushered in the modern age of boxing.[6]

The champion entered the ring accompanied by the jeers of the crowd, who serenaded him with "All Coons Look Alike to Me," a popular song inspired by Jeffries' remark when as champion he refused a challenge from Johnson. An eagerly and confidently awaited demonstration of white supremacy was quickly shattered. As he had done with Burns, Johnson taunted and toyed with Jeffries and flashed his imperturbable "golden smile" at his opponent and the hostile fans. Most Americans anticipated that Jeffries would wreak Caucasian vengence upon the black intruder in the racially sacred turf of the heavyweight championship. The unexpected outcome of the bout evoked widespread rage, dismay, and fear. Bob Fitzsimmons and Jim Corbett (Jeffries' manager) wept at Reno and newspaper headlines blared "JEFF MASTERED BY GRINNING, JEERING NEGRO." The mass media and white America had built up the fight as a contest for racial supremacy—now they proclaimed that it merely proved that "the best fighter comes from the lowest and least developed race" and that boxing was a brutal sport that should be outlawed. Blacks were warned against deriving "false pride" or "disastrous ambition" from Johnson's victory and whites rued his triumph as a setback for race relations. "For the colored population we fear that the victory of Mr. Johnson will prove a misfortune," the *New York Times* editorialized. "It will be natural for negroes to proclaim Johnson's victory as a racial triumph . . . and in doing so they incite hostility." The *Times* noted that "supremacy in a civilized State does not rest on physical force'' and hoped that America had seen the last "prizefight between representatives of different races. . . . '' The "unpopularity" of Johnson's "victory," however, would cause the *Times* "no regret" if it ended "prizefighting within the United States.''[7]

The fear, frustration, and anger generated by the Reno debacle was not confined to criticism of the victor, blacks, and boxing, rationalizations about the meaninglessness of Jeffries' defeat or advice to Negroes not to depart from the servility that reassured whites about the "race problem" in America. Violence was still the ultimate weapon against the "uppity nigger" and many Americans were not reluctant to resort to it when they felt the need to "keep the Negro in his place." Although recorded lynchings in the early 1900s averaged 60 to 70 per year compared to the 150 annual total of the 1890s, race riots occurred with rising frequency during the Progressive Period. Such conflict broke out in New York (1900)—the first in a Northern city since the Civil War—Atlanta, and Brownsville, Texas (1906), and Springfield, Illinois (1908). This turbulence, coinciding with what many considered a blow to their dominion, triggered the riots that flared as blacks celebrated and whites mourned the Johnson-Jeffries contest. A national race riot ensued virtually simultaneously with the news of Jeffries' loss. Eight people were killed in a whirlwind of disorder that swept over New York, Philadelphia, Pittsburgh, Baltimore, Washington, D.C., Chattanooga, Tennessee, New Orleans, St. Louis, Cincinnati, Louisville, Atlanta, and smaller towns in Georgia, Virginia, West Virginia, Arkansas, and Colorado. Lower-class whites, often sailors and soldiers, were the chief attackers, and the victims, as in the earlier disturbances, were mostly black.[8]

Riots and racism combined with the moral fervor of Progressivism to produce a ban on the national distribution of the fight films. Progressive reformers and racists, the two impulses often coexisted in the same person (as in the case of Woodrow Wilson), in fact had nearly prevented the fight from taking place. Clergymen in New York, Chicago, San Francisco, and Oakland, California, opposed the bout. The Presbyterian Ministerial Association of Chicago petitioned President William Howard Taft to stop the contest and fifty ministers knelt in prayer at the state capitol to convince the governor of California to reverse his acceptance of San Francisco as the site of the contest. Racists, reformers, and reverends prevailed upon the governor and the mayor of San Francisco, but Reno was a wide-open frontier town more attached to lucre than the Lord, and Nevada voters were less likely than those in California to wreak Progressive retribution against backsliding politicians. The arguments against holding the fight resounded with greater intensity after Jeffries' defeat and the subsequent mob violence. If the fight could no longer be stopped, at least the movies would not be shown. Theodore Roosevelt; the governors of Texas, California, Virginia, South Carolina, Arkansas, South Dakota, Maine, Michigan, and Utah; the mayors of Atlanta, Springfield, Illinois, Boston, San Francisco, Cincinnati, Chattanooga, Louisville, and Spartanburgh, South Carolina; the police chiefs of Washington, D.C., Baltimore, and Cincinnati; ministerial associations and religious leaders in Pennsylvania, Virginia, Wilmington, Delaware, Pittsburgh, and Dayton, Ohio; the United Society of Christian Endeavor (4 million members); and many civic leaders and organizations and antivice leagues and magazine and newspaper editors opposed screenings of the fight. They sought to spare American youth the spectacle of mayhem in the ring, destroy a corrupt and commercialized sport, prevent Negroes from harboring delusions of superiority and Caucasians from further humiliation, avoid racial strife, and make interracial bouts unprofitable, if not impossible. This wave of protest prevented the films from appearing in most large American cities and throughout the South.[9]

The campaign against fight films achieved complete success in 1912 when Congress, in a bill obviously aimed at Johnson, prohibited their interstate transportation. The Johnson-Jeffries fight was "the grossest instance of base fraud and bogus effort at a fair fight between a Caucasian brute and African biped beast," declaimed Representative Seaborn A. Roddenberry (Georgia) in the House legislative debate. "No man descended from the old Saxon race can look upon that kind of a contest without abhorrence and disgust."[10]

Conquering the white paladin ravaged Johnson's public image. London, Beach, and Sullivan, however, conceded that the champion fought fairly and courageously and even praised his character. Fight reports in the *New York Times*, the *New York Tribune*, and *Harper's Weekly* and by a *Chicago Tribune* correspondent concurred in this assessment. A *Times* editorial even ventured an unfortunately unique (in the establishment press) observation on the larger significance of the fight. Noting Johnson's "fair, manly and honorable standard of behavior," it asserted that such "a representative of the race" in "win[ing] a substantial triumph in the lowest of these [occupations] will instinctively be recognized as giving the race a somewhat different and higher title to respect." The editorial expressed the hope that this recognition would contribute to the "steady growth among the blacks of a definite race pride, analogous to that among the whites, which is slowly but constantly tending toward a social organization within the race similar to that existing in other races." These comments on Johnson's behavior and character at Reno led Nat Fleischer, a friend of the champion and a reporter at the fight and later America's leading boxing historian, to recall that the "editorial comment favored him." Johnson himself felt that "the bitterness which had actuated some of those interested in boxing had subsided. Some of my greatest enemies were silenced and many who had been almost venomous toward me grew a little more restrained." [11]

The postfight brawls, search for a white hope, criticism of Johnson, the blacks, the bout, and boxing, and the campaign against the fight pictures indicate that Fleischer and Johnson were unduly optimistic. Compared to the abyss into which "Little Arthur's" reputation soon plunged, the titleholder nevertheless enjoyed a respite from unceasing attacks. The halcyon days passed when Johnson offended the moral scruples of Progressivism and defied a host of racial taboos. In 1911 the champion opened an integrated night club on the edge of Chicago's red light district. The centerpiece of the cabaret's furnishings was a larger-than-life–sized painting of its owner embracing a white woman whom he married earlier in the year. In 1912 his spouse committed suicide and three weeks later Johnson was charged with abducting a Caucasian female who, immediately after the trial, married him. Before acquittal Johnson was accused of violating the Mann Act. In this case the alleged victim (a Caucasian superstar of the Chicago brothels whom the boxer had jilted) cooperated with the prosecution and in 1913 the champion was convicted. In order to avoid a prison term, Johnson fled the country. [12]

The titleholder rebelled against the color line during a peak period of race prejudice. The least of his transgressions was owning a cafe where blacks and whites ate and drank together. A generation later, during an era of relative tolerance, over two-thirds of Americans in a 1942 public opinion survey still felt that restaurants should be segregated. Lesser forms of segregation, as in separate public accommodations, were primarily motivated by white fears of miscegenation. When the civil rights movement was at its height in 1963, between three-fifths and four-fifths of white Americans responded affirmatively when polled on issues of equal access for blacks to jobs and integration of schools, transportation systems, parks, restaurants, and hotels. Yet only 36 percent agreed that there should be no laws against intermarriage. Nine years later only 25 percent of a national sample of whites approved of intermarriage. Americans have always regarded sexual relations between black males and white females as the basic racial taboo. Such unions are especially deplored when institutionalized by marriage because this arrangement implies social and legal sanction of the most intimate interaction between the races and therefore of the most fundamental violation of the caste system. In the 1940s intermarriage between blacks and whites was forbidden in thirty states. Johnson's encounters with white women, highlighted by three marriages, a suicide, an alleged abduction, a Mann Act conviction, and an escape from punishment for these humiliations of Caucasian pride, materialized for the white majority the lurid fantasies of the most ardent Ku Kluxer.[13]

These acts, which made Johnson a blackguard in the racial and sexual wasteland of white America, loomed particularly ominous in an age of rampant self-righteousness. The Progressive reform movement nobly attempted to improve the working and living conditions of poor women and children and inspired a generation of heroic settlement house and social workers. But the spirit of the era also stimulated a moral arrogance that encouraged judgmental crusaders to intervene in matters where equity and decency dictated forebearance. This type of reformer, unfortunately, was most likely to react to the sins of "Little Arthur."

Agitators for moral and racial purity were already mobilized before the champion inflamed their passions and aggravated their fears. Congress passed the Mann (White Slave Traffic) Act in 1910, and the year before Johnson was prosecuted under it federal judges handed down more prison terms for Mann Act violations than in any previous ten-year span for smuggling or counterfeiting. Chicago, the second-largest city in the country and its foremost manufacturing metropolis, represented for many Progressive reformers and other citizens the incarnation of the vice, corruption, and volatility that they regarded as endemic in urban, industrial America. Johnson's cafe and home were in Chicago and his wife's suicide, his subsequent remarriage, and his trials took place in that city. Bigotry was even worse there, where a race riot would occur in 1919, than in the Northeastern metropolises, and the local press was more stridently racist than in Boston or New York. Chicago also experienced a series of antivice crusades in 1911 and 1912, which exacerbated the seeming monstrousness of the champion's acts. During "Little Arthur's" abduction trial the antivice organizations put on a great parade and the city council passed a resolution condemning him and urging cancellation of his liquor license. At the time he was charged with violation of the Mann Act the Chicago mayor began a campaign against the town's saloons and brothels. In the interval between the two trials the champion's liquor license was lifted and his cafe closed.[14]

The judicial proceedings provoked a torrent of racial abuse and death threats against Johnson. At his arraignment for abduction a mob of 1,000 gathered outside the courthouse screaming, "Kill Him! Lynch him!" and several Chicago women's groups backed the prosecution. During the Mann Act trial hostile crowds surrounded the titleholder's automobile and he was hung in effigy. Comic books circulated titled *Jack Johnson and His Girls* and *Black Ape Splitting the White Princess*. The press, sports heroes, prominent businessmen, the governors of South Carolina, Maryland, Virginia, and New York, ministers and ordinary citizens raged against the black fighter's marrying and allegedly mistreating white women, and all demanded that he be sent to prison. The governors of Ohio, Pennsylvania, Massachusetts, and Connecticut called for laws to prohibit interracial marriages; such bills appeared in twenty state legislatures and a constitutional amendment for this purpose was introduced in Congress. Legal prohibition and punishment of Johnson's deeds seemed inadequate to many caught up in the national hysteria. Cries for lynching (an appeal to disorder to preserve racial order) the heavyweight champion thundered throughout the land—no idle threat, for during his reign 354 blacks were lynched, 89 for so-called offenses against Caucasian females.[15]

White America tended to treat Johnson not as an individual or even a criminal, but as a symbol of black evil. "This defendant is one of the best known men of his race," said Federal District Court Judge George Carpenter in explaining why he sentenced the champion to 366 days in prison for violating the Mann Act. "His example has been far reaching and the court is bound to consider the position he occupies among his people. In view of these facts, this is a case that calls for more than a fine.'' Congressman Roddenberry's speech in the House of Representatives on behalf of the proposed constitutional amendment against interracial marriage summoned every demon from the racial-sexual nightmare of fanatical bigotry. Such unions make ''a white girl . . . the slave of an African brute,'' encourage ''the viscious element of the negro race,'' and result in ''the descendants of our Anglo-Saxon fathers or mothers'' having ''mixed blood descended from the orangutan shores of faroff Africa.'' Intermarriage is ''abhorrent and repugnant to the very principles of pure Saxon government. It is subversive of the social peace. It is destructive of moral supremacy, and ultimately . . . will bring this nation to a conflict as fatal and bloody'' as the Civil War. The gentleman from Georgia evoked applause from his colleagues when he referred to ''an African prizefighter-saloon keeper'' who ''bound in the wedlock of black slavery'' a ''woman of our own race'' as exemplifying the disastrous consequences of intermarriage.[16]

Johnson's ill repute peaked between 1910 and 1913. In leaving the country the champion became a less-dire threat to Caucasian supremacy because his flight fulfilled the white wish to exclude him from American society and reduced the likelihood of his inspiring other blacks to emulate his behavior and challenge the caste system. When he lost the title in 1915 the potency of this mythic antagonist was further diminished. A *Chicago Tribune* editorial accurately noted that the ''great mass of our white citizenship simply rejoiced'' at the outcome of the fight. ''It is a point of pride with the ascendant race not to concede supremacy in anything, not even to a gorilla.'' The editorial also captured the deeper meaning of Johnson's defeat. Jesse Willard's ''triumph'' enabled ''millions of his fellow citizens to sit down to their dinners last night with renewed confidence in their eight inch biceps, flexed, and twenty-eight inch chests, expanded. . . . '' Willard further obliged his ''fellow citizens'' by declaring that he would fight no black challengers. This bout, however, unlike the Johnson-Jeffries match, did not make the front page of the Chicago daily. The Johnson phenomenon had been displaced by a new event—World War I.[17]

''Little Arthur,'' now an ex-champion living abroad while America was at war, no longer magnetized public attention. He returned home in 1920 and quietly served his prison term. Johnson's third white wife, wedded in 1925, did not offend Jazz Age mores as gravely as his previous unions had upset prewar America—partly because he had lost the title and no black was permitted to fight for the championship. According to his own account, Johnson's image improved in the 1920s. He was well treated in jail and later toured the lecture circuit promoting evangelical religion and temperance. One of his talks was favorably received by an audience consisting of Ku Klux Klan members. Another example of the abatement of hostility was a commendation for clean sportsmanship conferred upon the ex-champion by the 25th U.S. Army Infantry Regiment, whose camp he used to train for one of his last fights. Johnson never reattained celebrity status or achieved complete rehabilitation in public repute. But in the 1920s and 1940s, when a popular black ruled the heavyweight division and racism was identified with an enemy ideology and country, Johnson finally won recognition among history's premier prizefighters.[18]

When Jack Johnson was a notorious public figure, white America perceived him as a racial force or emblem rather than as a human being. He bore the "bad nigger" stigma, the "uppity" and villainous label that was the negative correlative of the virtuous white man and the "humble" Negro who accepted a submissive and segregated status. This stereotype personifies the fear of the "black brute," that envied but ominous counterforce to western civilization. Some students of race relations suggest that it represents the id in the white psyche. According to Freudian psychology, the id harbors the so-called primal instincts of physical indulgence that threaten the impulse control (superego) necessary to maintain social order. Suppression of these forbidden drives, however, creates anxieties and frustrations that are projected onto an outgroup (the blacks) in society. The most powerful instinct is the drive for sexual gratification, and the "primitive" black is popularly considered to be more potent in this respect than the "civilized" white. Consequently, the latter turns his feelings of sexual inadequacy into fear and condemnation of the former. To many white Americans, Johnson embodied the id. The champion's love of food, drink, and good times, his "golden smile" and easy laughter, his fancy clothes and cars, his humiliation of Caucasian opponents, and above all his promiscuous contacts with white women confirmed the widely held view of the black man as at best a simple child and at worst a superstud—savage brute. Whites envied Johnson's imputed (and by extension, his race's) capacity to gratify physical desires and emotional needs and detested the champion's defiance of the color caste system. For the dominant race he loomed as a demonic figure who demeaned its status and endangered social order. Johnson had traits—courage, virility, strength, independence, cleverness, and wit—widely admired in whites but generally considered "uppity" and disruptive of the racial hierarchy when they appeared in blacks. In ridiculing opponents, flaunting flashy dress, automobiles, and women, and owning and frequenting night clubs, he behaved no differently than other successful boxers. "Little Arthur" wanted to be treated just like his professional peers and this champion's demand for the usual perquisites and privileges of victory in the ring would have been granted if only he had been white.[19]

Twenty-two years after Johnson was dethroned a second black won the heavyweight crown. A sharp drop in the profits and popularity of boxing again enabled a black fighter to cross the color line. Mediocre title holders, suspicious championship fights, and the Great Depression made the Dempsey-Tunney era, which ended in 1928, a retrospective golden age—glorious but unrepeatable. If Jack Johnson and Joe Louis reached the top because prizefighting was in the doldrums, their careers had little else in common. The old champion was an improviser in the ring, fast on his feet and a superb defensive boxer; the new champion was a methodical slugger with awesome punching power. "Little Arthur" was flamboyant and defiant, the "Brown Bomber" was phlegmatic and obedient. Johnson was the "bad nigger" in an age of strident racism; Louis was "a credit to his race" in a time of patronizing tolerance.

Global and domestic developments, even more than personality differences, created greater approval of Louis' reign. During World War I many blacks moved to Northern cities in search of defense industry jobs. Civil rights were better protected in the urban North and the new immigrants slowly began to acquire political leverage. These advances produced visible gains in the 1930s. Although some New Deal policies hurt blacks, the federal agencies responsible for public aid to the poor and unemployed helped all races. Franklin Delano Roosevelt's administration also reversed the long decline in federal positions held by blacks, and Eleanor Roosevelt vigorously campaigned for progress in race relations and minority rights. Improvements also appeared in labor organizations. The newly formed Congress of Industrial Organizations was not as racist as the American Federation of Labor, and blacks enrolled in some key industrial unions. The gradual, though slow and imcomplete, inclusion of blacks in the industrial and political systems proceeded from (and in turn spurred) an amelioration in the public image of the race. During Johnson's championship scientists almost unanimously agreed upon the genetic inferiority of the Negro. In the 1920s several prominent anthropologists questioned this assumption, and in the 1930s the majority of anthropologists and social psychologists attributed to environmental conditions racial differences on such matters as IQ scores. A 1930 questionnaire circulated among scholars in the field of racial variances disclosed that only 4 percent of these experts believed in racial superiority. The change in academic opinion and the limited but significant political and economic gains of blacks began to modify the thoughts and behavior of the white masses. The yearly average of black lynchings, over fifty during Johnson's championship, fell to slightly over ten in the 1930s. A 1940 Gallup Poll showed that 55 percent of the respondents with an opinion approved a proposed federal law against lynching. Americans also revealed a growing distaste for other forms of prejudice. When the Daughters of the American Revolution in 1939 prohibited black singer Marian Anderson from performing in its Constitution Hall in Washington, D.C., Mrs. Roosevelt resigned from the organization. A Gallup Poll of that year disclosed that 67 percent of the respondents with an opinion supported her action. Even boxing was not immune to the rising tide of tolerance. When asked in a 1939 Gallup survey, "Who would you like to see win the Louis-Tony Galento Fight," 53 percent of the respondents with an opinion picked the champion.[20]

International events contributed heavily to these advances. Germany and Italy, increasingly perceived as the nation's foes, were committed to fanatical racism. As the country drifted toward war with these powers, the virtues of our society were contrasted to evils of Nazism and Fascism, thus further discrediting bigotry. The United States now focused on a geographical rather than a racial outgroup as its main enemy, a circumstance that promoted domestic harmony and better race relations. During World War II the blacks made their greatest political and economic progress since Reconstruction, and negative Negro stereotypes encountered increasing disfavor. In 1939, for example, 22 percent of the respondents in a public opinion poll felt that blacks had the same intelligence as whites; 42 percent of the respondents in a 1942 poll held this view. Diminished racism elevated the public esteem of Joe Louis, but the limitations of this progress also shaped the champion's image. During the war, changes were just beginning in the de facto and de jure structure of racial segregation and in the traditional belief in Negro inferiority. Public opinion surveys showed that large majorities still favored racial separation in public transportation facilities, residential areas, and schools.[21]

The sports scene, as always, reflected prevalent social currents. Major and minor league baseball remained segregated and the few blacks in the National Football League ended their careers in the early 1930s. But the gains of black athletes outweighed their exclusion from professional football. Track was becoming an interracial sport and a black held the heavyweight title. More important, in this decade Jesse Owens and Joe Louis emerged as the first black national athletic heroes, a sign that the nation was beginning to recognize blacks as legitimate American citizens. Black athletes, notably Owens, created a sensation in the 1936 Olympics. The games were staged in Berlin to provide a showcase for Nazism and Aryan supremacy. In this climate the medal-winning American blacks assumed, for the first time in our history, the status of patriotic symbols. Unlike previous athletic contests, where white Americans rooted for foreigners against Afro-Americans, these champions were heralded for sustaining national prestige in the initial confrontation between American democracy and German racist totalitarianism. Adolf Hitler further enhanced the symbolism of their victories by leaving the stadium to avoid congratulating the black track stars. Owens proved to be a temporary national hero and returned home to bear his share of the humiliation inflicted by a racist society. Louis, however, was a more celebrated and enduring idol. The conqueror of Primo Carnera and Max Schmeling, he became the athletic emblem of America's struggle against the Axis countries and the praise he received for these triumphs elevated the stature of his people.[22]

The Louis image was carefully crafted to minimize resistance to a black heavyweight challenger. It derived from his own personal qualities, from shrewd exploitation of the incipient relaxation of caste rigidity, and from the necessity of presenting a Negro stereotype designed to allay white fear and hostility. The Louis legend was born when his black managers (John Roxborough and Julian Black) and trainer (Jack Blackburn) realized that they were handling a potential champion. Refusing to adopt Uncle Tom tactics, they successfully resisted white takeovers of their protégé and rejected demands that their fighter, as often occurred when blacks faced whites, pull punches or take "dives." To breach the color bar, however, necessitated certain concessions to white opinion. Roxborough taught the young boxer the rudiments of personal hygiene and dinner table etiquette and hired a tutor to upgrade his grammar and manners. Paramount in the grooming of the future titleholder was the formation of a black antithesis to Jack Johnson. Roxborough, Black, and Blackburn told Louis that he could not be a champion if he behaved like "Little Arthur" and ordered him never to have his picture taken with a white woman, to go alone to a night club, or to gloat over an opponent and always to keep a "dead pan" in front of the camera and to live and fight cleanly. The contrast between the black heavyweights would be reinforced in the public mind by making sure that the "Brown Bomber" never became involved in a fixed fight or faced a misfit opponent. Measures were taken against any possible association or resemblance between the fighters. Johnson, a reckless driver, collected many speeding tickets; when Louis was caught speeding Roxborough took his license and hired a chauffeur for him. Early in Louis' career his managers even barred the ex-champion from their boxers' training camp.[23]

An anti-Johnson image was part of the strategy to portray Louis as the black savior of prizefighting. In an age of nonfighting champions, fixed bouts, and gangster influence (most notoriously in the case of recent champion Primo Carnera), the "Dark Destroyer" fought honestly and often. Since the heavyweight titlists of this era were widely criticized as mediocre fighters, bragging brutes, or uncouth playboys (another recent champion, Max Baer acquired the reputation of a white Jack Johnson), Louis was depicted as a modest man who hated to hurt opponents, read the Bible, went to church, neither smoked nor drank, and donated his earnings to charity and his family. The Louis buildup was vividly expressed in a 1939 interview with his mother published in the Hearst newspaper, the *New York Mirror*. "I know that if Joe wins the championship he is going to make Jack [Johnson] feel ashamed of himself again," said Mrs. Lillie Barrow Brooks after noting that she had taught her loving and obedient son to read the Bible. "Joe wants to win to show the white folks that a colored man can bring dignity and decency to the title just as well as a white man."[24]

The Louis image aimed to counteract the "bad nigger" myth epitomized by Johnson. Consequently, the heavyweight challenger was not presented to the public as an autonomous adult entitled to political and social equality. Portrayed as docile and child-like, Louis was merely imprisoned in a more acceptable racial stereotype. "Always be . . . modest and humble," Roxborough shrewdly advised Louis, "and nothing can stop you.'' The condescending tolerance that passed for enlightened race attitudes in the 1930s made this kind of Negro a viable title contender.[25]

This carefully prepared image first paraded before the public in 1935 when Louis came east to score sensational triumphs over Baer and Carnera. The athlete from Detroit got his big chance when Mike Jacobs arranged a match with Carnera. By donating part of the gate to a favorite charity of Mrs. William Randolph Hearst, the New York promoter made the potential title challenger palatable to the public. Thus did Louis acquire a reputation for benevolence and the support of the Hearst press. During the prefight media "hype" Quentin Reynolds and other writers hailed Louis' attachment to his mother and his faith. Reynolds assured the readers of *Collier's* magazine that if the young Detroiter became champion "the boxing game will have a leader of whom it will not be ashamed and . . . the Negro race will have a representative that it can point to with pride." The ring announcer told the crowd at the fight: "In America we admire the athlete who can win by virtue of his skill. Let me then ask you to join me in the sincere wish that regardless of race, color or creed the better man may emerge victorious." This message reflected the anxieties of the boxing establishment over the reception of a black heavyweight, but also showed that a new spirit of tolerance had entered the ring. Sixty thousand saw Louis knock out Carnera on a hot June night at Yankee Stadium, the best attendance at a New York bout since 1927. Harry Balough's salutation proved unnecessary—the postfight commentary in the *Mirror* and other dailies praised Louis' ring skills and his "God-fearing, Bible-reading, cleanliving . . . modest, quiet and unassuming manner."[26]

Three months later the Louis-Baer contest brought back the $1 million gate. "American sportsmanship, without regard to race, creed or color, is the talk of the world," said Balough in welcoming the largest crowd to attend a fight except for the two Dempsey-Tunney battles. The defeat of Baer made Louis more popular than any previous black boxer. In 1935 *Ring* magazine named him fighter of the year and the Associated Press sportswriters voted him Athlete of the Year. He visited the mayor of New York at City Hall and was told by the governor of Michigan that he would someday win fame and money even though his "people have been denied equal opportunity." From 1935 until his June 1936 match with Max Schmeling a multitude of articles celebrating Louis as a fighter and a person prompted the *Literary Digest* to remark that he "attracted more press 'raves' than any other non-champion in history." Sportswriters predicted that the "Dark Destroyer" would become champion. Modesty, religious faith, family feeling, "excellent habits," and "racial restraint," the press asserted, would make him an ideal example for blacks and, unlike Johnson, acceptable to whites.[27]

Despite a rising reputation, the contender still faced considerable hostility. Newspaper cartoons and reports stereotyped the "Brown Bomber" as a savage brute—simple child. Dempsey and others renewed the search for a white hope to stop the young challenger, and columnist Westbrook Pegler viewed the Carnera match as an invitation to racial conflict. Pegler and other writers also claimed that Louis was dominated by black racketeers. The State of Virginia barred the showing of the Louis-Baer fight films because—shades of Jack Johnson—their exhibition would "arouse racial animosity." And Louis was not permitted to spar with whites in New Orleans. Unfriendly observers called him "an ordinary colored boy, slow thinking and emotionless." Even neutral or positive commentators frequently alluded to his "savage" and "animal-like" traits in the ring, which they traced to the alleged "jungle" origins of his people. Noted sportswriter Paul Gallico saw in Louis' "poker face" a "nerveless, emotionless ice-cold killer." Anti-Louis feeling intensified after his 1936 loss to Max Schmeling. Touted by Hitler and Joseph Goebbels as an exemplar of Aryan supremacy, the triumphant Schmeling nonetheless received a "wild ovation" from the crowd at the fight. This testament to the enduring priority of racial over national affinity took place in New York City, a center of American liberalism, racial tolerance, and opposition to Nazism. "Schmeling's victory," said Dempsey, "is the finest thing to happen to boxing in a long time." The outcome evoked cheers in the gallery of the U.S. House of Representatives and the reborn Siegfried got more congratulatory telegrams from the United States than from any other country. Gallico and *Time*, no friends of Louis, now belittled his reputation as a publicity stunt and the former speculated whether the black boxer's low blows were deliberate while ignoring the fact that the German once hit Louis after the bell.[28]

The defeat, the low blows, and the notoriety surrounding the felonious activities of his trainer and managers did not permanently damage the Louis image. When he took the heavyweight crown from James

Braddock in 1937, "the white hope" campaign was not revived. Braddock proclaimed that he cared "not two hoots in Hades about the old 'color line,' " and Jim Jeffries called the "honor of the white race" a "kind of hokum" that he was no longer "handing out." [29]

The new champion's popularity grew because, unlike his recent predecessors, he fought honestly, regularly, and skillfully. Acceptance, however, did not turn into adulation until Louis became a national hero. The transformation of the Louis image into the Louis legend occurred from 1938 to 1945. The apotheosis of the Alabama sharecropper's son into the nation's most beloved sports figure began when he demolished Schmeling in a return match in June 1938. Unlike their first meeting, this encounter was widely viewed as a contest between America and the enemy. Since 1936, the Nazis had taken Austria and displayed a rabid streak of anti-Semitic violence. Hostility toward the Third Reich was further aroused when shortly before the fight eighteen suspected German spies were indicted for espionage. Hitler and other Nazi leaders regarded Schmeling as a national hero and the bout as a contest between decadent democracy and Aryan racial superiority. These sentiments were widely criticized in the American press and the nation rallied behind Louis as its representative in a confrontation with the foreign foe. A few weeks prior to the fight the champion was invited to the White House, where the president said, "Joe, we need muscles like yours to beat Germany." White citizens told him that they "were depending upon [him] to k.o. Germany," and Tunney, hitherto not an admirer of Louis, advised the titleholder on boxing tactics because he wanted the championship to remain in the United States. [30]

In Johnson's day the national majority put race above nationality and rooted for "Little Arthur's" opponents to beat him even when it meant that the title would pass to foreign hands. In the 1930s these priorities, at least in the case of a German challenger, changed. Louis' victory, therefore, was seen as an American triumph, and he became the first national black hero. Michigan Governor Frank Murphy was "full of hero-worship" for Louis and *Ring* reporter Ted Carroll, in a statement typical of a large sector of American opinion, asserted that "Schmeling's defeat symbolize[d] . . . the complete deflation of any and all 'isms' or claims to natural supremacy of any particular race or group." Louis' victory meant the "collapse of the Aryan theory . . . before the eyes of the whole world. . . . " [31]

The champion's fame soared after 1938 and peaked during World

War II. His refusal to seek a draft deferment, a striking contrast to Willard's and Dempsey's evasion of World War I military service, his patriotism and sacrifice of money and career for the war effort, his donation of two title defense purses to the Army and Navy Relief Funds, and his boxing exhibitions at and visits to military camps and hospitals made him America's most-revered athlete. Franklin and Eleanor Roosevelt, Wendell Willkie, governors, senators, cabinet officers, movie stars, and the public media admired him. A white Southerner named his child after Louis, whites wanted their sons to imitate his behavior, and a warplane was christened the "Brown Bomber." A 1947 Gallup Poll placed him among the fifty-eight most popular Americans—Babe Ruth was the only other athlete on the list. Dempsey, Tunney, Gallico, Pegler, and *Time* now lauded Louis as a Horatio Alger type, a great patriot, a superb champion, and an exemplary human being. Congress repealed its ban on interstate shipment of fight films and in 1942 Louis received boxing's highest award, the Edward J. Neil Memorial Plaque. The champion was also decorated by the U.S. Army for wartime contributions. A typical example of these sentiments appeared in historian John G. Van Deusen's *Brown Bomber*. "I give you here the story of a great man," wrote the author in dedicating the biography to his son. "He is great because his achievements were made despite handicaps that might well have been overwhelming. With little formal education, without cultural background, possessing neither money nor pull, he has fought his way to the top of the profession." The triumphant hero, however,

is still the same modest, unassuming lad we might have seen before his rise to fame. As you read these pages, you will find qualities that young men might well emulate. Courage, good sportsmanship, hard work, clean living, loyalty, obedience and thrift are desirable traits in any race or situation.[32]

In the late 1940s the halo begin to slip. Louis was still loved but the media and the public felt that he humiliated himself by continuing to fight after he lost the title and by briefly turning to professional wrestling when his ring career ended. Divorces and money problems and in the 1960s paternity suits, a mental breakdown, and drug addiction made him a pitiful rather than an inspirational figure. Involvement in a public relations firm hired by Fidel Castro, endorsements of cigarettes and liquor, showing up at fight camps to "puff" a boxer for "walking around money," and acting as a paid host at Nevada gambling casinos further faded Louis' glory. The social upheavals of the 1960s and early 1970s undermined traditional beliefs and idols and the ex-champion suffered from having been a hero and supporter of the establishment. A new generation of liberals, blacks, and sportswriters found his patriotism, 1940s stance on race relations, and criticism of Muhammad Ali irrelevant or Uncle Tomish in an era of civil rights and antiwar crusades.[33]

Popular heroes are figments of the public's imagination—incarnations of the needs and values of the times. During Louis' long championship America underwent dramatic changes. The country moved from outspoken racism to limited tolerance, from depression to prosperity, and from peace to war and then back to peace. Under ordinary boxing circumstances several heavyweight champions would have reigned in these years and embodied the different national impulses released by these changes. Since Louis held the title throughout this time, his image was modified to reflect national transformations. Until the second Schmeling fight the "Brown Bomber" was on trial. Most citizens harbored traditional prejudices and shuddered at the prospect of another black champion. But Louis restored to boxing the glory and money of its 1930s Golden Age and America was more racially tolerant than at any time since the 1860s. The new attitudes and the old bigotry, the promise of Louis and the spectre of Johnson, created ambivalent feelings. Even liberals needed persuasion that Louis was a faithful "darky" rather than a defier of the caste system. In 1938 Gallico shrewdly assessed why "Louis has enjoyed an extraordinary vogue" and an exemption from "the rules that have applied to the general run of negro fighters." The *New York Daily News* columnist noted that he "appeared at just the right time, when the public was sick and tired of the clowns, fakes, phoneys, and misfits they had been looking at in the guise of white champions." Gallico conceded that shrewd management and rare fistic talent helped Louis' career, but he emphasized that the black boxer's public image and the spirit of the times enabled him to win the championship. "Louis is what is known definitely as a 'good nigger who knows his place,' " observed Gallico. "He has been carefully trained in the sly servility that the white man accepts as his due." The well-managed, deferential "darky" and "box office draw" emerged "during an era of tolerance. The white man's ego was still a little shakened by the depression. The pale-faces patronized him and permitted him . . . and preened themselves'' about being '' 'fine people and sportsmen' '' who let '' 'a nigger earn a fortune in the ring just like any white man.' ''[34]

Louis' humility, generosity, Christianity, obedience to authority whether in the form of his mother, his managers, or the caste code, and his gratitude to the establishment for its favors remained permanent elements of the Louis legend. Other aspects of his image—references to his savage or animalistic traits, his calm ruthlessness in the ring, and his crude simplicity—began to disappear when Louis became a national hero. By 1938 the ambivalent trial period was over and Louis was no longer treated as an outsider accorded special privileges otherwise denied to members of his race. As an American idol Louis' patriotism, fairness, gentleness, dignity, respect for education, self-restraint, clean living, climb from obscure poverty to riches and fame, and his sense of obligation to his family, profession, and country were now stressed. When he became a national icon the "Brown Galahad" represented the middle-class virtues of the American creed. In the twilight of his life, Louis was increasingly seen as a figure of the past. Nostalgia for what he was mixes with sorrow for the exploited and troubled man he became in later years. Once again he was seen as childlike, manipulated, and limited, but this reversion to an early Louis image was perceived by the public and the media as a personal tragedy instead of an inevitable recurrence of a racial stereotype. The glorification of Louis as a national emblem and the nostalgic pathos that enveloped his declining years to his death in 1981 prevented the ex-champion from becoming a confirmation of that stock figure—the failed Negro. These well-meaning and sometimes admirable sentiments, however, effectively deracinated him. The hero worship that made Louis a model for all Americans, and especially the liberal view of him as a symbol of racial progress and white benevolence, abstracted him from his black identity. The next test for American liberals was whether they would accept a titleholder who could not be cut off from his roots and wished to be a black heavyweight champion as well as an American heavyweight champion.

The next great black heavyweight refused to adopt Louis' accommodating or Johnson's intrusive posture vis-à-vis the white power structure. Muhammad Ali won the championship in 1964, was stripped of his title in 1967, regained the crown in 1974, lost and retook it in 1978, retired in 1979, and returned in 1980 but was defeated in a title bout. From 1964 to 1967, when his career was caught up in contemporary social and political conflicts, he became the champion not only of the heavyweight division, but of black militance against white bigotry and tepid tolerance, of peace against war, of youth against age, of 1960s radicalism against 1940s liberalism, and of all forms of resistance to the establishment.

The dialectic in Ali's opposition to the Louis myth and the racial and political settlements of the previous generation was that the old champion and the gains of the earlier period prepared the way for the new champion and the upheaval he symbolized. Progress in civil rights and race relations, combined with the realization that these advances still left the blacks in a weak position, helped produce the explosions of the 1960s and pushed Ali to the forefront of racial strife. The Supreme Court school desegregation decision of 1954 and the crusade for equality that a few years later began in the South and culminated in the civil rights legislation and race riots of the 1960s simultaneously reflected improvements in white attitudes toward blacks and dramatized the severe and seemingly permanent economic and social disadvantages of the Afro-Americans. In these years the blacks finally received substantial legal recognition of their citizenship rights. Public opinion polls between the 1940s and 1960s showed a major shift in mass opinion about blacks. Between 1942 and 1963 the percentage of respondents believing that blacks were as intelligent as whites increased from 42 to 80. Between 1944 and 1965 the percentage of Americans favoring integrated schools rose from 30 to over 75. During these years the percentage of whites who said they would not move if a black family of the same income or education moved to their block climbed from 35 to 63. Between 1944 and 1963 the percentage of whites who thought that blacks should have as good a chance as whites to obtain any kind of job increased from just under 40 to over 80. Between 1942 and 1963 the proportion of Americans supporting integrated public transportation rose from under one-half to over three-quarters. Between 1942 and 1965 the percentage of those who felt that whites and blacks should use the same restaurants went from 27 to 75. Advances in law, public opinion, and level of black education, however, did not end residential and school segregation or close the income gap between the races. Furthermore, the advent of the Vietnam War diminished the national commitment to racial equality. These developments generated tension between the rising expectations of blacks and the reality of continued prejudice and a growing white backlash against attempts to reduce racial oppression. Frustration and anger, especially among the young blacks, triggered uprisings in the ghettos of New York, Los Angeles, and other cities and enlarged the membership numbers and intensified the militance of radical civil rights and black nationalist organizations. During these years, Cassius Clay, a patriotic cheerful Negro, won the heavyweight championship and changed into black nationalist Muhammad Ali.[35]

The repute and profitability of boxing was in one of its periodic recessions when Ali appeared on the scene. Between the 1956 retirement of Rocky Marciano and the reign of Ali, Floyd Patterson, Ingemar Johansson, and Sonny Liston held the title. Patterson acquired a reputation for ducking tough contenders; Johansson, an unskilled Swede, dethroned Patterson with a lucky punch and was defeated by him a year later; Liston was a convicted felon allegedly controlled by mobsters.

Cassius Clay, as had Jack Johnson and Joe Louis, emerged as the most talented and "bankable" challenger when mediocrity and mendacity threatened to make the heavyweight division moribund. Before winning the title Clay was widely praised as a likable young athlete with uncommon wit, talent, and crowd appeal. His debut in the public media occurred in the 1960 Olympics when, as the light heavyweight gold medalist, he told a Russian reporter that the "U.S.A. is the best country in the world, including yours." During these years Clay was publicly portrayed as warm, patriotic, clean-living, enthusiastic, friendly, articulate, humorous, and obedient to his white managers. The press hailed him as a rejuvenating force in the stagnant fight game. The syndicate of prominent Louisville businessmen who managed the contender was considered an honest, generous, and enlightened brain trust that would prevent the young Negro from suffering the fate of the bankrupt Louis. It was widely noted that Clay took a good-humored view of race relations and seemed aloof from the civil rights turbulence. "You know I'll be a credit to my race," he proclaimed in the best Louis tradition, "and I'll let my fists do the talking." When the Olympic victor returned to Louisville the mayor proudly declared that "he acts like you would like a young American to act after receiving so much acclaim and so many honors. If all young people could handle themselves as well as he does, we wouldn't have any juvenile problems. He's a swell kid."[36]

When Clay appeared on the March 1963 cover of *Time*, it became obvious that the media and the sports establishment were grooming a contender who would rescue boxing from the doldrums. Amid the early plaudits, however, were criticisms of the young fighter's bragging, egoism, taunting of opponents, and manipulation of the media for self-promotion and self-dramatization. Reminiscent of the ways and obloquy of Johnson, these comments foreshadowed the infamy that awaited Ali after he became champion. Sportswriters called him the "Louisville Lip," "Mighty Mouth," and "Cassius the Brashest," and many fans came to Clay's fights rooting for his comeuppance.[37]

Despite the shadows in Clay's image he wore the "white hat" at the February 1964 championship match. Titleholder Sonny Liston, the "bad nigger" of the early 1960s, had served two prison terms for robbery and assault. According to testimony given to U.S. Senator Estes Kefauver's committee investigating professional boxing (1960–1961), gangsters owned his contract; several state boxing commissions barred him from the ring; and he had won the crown from Floyd Patterson, a fighter revered for his Louis-like humility and gratitude to white America. When Clay unexpectedly beat Liston the Kentucky House of Representatives passed a resolution praising his triumph.[38]

This popularity rapidly vanished when the new champion precipitated the first of a series of crises that brought him denigration unrivaled in the sports world since the time of Johnson. On the day following his victory, Clay announced his membership in the Black Muslims, a militant black nationalist organization widely (and exaggeratedly) regarded as the vanguard of a violent revolution against Caucasian supremacy and the social order. "I don't have to be what you want me to be," Clay told the press. "I'm free to be who I want." Clay's public notification of Black Muslim membership evoked instant outrage. Rumors spread that Liston, intimidated by the organization, threw the fight. Ali's friendship for Black Muslim leader Malcolm X, his rejection of America as a racially oppressive society ("I'm not no American, I'm a black man"), and his discarding of "the slave name" Cassius Clay for Muhammad Ali intensified the uproar against him. Ali's renunciation of America and Christianity for Islam and negritude antagonized a vast majority encompassing integrationist liberals such as sportswriter Jimmy Cannon and columnist Jimmy Breslin, redneck racists, members of the white establishment, and ordinary citizens. Dempsey, Louis, and Patterson attacked his new religious beliefs and

associations as subversive of the nation and the heavyweight championship. "Clay is likely to hurt the sport badly by his ideologization
of it," argued William Buckley when Ali proclaimed his allegiance to
the Black Muslims. Buckley hoped for Ali's defeat "before he is done
damaging the sport and the country which, however much he now dis-
dains it, gave him the opportunity to hate it from a throne." U.S. Senator Kenneth Keating (New York) wanted Ali stripped of the title because of his association with Black Muslims, an organization that the
politician charged promoted racial violence and hatred. President Edward Lassman of the World Boxing Association (WBA) declared that
"Clay is a detriment to the boxing world." The "conduct of the
champion . . . has caused my office to be deluged with letters of tor-
rid criticism from all over the world—to say nothing of the unfavorable reaction of newspapers in this country and others. The entire nation is bitter about it." Lassman assailed the champion—who neither
smoked nor drank, rarely visited nightclubs, never caroused with women,
and explicitly stated that he wanted no white females—for "setting a
very poor example for the youth of the world." Within two months
after the Liston fight the WBA withdrew recognition of Ali as champion.[39]

A month after Ali won the title, a shrewd commentator perceived
that the prefight hero and villain had exchanged roles. "Liston used to
be a hoodlum," wrote social critic Murray Kempton. "Now he was
our cop, he was the big Negro we pay to keep the fresh Negroes in
line and he was just waiting until his boss told him it was time to throw
this kid out." When Ali returned to the ring in May 1965 for another
title match with Liston, the first summer of urban riots had heightened
the hostility against the young champion. The contest was shifted to
Lewiston, Maine, because veterans' groups caused its cancellation in
Boston. The fighters entered the ring accompanied by jeers for Ali and
cheers for the challenger. Ali's first-round knockout of Liston aroused
a storm of protest. Many observers again claimed that the contender
had been terrorized into submission by the Black Muslims. The WBA
legal council called the KO "a farce and a fraud" and Tunney considered the bout the "most offensive debasement of boxing that I have
ever seen or even read about." U.S. senators and representatives demanded a congressional investigation of the match, and bills to ban or
investigate boxing were introduced in the Massachusetts, Pennsylvania, Missouri, and California legislatures. The New York Senate ma-

jority leader wanted to outlaw professional prizefighting in that state and Dempsey called for a national boxing commission.[40]

Six months after the Lewiston fiasco, Ali confronted the Louis tradition in the form of Floyd Patterson. Recent convert to Catholicism, redeemed juvenile delinquent, NAACP integrationist, and friend of the Kennedys, Patterson was another "brown Galahad." He agreed with the WBA decision to take away its part of Ali's championship and offered to fight him for nothing in order to "bring the title back to America." For the contestants and the people the Ali-Patterson fight was a battle of the ingrate against the grateful, the traitor against the patriot, the crescent against the cross, and the defiant, uncontrollable black against the loyal, humble Negro. Ali was infuriated by Patterson's attacks, his refusal to call him by his Islamic name, and the ex-champion's role as an establishment paladin. He called Patterson an "Uncle Tom," the "black white hope," a "white man's nigger" and vowed to humiliate him in the ring. The circumstances surrounding this bout brought out in the titleholder (always a clean and often a merciful fighter) a hitherto undisclosed streak of cruelty. For twelve rounds he taunted Patterson and hit him hard enough to inflict maximum damage without knocking him out. The public was sickened and angered by the exhibition and the press denounced Ali in terms reminiscent of the racial and other epithets hurled at Johnson. Louis called the victor "selfish and cruel," Cannon discovered that he was "streaked with savagery," famed sportswriter Red Smith accused him of being a "practicing sadist," and one columnist urged boxing authorities to "outlaw this cannibal Clay."[41]

Ali administered similar punishment in 1967 to Ernie Terrell, the WBA titlist and another patriot-integrationist who regarded him as a black renegade. A torrent of abuse again was heaped upon Ali and the negative Negro stereotype reemerged. Traditionally sullen about black heavyweight champions, *Time* labeled him "the sideshow clown" who wore "jazzy clothes" and uttered "incoherent ravings on race . . . puerile dirty jokes" and an "endless stream of babyhood reminiscences." Now, however, the champion's conduct outside the ring constituted a graver threat to his image and career.[42]

Dismantling Patterson made Ali the most reviled American athlete since Johnson. But this opprobrium was merely a prelude to the hatred he incurred by opposing the Vietnam War and refusing military service. When Ali twice failed the mental part of the draft examination angry citizens protested to their congressmen, and his draft board received over 1,000 letters demanding that the champion be inducted. Amid the controversy over his draft status, the titleholder in 1966 remarked that he had "no quarrel with the Viet Cong" and declared that he was "not going 10,000 miles from here to help murder and kill poor people simply to help continue the domination of white slave masters over the darker people." If ordered to serve, Ali declared he would seek conscientious objector status because of his religious beliefs. These statements resulted in Governor Otto Kerner of Illinois, Mayor Richard Daley of Chicago, and the Illinois Athletic Commission's preventing the forthcoming Ali-Terrell fight from taking place in Chicago. Seven other American cities also rejected the bout, bowing to pressure from the Veterans of Foreign Wars and the American Legion. L. Mendel Rivers, chairman of the House Armed Services Committee, threatened to investigate Ali's draft board if it deferred him, and the Kentucky State Senate demanded Ali's induction into the U.S. Army. The champion received hate mail and death threats, Tunney told him that he "disgraced" the "title and the American flag," and Dempsey asserted that it was "not safe for him to be seen on the streets." Liberal newspapers such as the *New York Post* urged him to follow Louis' World War II example and called him a dangerous model for American youth.[43]

The uproar evoked by Ali's encounters with the Selective Service System caused it to lower the passing grade on the mental exam and reclassify Ali 1A. The Department of Justice then rejected Ali's application for conscientious objector status on the ground that he was "politically and racially motivated." In April 1967 the champion refused to step forward for induction into the army. Within twenty-four hours and long before Ali would be tried and found guilty of refusing military service, the WBA took away his title and the New York Athletic Commission (which had licensed ninety felons, including rapists and murderers) lifted his boxing license. In June, an all-white Houston jury convicted him of violating the U.S. Selective Service laws. The chief prosecutor asked for leniency (the average sentence for refusing induction was eighteen months), but Ali received the maximum penalty of five years in prison and a $10,000 fine. U.S. Attorney Morton Sussman, prosecutor of the case against Ali, attributed the champion's guilt to his membership in the Black Muslims.[44]

The vast majority of white Americans, enraged by Ali's draft refusal, applauded the vengeance wrought in the courts and the boxing organizations. Louis thought Ali should serve and agreed with Dempsey that he was justly deprived of the title. Kerner and Daley denounced the beleaguered champion and California Governor Ronald Reagan called him "unpatriotic" and "ungrateful." The American Legion, the Veterans of Foreign Wars, and the White Citizens' Council threatened to boycott any arena in which he fought. *Time* scorned him and the *New York Times* advocated judicial punishment of his actions. The *National Review*, the right-wing intellectual organ, labeled him a "brainwashed puppet" whose "defiance of the draft law" exemplified the "vicious dissent" of the "New Left" and "Black Power" which threatened "the safety and even survival of the nation." A *Chicago Tribune* editorial expressed the *vox populi* in calling Ali "a flagrant draft dodger" and the Houston verdict an act of "justice," and blaming his troubles on a "race hate sect."[45]

Appealing a jail sentence, detested by most Americans, and barred from the ring, Ali seemed to be replaying the fifty-year-old drama of Jack Johnson. Both boxers were despised as "uppity niggers" who defied American racial conventions. But Johnson was attacked for violating the color caste system, particularly and fundamentally for consorting with white women. Ali and the Muslims, on the other hand, practiced racial segregation. Their espousal of separatism did not derive from acceptance of black inferiority and submission, however. It sprang from a belief that blacks were superior to the Caucasian enemy. These departures from the canons of American racism focused Ali's defiance, and the hostility against him, on politics rather than on sex or masculinity. It made him resolve not to flee the country as had Johnson and led him to oppose liberal tolerance as well as blunter modes of racial oppression.

If Ali's emergence as a political counterforce to the establishment brought him vilification, it also prevented him from becoming as isolated as Johnson. Ali's execration of the war, racism, boxing commissions, the federal government, the mass media, and other institutions associated with power elites, and his willingness to sacrifice money and fame for his ideals, won him adherents among younger sportswriters, college students, and others antagonized by current domestic and foreign policies and alienated by traditional social and cultural values. During his suspension from the fight game a national public opinion poll showed the ex-champion to be the third most sought-after speaker in the country. Ali's public image brightened in the late 1960s as black militance, Muslim antiwhite rhetoric, and racial conflict diminished and disenchantment with the war and opposition to the draft began to spread. Increased public acceptance of athletes' resistance to racism and establishment sports policies and organizations also generated support for the dethroned boxer. During his ordeal, *New York Times* sportswriter Robert Lipsyte, Howard Cosell, and articles in sophisticated magazines such as *Esquire*, *Newsweek* (the liberal counterpart of *Time*), *Sports Illustrated* (designed to reach the young "with-it" reader), and the liberal religious journal, *Christian Century*, lauded Ali's nobility and sincerity, mocked his opponents as self-righteous hypocrites who arbitrarily prosecuted him and took away his title, and gave him a forum for castigating the war and racism and extolling Allah. Ali became a "radical-chic" cause when entertainers, writers and intellectuals, Elizabeth Taylor, Richard Burton, Norman Mailer, George Plimpton, Elia Kazan, Dick Cavett, Gloria Vanderbilt, and others issued a statement that "Muhammad Ali, Heavyweight Champion of the World, should be allowed to defend his title." Even more-powerful figures and institutions rallied behind Ali: Robert Kennedy defended his right to fight and express his views. Roone Arledge, president of the sports department of the American Broadcasting Company, successfully resisted government pressure to have the network cancel Ali's television commentary on an amateur boxing tournament between the Soviet Union and the United States. The conservative Henry Luce publication, *Life*, published a sympathetic article in 1969 about the black boxer.[46]

Ali's public rehabilitation was a consequence of shifting sentiment about the war, the draft, the prospects of racial friction, and the legitimacy of nonconformist athletes. The resurrection was further inspired by the feeling that the former champion's persecution by the establishment made him, for the first time since winning the title, an underdog. Public approval was swinging toward Ali when, in 1970, the New York Supreme Court ruled that he be given a boxing license. Nevertheless, when he returned to the ring in that year, Ali was still a *bête noire* to many Americans. Lipsyte and Cosell received hundreds of letters excoriating their defense of that "Nigger draft dodger." Hate mail and death threats continued to plague the black boxer and an attempt was made to assassinate him. Ali's first fight in forty-three months took place in Atlanta, and Georgia Governor Lester Maddox declared the occasion a day of mourning and, along with the mayor of Macon, Georgia, called for a boycott of the bout. Advertisers refused to sponsor the radio broadcast of the match because of Ali's notoriety and many regarded his opponent, Jerry Quarry, as the "white hope" who would end the "uppity nigger's" comeback. "I think it will be the great American public who puts the kiss of death on the fight and on Clay," wrote *Chicago Tribune* sports editor Gene Ward in a statement typical of the feelings of many furious citizens. But the crowd at the Madison Square Garden closed-screen televising of the contest cheered Ali, and Lipsyte also received congratulatory messages for his defense of the ex-titleholder.[47]

Ali's resurgence steadily progressed in 1971. In March he met Joe Frazier for the heavyweight crown, a bout that produced the first $1 million gate since Ali's exclusion from the ring. Even *Time* admitted that boxing had floundered during Ali's suspension because "the really good [heavyweight] fighters are few and colorless." The Ali-Frazier match at New York's Madison Square Garden was publicized and perceived as carrying considerably more significance than the usual battles for boxing's paramount title. "Not since the days of Joe Louis has a black man [Frazier] done so much for his race," read the Garden Press Kit on the fight, and "brought so much credit to boxing." Ali "will be Battling not just Frazier but all the Establishment forces that drove him from the ring for political reasons," reported *Newsweek* sports editor Pete Axthelm. Frazier was a "black 'white hope,' " representing "the forces of law and order against Ali, the Black Muslim and draft resister who has taunted white America. . . . " Axthelm saw Ali as "one of the country's folk heroes." Jerry Perenchio, who organized the closed-circuit TV presentation of the bout, regarded Ali as "a matinee idol. This isn't a fight. It's a happening. It's Woodstock all over again." *New York Times* columnist Arthur Daley, a bellwether of respectable opinion, rooted for the challenger and *Time* conceded that a man of "firmly entrenched conviction" had been "stripped of his rights" by "a pretentious body of boxing executives."[48]

Ali lost the fight but won a more important victory in the courts. In June 1971 the U.S. Supreme Court unanimously cleared him of the charge of refusing induction. The nation's highest tribunal concluded that the Justice Department misled Selective Service authorities by asserting that Ali's objections to the draft were insincere and improperly

based. The decision was favorably received and the boxing solons' unseemly haste in taking away his title was now widely condemned, even
by such former detractors as Cannon, *Time*, and the *Chicago Tribune*.
Robert Markus, a *Tribune* sports columnist, noted that when Ali was
convicted of draft evasion "near unanimity" prevailed—"at least in
white America—that he was guilty and should go to prison. But in the
intervening time there have been dramatic changes in this country's
thought." The war "has lately become so unpopular with many Americans that there are doubtless many who would condone his conduct."
Markus argued that Ali sincerely opposed the war, that "there may
have been some discrimination against Ali because he was who he was,"
and that the sentence was too severe. *Look* sports editor Leonard Shecter echoed these views and significantly added the observation that the
"Black Muslims are now considered . . . pussycats next to militant
blacks like the Panthers."[49]

A few right-wingers and die-hard patriots remained unreconciled. New
England newspaper chain publisher William Loeb refused to print ad-
vertisements and news accounts of the Frazier-Ali fight and the head
of the Veterans of Foreign Wars denounced the Supreme Court finding. But Ali's detractors at best mounted a futile rearguard resistance.
The cessation of the civil rights, youth, antiwar and antiestablishment
onslaught gradually mellowed Ali's image. Once though arrogant, he
was transmitted into an underdog hero matured and humanized by his
tribulations. Like Louis, he was now depicted as a model for youth,
fond of children, a loyal family man, and a philanthropist and became
the subject of several beatifical biographies. The new Ali persona
prompted novelist-critic Wilfrid Sheed to informally survey the champion's standing with taxi drivers, liquor store owners, and other members of the hoi polloi. The "squares love him now," said Sheed. "He
is, in some ways, their kind of nigger; self-reliant, keeps to his own
kind, and is harmlessly entertaining."[50]

Although his image was transformed, Ali had not completely changed.
He still demeaned his opponents and celebrated his beauty, skill, and
fame. Shortly before the 1974 bout with George Foreman, in which
Ali regained the crown, he said that "America has 40 million of my
people in slavery." At the 1968 Olympics, where several black sprinters refused to salute the American flag raised over the victory podium,
Foreman waved "Old Glory" and trumpeted his patriotism. "This Foreman," remarked Ali, "represents Christianity, America, the flag. I

can't let him win." During their fight Ali taunted Foreman. But these antics, now that Ali and the Muslims no longer loomed as an implacable foe, were looked upon as ruses to publicize his fights.[51]

The restoration of Ali was complete by 1974. The recrowned champion was the crowd favorite against Foreman and in subsequent bouts. Several of his title defenses were close fights but, as was the custom with incumbent champions, doubtful decisions went to Ali. Outside the ring Ali was accorded the full honors of a heavyweight titlist esteemed by the public and the establishment. In 1974 he visited President Gerald Ford at the White House and was designated "Sportsman of the Year" by *Sports Illustrated*. Two years later he campaigned for Jimmy Carter. In 1980 he went to Africa as a presidential good will ambassador, and the city of Philadelphia celebrated "Muhammad Ali Day." Regained popularity and changing times softened Ali's racial convictions and reawakened his youthful appreciation of America. In 1975 the champion noted that "there are good and bad regardless of color." Three years later, on a visit to Russia, he said: "I love my country. I think it is the best in the world. I don't want to live in any other country but America."[52]

After his epic contests with Foreman and Frazier, Ali descended into the twilight of his career. Now, more than ever, he was accorded the treatment of another noble champion, Joe Louis. The press noted that he continued to fight because he needed money for his children and charities. Reporters, friends, and associates begged the champion to stop fighting before he suffered defeat and irreparable physical and mental damage. Lance Morrow in *Time* described his loss of the title in February 1978 in terms reminiscent of the attitude toward Joe Louis at the end of his career: "In the last few rounds those watching felt a growing and almost unreasonable pathos. It was an emotional force . . . and accumulation of memories and meaning that are involved in the drama of great athletes aging and failing." Ali, however, defied yet one more adversary by regaining the title in September, thus becoming the only three-time heavyweight king. He retired in 1979, but restlessness and the need for adulation and money brought him back, in October 1980, for an unsuccessful attempt to regain the title.[53]

When he won the title and turned Muslim in 1964, Ali joined a select company of heavyweight champions, Sullivan, Dempsey, Johnson, and Louis, who transcended the ring to become mythic figures. After Ali assumed iconic status, inevitable comparisons were made with

Johnson and Louis. The three champions were supremely talented fighters who revived the fight game and became emblems of their respective eras. To white America, Johnson and Louis were polar opposites. The former was demonized as the stereotyped "bad nigger" who violated the caste system, the latter was deified by racial liberals and conservatives as the loyal, humble, patriotic Negro. Ali admired "Little Arthur" and denigrated the "Brown Bomber." Louis, the traditional ideal black athlete, reinforced his successor's contempt by attacking Ali's religious, racial, and political beliefs. Ali and Johnson, on the other hand, had marked similarities in style, personality, and image. Superb defensive boxers, quick with a punch or a quip and flamboyant egotists, neither conformed to the modest, controllable sports hero model. The traits of this traditional type of idol were also prescribed for blacks. White America expected humility and accommodation to established authority and values in athletes and Negroes. Louis was rewarded and glorified for fulfilling these expectations; Johnson and Ali endured rejection, deprivation, and punishment for transgressing racial and sports norms and thus threatening social order. But the beleagured champions lived in different eras, had different aspirations, differed in the nature of their defiance, and ultimately encountered different fates. Johnson responded to prejudice by breaching the color line. Ali reacted to bigotry by espousing racial separatism, thus emphasizing black authenticity. Louis, at least until World War II, also accepted segregation. But he submitted to exclusion as a social arrangement that made black inferiority a condition of racial harmony. Ali avoided this stigma by maintaining that blacks were superior to their Caucasian enemy. His embrace of segregation, therefore, constituted an attack on social convention that alarmed and enraged the white majority. Johnson wanted full participation in the American system, possibly at the expense of his racial identity. (After becoming champion he refused to meet black challengers.) Ali's route to manhood in the 1960s involved an assertion of negritude that meant rejection of American society. Unlike Johnson, he did not seek entry into the system; unlike Louis, he was not grateful for the rewards it gave him. Consequently, he epitomized the domestic and Third World insurgence against the American power structure. A symbol of rebellion in a decade of turmoil, Ali never won the plaudits showered on Louis, but he avoided the isolation of Johnson. White America almost universally condemned "Little Arthur," but the middle-class–led dissident movement rallied to Ali. "The athlete of the decade has to be Cassius Clay," wrote Cannon in 1970.

He is all that the Sixties were. It is as though he were created to represent them. In him is the trouble and the wildness and the hysterical gladness and the nonsense and the rebellion and the conflicts of race and the yearning for bizarre religions and the cult of the put-on and the changed values that altered the world and the feelings about Vietnam in the generation that ridicules what their parents cherish.

To a nation adrift in a wave of turbulence, Cannon's portrayal became Ali's image. Novelists Budd Schulberg and Norman Mailer, sportswriters Robert Lipsyte and Pete Axthelm, commentators in *Time* and *Newsweek*, and other analysts regarded him—in tribute or in trepidation—as a firebrand in the conflagration that swept over America in the 1960s and early 1970s.[54]

Johnson went down in history as the epitome of the "bad nigger"; Louis was revered as "a credit of his race" and the nation and a token of liberal tolerance. These images persisted through most of their careers, but Ali's mixed reception and the changing perceptions of the issues he represented made him a more volatile and complex celebrity. Once a popular young contender for the heavyweight crown, from 1964 to 1969 his standing plummeted, yet in the 1970s he regained public favor. Ali eventually became a positive "symbol," a "hero," a "Folk hero," "our favorite defender of the truth and resister of authority," the "prince of mass man and the media," a "World Social Force," the "mightiest victim of injustice in America," the "most famous man in the world," a "personification of the negro metamorphosis," a "giant," an "idol," a "martyr," the "most vital symbol of black resistance," and the "protagonist of a vast popular melodrama."[55]

In triumph or tribulation, in celebration or contempt, Ali was invested with white America's conflicts and contradictions. "For us white liberals he helps us assuage our guilt for having negative feelings about blacks," wrote Ali biographer Henry Korn. "For other whites, he may represent confirmation of their favorite notions about blacks: pushy, uppity, exploitative of others, radical, potent, even magical." Since white America burdened Ali with its anxieties and ambivalences, its opinions of the champion reflected its own confused self-assessments. Unable to comprehend itself, it could not understand Ali. Detractors and defenders of the champion ultimately concluded that he was "confusing," "contradictory," "at once a saint and a monster," an "enigma," "impenetrable," a "chameleon," a "man of many moods," a "strange, uncommon man," a "mix of con and conviction," a "paradox" of "clown, thinker," and "socio-political spokesman," a "troubled and searching man," "one of the most abundantly complicated figures in the history of games," and a "kaleidoscope."[56]

Johnson, Louis, and Ali, through their exploits in and out of the ring, forced whites to perceive or accept a new social role for blacks. Each boxer, therefore, compelled Caucasians to confront their feelings about blacks, thereby helping to precipitate crises or turning points in American race relations. Johnson's capture of the heavyweight title and his subsequent behavior presented demands for the elimination of the color line in everything from boxing to the bedroom. The white response to this crisis was exclusion and oppression. Race riots broke out, the champion was convicted of a felony, and the title was denied to blacks for another twenty years. Johnson did not permanently modify the balance of power between the races, but everyone—black or white—now realizes that the reassertion of the caste system in athletics depended upon segregation instead of genetic superiority. Since the heavyweight crown epitomized virility, Johnson's victories reverberated in the deepest recesses of white manhood. Louis' championship generated a crisis in race relations that was more agreeably and lastingly resolved. This crisis involved the adjustment of traditional prejudices in an era of limited but expanding tolerance and the securing of black allegiance to a racially repressive society threatened by a world war. Although he accommodated to the racial stereotype of the submissive Negro, Louis (partly as a result of this accommodation) became the first black national hero. This achievement represented a new role for blacks and a major concession by the dominant race. Most white Americans now altered their vision of their national identity to include Afro-Americans. Louis convinced whites that blacks could be virtuous as well as virtuoso athletes and, by extension, worthy citizens. By alleviating Caucasian anxieties regarding changes in race relations and black patriotism, Louis' example regularized black contention for the heavyweight crown. This accomplishment paved the way for a new kind of Afro-American titleholder who assumed a new role for blacks in this country and presented the nation with a new type of racial crisis. Ali dropped the accommodationist stance of previous black titleholders (his predecessor, Liston, was a partial exception to this convention) and forced America to deal with the rebellion of black pride against patronizing, self-indulgent liberal tolerance. When Ali's challenge to American society moved from racial matters to other issues he exposed our weaknesses and faults to ourselves and the world. The renegade champion accused America of being a failed utopia corrupted by injustices from which it had historically and hypocritically claimed immunity. He called our bluff by telling us that he (as did other blacks such as Malcolm X or Martin Luther King) would not accept us on our terms, but on his terms or perhaps not at all. The liberal consensus—which glorified Louis and cleared the consciences of many white Americans—and faith in American rectitude and supremacy ended in the furor over civil rights, Vietnam, and the structure and destiny of our society. An uneasy truce, unlike the overwhelming condemnation of Johnson or commendation of Louis that emerged from the crises of their eras, finally descended upon the battlefields of the 1960s and early 1970s. None of the principal combatants was completely victorious or vanquished and no universal consensus resolved the conflicts. Ali, prominent both as an object and a catalyst of this turbulence, reflected the ambivalence of the aftermath. He no longer leads the charge against the American establishment, but he had not become a grateful Negro; he shares neither the castigation of Johnson nor the canonization of Louis. Johnson, Louis, and Ali, bearing the fears and fantasies of white America, became half men and half myth. As demons or heroes they reflected forces at play in the national and international rather than in the boxing arenas. But they were more than passive representatives of their respective eras. The three champions were protagonists of the crises they symbolized and it is as creators as well as creatures of their times that they became historic figures who transcended their athletic attainments.

NOTES

1. John Larner, *White Hopes and Other Tigers* (Philadelphia: J. B. Lippincott, 1951), 21; *Chicago Tribune*, April 4, 1915, part 3, p. 1, April 6, 1915, p. 12.

2. Gunnar Myrdal, *Am American Dilemma*, 2 vols. (New York: McGraw-Hill, 1964), 1, 327–28, 402, 504, 11, 561; August Meier and Elliott M. Rudwick, *From Plantation to Ghetto* (New York: Hill and Wang, 1966), 157, 162–65, 167–71.

3. John A. Lucas and Ronald A. Smith, *Saga of American Sport* (Philadelphia: Lea & Febiger, 1978), 269–80.

4. Nat Fleischer, *Black Dynamite*, 8 vols. (New York: C. F. O'Brien, 1939), IV, 66–67; Finis Farr, *Black Champion—The Life and Times of Jack Johnson* (New York: Charles Scribner's Sons, 1964), 55–56; Jack London report of the fight for the *New York Herald*, December 27, 1908, reprinted in King Hendricks and Irving Shepard, eds., *Jack Johnson Reports* (Garden City, N.Y.: Doubleday, 1970), 258. For accounts of the Burns-Johnson bout see ibid., 261–63; *New York Times*, December 26, 1908, p. 8; Jack Johnson, *Jack Johnson in the Ring and Out* (Chicago: National Sports, 1927), 155, 165–67; Jim Corbett, *Chicago Tribune*, December 27, 1908, part 3, p. 1. For more moderate comments see Jack Johnson, *New York Herald*, December 27, 1908, reprinted in Hendricks and Shepard, eds., *Jack Johnson*, 259; *New York Times*, December 26, 1908, p. 8; Randolph Roberts, "Heavyweight Champion Jack Johnson: His Omaha Image, a Public Reaction Study," *Nebraska History*, 57 (Summer 1976), 231; Al-Tony Gilmore, *Bad Nigger! The National Impact of Jack Johnson* (Port Washington, N.Y.: Kennikat Press, 1975), 29–31.

5. Jack London, *New York Herald*, July 4, 1910, reprinted in Hendricks and Shepard, eds., *Jack London*, 293. For the press reaction see *Chicago Tribune*, July 1, 1910, part 1, p. 13, July 2, 1910, part 1, p. 11; Roberts, "Heavyweight," 233–34; Arthur Ruhl, "The Fight in the Desert," *Collier's*, 45 (July 23, 1910), 12–13; "The Psychology of the Prize Fight," *Current Literature*, 44 (July 1910), 57–58; Gilmore, *Bad Nigger*, 36–39; Farr, *Black Champion*, 76–77. For the opinions of clergymen see *Chicago Tribune*, July 4, 1910, part 1, p. 4; Gilmore, *Bad Nigger*, 36–37; Roberts, "Heavyweight," 233. William Jennings Bryan quoted in Robert H. deCoy, *The Big Black Fire* (Los Angeles: Holloway Press, 1969), 114. For the views of boxing experts and the betting odds see *New York Times*, July 2, 1910, p. 3, July 4, 1910, p. 14; *Chicago Tribune*, July 1, 1910, part 1, p. 13.; "Psychology," 57–58; Ruhl, "Fight," 22; London, *New York Herald*, July 4, 1910, reprinted in Hendricks and Shepard, eds., *Jack London*, 301; Fleischer, *Black Dynamite*, IV, 92.

6. *New York Times*, July 5, 1910, p. 12. For these features of the fight see ibid., pp. 3–4; *Chicago Tribune*, July 3, 1910, part 1, p. 1; London, *New York Herald*, July 4, 1910, reprinted in Hendricks and Shepard, eds., *Jack London*, 295; "Johnson Wins the Great Fight," *Harper's Weekly*, 54 (July 9, 1910), 8; Ruhl, "Fight," 22; "The Wonderful Refining Influence of the Prize Fight," *Current Literature* 49 (July 1910), 126–27; Fleischer, *Black Dynamite*, IV, 92; Nat Fleischer, *The Heavyweight Championship: An Informal History of Heavyweight Boxing from 1719 to the Present Day* (New York: G. P. Putnam's Sons, 1949), 150; Farr, *Black Champion*, 98–100; deCoy, *Big Black Fire*, 111–12; Box Lucas, *Black Gladiator: A Biography of Jack Johnson* (New York: Dell, 1970), 106–7; Gilmore, *Bad Nigger*, 39–41.

7. *New York Times*, July 5, 1910, part 1, pp. 1–4; *Chicago Tribune*, July 5, 1910, p. 1, "Wonderful," pp. 126–30, "Johnson Wins," pp. 7–8; London, *New York Herald*, July 4, 1910, reprinted in Hendricks and Shepard, eds., *Jack London*, 293–301; Ruhl, "Fight," 12, 22; Roberts, "Heavyweight," 235–37; Johnson, *Jack Johnson*, 62, 128, 171, 176–77, 185; Fleischer, *Black Dynamite*, IV, 92–102; Fleischer, *Heavyweight Championship*, 140–53; Denzil Batchelor, *Jack Johnson and His Times* (London: Phoenix, 1956), 77, 82–85; Lucas, *Black Gladiator*, 117; "Wonderful," pp. 126, 131; *Chicago Tribune*, July 5, 1910, part 1, p. 10; Theodore Roosevelt, "The Recent Prize Fight," *Outlook*, 95 (July 16, 1910), 51; Roberts, "Heavyweight," 235–37; Gilmore, *Bad Nigger*, 42–45, 68–69; Farr, *Black Champion*, 127; *New York Times*, July 5, 1910, p. 12.

8. Meier and Rudwick, *Plantation*, 157, 164, 167, 169–70; *New York Times*, July 5, 1910, pp. 1, 4; *New York Tribune*, July 5, 1910, pp. 1–2; *Chicago Tribune*, July 5, 1910, part 1, p. 1, "Wonderful," pp. 130–31.

9. Farr, *Black Champion*, 35–39, 132–33; Gilmore, *Bad Nigger*, 34–35, 75–83; Roosevelt, "Recent Prize Fight," 51; editorial in *Outlook*, 44 (July 16, 1910), 541–42; *New York Tribune*, July 6, 1910, p. 4.

10. For the debate on the bill see *Congressional Record*, 62d Cong., 2d session, XLVIII: Part VIII (June 15, 1912), 8234–36; Part IX (July 1, 1912), 885, (July 19, 1912), 9304–09. Representative Roddenberry's speech is on 9305.

11. London, *New York Herald*, July 4, 1910, reprinted in Hendricks and Shepard, eds., *Jack London*, 294–96; Rex Beach, *Chicago Tribune*, July 5, 1910, part 1, p. 1; John L. Sullivan, *New York Times*, July 5, 1910, p. 1. For favorable reports and editorials see *New York Times*, July 5, 1910, p. 12, July 6, 1910, p. 6; *New York Tribune*, July 5, 1910, p. 1; *Chicago Tribune*, July 5, 1910, part 1, p. 23, "Johnson Wins," p. 7; Fleischer, *Black Dynamite*, IV, 102; Johnson, *Jack Johnson*, 63–64.

12. *Chicago Tribune*, December 12, 1912, part 1, p. 3, June 5, 1913, part 1, p. 1; *Chicago Daily News*, November 19, 1912, p. 1; November 21, 1912, p. 3; Johnson, *Jack Johnson*, 68, 76–88; Gilmore, *Bad Nigger*, 95–121; Farr, *Black Champion*, 146–75; Lucas, *Black Gladiator*, 124–44.

13. National Opinion Research Center survey (1942) reprinted in Mildred A. Schwartz, *Trends in White Attitudes Toward Negroes*, NORC Report No. 119 (Chicago: University of Chicago Press, 1967), 83; NORC survey (1963) reprinted in Talcott Parsons and Kenneth B. Clark, eds., *The Negro American* (Boston: Beacon Press, 1967), 310; Gallup Poll (1972) reprinted in *The Gallup Poll: Public Opinion 1972–1977*, 2 vols. (Wilmington, Del., 1978), I, 72.

14. Farr, *Black Champion*, 168; ibid., 150–53, 157–58, 162–63, 166–67; Lucas, *Black Gladiator*, 125, 137–38, 144.

15. For the response in Chicago see *Chicago Daily News*, November 19, 1912, p. 1, November 21, 1912, p. 3; *Chicago Tribune*, December 20, 1912,

part 1, p. 3, December 21, part 1, 1912, p. 3; Johnson, *Jack Johnson*, 68, 81–88. For the national reaction see *Crisis*, 5 (December, 1912), 72; Roberts, "Heavyweight," 236–37; deCoy, *Big Black Fire*, 59–61; Farr, *Black Champion*, 152–59; Gilmore, *Bad Nigger*, 95–109, 119. For the introduction of anti-intermarriage legislation see Gilmore, *Bad Nigger*, 108–9; *Congressional Record*, 62d Cong., 3d session, XLIX, Part 1 (December 11, 1912), 502–3. For the statistics on lynching see Gilmore, *Bad Nigger*, 13.

16. Judge George Carpenter quoted in the *Chicago Tribune*, part 1, p. 1. Roddenbury quoted in *Congressional Record*, December 11, 1912, 502–3.

17. *Chicago Tribune*, April 5, 1915, part 3, p. 1. For another expression of satisfaction over Willard's victory see the *New York Times*, April 6, 1915, p. 10.

18. Johnson, *Jack Johnson*, 128–30, 245–47; Ed Van Every, "Louis' Rise Meteoric," *Ring*, 25 (August 1946), 26; Fleischer, *Black Dynamite*, IV, 107–8, 120.

19. H. C. Brearly, "Ba-ad Nigger," *South Atlantic Quarterly*, 38 (January 1939), 78–81; William H. Wiggins, Jr., "Jack Johnson as Bad Nigger: The Folklore of His Life," *Black Scholar*, 2 (January 1971), 35–41; Gilmore, *Bad Nigger*, 16–17, 153. For discussions and data on this view of race relations see Bruno Bettelheim and Morris Janowitz, *Social Change and Prejudice* (New York: The Free Press, 1964), 145–47; Thomas F. Pettigrew, "Complexity and Change in American Racial Patterns: A Social Psychological View," in Parsons and Clark, eds., *Negro American*, 326–48; Myrdal, *American Dilemma*, I, 97–107, 140, II, 957–68.

20. For political and economic advances of blacks see Myrdal, *American Dilemma*, I, 267–70, 327–29, 343–47, 354–61, 402–3, 503–4; Meier and Rudwick, *Plantation*, 211–14; William E. Leuchtenberg, *FDR and the New Deal: 1932–1940* (New York: Harper Torchbooks, 1963), 186–87, 192. For the improvement in "expert" opinion about blacks see Myrdal, *American Dilemma*, I, 90–93, 144–50; Richard Weiss, "Ethnicity and Reform: Minorities and the Ambience of the Depression Years," *Journal of American History*, 66 (December 1979), 566–85. For statistics on lynching see Myrdal, *Dilemma*, II, 561. *The Gallup Poll: Public Opinion 1935–1971*, 3 vols. (New York: Random House, 1972). The 1940 poll is reprinted in I, 209; the 1939 polls are in I, 142–61.

21. For black political and economic gains during World War II see Meier and Rudwick, *Plantation*, 218–19; Geoffrey Perrett, *Days of Sadness, Years of Triumph: The American People, 1939–1945* (Baltimore: Penguin Books, 1974), 151, 317–24. The Roper Center for Public Opinion Research poll (1939) and the NORC poll (1942) are reprinted in Schwartz, *Trends*, 19–20. See the wartime NORC polls reprinted in ibid, 19–20, 23, 54–55, and in Paul B. Sheatsley, "White Attitudes Toward the Negro," *Daedalus*, 95 (Winter 1966), 218, 222.

22. Lucas and Smith, *Saga*, 374–84.

23. Joe Louis with Edna Rust and Arthur Rust, Jr., *Joe Louis: My Life* (New York and London: Harcourt Brace Jovanovich, 1978), 35–39, 47, 67; Joe Louis, "My Story," *Life*, 25 (November 8, 1948), 142, 145–46; Alexander J. Young, Jr., "Joe Louis Symbol: 1933–1949" (Ph.D. dissertation, University of Maryland, 1968), 15–16; Gerald Astor, " . . . *And a Credit to His Race:*" *The Hard Life and Times of Joseph Louis Barrow, a.k.a. Joe Louis* (New York: Saturday Review Press/E. P. Dutton, 1974), 37, 42, 50, 59–60, 85–86, 134; Barney Nagler, *Brown Bomber* (New York: World Publishing, 1972), 42–43, 54–55; Anthony O. Edmonds, *Joe Louis* (Grand Rapids, Mich.: William B. Erdman, 1973), 29, 31–32; Margery Miller, *Joe Louis: American* (New York: Current Books, 1945), 33–35.

24. Mrs. Lillie Barrow Brooks quoted in Edmonds, *Joe Louis*, 35–36. For the Louis image also see ibid., 31–32, 35–37, 41, 55–56; Louis, "My Story," 146; Astor, *"And a Credit,"* 59–62, 86; Young, "Joe Louis Symbol," 18–24, 27–29; Nagler, *Brown Bomber*, 42–44, 54–55; Miller, *Joe Louis*, 35–36.

25. John Roxborough quoted in Edmonds, *Joe Louis*, 36.

26. Quentin Reynolds, "Dark Dynamite," *Collier's*, 95 (June 22, 1935), 16, 34, quote on 16; "Brown Bomber," *Literary Digest*, 119 (May 4, 1935), 35; Harry Balough quoted in Astor, *"And a Credit,"* 100. For the details of the Louis-Carnera fight and the reception of Louis' victory see Louis, *Joe Louis*, 50, 58; Young, "Joe Louis Symbol," 45; Edmonds, *Joe Louis*, 32–36, *New York Mirror* quote on p. 35.

27. Balough quoted in Jonathan Mitchell, "Joe Louis Never Smiles," *New Republic*, 84 (October 9, 1935), 239. For details of the Louis-Baer fight see Young, "Joe Louis," 41; Astor, *"And a Credit,"* 118; Nagler, *Brown Bomber*, 61; Louis, "My Story," 145; Louis, *Joe Louis*, 82; Young, "Joe Louis Symbol," 42; Governor Frank D. Fitzgerald quoted in Astor, *"And a Credit,"* 111; "Dusky Meteor," *Literary Digest*, 121 (June 13, 1936), 36. For pro-Louis commentary see Frank Scully, "Young Black Joe," *Esquire*, 4 (October 1935), 34; Mitchell, "Joe Louis Never Smiles," 239–40; "Dusky Meteor," 26; Ed. W. Smith, "The Value of a Swagger," *Ring*, 15 (May 1936), 46; Ed. W. Smith, "Louis Better Than Johnson," ibid. (March 1936), 10.

28. Louis, *Joe Louis*, 73, 91; Louis, "My Story," 145; Edmonds, *Joe Louis*, 45–46, 50, 91–92, 112; Young, "Joe Louis Symbol," 108, 124–25; Astor, *"And a Credit,"* 11, 33–34, 105–6. For the characterizations of Louis as an animal and cold-blooded see Jack Trucott in the *New York Herald Tribune*, quoted in Astor, *"And a Credit,"* 120; sportswriters quoted in Edmonds, *Joe Louis*, 41–42, 50, 52; Max Schmeling as told to Paul Gallico, "The Way I Beat Joe Louis," *Saturday Evening Post*, 209 (September 5, 1936), 10; Ed W. Smith, "Picking 'Em Apart," *Ring*, 15 (June 1936), 2–3, criticized Dempsey for drawing the color line, Max Baer for belittling Louis and making other unfavorable and racist comments about the young boxer. For details of

the fight and the pro-Schmeling sentiments see Nat Fleischer, ''The Fall of the Mighty,'' *Ring*, 15 (August 1936), 2; James T. Farrell, ''The Fall of Joe Louis,'' *Nation*, 142 (June 24, 1936), 834–35; Astor, *''And a Credit,''* 139; Dempsey quoted on 138. For the comments of Gallico and *Time* see Schmeling and Gallico, ''Way,'' 34; *Time*, 27 (June 19, 1936), 35–36.

29. James Braddock and Jim Jeffries quoted in Edmonds, *Joe Louis*, 89. For another attack on the ''white hope'' campaign see Daniel M. Daniel, ''White Hope Campaign Leaves Us with Max,'' *Ring*, 16 (May 1937), 3.

30. Louis, *Joe Louis*, 137–40; *New York Times*, June 22, 1938, p. 28; Nagler, *Brown Bomber*, 93–98; Astor, *''And a Credit,''* 166–81; Edmonds, *Joe Louis*, 77–93; Young, ''Joe Louis Symbol,'' 126–29. Franklin D. Roosevelt quoted in Louis, ''My Story,'' *Life*, 25 (November 15, 1948), 1, 133. For Tunney's role see Ted Carroll, ''A Great Champion Arrives,'' *Ring*, 17 (September 1938), 81.

31. Governor Frank Murphy quoted in the *New York Times*, June 23, 1938, p. 14; Carroll, ''Great Champion,'' 18. For similar views see Daniel M. Daniel, ''Schmeling's Squawk Makes Kidney Famous,'' *Ring*, 18 (September 1939), 14; Young, ''Joe Louis Symbol,'' 143; Edmonds, *Joe Louis*, 79–83.

32. The 1947 Gallup Poll is in ''America's Ten Favorite People,'' *Look*, 11 (June 24, 1947), 58. For other examples of the reverence given Louis during these years see Louis, ''My Story,'' *Life* (November 8, 1948), 136, 140; Louis, *Joe Louis*, 171–72, 189–90; Nat Fleischer, ''Max Fouled, Bunk,'' *Ring*, 17 (September 1938), 4: Lester Bromberg, ''Joe Louis Deplores Lack of Schooling,'' *Ring* 17 (August 1938), 12–13, 135, *Ring*, 21 (March 1942), 16; *Ring* 21 (April 1942), 16; Miller, *Joe Louis: American*, 35, 136–37; Joe Louis and Gene Kessler, ''I Hate to Hurt Anybody,'' *Look*, 4 (May 7, 1940), 50; Caswell Adams, ''Introducing the New Joe Louis,'' *Saturday Evening Post*, 214 (May 10, 1941), 26, 106, 108; Earl Brown, ''Joe Louis, The Champion, Idol of His Race Sets a Good Example of Conduct,'' *Life*, 8 (June 17, 1940), 49–55; Arthur Daley, ''Ten Years a Champion,'' *New York Times*, June 26, 1947, reprinted in Arthur Daley, *Sports of the Times* (New York: E. P. Dutton, 1959), 129–31; John G. Van Deusen, *Brown Bomber: The Story of Joe Louis* (Philadelphia: Dorrance, 1944); Jack Sher, ''Brown Bomber: The Saga of Joe Louis,'' in Ernest V. Heyn, ed., *Twelve Sports Immortals* (New York: Bartholomew House, 1949), 272; Nagler, *Brown Bomber*, 123, 126; Young, ''Joe Louis Symbol,'' 50–53, 58–60, 62, 108, 112, 114–16, 145–57; Astor, *''And a Credit,''* 210, 224–25; Edmonds, *Joe Louis*, 74, 85–86; Paul Gallico, ''Citizen Barrow,'' *Reader's Digest*, 40 (June 1942), 21–25; ''Black Moses,'' *Time*, 38 (September 29, 1941), 60–64; Van Deusen, *Brown Bomber*, 3.

33. For sentiments and details regarding Louis after the late 1940s see ''The Greatest Is Gone,'' *Time*, 103 (February 28, 1978), 79; Robert Lipsyte, *Sports World: An American Dreamland* (New York: Quadrangle/New York Times, 1975), 75; Jimmy Cannon, *''Nobody Asked Me, But''* . . . *The World of Jimmy*

Cannon (New York: Holt Rinehart and Winston, 1978), 115; Louis, *Joe Louis*, 125, 220, 230, 347, 252, 254, 259–60; Sher, "Brown Bomber," 265–66; Astor, *"And a Credit,"* 264–301; Nagler, *Brown Bomber*, passim; Edmonds, *Joe Louis*, 102–4, 106.

34. Paul Gallico, *Farewell to Sport* (Freeport, N.Y.: Books for Libraries, 1970), 307–8.

35. NORC surveys reprinted in Schwartz, *Trends*, 19–20, 23, 54–55, 73–74, 78–79, 83. For similar results of Gallup Polls on these issues see *Gallup Poll 1935–1971*: I, 528, II, 783, 1405, III, 1824, 1863, 1940–41, 2010, 2211; *Gallup Poll 1972–1977*, I, 179, 567.

36. Muhammad Ali quoted in "The Dream," *Time*, 81 (March 22, 1963), 79; Dick Schaap, "The Happiest Heavyweight," *Saturday Evening Post*, 234 (March 25, 1961), 36, 100–102, Ali quoted on 100–101; Huston Horn, "Who Made Me—Is Me," *Sports Illustrated*, 15 (September 25, 1961), 39; Huston Horn, "Cautious Comes of Age," ibid. (October 16, 1961), 25; A. J. Liebling, "Poet and Pedagogue," *New Yorker*, 38 (March 3, 1962), 108; Myron Cope, "Feats of Clay," originally published in 1962 and reprinted in Irving T. Marsh and Edward Ehre, eds., *Best of the Best Sports Stories* (New York: E. P. Dutton, 1964), 433; Howard Tuckner, " 'Man, It's Great to Be Great,' " *New York Times Magazine*, December 9, 1962, 47–48; "Dream," 79–80; Tom Wolfe, "The Marvelous Mouth," *Esquire*, 60 (October 1963), 190, 195–96; mayor of Louisville quoted in Jack Olsen, *Black Is Best: The Riddle of Cassius Clay* (New York: G. P. Putnam's Sons, 1967), 86.

37. "Dream," 79–81; Tuckner, " 'Man,' " 47; Cope, "Feats," 429–31; "Louisville Lip," *Time*, 80 (November 23, 1962), 38; Wolfe, "Marvelous," 146, 189–92, 195; Huston Horn, "A Rueful Dream Come True," *Sports Illustrated*, 19 (November 11, 1963), 26–27; John Cottrell, *Man of Destiny: The Story of Muhammad Ali, Formerly Cassius Clay* (London: Frederick Muller, 1967), 61, 85, 92, 99–100.

38. A. S. Young, *Sonny Liston, The Champ Nobody Wanted* (Chicago: Johnson Publishing, 1963), 55–56, 79–86, 92–95, 100–102, 107, 109, 135, 162; Jack Newcombe, *Floyd Patterson: Heavyweight King* (New York: Sport Magazine Library, 1961); Lipsyte, *Sports World*, 84; Cottrell, *Man of Destiny*, 66–73, 146–51. For the pro-Ali sentiment in the title fight see *New York Times*, February 27, 1964, p. 27, February 27, 1964, p. 334; Daley, "Another Surprise," ibid., February 26, 1964, p. 27; Robert Lipsyte, "Cassius Clay, Cassius X, Muhammad Ali," *New York Times Magazine*, October 25, 1967, p. 29.

39. *New York Times*, February 27, 1964, p. 34, February 28, 1964, p. 22. Ali quoted in Lipsyte, *Sports World*, 92. For the negative reaction to Clay's announcement of Black Muslim membership and the Ali-Liston bout see *New York Times*, February 27, 1964, p. 34, February 28, 1964, p. 22; Tex Maule, "Yes, It Was Good and Honest," *Sports Illustrated*, 20 (March 9, 1964), 20,

23–24; Murray Kempton, "I Whipped Him and I'm Still Pretty," *New Republic*, 150 (March 7, 1964), 9; George Plimpton, "Miami Notebook: Cassius Clay and Malcolm X," *Harper's*, 22 (June 1964), 54; Lipsyte, "Cassius," 143; Lipsyte, *Sports World*, 87; "Bull v. Butterfly: A Clash of Champions," *Time*, 97 (March 8, 1971), 68; Muhammad Ali with Richard Durham, *The Greatest: My Own Story* (New York: Random House, 1975), 40–41. William F. Buckley quoted in Olsen, *Black is Best*, 52; Senator Kenneth Keating's view in Cottrell, *Man of Destiny*, 154; Edward Lassman quoted in ibid., 180–81, and Jose Torres, *Sting Like a Bee: The Muhammad Ali Story* (New York: Abelard-Schuman, 1971), 128. For the sentiments of Breslin, Cannon, Dempsey, Louis, and Patterson and other examples of disapproval see Olsen, *Black is Best*, 185; Ali, *Greatest*, 203; Torres, *Sting*, 137–38; Don Atyeo and Felix Dennis, *The Holy Warrior: Muhammad Ali* (New York: Fireside Books, 1975), 57; Cottrell, *Man of Destiny*, 154, 177–78, 183.

40. Kempton, "Whipped," 9; Jim Murray, "The Drubbing," *Sports Illustrated*, 22 (June 7, 1965), 53. For the pro-Liston fight crowd, the quotes from Tunney and the WBA legal counsel, the charges of state and federal legislators, and Dempsey's recommendation see *New York Times*, May 26, 1965, p. 54, May 27, 1965, pp. 1, 42; Murray, "Drubbing," 53; Tex Maule, "A Quick Hard Right and a Needless Storm of Protest," *Sports Illustrated*, 22 (June 7, 1965), 23; Howard Cosell, *Cosell* (Chicago: Playboy Press, 1973), 181–82; Lipsyte, *Sports World*, 93; Pete Axthelm, "The Return of an Exiled Champ," *Newsweek*, 76 (November 9, 1970), 60.

41. For Patterson's attitude toward the fight see Floyd Patterson, "Cassius Clay Must Be Beaten," *Sports Illustrated*, 34 (October 11, 1965), 80, 98. For further commentary on Patterson's role, Ali's response, and the champion's tactics in this fight see Rogin; "Rabbit Hunt in Vegas," ibid. (November 29, 1964), 22, 24; "Not a Great Fight, But It Was a Real One," ibid. (December 9, 1965), 45, 108; Lipsyte, *Sports World*, 108–10; " 'I Don't Have to Be What You Want Me to Be,' Says Muhammad Ali," *New York Times Magazine*, March 7, 1971, p. 57; " 'I'm Free to Be Who I Want,' " ibid., May 28, 1967, pp. 50, 52; Cosell, *Cosell*, 182–83; Torres, *Sting*, 143; Ali, *Greatest*, 132, 217–19; Cottrell, *Man of Destiny*, 232, 239, 243, 270; Atyeo and Dennis, *Holy Warrior*, 61. Louis quoted in Atyeo and Dennis, *Holy Warrior*, 62; Cosell, *Cosell*, 182; the other quotes are in Ali, *Greatest*, 133–34.

42. "Theater of Cruelty," *Newsweek*, 69 (February 20, 1967), 87; Cosell, *Cosell*, 197; Ali, *Greatest*, 164–65; Lipsyte, *Sports World*, 120; Lipsyte, " 'I'm Free,' " 52; Cottrell, *Man of Destiny*, 309–17; "Gee, Gee," *Time*, 80 (February 10, 1967), 100.

43. The Ali quotes and statement regarding conscientious objector status are all in Ali, *Greatest*, 124–25, 160, and Cottrell, *Man of Destiny*, 335. For the uproar over his stand on the war and the draft see Ali, *Greatest*, 124–25, 128, 144, 150–53, 160, Dempsey and Tunney are quoted on 143; Lipsyte, " 'I

Don't,' " 57; Lipsyte, " 'I'm Free,' " 57; Torres, *Sting*, 148–50; Cottrell, *Man of Destiny*, 178–80, 253–54; Olsen, *Black is Best*, 332–37; "Government's Round," *Newsweek*, 70 (July 3, 1967), 24; Gordon Parks, "The Redemption of the Champion," *Life*, 61 (September 9, 1966), 79.

44. *New York Times*, April 29, 1967, p. 1, June 21, 1967, pp. 1–2; *Chicago Tribune*, April 29, 1967, section 2, pp. 1, 4, April 20, 1967, section 2, p. 6, June 21, 1967, section 1, p. 1, section 3, p. 2; Edwin Shrake, "Taps for the Champ," *Sports Illustrated*, 26 (May 8, 1967), 19–24; "Into the Fiery Furnace," *Newsweek*, 69 (May 8, 1967), 72; "Government's Round," 29; Axthelm, "Return," 56, 59; Lipsyte, " 'I Don't,' " 62; Lipsyte, " 'I'm Free,' " 28; "Gaseous Cassius," *Time*, 89 (May 5, 1967), 24; "The Draft," ibid. (June 20, 1967), 20, Ali, *Greatest*, 75, 172–74, 227–39.

45. Ali, *Greatest*, 75, 138–39, 175–76, 251, Ronald Reagan quoted on 136; Cottrell, *Man of Destiny*; Shrake, "Taps," 22; "Gaseous," 23–25; "The Draft," 20–21; *New York Times*, April 29, 1967, p. 34; "The Dissenting Champion," *National Review*, 19 (May 16, 1967), 504, 506; *Chicago Tribune*, June 22, 1967, section 1, p. 20.

46. Lipsyte, " 'I'm Free,' " 57, 60; " 'I Don't,' " 62, 67; "Cassius Clay," 29, 140–41, 143; Lipsyte, *Sports World*, 195; Cosell, *Cosell* 176–77, 184, 203, 205–7, 219; Leonard Shecter, "The Passion of Muhammad Ali," *Esquire*, 69 (April 1968), 131, 140, 156, 158; Mark Kram, "After Muhammad, A Graveyard," *Sports Illustrated*, 26 (April 3, 1967), 29; Tex Maule, "For Ali, A Time to Preach," ibid., 28 (February 19, 1968); James L. Kidd, " 'Yes Sir, Mr. Ali'—The Tale of a Talk," *Christian Century*, 85 (October 30, 1968), 1384–85; Joseph Morgenstern, "Knock Down, Put On," *Newsweek*, 74 (December 8, 1969), 124; "Government's Round," 24, 29; Pete Hamill, "Muhammad Ali: This Is About Me," *Life*, 65 (October 25, 1968), 66B. For the list of luminaries supporting Ali see Irwin Shaw, "Muhammad Ali and the Little People," *Esquire*, 70 (November 1969), 124–25; Ali, *Greatest*, 136; "The Draft, Protest, Debate, Renewal," *Newsweek*, 69 (May 22, 1967), 25; Torres, *Sting*, 167.

47. Ali, *Greatest*, 304, 310, 312, 316–17; Cosell, *Cosell*, 287; Lipsyte, *Sports World*, 195; Torres, *Sting* 19, 162–63; Axthelm, "Return," 62; Gene Ward quoted in Ali, *Greatest*, 312. *New York Times*, October 27, 1970, p. 56; Lipsyte, *Sports World*, 195.

48. "Bull," 63, 66; Madison Square Press Box Kit quoted in Lipsyte, *Sports World*, 197; Pete Axthelm, "More Than a Fight, A Crunch of Values," *Vogue*, 157 (March 1, 1971), 115; Jerry Perenchio quoted in "Take the Money and Run," *Newsweek*, 77 (March 8, 1971), 74; Arthur Daley, "The Fight," *New York Times*, March 7, 1971, section 5, p. 2; "Bull," 63, 69. For other examples of pro-Ali feeling and the perception of the Ali-Frazier fight as a clash between symbols of the establishment and its attackers see Lipsyte, " 'I Don't,' " 67; "Bull," 66; Mark Kram, "At the Bell," *Sports Illustrated*, 34

(March 8, 1971), 20–21; Norman Mailer, *"King of the Hill"* (New York: New American Library, 1971), 67; Budd Schulberg, *Loser and Still Champion: Muhammad Ali* (Garden City, N.Y.: Doubleday, 1972), 98, 102, 109–10; "Now There Is One Champion," *Newsweek*, 77 (March 22, 1971), 72.

49. *New York Times*, June 29, 1971, section 1, p. 1; *Chicago Tribune*, June 29, 1971, section 1, p. 1; "Decision for Allah," *Newsweek*, 28 (March 12, 1971), 61; "Winner If Not Champion," *Time*, 98 (July 12, 1971), 53; Cannon, *"Nobody Asked Me,"* 155–57; "Winner," 53; "Decision," 62; Robert Markus, *Chicago Tribune*, June 20, 1971, section 3, p. 3; Leonard Shecter, "The Fall and Rise of Muhammad Ali," *Look*, 335 (March 9, 1971), 62, 65.

50. *New York Times*, March 9, 1971, p. 30, June 29, 1971, p. 1. Kram, "At the Bell," 21; Tex Maule's articles in *Sports Illustrated*: "He Has Heavy Things on His Mind," 35 (July 26, 1971), 24–26, "End of a Beautiful Friendship!" (August 23, 1971), 11, "Got to Be Like Allah," (November 29, 1971), 28–29; Axthelm, "More Than a Fight," 115; "Now," 75D, Lipsyte, *Sports World*, 244, 255–56; Dick Schaap, "Muhammad Ali, Then and Now," *The Best of SPORT: 1946–1971*, ed. Al Silverman (New York: Viking Press, 1971), 605–15; Mailer, *"King"* 57, 74; Maurice R. Berube, "The Defeat of the Great Black Hope," *Commonweal*, 55 (March 26, 1971), 55; Carey McWilliams, "Muhammad Ali for Congress," *Nation*, 227 (July 22, 1978), 60–70. For worshipful biographies see Schulberg, *Loser*; Henry James Korn, *Muhammad Ali Retrospective* (New York: Wild & Wolley, Sydney Assembling Press, 1974); Atyeo and Dennis, *Holy Warrior*; Wilfird Sheed, "Ali," *Esquire*, 84 (October 1975), 113, 218.

51. "Muhammad on the Mountaintop," *Time*, 104 (November 11, 1974) 84; "Ali—You Gotta Believe," *Newsweek*, 84 (November 11, 1974), 70–71; Ali quoted in Will Grimsley, "Muhammad Ali: Athlete, Folk Hero, World Social Force," *Best American Sports Stories, 1975*, ed. Irving T. Marsh and Edward Ehre (New York: E. P. Dutton, 1975, 166; Ali Quoted in Atyeo and Dennis, *Holy Warrior*, 103.

52. Red Smith, "Funny Thing Happened in Zaire," *New York Times* (October 30, 1974), p. 53; Pete Axthelm, "Mirror, Mirror on the Wall," *Newsweek*, 88 (October 11, 1976), 82–83; Roger Kahn, "Doing It Just One More Time," *Time*, 108 (October 11, 1976), 74; D. Keith Mano, "Muhammad Ali," *National Review*, 28 (November 26, 1976), 1292; Benjamin DeMott, "Real Name: Champ," *Atlantic*, 238 (December 1976), 109–10; A. B. Giamatti, "Hyperbole's Child," *Harper's*, 235 (December 1977), 117; Phil Berger, "Ali's Made-for-TV Challenger," *New York Times*, January 29, 1978, p. 30; Ali, *Greatest*, 140; George Plimpton, "Return of the Big Bopper," *Sports Illustrated*, 41 (December 23, 1974), 98; *New York Times*, July 2, 1980, section A, p. 22, August 23, 1980, section 1, p. 3. The Ali quotes are in Lipsyte, *Sports World*, 257; McWilliams, "Muhammad Ali for Congress," 69.

53. Pete Axthelm and Peter Bonventure, "Ali: Born Again," *Newsweek*,

92 (September 25, 1978), 770; Kahn, "Doing It," 75; Lance Morrow, "To an Athlete Getting Old," *Time*, 111 (February 22, 1978), 86.

54. For comparisons between Ali, Louis, and Johnson see Shrake, "Taps," 22; Cottrell, *Man of Destiny*, 112–13, 317; Shecter, "Fall and Rise," 62; Hamill, "Muhammad Ali," 66B; Lipsyte, " 'I Don't,' " 54, 56; Jack Richardson, "Ali on Peachtree," *Harper's*, 242 (January 1971), 47; Axthelm, "Return," 59; Schulberg, *Loser*, 18, 48; Korn *Retrospective*, 44; Jervis Anderson, "Black Heavies," *American Scholar*, 47 (Summer 1978), 289–90; Ali, *Greatest*, 114. For Ali's comments on Johnson and Louis see Ali, *Greatest*, 321; Hamill, "Muhammad Ali," 66B, 68; Shrake, "Taps," 22; Cosell, *Cosell*, 203; Atyeo and Dennis, *Holy Warrior*, 57; Shecter, "Fall and Rise," 62. For Louis' attitude toward Ali see Ali, *Greatest*, 185; Lipsyte, " 'I Don't,' " 54; Martin Kane, "The Greatest Meets the Grimmest," *Sports Illustrated*, 23 (November 15, 1965), 36; Lipsyte, *Sports World*, 75; Atyeo and Dennis, *Holy Warriors*, 57; Cannon, *"Nobody Asked Me,"* 149; Schulberg, *Loser*, 32, 35, 48–50, 68–69, 102, 127–28; Mailer, *"King,"* 74; Lipsyte, " 'I Don't,' " 67; Axthelm, "More," 115; Axthelm, "Return," 56, 59; "Now," 72; "Bull," 66; Korn, *Retrospective*, 41–42; "Greatest Is Gone," 72, 74; Giametti, "Hyperbole," 122; Richardson, "Ali," 47; Berube, "Defeat," 55; Morrow, "To an Athlete," 86; Kram, "At the Bell," 20–21; Grimsley, "Muhammad Ali," 164–65.

55. Berube, "Defeat," 55; Richardson, "Ali," 47; Mailer, *"King,"* 11, 57; Schulberg, *Loser*, 32, 49, 128; "Now," 71; Grimsley, "Muhammad Ali," 164–65; "Ali—You Gotta Believe," 70; "Greatest Is Gone," 72; Morrow, "To an Athlete," 86; Korn, *Muhammad*, 41–42.

56. Korn, *Retrospective*, 41; Grimsley, "Muhammad Ali," 164; Mailer, *"King,"* 75; Schulberg, *Loser*, 138, "Greatest Is Gone," 72; Morrow, "To an Athlete," 86; Rogin, "Champion," 24; Sheed, "Ali," 113; "Bull," 66; Cosell, *Cosell*, 173–74, 187; Lipsyte, "Cassius," 29; Olsen, *Black*, 128; Atyeo and Dennis, *Holy Warrior*, 7.

VIII

Women and Sport

Stephanie L. Twin

In 1970, WHEN THE STUDY OF SEX ROLES was accelerating, a
member of the Association for Humanistic Psychology challenged her
newsletter's male readers to imagine life in a female-dominated society. Language would be feminine; *woman* and *she* would refer to human beings of both sexes. Women would be the political and economic powerbrokers, and men would naturally fulfill themselves as
husbands and fathers—"naturally" for the obvious biological reason
of men's physical and emotional passivity. "By design," the writer
explained,

> female genitals are compact and internal, protected by her body. Male genitals
> are so exposed that he must be protected from outside attack to assure the per-
> petuation of the race. His vulnerability obviously requires sheltering . . . [A
> boy] remembers his sister's jeering at his primitive genitals that "flap around
> foolishly." She can run, climb and ride horseback unencumbered. Obviously,
> since she is free to move, she is encouraged to develop her body and mind in
> preparation for her active responsibilities of adult womanhood. The male vul-
> nerability needs female protection, so he is taught the less active, caring vir-
> tues of homemaking.[1]

This particular rendering of "anatomy is destiny" may strike us as
ridiculous, certainly laughable, because it reverses the actual conceptions of the body with which each sex is raised. Yet it is no more ri-

diculous than those "real" conceptions. Girls learn from a young age that their bodies restrict their range of behavior. The way sports are encouraged and organized for boys is perhaps the most impressionable way girls observe that males are to be active while females are not. Psychological theories, custom, and popular prejudice combine to measure women negatively against men. The fact that females generally grow to be shorter, lighter, and less muscular than males is exaggerated to mean that femininity equals weakness, softness, and inertia. Athletic women are thus seen as masculine. In 1912, Harvard's famous Dr. Dudley Allen Sargent went so far as to suggest that women who excelled at competitive sports might have inherited masculine characteristics. A contemporary variation is that muscular, first-rate female athletes take male hormones (steroids). The implication, both in 1912 and today, is that true females are physically limited.[2]

This perception of the female form goes back centuries. Despite speculation about matriarchal (female-dominated) cultures and the existence in mythology of female hunting, fertility, and athletic goddesses, in most known cultures physical contests have been primarily for men. In numerous societies, male economic activities evolved into sports—as with hunting, fishing, riflery, and archery—but female ones did not.

Beyond sport's relation to men's work, however, many cultures have linked athletics with male physical energy in an almost mystical bond. The classical world's conviction that vitality was exclusively masculine is found in Aristotle's theory of human conception. The fetus was a mixture of semen and menstrual liquid, he believed, and the semen was actually purified blood and the active, critical "germinating fluid." In the formation of life, man was to woman what the carpenter was to a block of wood: the creative shaper of a passive substance. Indeed, the word *semen*, meaning seed, reflects this view, as does the adjective *seminal*, meaning germinative or original.

If men biologically monopolized vitality, then excluding females from the Greek Olympics was logical. Women were permitted neither to watch nor to participate in the ancient games which, along with literature and music competitions, formed a religious festival dedicated to Zeus. The winners emerged as political and religious heroes. They were honored with civil privileges and titles and, in Athens, supported for life at public expense. One writer noted that a "beautiful and good woman for wife" was often promised as a reward for winning the running high jump.

"History does not relate," she sardonically added, "whether or not the Spartan girls were awarded a 'beautiful and good man for husband' in their competitions."[3]

The women of the Greek city-state Sparta were only partial exceptions to the classical world's faith in male physical energy. They were trained from girlhood in running, jumping, wrestling, and javelin and discus throwing to enhance their future role as breeders. Their sports were designed to build the health and emotional stamina needed to bear great warriors for the state; their athletics held no wider political or religious significance. Most Grecian women were denied even this minimal justification for sports. Thought weak and timid, they were assigned to indoor, domestic tasks, the more difficult of which fell to slave women. "The oddity" of the Greek woman's life was striking, the classicist Emily James Putnam remarked in 1911. "She lived in the house among a people that lived out of doors. . . . Among a people who gave great importance to physical training she was advised to take her exercise in bedmaking." Plato referred to females as "a race that are used to living out of the sunlight."[4]

Sparta remains one of the few patriarchal (male-dominated) states to have associated birthgiving with female physical strength. In most cultures, the belief in female passivity and bodily inferiority—or the ideal of feminine fragility—has existed alongside the physically strenuous reality of childbirth. Modern estimates are that the uterus exerts the equivalent of 100 pounds of pressure in expelling a full-term fetus. The paradox of actual biological and physical strength interpreted as feminine weakness casts an ironic perspective on the past, as one historian has noted. In his study of early seventeenth-century France, David Hunt described childbirth as that period's most demanding physical activity:

Ironically, in a society which put such a high premium on bravery and endurance, and in which masculine prerogatives were so aggressivly formulated, childbearing was probably the single experience which made the heaviest demands on the courage and fortitude of the participant. For all their vainglorious pretentions, men were obliged to watch helplessly from the sidelines as women faced this ultimate trial.

This paradox suggests that traditional notions of female limitations have seriously underestimated women's actual physical experience and capacity.[5]

Though long-held, the belief in feminine physical frailty reached its peak, perhaps, in nineteenth-century America. It became a self-fulfilling prophecy for numbers of middle-class women. The "woman on the pedestal," whose strengths were moral and emotional and non-physical—indeed antiphysical—emerged as the ideal by the 1830s. Popular and scientific opinion alike upheld physical inertia as both natural and desirable for women. Physicians warned that too much activity unnerved females, creating everything from hysteria to dyspepsia. Since the uterus, they thought, was connected to the nervous system, nervous shocks induced by overexertion threatened reproduction and might lead to "weak and degenerate offspring." Women were to conserve the little energy that they had. By 1850, these notions had crystallized into a cult of ill health in which women proved their feminity with invalidism.[6]

A logical extension of this perception of females as weak was a belief in girls' and women's recreational passivity. Furthermore, sports were believed irrelevant to girls' future roles. Ball playing was encouraged among boys because it tested speed, strength, skill, and agility but discouraged among girls, who were thought to need none of those qualities. Girls might occasionally toss a ball or, for health's sake, go "bathing." Horseback riding was permitted as transportation; the gentry considered it appropriate recreation for both sexes. Young women sometimes rolled hoops or ice skated, but an historian has related how, during the 1850s skating revival, at least one woman was urged to hold her partner's coattails so as to have fun without "incurring any of the fatigue of the exercise."[7]

Though articulated for all women, this standard of delicacy pertained in reality to a minority. As Barbara Ehrenreich and Deirdre English have explained in *Complaints and Disorders: The Sexual Politics of Sickness* (1973), "For the affluent women, society prescribed lives of leisured indolence; for the working class women, back-breaking toil." On farms, where most Americans lived, women worked long, hard hours. In mills, factories, and private homes farmers' daughters and immigrant women labored as industrial workers and domestic servants. Slave women provided the most flagrant disproof of supposed female debility, as the freed slave Sojourner Truth reminded a women's rights audience in 1851:

The man over there says women need to be helped into carriages and lifted over ditches, and to have the best place everywhere. Nobody ever helps me into carriages or over puddles, or gives me the best place—and ain't I a woman? Look at my arm! I have ploughed and planted and gathered into barns, and no man could head me—and ain't I a woman? I could work as much and eat as much as a man—when I could get it—and bear the lash as well! And ain't I a woman?[8]

While she roused her listeners to a standing ovation, not all Americans would have agreed that she was, indeed, a woman. That is, they would have concurred in her being anatomically female, but not feminine. Lacking femininity, she was not really a woman: genuine women were physically weak. Thus working women, who were the majority, used their bodies at the price of their sexual identity—at least the identity determined by orthodox opinion. Athletic women in the twentieth century have suffered the same penalty.

In a 1901 *Harper's Bazar* Dr. Grace Peckham Murray analyzed women's dilemma in this way:

Women were strong enough for the drudgery of life—men never disputed that—but when it came to entering fields of labor which yielded the crops of dignity and remuneration, women who were pioneers received great reprobation and were accused of unsexing themselves.

In other words, women were permitted to do certain kinds of hard physical labor—someone had to. But if women demanded recognition or payment for their labor, took pride in their physical ability, or tried new kinds of work, they were chided for defying nature and social norms.[9]

This attitude hindered pioneer educators' and health reformers' attempts to strengthen women physically. Until the late 1800s, even the mildest female exercise regimens won little public approval. The earliest known experimenter with female gymnastic instruction was William Bentley Fowle, who in 1826 vainly searched for precedents:

You know the prevailing notions of female delicacy and propriety are at variance with every attempt to render females less feeble and helpless. . . . I read all the books I could find, but met with very little applicable to the instruction of females. It seemed as if the sex had been thought unworthy of an effort to improve their physical powers.

Some female seminaries and colleges required housework as a form of exercise. Reformers such as Catherine Beecher, Dio Lewis, and Dr.

Dudley Allen Sargent devised calisthenic and dumbbell routines which, despite denials, were hardly different from or more invigorating than dance quadrilles.[10]

In stark contrast, males were regarded as repositories of energy. One historian has found that "energy was one of the most frequent and most characteristic terms associated with male activity" in the middle third of the nineteenth century. As in the ancient world, men's physical vitality was traced to sperm and seen as the basis of both their work roles and their aggressive social roles. Men were warned that masturbation and nonprocreational intercourse wasted their precious energy supply. In other words, women, lacking energy themselves, might also drain men of theirs and debilitate them in the work world.

An anthropologist noted in 1975 that many cultures, sharing this view, have isolated men from women before important male rituals such as hunting, warfare, or, in our society, sports. He compared twentieth-century male athletes' pregame sexual abstinence to the Cheyenne feeling that male sexuality was "something to be husbanded and kept in reserve as a source of strength for the great crises of war." Victorian America felt this way apart from war and before the rise of organized sport: male sexuality energized men for business and work.[11]

To grasp American women's changing relation to sport over the last 150 years, we must understand the evolution of sport itself in the United States. The media-popularized, multibillion-dollar spectator and sporting goods industries which shape athletics today were barely discernible even 100 years ago. In the predominantly rural, small town society that America was up through the Civil War, games were casual, occasional, and usually work-related. This does not mean that hunting, trapping, and the like comprised all play. An assortment of bat and ball games did exist. Puritan men and boys played an informal version of football, using inflated pigs' bladders filled with peas. However, unlike modern games, such play lacked fixed rules and varied dramatically by region and class.

After the Civil War, industrialization transformed American life. The factory replaced the farm, the worker the entrepreneur, the clock the sun, and the city the town. Work and play were divorced, as life became compartmentalized. As people worked in set places for a set time, play had to be conducted separately. In this way, industrialization encouraged the development of organized athletics, which also benefited from emerging national communication and transportation networks.

As industrialization proceeded, long-standing but casually played games acquired formal rule structures and permanent teams. College football and professional baseball, having unfolded in the late 1860s, steadily gained popularity throughout the 1870s. In that decade, sports journalism materialized, A. G. Spalding and Brothers opened, the first bicycle was invented, and national associations were founded for various sports. These trends continued in the 1880s which also witnessed the construction of the modern "safety" bicycle that created a sensation in the 1890s. Besides the bicycling fad, the 1890s gave rise to basketball and volleyball, as well as the first public sports scandals and an increasingly aggressive physical education movement. In 1900, America's first mass circulation sports magazine, *Outing*, appeared.

Sports were considered increasingly important for men as changes in the work world brought about by industrialization created the fear that effeminacy was sapping male vitality. People were disturbed by the decline of outdoor farm life. Sedentary urban occupations were interpreted as passivity and lethargy overtaking an earlier dynamic frontier virility. In addition, the once sex-segregated work world was steadily encompassing women, as females moved into professions and grew visible as industrial laborers. As the new century turned, articles proliferated with titles like "The Effeminization of the United States," "The Feminizing of Culture," "Feminizing of Schools," and "Feminization in School and Home." Observers worried especially about the effect on boys of women's predominance as school teachers. Since urban jobs separated men from their families for most of the day, many people feared that boys were losing role models both at school and at home. Organizations such as the Boy Scouts were meant to serve as compensation, and, in large measure, so were sports.

Americans believed that sports revitalized "masculine" instincts, which were loosely referred to as virility. In 1893, nearly a decade before he became president, Theodore Roosevelt delivered his famous address, "The Value of an Athletic Training," in which he used the word "manly" at least a dozen times to describe the sort of national character and lifestyle athletics created. In a key passage he warned:

In a perfectly peaceful and commercial civilization such as ours there is always a danger of laying too little stress upon the more virile virtues—upon the virtues which go to make up a race of statesmen and soldiers, of pioneers, and explorers by land and sea. . . . These are the very qualities which are fostered by vigorous, manly out-of-doors sports. . . . [12]

Writers, educators, psychologists, reformers, priests, and politicians endorsed sport as a solution to social problems attributed to male energy imbalances. Crime and fornication, the products of too much energy, were thought to affect lower-class boys; effeminacy and homosexuality, the products of too little energy, were believed to threaten males of the upper class. To refine yet preserve boys' supposed "animal nature," civic leaders and private promoters founded numerous summer camps and religious, community, and school athletic leagues. Many of these, such as the Police Athletic League, survive today and still administer sports mainly to boys.

If sports were regarded as an expression of male sexuality, they were also believed to teach men values that were especially important in the post-Civil War era. The labor struggles and urban poverty growing from rapid industrial change showed class tension and unequal opportunity to be realities of American life. Scores of middle-class Americans came to believe that sports called forth the very qualities long held to be prerequisites for success: hard work, ambition, diligence, perseverance, humility, and respect for authority. By playing sports, they claimed, disadvantaged males could acquire attributes and attitudes which could help them strive toward the American Dream. Rich men, they continued, could learn the virtues of effort and equality since sports were a social leveler; on the playing field, wealth and status gave no advantage. Spectators could supposedly absorb all these lessons. In inspiring character as well as virility, the argument concluded, sports might thus blunt the malaise arising from tumultuous change. This theory did not hold up in practice. Yet the contention that "sports build character" has enjoyed a long, little-criticized life, although public scandals, open corruption, and colorfully "uncouth" players have convinced numbers of people otherwise.

Since the sort of character sports was believed to build was thought irrelevant to womanhood, women were deprived of a philosophical basis for sports participation as well as a biological one. Hard work, ambition, diligence, and perseverance were considered unfeminine and so were women who displayed them. Women's evolving athleticism, beginning in the 1880s and strengthening with each succeeding decade, therefore came from other sources.

One source was the rise of an industrial leisure class. The "captains of industry" and their families, like most social elites, pursued sport as a form of art; it was a "refined" way for the sexes to spend time together. Aristocratic women in the Middle Ages had sometimes engaged in fox hunts and early forms of tennis and golf. When the modern versions of those games appeared in the late 1880s, elite women immediately took part. A woman, Miss Mary Ewing Outerbridge, is credited with bringing tennis to the United States from abroad. Women's colleges rapidly adopted it, and in 1887, the first female tournament occurred. (The earliest in golf was in 1895.) Thus, though numerically few and socially remote from the larger population, upper-class women contributed to the budding athleticism of their middle-class sisters.

Middle-class women's introduction to sports came primarily as a consequence of female higher education. Ironically, it was the critics of female education who were partially responsible for this development. These opponents, backed by the period's dominant medical opinion, considered intellectual effort physically harmful to women, especially to their reproductive systems. In 1873, Harvard Medical School's eminent Dr. Edward H. Clarke published his controversial *Sex in Education; or, A Fair Chance for the Girls*. In it he blamed college education for a range of female ailments, among them neuralgia, uterine disease, and hysteria. Female educators and proponents of women's education strongly disagreed and countered the next year with *No Sex in Education; or, An Equal Chance for Both Girls and Boys*. However, because of the popularity of Clarke's position, they have made efforts to guard against possible female invalidism. Advocating mild physical activity as a way of keeping the female body—especially the sedentary, intellectual one—healthy, women's and coeducational colleges carefully included physical departments to ensure female students' physical health.

By the early 1890s, studies showed college women to be healthier than their noncollege counterparts, and female physical education spread. Popular magazine articles on these programs encouraged a wider audience to view women's sports more positively. In addition, numbers of native-born white protestants became interested in female physical strength through the eugenics movement. The leaders of this movement claimed that because the immigrant population was growing as the native-born white protestant birth rate was declining, the survival of the native-born white protestants as a race was threatened. The healthier female body would, it was hoped, be able to bear more, healthy children and "save" the race.

Although there were advances in the early 1900s, contemporaries exaggerated the extent of women's pre-World War I athleticism because the sight of even a few women cycling, rowing, exercising, and playing golf, tennis, basketball, and field hockey was a startling deviation from the nineteenth century. Supporters hailed the era of the tomboy and pronounced the sickly, corseted Victorian woman dead. Critics blamed everything from divorce to delinquency on women's growing physical assertiveness and judged the selfless, maternal Victorian woman dead. The truth was somewhere in between: the tomboy was not a favored ideal, most women still wore layered, corseted clothing, remained physically undeveloped, and aspired primarily to marriage and motherhood. Even college women's athletic involvement was nominal, a *Collier's* writer claimed in 1910. Jane Addams, the social work pioneer who would one day win a Nobel Peace Prize, charged correctly, in 1908, that Americans still refused to acknowledge the energies of girls.[13]

The dominant perception of the female body had not changed dramatically. In 1907, the University of Chicago sociologist William I. Thomas published *Sex and Society; Studies in the Social Psychology of Sex*, a compilation of his scholarly articles from the past decade. He saw the "emergence of the adventuress and the sporting-woman" as a negative reaction to society's insistence on passivity. Women needed exercise, he agreed, but athletics were beyond their physical capacity. He explained that females were physically inferior to males because their reproductive function arrested their development early. Woman "resembles the child and the lower races, *i.e.*, the less developed forms," he wrote, in having "relatively" shorter limbs and a longer trunk than man. Such proportions constituted "a very striking evidence of the ineptitude of women for the expenditure of physiological energy through motor action."[14]

Dr. Dudley Allen Sargent offered a somewhat more liberal interpretation of female physiology in 1912. The sexes, he said, were structurally similar. Therefore, women not only needed exercise, but could even be quite capable athletes. However, he added, sports broadened and strengthened women, making them more "masculine" physically, and only women with such acquired or else inherited masculinity could

excel at men's sports. Since this was socially undesirable, he concluded, women's sports should be modified versions of men's: shorter
and less strenuous, like the female body itself.

This line of thinking had already won a wide following, especially
among the first generation of female physical educators. In 1899, a
group of them had created special women's basketball rules, designed
to minimize exertion and physical contact. Believing women more
vulnerable than men to heart strain, exhaustion, and jarred reproductive organs, the educators had divided the court into three sections and
confined certain players to each. A five-person team (nine were also
permitted) had two forwards in one section, two guards in another, and
a center in the middle. A player could not grab or strike the ball from
another player's hands, hold it longer than three seconds, or bounce it
more than three consecutive times or at a height lower than her knee.
In other words, the game allowed only brief, broken movements in a
small space with too many people who could not touch one another.
It undoubtedly eliminated overexertion. In 1908, a permanent panel was
formed to enforce acceptance of the separate rules. With the growth of
national women's sports organizations after World War I, the wom-
en's game became standard in most schools and colleges. Its main feature, the divided court, generally lasted until the early 1970s.

Other sports were similarly modified to conform with women's assumed or desired physical limitations. In 1902, female tennis tournaments were reduced from three of five sets to two of three, despite
players' protests. In bicycling and field hockey, clothing reinforced rules
to modify movement. The absence of competition had made bicycling
more of an outdoor gymnastic exercise than a sport among women.
Yet "lady cyclists" had been mercilessly ridiculed for their necessarily loose attire, especially their bloomers, and had eventually stopped
cycling altogether. In field hockey, which became a favorite team sport
in women's schools and colleges in the early 1900s, women clad in
long-sleeved, petticoated, ankle-length dresses attempted to wield hockey
sticks forcefully and dash across a field. Their uncorseted, ankle-rather-
than-ground-length costume was widely considered a reform.

Hopelessly "masculine" sports were thought beyond modification.
Baseball, boxing, football, and track, except for short sprints, were
unanimously opposed for women by physical educators and publicists.
Competition was likewise discouraged, even in "feminized" sports,
because its essential elements—contention, ambition, and exertion—

were believed unfeminine. Women were not to play seriously; they were not to win, which was masculine, but to play for fun, companionship, and health. As late as 1917, the New York City Board of Education's Inspector of Athletics for Girls characterized dancing as the best female sport. The most widely approved form of female physical activity was physical culture: mild calisthenics designed to strengthen, beautify, or correct various parts of the body.

In nurturing women's athleticism, then, the late 1800s and early 1900s lifted some but not all of the Victorian constraints on female physical expression. Although more restraints would vanish after World War I, the groundwork for women's twentieth-century sport participation was laid in the prewar period. Women's physicality was acknowledged in those formative years, but was assumed and hoped to be limited. Her body, a means to social ends—beauty, motherhood, education—rather than something to be mastered in itself, simply needed to be kept healthy. Some educators argued that a healthy body was the basis of women's new work and community roles, but most women's sports sympathizers only cared that the body be kept healthy to strengthen the old roles of wifehood and maternity. Few suggested that, through sports, women might gain mastery over their bodies, and most doubted even that they could.

The second generation of female physical educators and their allies built on this ambivalent legacy after World War I. Through various national organizations, they persuaded innumerable school districts and colleges to use separate rules and sponsor only certain sports for women. They campaigned hard against female interscholastic competition and in favor of "play days": regional, one-day meets in several sports between shifting, temporary teams. Baltimore physical educators decided that girls could participate in state basketball championships after "building up to it" for nine years with dodge ball, captain ball, and volleyball. Other cities warded off or eliminated girls' tournaments for mildly competitive intramurals. The justification was that strenuous, highly competitive athletics undermined women biologically and socially. In 1923, a *Ladies' Home Journal* writer insisted that, despite women's growing competitiveness in sports, "physiological necessity . . . decidedly stands in the way of unrestricted physical achievement." Menstruating females were believed particularly handicapped, which was why women's teams were to be larger than men's. A Texas physical educator described the "ideal girl" in 1927 as "one who is active, graceful, skillful in at least one sport, but at the same time a girl who is mentally alert and socially attractive, who does not make her athletic ability her chief hobby. . . . " As late as the early 1960s, national women's sports groups maintained that most out-of-gym competition was unnecessary and undesirable.[15]

Not everyone, of course, agreed. Competitive female athletics blossomed in the 1920s and 1930s. American women entered the Olympics in 1920, and in 1922, the Federation Sportive Feminine Internationale hosted the first Women's World Games. In the "feminine" sports of tennis, swimming, ice skating, and golf top female competitors became popular personalities. They were admired for their skills, imitated in advertising, and discussed in magazines. Even in the less "feminine" sports of softball and basketball, companies sponsored successful, profit-making, spectator-oriented leagues. In some regions, women's softball outdrew men's during the 1930s. In 1936, a knowledgeable observer claimed that basketball, played by a million girls and women, was the most common female game.[16]

To some extent, the emergence of popular competitive female athletes represented a liberalized perception of women's bodies. During World War I, women had assumed many of the heavy industrial jobs vacated by men. This fact was not lost upon the public, although women lost these jobs after the war. Dr. Clelia Duel Mosher had observed that women were performing tasks thought beyond their capability. This prompted her to study the comparative strength of physically active but nonathletic college women and athletic college men, and conclude that "there is no difference in the muscular strength of women and men which is due to sex as such." Differences resulted from cultural limitations, such as restrictive clothing, poor eating habits, and inadequate training. Educators who would not go that far did agree that the war had shown women physically capable of more than expected. At their postwar conventions, educators increasingly tied sports to women's roles as citizens and workers, not simply to motherhood as in the past. Government and military leaders, also impressed with women's wartime contribution, established the National Amateur Athletic Federation in 1922. They hoped to include "men and women and boys and girls . . . on equal footing, with the same standards, the same program and the same regulations." However, Girl Scouts President Mrs. Herbert Hoo-

ver opposed equal standards. Reflecting the still-dominant belief in female physical limitations, she presided over a Women's Division within
the NAAF which took the lead in anticompetition efforts.[17]

This growing awareness of women's physical potential had, significantly, another dimension. The female form was becoming a market-
able item, used to sell numerous products and services. It emerged as
a staple of American life in the 1920s, part of what sociologist Martha
Wolfenstein later called "fun morality." The old fear of having too
much fun gave way to the new fear of having too little and was exploited by advertisers to create consumer demand for products. The
message, "Sex is fun, and so is my product (body)," made women
physically profitable.[18]

The commercialization of women's bodies provided a cultural opening for competitive athletics, as industry and ambitious individuals used
women to sell sports. Leo Seltzler included women in his 1935 inven-
tion, roller derby, with "one eye to beauty and the other on gate receipts," according to one writer. It was a novelty, a successful publicity gimmick, since athletic marathons were usually for men. Similarly,
money-making sports ventures benefitted from women's shortened
postwar clothing. Colonel Melvorne McCombs, the insurance company women's basketball coach who "discovered" Babe Didrickson,
claimed that a 1920s Dallas press controversy over players' shorts had
increased regular game attendance from 150 to 5000.[19]

While women's physical marketability profited industry, it also allowed females to do more with their bodies than before. It allowed
them to become not merely athletic but athletes—as long as they un-
derscored their femininity with the right sports and attire. No longer
condemned as masculine or "Amazons," competitive female tennis
players, ice skaters, and sprinters were called goddesses, and swimmers were referred to as mermaids. Helen Wills, the top female tennis
player between 1923 and 1935, was praised for upholding "the wonderful womanhood that uses sports to enhance its womanly charm instead of to affect an artificial masculinity." Producer Flo Ziegfeld and
Hollywood agents regularly scouted swimming and tennis meets in
search of attractive females for nonathletic, nondramatic stage and film
roles. And Marty Fiedler, promoter of women's softball teams with
names like Slapsie Maxie's Curvacious Cuties and the Balian Ice Cream
Beauties, was called sport's Ziegfeld—"to wit, the glorifier of the
American girl athlete." The beauty queen, movie star, and athlete were

related examples of the nature of women's expanded postwar physical freedom. In fact, the beauty queen and the woman athlete were officially recognized within a year of each other: 1921 introduced the first Miss America pageant and 1922, the first ''Women as Athletes'' category in the *Reader's Guide to Periodical Literature* (an annual index of magazine articles.)[20]

Female physical educators saw these cultural connections and protested. Competition was exploitation, they charged, cheap prostrations of women for publicity and money. They claimed that women were being pushed beyond themselves physically and emotionally to satisfy crowds. They predicted that nervous instability, premature pelvic ossification, narrowed vaginas, difficult deliveries, heart strain, and spinsterhood were the high prices women would pay for being serious contenders. Furthermore, educators agreed, competition turned play into work.

The Women's Swimming Association of New York, which trained most of the top Olympic swimmers in the 1920s and 1930s, was critical of an overemphasis on competition and had as their motto, ''Sportsmanship is more important than winning.'' However, they also believed that contention did not inherently contradict health and fun, and they refused to separate the basics of racing from recreational swimming:

A stroke succeeds in all-round competition because it exploits . . . human strength and stamina; because it enables contestants to draw greater speed, or endurance from their physical resources. It will be obvious then that such a stroke must afford the same advantages to those who swim for recreation, physical improvement or to save their lives.

Didrickson's coach, McCombs, similarly argued that certain techniques were necessary to play sports well, whether for recreation or recognition. He said colleges' restrictions produced inferior women's teams.[21]

Educators and allied civic leaders grew particularly outraged over women's participation in the Olympics and Women's World Games. Disapproval was nearly unanimous, a 1923 *Ladies' Home Journal* writer observed, among physicians, physical educators, and national organizations involved in women's sports. Many of these groups and persons joined in a formal protest after the 1938 Olympics, asking officials to suspend the newly added female track and field competition and, if possible, women's participation altogether. Their petition noted that Pierre de Coubertin, the founder of the Olympics, had not wanted females included and that, as a male organization, the Olympics should not conduct sports for women.

Actually, women's involvement was strictly supervised. The Olympics Medical Sub-Commission decided in 1925 that women's "special functions" and "special organization" necessitated "carefully chosen" events "reduced considerably from those arranged for men." Women were medically examined more frequently than men, and clothing regulations existed "to prevent regrettable exhibitions." In addition, the Olympic Congress partially acceded to the educators' wishes by dropping the women's 800-meter race.

Though rooted in physiology, female physical educators' objection to competition had other dimensions. It attacked both men's athletics and American culture. "It isn't the competition which so many of us decry," insisted Barnard College's prominent Agnes R. Wayman, "but the highly intense type of do-or-die play, . . . a desire to 'defeat someone.' " Competition was the vital "soul" of sport, she continued, but Americans' compulsion to win "tends to tear down real values and set up false ones." She and her colleagues characterized men's intercollegiate athletics as joyless, elitist, exploitive, money-making enterprises without educational value. Men's sports were the overcoached, intensive training of the few instead of the democratic, extensive training of the many.[22]

In 1929, the Carnegie Report's famous "Bulletin 23" similarly indicted intercollegiate sports for exclusivity, excessive commercialism, corrupt practices, and overspecialized training. The NAAF Women's Division flourished its motto, "A Game for Every Girl and a Girl for Every Game," in contrast. In 1937, the national Section on Women's Athletics of the American Physical Education Association composed a statement of principles, the Standards Report, affirming the superiority of nonprofit, noncompetitive women's sports. Sportswriter John Tunis called it "a clear definition of what sport should be in a democratic regime. It ought to be studied by all those charged with supervising men's athletics." Others involved in men's athletics praised women educators' emphasis on "the right to participate." One coach wrote that college women were half a century ahead of college men.

"The co-ed is blazing a modern trail through the educational wilderness for her brother, one that he must ultimately follow. . . ."[23]

As a cultural critique, organized women's opposition to competitive athletics reflected their feminism. Feminism is said to have died with the victory of the suffrage movement in 1920, but in reality, a feminist perspective survived among professional women educated in preceding decades. Early twentieth-century feminists had turned antifeminist arguments inside out by describing women's limitations as virtues. Were women too pure for politics, or too inexperienced for government? On the contrary, feminists had argued, government was just enlarged housekeeping and women's higher morality would clean it. Essentially, postwar female physical educators did the same thing, first declaring women incapable of competition and then calling "play for play's sake" superior. They consciously converted a physiological argument into an alternative philosophy of sport.

This philosophy was vigorously trumpeted by *The Sportswoman*, an "amateur magazine . . . by and for women who love sports for sport's sake." It was published between 1924 and 1936 by the U.S. Field Hockey Association, a women's organization. The magazine had its own staff consisting largely of college students and teachers, and included high school students as contributors.

The Sportswoman did not oppose all competition. It endorsed nonprofit, medically supervised amateur competition, played by women's rules. It reported standings and results of tournaments and meets, and ran profiles on female athletes. In 1931, it even disputed American Physical Education Association (APEA) President Mabel Lee for saying intercollegiate sports equaled "throwing women's ideals to the winds." Intercollegiate competition, the editors countered, was "highly beneficial as a broadening and character-developing influence" if not overdone.

However, the magazine applauded whenever a school district or urban area substituted intramurals or field days for championship structures. It energetically promoted play days, minimized Olympic coverage, and denounced professionalism and scholastic "semiprofessionalism." Calling the latter a "perverted form of enthusiasm," it periodically editorialized against spectator-oriented basketball programs and tournaments. "Women desire the promotion of sport for recreation rather than for commercialism," the editors explained. A 1927 writer categorized fierce personal competitiveness and striving as "infantile characteristics" which experienced female teams and athletes outgrew.

The athletes themselves thought otherwise. In 1931, former Women's Swimming Association Olympian Ethel McGary suggested, to *The Sportswoman* readers, that "since there always exists a certain amount of competition, it really seems more logical to work for improved conditions in this through education" instead of alienating athletes by opposing competition. Other prominent athletes wrote similarly.

Egalitarian as it sounded and accurate as the physical educators' perception of American sports was, "play for play's sake" was a problematic alternative. It could hardly have succeeded in such a highly competitive society. But beyond that, modified stakes in modified games did not inspire girls to participate, nor schools to provide facilities and funding. Wayman's denial aside, most female physical educators were hostile to competition itself, not just to its excesses. The play days they advocated were trivial and boring. Why, asked a dissenting teacher in 1939, did college women hate gym class and shun sports in their spare time? "Heretical as it sounds," she answered, slogans such as "A game for Every Girl and A Girl for Every Game" were meaningless "theme songs" which had failed. Not every girl wanted a game, she claimed, especially the games educators liked.[24]

The Sportswoman's dissolution in 1936 ended the first wave of athletic feminism. The second, beginning in the early 1970s, came after more than three decades of inactivity. Between the 1930s and the 1970s, the basic premises of women's athletics remained unchanged. Player pressure steadily forced educators to liberalize basketball rules, but modified games and play days continued at least through the early 1960s. In 1967, an article in *Today's Health*, published by the American Medical Association, advised for "sound reasons" that girls refrain from contact sports. "The female breasts and other organs can be injured seriously by a sudden blow. The danger of scars, broken teeth, or other results of injury probably are more of a psychological hazard for girls than for boys." Two years later, Yale philosopher Paul Weiss suggested, like countless educators before him, that women be viewed as "truncated males" capable of men's sports in "foreshortened versions."[25]

Athletic women from the 1930s through the 1960s had few options if they wanted to avoid the masculine stereotype. Sportswriter Paul Gallico had wryly remarked in 1936 that women looked beautiful in only eight of twenty-five sports. Some sports, including ball games, were out for making women perspire. The acceptable included archery, shooting, fishing, riding, flying, and skating because women moved gracefully, if at all, and wore "some pretty cute costumes." Thirty years later, a similar attitude prevailed. A majority of the people interviewed by *Today's Health* writers thought most sports unfeminine except the traditional ones of swimming, tennis, golf, girls' basketball, and a little track. Even these sports were considered unfeminine if serious competition was involved.[26]

One 1934 study had found athletic high school girls no different— no more "mannish" though perhaps more outgoing—than their non-athletic peers. However, the work of psychologist Lewis M. Terman later in that decade showed otherwise, and it was the Terman study that was widely publicized. In 1939, *Good Housekeeping* reported that Terman had devised a Masculinity-Femininity Quotient test for his book *Sex and Personality*. By conventional standards, male engineers and college athletes had responded the "most masculinely" and female athletes and physicians the "least femininely" to the questions. Both Terman and the magazine observed that such judgments could change as society's standards changed. But neither noted that mastery or total control of the body was a power shared by athletes and physicians and was what probably made them equally "unfeminine."[27]

In the post-World War II era, athletic women improved their skills and records, but not their numbers or image. A 1950 estimate was that merely five percent of professional athletes were female. Athletic women's "masculinity" became popular and academic dogma, with Terman's study setting the tone for postwar analyses. Sports sociologist Gregory Stone observed, in 1955, that little was known about the female player except that she was masculine. In 1967, a psychiatrist writing on "The Superior Athlete" paused to consider women:

Someone is bound to ask: "What about female athletes?" Female athletes, no less than female nonathletes, present special problems in evaluation. I am aware of no one who claims any special competence in assessing either group. . . . The real enigma is in the reconciliation of the soft, physiologically, socially and culturally determined maternal inclinations with the harsh phallic requisites of competitive sports at a superior level.[28]

Throughout the twentieth century, women's growing autonomy, education, and economic productivity have blurred the once clear distinction between masculine and feminine. The changes in work and family relationships begun by industrialization a century ago have intensified since World War II. Forty percent of the work force was female in 1975, double the 1920 figure. Between 1965 and 1975, women accounted for three-fifths of the expansion in nonmilitary fields of work. In 1976, the Department of Labor announced that the two-income family had become the norm. Other statistics confirm an increase in single-parent households. This blurring of sex roles has left some people frightened and confused, although others see it as a healthy development for both sexes.

In his 1967 "psycho-social" study of sport, psychiatrist Arnold R. Beisser observed that the athletic world's traditional ordering of relationships has helped blunt the impact of change elsewhere:

It is small wonder that the American male has a strong affinity for sports. He has learned that this is one area where there is no doubt about sexual differences and where his biology is not obsolete. Athletics help assure his difference from women in a world where his functions have come to resemble theirs.

Beisser concluded that "sports represent the cultural safety valve . . . the great arena in which the historical traditional roles of the sexes can be played." If so, then attempts to unplug the valve by altering roles inside this last bastion of tradition understandably meet strong resistance.[29]

The changes of recent years have not, however, bypassed athletics; today's women's movement has revived sports as a feminist issue. The athletic feminism of the seventies is different from that of the past in its legal, equal-rights orientation and its appeal to female athletes. The two go together. Though all women involved in sports and physical education in the 1920s and 1930s complained of having less staff, funding, and facilities than men, top players could hardly have joined in the demands of women's sports organizations for less competition. A sisterly alliance between athletes and educators was thus impossible.

Today's athletic feminism is different because feminism is different. Unlike their predecessors, contemporary feminists rarely argue for goals on the basis of women's moral superiority or physical inferiority. The roots of modern feminism lie in the civil rights and antiwar movements of the 1960s—hence the emphasis on equality and the search for legal solutions. In sports, this has led to a rash of court cases invalidating sex segregation in Little League, and to Title IX, the 1975 HEW directive prohibiting sex discrimination in sports conducted by federally assisted institutions and organizations. Almost all schools and colleges receive some federal assistance, and so schools and colleges receive some federal assistance, and so Title IX applies to a huge number of institutions. Some schools, such as Stanford University, have merged the men's and women's athletic departments, a controversial move that any previous generation of physical educators would have opposed, and that many still question. Noticeably, today's athletic feminism is more the work of lawyers and athletes than of physical educators. *The Sportswoman* was published by the U.S. Field Hockey Association, a women's organization dominated by educators. *Women Sports*, the major women's athletic magazine of the 1970s, was published by athlete Billie Jean King and advocated total sexual equality in competitive sports.

Attitudinal gains lag behind the legal ones. Despite favorable decisions, few girls participate in Little League and related organizations because females are still discouraged from team and contact sports. Those who attempt involvement are frequently harassed. In 1974, a suburban Little League in Michigan insisted that a female player comply with regulations by wearing an athletic supporter. In his 1976 *Sports in America*, novelist James Michener considered the "problems" of sex-integrated teams, especially for girls and boys aged eleven to twenty-two. He shared the concern of coaches who had "warned [him] that they would not wish their thirteen- and fourteen-year-old boys to compete against girls in public situations in which a defeat might be interpreted as a failure in manliness."[30]

Athletics are still largely viewed as an expression of male sexuality and power, a world in which women are intruders but not rightful heirs. In 1973, the authors of a three-part series in *Sports Illustrated* on female athletics found physicians, educators, and athletic personnel across the country indifferent or hostile to the subject. Most claimed that sports did not provide the same educational and physical benefits for women as for men, that women did not want sports, and that women's sports were economically unprofitable. The writers painstakingly refuted each point: if sports were educationally valid, then they were as valid for women as for men; women's physical capabilities were unknown, untested, and submerged in myths; and the popularity of women's tennis, girls' basketball in Iowa (where it is a major spectator sport), and roller derby (a violent sport and the only one in which women have numerical parity) proved women's athletic marketability. A year later the writers reported that many of the schools and colleges had improved their resource allocations and their attitudes, though not enough. Zealously guarding the status quo, a well-financed male college sports lobby successfully diluted the final version of Title IX in 1975. Their desire to share athletic budgets with women was, to understate it, minimal. The vagueness of the guideline makes meaningful program reform, let alone equality, unlikely.[31]

Still, activists have done much to open sports' professional and material rewards to women. They have won larger budgets, staffs, and programs in many schools and colleges. They have provided role models and helped foster an atmosphere supportive of women's athleticism. They have promoted "unfeminine" and contact sports as well as the traditional ones. In 1976, the *New York Times* reported that about 10,000 American women were weight lifting, compared to a few hundred in 1974. Weight lifting has always been among the most masculine of sports, though female athletes have done it moderately for conditioning. The *Times* quoted a California YMCA instructor who said the sport was growing fastest among housewives and office workers, "women under twenty-five who aren't crushed by the old stereotypes" and accepted "the idea that there is no such thing as a masculine or feminine sport."[32]

At some point, however, activists will have to regain earlier generations' awareness of the limitations of equality. In transcending their restricted past, women are uncritically courting an athletic structure which heaps enormous resources on a few participants and underserves most of the populace. A growing number of male athletes have deserted or denounced the sports world in recent years, charging that its exaggerated pursuit of victory and profit leaves players overworked, underpaid, and physically subservient to coaches and owners. "I would never say that athletes are exactly like slaves were," former New York Jets player George Sauer has claimed. "But there is something about organized athletics that treats an athlete somewhat as a slave. The attitude still exists that we are a body and that we are property. . . ."[33]

For these reasons, some feminists are urging women to reject athletic scholarships. A 1972 writer described the scarcity of women's athletic scholarships not as discrimination but as "a blessing in disguise, since without athletic scholarships the possibility of maintaining sport as an experience to enhance the individual exists to a greater degree for women than for the male collegiate athlete." Female physical educators traditionally made this claim; it was a staple of athletic feminism in the past. Its truth is debatable, given most women's limited economic resources. And its parallels with "play for play's sake," which activists today blame for holding women back, make it unpopular.[34]

Women's effort to liberalize the sports structure that exists rather than to oppose it or forge an alternate one is momentarily their best option. Like all discriminated-against groups, women stand to gain more from equality than they would lose. If they can erase sport's masculine identity, as blacks have changed sport's earlier racist character, and acquire athletic habits, as men do from childhood through adolescence, women will have gained a great deal. In fighting for equality, however, women ideally would keep in mind what Jack Scott, director of the Institute for the Study of Sport and Society and former physical education chairperson of Oberlin College, calls sports' "radical ethic": the belief that athletic excellence is obtainable within a humane, democratic, and widely accessible structure. Women can work to avoid the most authoritarian, alienating, and corrupt aspects of men's sports, while still striving for mastery and achievement.[35]

Sport is part of a larger movement for female physical autonomy, a movement in which efforts to gain control over pregnancy, birth, family size, and individual safety figure prominently. As this movement proceeds, athletics may well form its backbone.

NOTES

1. Theodora Well, "Woman—Which Includes Men, of Course . . . , An Experience in Awareness," *Association for Humanistic Psychology Newsletter* 7, no. 3 (December 1970).

2. For a humorous reversal of this, see the K.N.O.W. publication by psychotherapist Joyce Jennings Walstedt, "Corporeal Orgasm and Personality Development in the Human Male (A Spoof in the Manner of Freud)," (September 1970). Dr. Dudley A. Sargent, "Are Athletics Making Girls Masculine?" *Ladies' Home Journal* 29 (March 1912): 71.

3. Sophie C. Elliott-Lynn, *Athletics for Women and Girls: How to Be an Athlete and Why* (London: Robert Scott, Roxburghe House, 1925), p. 65. She was the vice president of England's Women's Amateur Athletic Association.

4. Emily James Putnam, *The Lady: Studies of Certain Significant Phases of Her History* (Chicago: University of Chicago Press, 1970), p. 13.

5. David Hunt, *Parents and Children in History: The Psychology of Family Life in Early Modern France* (New York: Basic Books, Inc., 1970), p. 88.

6. Carroll Smith-Rosenberg and Charles Rosenberg, "The Female Animal: Medical and Biological Views of Woman and Her Role in Nineteenth-Century America," *Journal of American History* 60, no. 2 (September 1973): 335.

7. Foster Rhea Dulles, *A History of Recreation; America Learns to Play*, 2nd ed. (New York: Appleton-Century-Crofts, 1965), p. 96.

8. Barbara Ehrenreich and Deirdre English, *Complaints and Disorders: The Sexual Politics of Sickness* (Old Westbury, N.Y.: The Feminist Press, 1973), p. 11. Eleanor Flexner, *Century of Struggle: The Woman's Rights Movement in the United States* (New York: Atheneum, 1970), pp. 90–91.

9. Dr. Grace Peckham Murray, "The Health of Professional Women," *Harper's Bazar* 34, no. 17 (27 April 1901): 1117.

10. Thomas Woody, *A History of Women's Education in the United States*, Vol. II (New York: The Science Press, 29), pp. 109–110.

11. Ben Barker-Benfield, "The Spermatic Economy: A Nineteenth-Century View of Sexuality," *Feminist Studies* 1, no. 1 (Summer 1972): 46. William Arens, "The Great American Football Ritual," *Natural History* (October 1975): 79–80.

12. Theodore Roosevelt, "Value of an Athletic Training," *Harper's Weekly* 27, no. 1931 (23 December 1893): 1236.

13. Florence E. Canfield, "Give the Girls a Chance," *Collier's* 44, no. 25 (12 March 1910): 20. Jane Addams, "Some Relfections on the Failure of the Modern City to Provide Recreation for Young Girls," *Charities and the Commons* 21 (5 December 1908): 365–68.

14. William I. Thomas, *Sex and Society: Studies in the Social Psychology of Sex* (Chicago: University of Chicago Press, 1907), chapter 1, based on an 1897 article.

15. Sarah Addington, "The Athletic Limitations of Women," *Ladies' Home Journal* 40 (June 1923): 144. Josephine Schmid, "Some Sport Activities at the University of Texas," *The Sportswoman* 33, no. 10 (June 1927): 23.

16. Frank G. Menke, sports encyclopedist, gave the figure and ranked swimming second.

17. Mary Roberts Coolidge, "Clelia Duel Mosher, the Scientific Feminist," *Research Quarterly* 12, no. 3, supplement (October 1941): 640–41. Alice Allene Sefton, *The Women's Division, National Amateur Athletic Federation: Sixteen Years of Progress in Athletics for Girls and Women* (Palo Alto: Stanford University Press, 1941), p. 2.

18. Martha Wolfenstein, "The Emergence of Fun Morality," in *Mass Leisure*, ed. Eric Larrabee and Rolf Meyersohn (Glencoe, Ill.: The Free Press, 1958), pp. 86–95.

19. Quentin Reynolds, "Round and Round," *Collier's* 98, no. 8 (22 August 1936): 15.

20. "Sketches from Helen: A Novel from Suzanne," *Literary Digest* 89, no. 3 (17 April 1926): 66. Frank J. Taylor, "Fast and Pretty," *Collier's* 102, no. 8 (20 August 1938): 23.

21. *Women's Swimming Association News* 7 (March 1927): 3.

22. Agnes R. Wayman, "Let's Take It in Our Stride," *The Sportswoman* 10, no. 7 (March 1934): 14; Sefton, *The Women's Division*, p. 29.

23. John R. Tunis, *Democracy and Sport* (New York: A. S. Barnes & Co., 1941), p. 42. H. W. Whicker, "Growing Up to Play," *The North American Review* 234, no. 5 (May 1933): 469–70.

24. Mary C. Baker, "The 'Love of Strenuous Activity Among College Women' Myth," *School and Society* 49 (18 February 1939): 208–12.

25. Rose and Hal Higdon, "What Sports for Girls?" *Today's Health* 45, no. 10 (October 1967): 21. Paul Weiss, *Sport, A Philosophical Inquiry* (Carbondale & Edwardsville, Ill.: Southern Illinois University Press, 1969), p. 125.

26. Paul Gallico, "Women in Sports Should Look Beautiful," *The Reader's Digest* 299 (August 1936): 12–14.

27. Dr. Edwin G. Flemming, "Personality and the Athletic Girl," *School and Society* 39 (10 February 1934): 166–69. Amram Scheinfeld, "A Test for Femininity," *Good Housekeeping* 108 (February 1939): 59–60.

28. Gregory P. Stone, "American Sports: Play and Dis-Play," in *Mass Leisure*, ed. Larrabee and Meyersohn, p. 260. *Ibid.*, p. 260. Stephen D. Ward, "The Superior Athlete," in *Motivations in Play, Games and Sport*, ed. Ralph Slovenko and James A. Knight (Springfield, Ill.: Charles C. Thomas, Publisher, 1967), p. 311.

29. Arnold R. Beisser, *The Madness in Sports: Psycho-Social Observations on Sports* (New York: Appleton-Century-Crofts, 1967), pp. 198, 225.

30. James A. Michener, *Sports in America* (New York: Random House, Inc., 1976), p. 126.

31. Bil Gilbert and Nancy Williamson, "Women in Sport" (3-part series), *Sports Illustrated* 38, no. 21 (28 May 1973); 38, no. 22 (4 June 1973); 38, no. 23 (11 June 1973).

32. Sharon Johnson, "A Little Weightlifting to Get into Feminine Shape," *New York Times*, 13 December 1976, p. 46.

33. Paul Hoch, *Rip Off the Big Game: The Exploitation of Sports by the Power Elite* (Garden City, N.Y.: Anchor Books, 1972), p. 111.

34. Darlene Kelly, "Women and Sports," *Women: A Journal of Liberation* 3, no. 2: 16.

35. Jack Scott, "A Radical Ethic For Sports," *Intellectual Digest* 2, no. 11 (July 1972): 49–50.

IX

Sports Violence and Social Crisis

Peter Levine and Peter Vinten-Johansen

During the summer of 1980, Representative Ronald Mottl from Ohio introduced the Sports Violence Act in the U.S. House of Representatives. The proposal received immediate attention in the national media and generated a wide range of opinion as to its merits. Supporters of the bill stressed the need for federal prosecution of excessive and unreasonable physical violence in professional sport. Opponents decried the introduction of burdensome and unwarranted federal litigation in matters best left to members of the sport family. Neither side, however, denied that the bill addressed fundamental problems: Instances of excessive violence in professional sport had increased to worrisome dimensions, with pejorative effects on the physical and psychological welfare of the players, on spectators for whom the players often served as role models, and on the general image of sport in American society.[1]

Similar controversy over the level of acceptable violence in college football at the turn of the century reminds us that concern about excessive violence in American sport has been a recurring, if episodic, theme. But why did President Teddy Roosevelt, the Rough Rider and hunting enthusiast, apply different expectations to the gridiron than toward Spanish soldiers and African rhinos when he jawboned university presidents into changing the rules of the game? And why were critics of violence in American sport largely ignored in the 1960s, whereas Mottl's bill, narrowly focused on violence in professional sport, has become the subject of congressional hearings in the early 1980s? In other words, why has publicly expressed concern about excessive violence become especially noteworthy at particular points in time, while at other times it remains ignored?

Clarification of such questions requires a historical perspective often overlooked by behavioral scientists interested in sport violence. The instinct-versus-learned-behavior debate continues to inform the literature, and there is little likelihood that either side will ever win an unqualified victory. What does seem likely, however, is that some irreducible quantity of individual aggressive behavior is associated with every form of social life. Since cultural norms and socialization processes vary widely, individuals in different societies will develop concomitant types of "surplus aggression" associated with their particular sociocultural and historical experiences. Sport is only one of a number of responses that a society may develop to sublimate aggressive feelings, be they inherent or surplus, into culturally acceptable forms of behavior. Consequently, the amount of violence tolerated in sport in any given society is a reflection of historically established and changing norms and expectations.[2]

Starting from that premise, this chapter argues that understanding a society's attitude about violence in sport provides important insights into its basic value structure and historical development. Specifically, an examination of situations in both the European and American experiences indicates that public recognition of and attention to what is deemed to be excessive violence in sport coincides with points in time when particular societies are undergoing fundamental socioeconomic upheavals and critical evaluations of their basic values.

The European experience is replete with examples that illustrate this thesis. Shifting attitudes about acceptable levels of violence in ancient Greek sport were directly associated with a breakdown in the cultural unity associated with the *polis*. In ancient Greece, sport was intricately linked with religious rituals and social principles for the distribution of wealth accumulated by elites. Over time, there emerged well-defined and well-enforced rules for each sporting event, with judges, umpires, and a variety of technological means to ensure compliance and a sense of ethical fair play. Although sport remained relatively nonviolent in comparison with the prevalence of political and social violence among the city-states in ancient Greece, some events (the chariot races and combat sports, for example) included levels of violence considered acceptable in terms of the principles of socialization in militaristic virtues accomplished through the continuance of these events. Thus the violence in sport that did occur during the formative states of the Greek *polis* was considered necessary for the welfare of the polity as a whole.[3]

Greek sports, like the early Greek theater, served cathartic purposes in that the participants were models of expected behavior—models of physical strength and mental acuity, but also models of fair play in situations involving keen competition. Consequently, sport in the Greek *polis* evolved its peculiar form in order to meet certain sociocultural needs in a particular historical context. Striving for "fairness," "honor," and "victory" in ancient Greek sport was but one element in an interlocking set of norms and values that evolved as part of a general cultural response to problems of survival and territorial expansion. No generalized perception that the violence in these sports was excessive appeared as long as these cultural values informed the daily actions of the citizens into a united *polis*.

But the relative sociocultural solidarity and cultural agreement that characterized the Athenian Empire during the middle of the fifth century B.C. began to disintegrate during the Peloponnesian War. Previously accepted values and norms were subjected to critical scrutiny, especially by an aristocratic elite that associated the democratic values of the *polis* with vulgarity and commonness. This elite evolved philosophical justifications for their retreat from religious and public life by emphasizing the contrary value of the private sector, including the personal satisfaction (rather than moral edification) found as a sports participant or spectator. Concern about this shift in the function of sport, from ritual to entertainment, was but one aspect of a generalized anxiety about the social implications of the fragmentation of the *polis* as a common cultural entity. Some fourth century B.C. commentators, for example, deplored the effects that commercialism and specialization had on the athletes themselves. What did it signify for the future of Greek society, they asked, if their athletes were models of greed and self-indulgence rather than "justice" and "the good life"? What social utility could be served by combat sports and chariot races if the spectators were expected to be passive subjects rather than active participants in the creation and defense of a unified society? These concerns antedate the Roman conquest, the introduction of the unregulated, violence-prone pancratium, and the development of a professional class of athletes, prized for their brutality and endurance. Consequently, contemporary Greek perceptions about excessive violence in sport reflected not problems specific to sports alone, but general anxiety about the cultural fragmentation under way throughout Greek society.[4]

Similar connections are apparent in modern European societies. In Sweden and Denmark, for example, military exigencies during the Napoleonic Wars; the confluence of romanticism, patriotic nationalism, and Enlightenment educational theories; and some restrictive factors imposed by living in a harsh climate contributed to the development of gymnastic exercises on a national scale rather than in organized games as in England. Belief in the use of gymnastics as an agent of social regeneration, modeled on the vigorous physical specimens of Nordic mythology, spread throughout Scandinavia early in the nineteenth century. Nonetheless, different climatic factors, historical events, and cultural developments in Sweden and Denmark resulted in significant variations in the role of sport in each of these societies. Consequently, perceptions about what constitutes excessive violence in sport differ as well.[5]

For Sweden, the loss of Finland to the Russians in 1809 inaugurated an intensification of the military values inherent in the gymnastics taught in its education system. Highly regimented, systematic exercises with little room for individual imagination were sustained past mid-century. This regimentation of the gymnastics movement expanded to adult sports clubs in the twentieth century and helps explain why Swedish contests today are still dominated by unmistakable overtones of "team spirit" and authoritarian behavior in comparison with the individual initiative and decision making expected of athletes in other countries.

A 1969 study of soccer players, for instance, shows that Swedish players expressed significantly higher concern for the priority of team interest, even to the point of condoning the use of violence, than did amateur players from England and Finland, where individual play and decision making are stressed. Moreover, the presence of regimented training in athletics and religion is detectable in the high percentage of Swedish players who registered acceptance of a coach's order to "knock out" a dangerous player on the opposing team, yet were unwilling to criticize referees or to make personal decisions about breaking the rules.[6]

An international attack on an opposing player, which might appear to an outside observer as an unwarranted, excessively violent act, represents instead a very complex set of attitudes about the priority of team interest and obedience, in constant tension with the demands of a rule-bound society. Player violence is socially acceptable if it remains within the framework of expectations established by these competing author-ities. But acts of violence are condemned as excessive by players and spectators alike when they appear to be individually motivated or in blatant disregard of the tone of play established by the referee, even though the violent acts, in and of themselves, are identical to those carried out in behalf of "team spirit." Consequently, assessments of the violence that does occur in Swedish sport, as well as suggestions about how to minimize this violence, are meaningless without an understanding of this historical and cultural context. In spite of current reevaluations of the role of the welfare state in the lives of Swedish citizens, the cultural foundations noted above remain intact; therefore, there is no generalized state of anxiety about Swedish culture, and this relative equanimity is reflected in the absence of any sustained debate about excessive violence in Swedish sport.

As in Sweden, Danish interest in gymnastics increased during the Napoleonic Wars. But the revenge spirit that evolved in Sweden after the loss of Finland and that propelled interest in military preparedness as a means to regaining status as a major world power did not come to dominate the Danish mentality. After the wars, Denmark's middle classes turned inward, blaming an aristocratic clique at court for Denmark's demise as a world power. At the same time, they recognized the impossibility of any change in that status. In the 1860s, when interest in sport as a means to national self-regeneration did appear, it reflected this acceptance by emphasizing the *idreat* ideal in sport instead of the militaristic tendencies found in Sweden.

This ideal recognized the use of sport as an agent for developing a combination of physical strength, mental perseverance, and creative skill in the individual. In comparison to Sweden, a less-regimented, more individually interpretative form of rhythmic, movement-oriented gymnastics developed in Denmark during the second half of the nineteenth century. This emphasis was incorporated in physical activity other than gymnastics and remains an essential component today in the local sports clubs (*idreatforbunder*) that compete with each other in both regional and national divisions in a variety of sports, including handball and soccer.

Contemporary opposition to violent behavior in Danish sport is a reflection of this historically evolved *idreat* ideal in the present geopolitical context. Since few Danes have any illusions that their country will ever become a world power, they have developed specific notions about the qualities that must be inculcated in young Danes if the country is to preserve its semi-Western, semineutral political position. These qualities are rational foresight, creative imagination in the use of scarce resources, and artful compromise. To them, therefore, "rough play" is dangerous, whether it occurs in politics or sport. The Danes look for technically superior and tactically imaginative, rather than hard or violent, play from their athletes. Although they often bemoan the losses to more team-spirited nations (especially the Swedes), there remains an undaunted devotion, as one commentator on Danish soccer notes, to "artistic ball-control, guided by intelligence," rather than to victories in and of themselves.[7]

Unmistakable tones of national self-congratulation about this devotion to the aesthetics of sport color Danish assessments of the role of sport in other countries. Italian soccer is described as hysterical, neurotic, and misguided because of player and spectator brutality in the service of winning at all costs. Danish reporters are shocked by the brutality in American football and Canadian hockey. Ethnocentric innuendo is often resorted to when describing East European teams. For example, after witnessing a particularly brutal game of international handball between national teams from Denmark and Rumania, a Danish reporter stated categorically that Rumanians were primarily responsible for the legalized mayhem that exists in international handball. Other teams are "forced" to retaliate with violence whenever playing the Rumanians, but find it difficult to alter their strategies when competing against other opponents.[8]

Although some of this outrage is undoubtedly justified, it needs to be viewed within the context of Danish feelings about their political impotence in the modern world. The Danish press often discusses the uncomfortable positions in which Denmark and the rest of northern Europe find themselves as a buffer zone between what they view as self-interested geopolitical conflicts among the super powers. The Danes also ally themselves with other northern European countries as advocates of quality, nonviolent sport. In doing so, they greatly exaggerate the sport violence occurring in the Eastern European–Soviet bloc countries and in the Americas, while minimizing the significance of violence in their own sporting events.

Nonetheless, there are emerging some very deep-seated anxieties about growing violence in Danish sport. Although rarely given as much attention as violence in international sport, the increase in injuries associated with organized sports and the increase in penalties called in officiated contests in Denmark concern many Danes. The problem is not overexaggerated. Fundamental principles of long historical duration are at stake as the country examines its notion of sport within a larger process of cultural reassessment. Can the *idreat* ideal in sport, emphasizing the aesthetic quality and personal growth associated with athletic competition in the past, survive the growing commercialization and profit-making mentality in Danish life? Can the carefully structured, if still tenuously balanced, collectivist principles in Danish society withstand the pressures for professionalizing spectator sports, thereby increasing the gulf between elite and mass sport participation already under way in the public schools? And to what degree is the increase in violence in Danish sport associated with the reductionistic interpretation placed on the value of competition associated with commercialization and elitism in Danish society as a whole? For the Danes, as for the members of any society, widespread concern about violence in sport is inextricably linked to more fundamental questions about the viability of a society's perceived values and self-expectations.

The American experience also suggests that focus on the question of sports violence coincides with points in time when reevaluation and questioning of the vitality of dominant values is taking place. Accompanying the western settlement of the United States in the nineteenth century, for instance, was real interest in animal-violence sports such as bearbaiting and gander pulling. Although these activities rarely involved the kind of organization or routine that is associated with modern sport, they clearly enjoyed active participation and spectatorship on the frontier and without question involved high levels of violent behavior.

Particularly grisly was gander pulling, which involved the efforts of a skilled horseman striving to break the neck of a defeathered, live, greased gander, hung upside down from a crossbar just above the reach of the rider's outstretched hands. If unsuccessful the first time, as was often the case, it could take hours for the "game" to end as the gander quickly realized that his only salvation lay in avoiding the rider's grasp. Yet the blood and gore involved in such amusement caused little discernible public outcry or concern.[9]

Rough-and-tumble wrestling, also referred to as "gouging," provided similar opportunity for excessive violence and bloodshed, but it too rarely engendered criticism. Indeed, at times Americans seemed to revel in their accomplishments in this area—witness Abraham Lincoln's reputation as a country wrestler. Mark Twain's description of a rough-and-tumble wrestler, from *Life on the Mississippi*, conjures up the image conveyed by such a person and the clear possibilities for violence and destruction his sport contained:

Whooop! I'm the old original iron-jawed, brass-mounted copper-bellied corpse-maker from the wilds of Arkansaw! Look at me! I'm the man they call Sudden Death and General Desolation! Sired by a hurricane, damn'd by an earthquake, half-brother to the cholera. . . . Look at me! I take nineteen alligators and a barrel of whiskey for breakfast. . . . I split the everlasting rocks with my glance, and I squench the thunder when I speak! Stand back and give me room according to my strength! Blood's my natural drink and the wails of dying is music to my ear! Cast your eye upon me, gentlemen, and lay low and hold your breath, for I'm 'bout to turn myself loose.[10]

In a society that prided itself on carving a nation out of a seemingly boundless, wild frontier, it is clear why such sports were not viewed as excessively violent. Celebration of self-reliant, courageous, strong individuals capable of using violence to subdue nature and the Indian went hand in hand with acceptance of activities that personified such characteristics. Moreover, frontier sports such as gander pulling or gouging hardly seemed excessive in a society that justified the virtual extermination of Indian cultures and that relied on extralegal violence to maintain law and order among segments of its white constituency and its black slaves.[11]

Accompanying westward expansion, however, was internal urban migration, European immigration to America, and the transformation of the United States into an industrialized society that, by the end of the nineteenth century, created social and cultural upheaval and a consequent reevaluation of basic values and goals. For a people whose dominant value structure was buttressed by social Darwinist theory with its emphasis on survival of the fittest, some wondered what areas of human life would not provide the opportunity to nourish the character, drive, and virtue that had enabled Americans to conquer a continent and establish the United States as a preeminent world power. What would take the place of the violent testing ground of the frontier that no longer existed? Complicating matters were highly articulated fears that the sedentary nature of middle-class life would soften the basic tissue of the American character already under seige. Finally, the sudden presence of East European immigrants with their own customs and cultures made many white native Protestants fearful that the purity of the American stock would be severely diluted.[12]

Responses to these fears were wide-ranging. They included an increasingly aggressive foreign policy, a variety of efforts, some often tinged with violence, to control and acculturate new immigrants, and, most important for our consideration, the promotion of sport as a means of building the proper kinds of citizens necessary to continue American greatness.[13]

Particularly for urban, middle-class Americans, the last quarter of the nineteenth century witnessed a virtual explosion of popular interest in sport. Whether measured by the bicycling craze of the 1890s, the growth of organized professional baseball, or the astounding success and expansion of the sporting-goods industry, promotion and acceptance of sport as legitimate leisure-time pursuit that served significant social ends marked these years. This point was not lost on Albert Goodwill Spalding, one of the founders of the National League, one-time owner and manager of the Chicago White Stockings, president of the sporting-goods company that made him a millionaire, and one of the key figures in shaping the leisure-time needs of middle-class, Victorian America.

In *America's National Game*, Spalding's autobiographical history of organized baseball published in 1911, he emphasized that a significant goal of sport was the development of character traits necessary for the continued growth and prosperity of the United States. Spalding saw baseball as exemplifying "American Courage, Confidence, Combativeness; American Dash, Discipline, Determination, American Energy, Eagerness, Enthusiasm, American Vim, Vigor, and Vitality." As he noted elsewhere, Americans "live in a strenuous age, and our boys . . . should be educated and developed along lines that will enable them to meet and cope with these conditions." Participation in athletics, and especially baseball, in his mind, was the best way to "fit a boy for the rough and tumble business life of today," not only because it provided him with the litany of traits already noted but also because it taught him "the absolute necessity of self-control" and the need to play by the rules as a member of a larger team. After all, baseball's "basic principle," he noted, is "subordination to the rule."[14]

The problem, as Spalding recognized, was not simply to preserve the values associated with the frontier existence of America but to adapt them in ways that would fit the more civilized, bureaucratic sedentary nature of American life as it was developing by 1900. This concern helps clarify his interest in promoting sport as an activity that would resolve the tension and anxiety about how to mesh traditional American values, still tinged with violent individualism and aggressiveness, with the emerging values of an urbanized society without causing chaos and destruction.

Spalding's vigorous promotion of baseball is only one example that sports activity could serve significant social purpose in a society undergoing dramatic change. The idea that participation in organized athletics might replace the frontier experience as a means of building character even found expression in the growing interest in country clubs. Indeed, one writer in 1901 referred to the spread of such elitist clubs as a "safety-valve of an overworked Nation," quite as responsible for American victory in the Spanish-American War as "Waterloo was won on the Rugby gridiron."[15]

In an atmosphere where sport was referred to as "artificial adventure, artificial colonizing, artificial war," it is not surprising that college football emerged as the most popular team sport in America. Like baseball, it offered the opportunity for individual skill and excellence to be subordinated to a team effort so that victory could be achieved. There were plays to be mastered, responsibilities to be carried out, and rules to be followed—all experiences tailor-made for a society interested in shaping character to conform to the demands of a more bureaucratic, industrialized state with new demands of efficiency, cooperation, and productivity.[16]

Yet football, played within proper limits, offered more. The very nature of the game—its demands of strength and its acceptance of violent physical contact—provided a means of preserving the savage instinct in man in ways that could still be utilized by a society no longer in its violent, frontier stage. It was a game, as one writer put it, played "according to the laws of natural selection—only the fittest survive."[17]

That the game was popular is undeniable. From the first intercollegiate game between Princeton and Rutgers in 1869, college football spread rapidly. By the 1890s colleges and universities throughout the country boasted teams and organized into conferences to facilitate scheduling and competition. Paid coaches such as Walter Camp at Yale,

Amos Alonzo Stagg at Chicago, and Fielding Yost at Michigan turned out winning teams that brought out the crowds and helped publicize and finance their institutions. By 1914, over 450 colleges and 6,000 secondary schools fielded teams.[18]

College football also enjoyed popularity because it allowed the identification of the player as a hero whom adolescents could emulate and admire. Perhaps the most telling evidence on this point, especially relevant to this discussion of violence and sport, was the vast success of Gilbert Patten's "Frank Merriwell" series, built around that wonderful muscular Christian who personified the strenuous ideal through sport. The exploits of this fictional Yale undergraduate demonstrated that the character traits necessary to American development could be shaped on the playing fields, because such activity provided an acceptable channel for violent behavior that could then be utilized in positive ways elsewhere. Descriptions of Frank churning through the Harvard eleven, fighting on despite the "hands clinging to him . . . with all the fierceness he could summon," striving to break away, "his lips . . . covered with a bloody foam . . . and a frightful glare in his eyes," clearly evoke a violent, savage image, but one that could be nurtured through sports and eventually channeled into socially productive outlets. Indeed, as Patten described Frank, he was the ultimate team player who followed the rules and who understood that his individual drive and aggressive, even violent, behavior served a larger, collective effort.[19]

In reality, however, not everyone who played college football was a Frank Merriwell. More to the point, football's potential was double-edged, as capable of encouraging uncontrollable, excessive, antisocial violent tendencies as it was of channeling them into ends acceptable to an urban, industrialized state. The controversy over the question of excessive violence in the college game between 1895 and 1915 reflected this concern and mirrored the larger debate in American society about how to influence its direction and values.[20]

The violent nature of college football in these years is indisputable. The flying wedge, mass plays, and general mayhem, coupled with a lack of protective equipment, resulted in numerous injuries and much-publicized gridiron deaths. An oft-quoted description from the *New York Times* of the 1895 battle between Yale and Princeton provides some sense of the scene:

Slap! Two masses of humanity would come together with a sound like the cracking of the bones of a tasty hot bird between the teeth of some hungry

giant. Legs and arms and heads and feet would be apparently inextricably intermingled, until it looked as if not even the fondest mother would be able to sort out the right parts of her one and only son. The whistle of the referee would blow sharply, and then the lot of legs and arms and hands and heads would sort themselves out once more, and there would be something like the sixteen or eighteen of the boys that seemed to be human beings once more, with all the members of their bodies intact.

The rest of the men that had been in the collision lay prone on the field and doctors Josh Hartwell and Boviard would rush on the field, followed by assistants with packages of sticking plaster, buckets of water, and cases of surgical instruments. A big gap in someone's head would be patched together with plaster, another man's leg would be pulled back until it assumed its normal shape, sprained wrists would be bandaged, and wrenched ankles bound up. Then the crowd would yell itself hoarse with the rival cries of the colleges, possibly because no one had been killed outright. Roaring bulls of Bashan never made one-half the noise!

Sharply the whistle of the referee would ring out its orders and then another human cyclone would be set in motion, and possibilities of carnage can be suggested by the merry cries of "eat 'em up, Princeton!" and "Kill 'em in their tracks, Yale!"[21]

Critics, appalled by such affairs, linked what they considered to be wanton violence to other problems associated with the sport. Most pronounced were fears that depraved elements of society only interested in debauchery and gambling were taking over the game and consequent concern that college football was undermining the university's role to train leaders for a new society. Underlying these concerns was real anxiety that violence that went beyond the rules and that served no useful ends called into question the vitality of the game as a means of encouraging the kind of character necessary to continue American greatness.[22]

Even firm supporters of football such as Theodore Roosevelt took seriously the criticism directed against it. Sport's "real purpose," Roosevelt argued, was "preparation to do work that counts when the time arises." Any deflection from that purpose could not be tolerated. Indeed it was out of the efforts of certain college administrators, brought together by Roosevelt, that reforms were initiated in 1906 and 1910.

The reduction of violence by legalizing the forward pass, introducing the six-man line, and eliminating mass plays sought to preserve the game as an activity that would build proper character while maintaining it as a popular and profitable source of entertainment.[23]

In the end the results of these reforms were limited. Although the game did "open up" and become more fluid, football on both the college and later the professional levels remained a violent contact sport with ever-present possibilities for real tragedy and destruction. This is understandable because Americans in the Progressive Era never completely shucked their aggressiveness for a more cooperative, communitarian ethic. Widespread concern and discussion about excessive sports violence at this time occurred precisely because a sense of crisis existed about traditional social values and the degree to which they could be retained.

The connection between public concern about excessive sports violence and a generalized sense of social crisis about values and direction is also relevant for understanding recent interest in the problem and meaning of sports violence. Increased American involvement in Vietnam in the 1960s, for instance, proceeded apace with the emergence of professional football as "America's game" and, for some people, increasing doubts about the correctness of American foreign policy and the value structure that underlay it. Although largely ignored by national media coverage, critics such as Robert Lipsyte, Harry Edwards, Jack Scott, and Paul Hoch offered analyses of excessive violence in sport linked to a critique of continuing American values that emphasized a "win at all costs," survival-of-the-fittest mentality. The fact that the National Football League proudly advertised its product as "vicarious warfare nurtured by the technology that is this land's hallmark" suggests why these critics frequently used professional football to illustrate their views.[24]

As in the 1890s, those who voiced concern about excessive sports violence in the 1960s saw it as a manifestation of a larger social crisis. Yet more so than their turn-of-the-century counterparts, their introspective analysis demanded a dramatic reordering and reevaluation of American goals and values that appeared too extreme and utopian for most Americans to accept.

Since the late 1970s, the issue of sports violence has been resurrected by more conservative critics who eschew the complexities of historical context and cultural values in favor of an obsession with sensationalized incidents such as the 1975 National Hockey League fight between Dave Forbes and Henry Boucha. While subsequent litigation failed to set a precedent for criminal prosecution in similar incidents, it did call into question the oft-used argument that certain sports are inherently violent and outside the realm of judicial control. These new legal critics also have their sights set on establishing legal limits on player violence in professional football, using "Booby" Clark's attack on Dale Hackbart and the Jack Tatum–Daryl Stingley incident as evidence that the leagues are unwilling to control intentionally excessive violence in the game. Even basketball is under scrutiny since the infamous Kermit Washington–Rudy Tomjanovic altercation in December 1977. The disposition of this case, with monetary awards of several million dollars, is cited by the law-and-order critics as one of the more hopeful landmarks on the way to establishing "an effective deterrent to violence in *all* professional sports."[25]

This deterrence mentality underlies the proposed Sports Violence Act of 1980–1981. The Mottl bill, as it is commonly called, assumes that the entire climate in professional sport can be changed by levying fines of up to $5,000 or imprisonment of not more than a year for deliberate, reckless, excessively violent infractions of rules during the course of a game. Supporters of the bill have described this attempt to interject the federal judiciary into professional sport as a "cohesive and rational approach" to reducing excessive violence in all sports, professional and amateur alike, due to an anticipated "trickle-down" effect.[26]

But the Mottl bill is hopelessly inadequate to accomplish these goals. Most obviously, how would a threat of protracted litigation, eventuating at most in a fine of $5,000 and a year in jail, dissuade behavior that has changed little in spite of the much larger financial penalties involved in both the Washington and Clark cases?

For those who believe in the deterrence established by financial penalties, there are other proposals, simpler and more direct than the Mottl bill. For example, Mark Mulvoy's suggestion for curbing on-ice violence in the National Hockey League places primary responsibility with the League itself. The commissioner should, quite simply, suspend a player for five games without pay (hardly an insignificant sum for most players today) the first time he drops his gloves or raises his stick. Equally important, the League should prohibit the club from replacing the penalized player during the period of suspension. Second offenses deserve ten-game suspensions for player and club alike. In other words,

Mulvoy believes that only immediate actions that hurt the players in their pocketbooks and diminish a club's ability to perform may have some effect on reducing the violence in the game. League commissioners, team owners, and coaches are as responsible for excessive violence as the players themselves. Or in John Underwood's words, "the problem is an orchestrated kind of violence that implicates the entire structure of pro[fessional] sport."[27]

But even Mulvoy's proposal, which is potentially more effective in reducing player violence than the Mottl bill, and Underwood's extension of responsibility for violence to other elements in professional sport are limited. Like the legalistic critics, their articulations of the problem and professed solutions ignore the connections between American sport and American values. Since Americans continue to define success and self-worth largely in materialistic terms, player violence may be curbed somewhat by immediate and drastic penalties. However, since the owners and coaches define themselves by an acquisitive ethic as well, they will only strive to curb sports violence in the face of spectator revulsion and consequent loss of income.

But there are few indications that the cultural values of American society in the 1980s have shifted that drastically since the days of Teddy Roosevelt and Frank Merriwell. In fact, the New Right's assertions of aggressive individualism are currently restitching most of the tears in the socioeconomic and cultural fabric of American life that developed during and after Vietnam. The parallel revulsion at excessive violence in American sport was similarly episodic and short-lived. There is in the early 1980s no crisis in American values sufficiently advanced to evoke lasting public sentiment for reducing the same violent behavior by professional athletes that less than twenty years ago was instrumental in shifting spectator interest from baseball to football and that has for decades been a source of plaudits from hockey fans.

Unlike previous examples we have discussed in this chapter, the conservative reformers of the 1980s have a narrow vision of the function sport has in socializing values in the American citizenry. Their approaches are representative of a crisis in American society more significant than violence in professional sport—an incapacity to formulate a synthetic conception of social problems and to evolve self-critical and analytical proposals for constructive solutions. Reformers of American sport must come to recognize that a correlation exists between a society's cultural values, its social and geopolitical framework, the place of organized sport in that setting, and its preference, toleration, or abhorrence of sports prone to high levels of violence.

Perceptions of what constitutes excessive violence will vary from society to society, but the historical examples noted above indicate that *widespread* expressions of concern about excessive violence in sport appear when a society is undergoing a crisis involving a reexamination of its established values. The issue of sports violence, albeit highly symptomatic of this general crisis, is minor compared to the entire spectrum of the social and cultural tensions it reflects. While such tensions did occur at the turn of the century, there is little evidence to indicate that they exist today. Consequently, current legislation aimed solely at curbing the violent tendencies of a few professionals is, at best, a superficial response to symptoms of the most serious problem facing American society in the last quarter of the twentieth century—an unwillingness to recognize the bankruptcy of our acquisitive ethic in a world characterized by diminishing resources and political conflict.

Where does this leave us? We believe that we must deal with the world as it is today rather than as traditional American values suggest it should be. We need a fundamental reordering of our values and goals, away from what C. B. MacPherson calls "possessive individualism" and toward an ethic that emphasizes a sense of collective responsibility and shared commitment toward creating a society where all people can live with mutual respect and understanding for each other and other societies. Only if current legislative proposals to curb excessive violence in sport become part of this larger process of reordering values in American society can they serve any significant purpose.[28]

We recognize, however, that the American historical experience offers little hope for dramatic reversals of this magnitude. Our society is likely to remain acquisitive and materialistic in the forseeable future. In this context, professional athletes represent a highly visible group whose behavior on and off the field serves as one of a number of acculturation forces for adolescents and children. The enactment of sports violence legislation along the lines of Mulvoy's proposals might encourage some diminution of blatant violent behavior that could filter down to young people.

Organized sport for children can play an important part in an effort to introduce our children to new attitudes about their society and place in the world. It does make a difference, for example, who coaches Little League teams or who runs organized athletic programs in our elementary schools, high schools, and colleges. Do these authority figures encourage a win-at-all-costs mentality that may be used to legitimate violence, or do these role models assist children in channeling aggressive drives and competitive values into some concern with a sense for technical mastery and aesthetic accomplishment in sports? It is in this context that groups such as Sports for People can positively affect the population's attitudes about sport and the types of communities in which we live. Since sport will always serve as an agency of socialization, let's at least make sure that those who have determined its character—and at times sought to control its excessive violence—in the past no longer maintain a monopoly over its direction in the future.

NOTES

1. H.R. 7903 (1980); H.R. 2263 (1981). H.R. 7903 was introduced on July 31, 1980. Hearings were held on September 30 and November 19, 1980, and May 19, 1981, before the Subcommittee on Crime of the House Judiciary Committee, chaired by Representative John Conyers, Jr. See *Congressional Record*, Extension of Remarks, July 31, 1980.

2. The aggressive-instinct interpretation is based largely on the writings of Freud and Lorenz. More-recent expositions occur in the works of Storr and Ardrey, as well as offshoots of sociobiology. See Nicholas Petryszak, "The Bio-Sociology of 'Joy in Violence,' " *Review of Sport and Leisure*, 2 (June 1977), pp. 1–16. The learned behavior, or environmental, theory gained renewed support after the 1967 Wolfgang and Ferracutti studies on violence as a learned response in primates. With respect to humans, the literature is cited in Joel Tirer, "The Psychological Perspective: Analysis of Violence in Sport," *Arena Review*, 5 no. 1 (February 1981), pp. 37–43. Other discussions of causal theories of violence are found in two collections of papers from the International Congress of Physical Activity Sciences (1976): Fernand Landry and William A. R. Orban, eds., *Ice Hockey* and *Physical Activity and Human Well-Being* (Miami, 1978). The idea of "surplus aggression" is derived from Herbert Marcuse's analysis of historically determined surplus repression, in *Eros and Civilization* (Boston, 1966) and *Five Lectures* (Boston, 1970).

3. The following comments about sport in ancient Greece are based in part on general information, as developed in Peter McIntosh, *Fair Play: Ethics in Sport and Education* (London, 1979), chapters 1 and 2. See also chapter 2, "The Olympic Ideal and Its Downfall," in McIntosh, *Sport in Society* (London, 1963).

4. McIntosh, *Fair Play*, pp. 13–19; William H. McNeill, *A World His-*

tory, 3d ed. (New York, 1979), chapter 8; H. A. Harris, *Sport in Greece and Rome* (Ithaca: Cornell University Press, 1972), pp. 25–26.

5. An overview, in English, of the historical background for the development of modern sport in Scandinavia is found in McIntosh's essay, "Therapeutic Exercise in Scandinavia," in J. G. Dixon et al., *Landmarks in the History of Physical Education* (London, 1957).

6. Data from this study by K. Heinila of the University of Jyväskylä, Finland, are discussed in McIntosh, *Fair Play*, chapter 9. The interpretation of the data is our own. Ibid., pp. 130–134. Swedish players registered the highest percentage of acceptance (60 percent) to the suggestion that "a fast opponent must be stopped by any means, lawful or otherwise," compared with 37 percent each for Finnish and English players. Moreover, 63 percent of the Swedes supported the notion that a coach's orders to knock out a dangerous player should be followed compared with 35 percent acceptance among English and 27 percent among Finnish players.

7. *Politiken* (Copenhagen), March 13, 1977, p. 31.

8. Ibid., June 25, 1977, Section 2, p. 1; ibid., June 5, 1977, p. 23; June 8, 1977, p. 30; ibid., July 17, 1977, p. 25; March 28, 1977, Section 4, p. 9.

9. Jennie Holliman, *American Sports, 1785–1835* (Durham, 1931), pp. 136–137, provides a good description of gander pulling.

10. Quoted in Foster Rhea Dulles, *A History of Recreation: America Learns to Play*, 2d ed. (Englewood Cliffs, 1965), pp. 73–74.

11. John Ward, *Andrew Jackson: Symbol for an Age* (New York, 1953), is the best-known discussion of such matters.

12. The literature encompassing these issues is immense. Two important synthetic works are Paul Boyer, *Urban Masses and Moral Order in America, 1820–1920* (Cambridge and London, 1978), and Robert Eiebe, *The Search for Order* (New York, 1967).

13. As early as the 1850s middle-class Americans began similar consideration. See Peter Levine, "The Promise of Sport in Ante-Bellum America," *Journal of American Culture* (December 1979), pp. 623–634. For a European parallel to the emergence of sport in response to concern about the enervating consequences of Victorian life, see Eugene Weber, "Gymnastics and Sports in *Fin-de-Siecle* France: Opium of the Classes?" in *The American Historical Review*, 776 (1971), pp. 70–98.

14. Albert G. Spalding, *America's National Game* (New York, 1911), p. 4; *Public School Athletic League of New York Handbook* (New York, 1906), p. 29; *Spalding's Official Baseball Guide* (New York, 1910), p. 325. Both excerpts come from speeches given before schoolboys in New York and Cleveland on occasion of the awarding of trophies donated by Spalding commemorating victories in organized baseball tournaments.

15. Gustav Kobbe, "The Country Club and Its Influence Upon American Social Life," *The Outlook*, LXVIII (June 1, 1901), pp. 255, 266. Quoted in

Gerald F. Roberts, "The Strenuous Life: The Cult of Manliness in the Era of Theodore Roosevelt" (Ph.D. diss., Michigan State University, 1970), p. 118. Roberts, pp. 78–134, provides an excellent discussion of late-nineteenth-century interest in sport and its relationship to social Darwinism.

16. Price Collier, "Sports Place in the National Well-Being," *Outing Magazine* XXXII (July 1898), p. 384, quoted in Roberts, "The Strenuous Life," p. 82.

17. "The Football Team," *Youth's Companion*, LXVII (February 22, 1894), p. 84, quoted in Roberts, "The Strenuous Life," p. 87.

18. John R. Betts, *America's Sporting Heritage, 1850–1950* (Reading, 1974), p. 129.

19. Quoted in Robert H. Boyle, *Sport: Mirror of American Life* (Boston, 1967), pp. 264–265.

20. Guy M. Lewis, "Theodore Roosevelt's Role in the 1905 Football Controversy," *The Research Quarterly*, 40 (December, 1969), pp. 717–724; John H. Moore, "Football's Ugly Decades, 1893–1913," *The Smithsonian Journal of History*, 2 (Fall 1967), pp. 49–63; and John Watterson III, "The Football Crisis of 1909–1910: The Response of the Eastern 'Big Three,' " *The Journal of Sport History*, 8 (Spring 1981), pp. 33–49 provide good coverage of this subject.

21. Quoted in Moore, "Football's Ugly Decades," pp. 51–52.

22. Ibid., p. 50.

23. Theodore Roosevelt, "The American Boy," *The Works of Theodore Roosevelt*, vol. XII (New York, 1900), p. 132. Quoted in an unpublished manuscript by Donald Mrozek, "Sport and the Americans' Experience, 1880–1910."

24. See Harry Edwards, *The Revolt of the Black Athlete* (New York, 1969); Paul Hoch, *Rip Off the Big Game: The Exploitation of Sport by the Power Elite* (New York, 1972); Robert Lipsyte, *Sports World: An American Dreamland* (New York, 1975); and Jack Scott, *The Athletic Revolution* (New York, 1971). Quoted in Lipsyte, *Sports World*, p. 50.

25. Although interest in particularly violent incidents is hardly novel, the formulation of solutions to prevent their recurrence has taken new forms. Most strident at the moment are the legal reformers who seek to invoke a law-and-order climate in American sport. The fundamental issue is whether participants in sport should behave in accordance with laws that apply in everyday life or in accordance with rules that are specific to each individual sport. See the articles by Michael D. Smith, "Sports Violence: A Definition," and Rick Horrow, "The Legal Perspective," in *Arena Review* 5, no. 1 (February 1981), pp. 2–18. Also among the conservative reformers who focus on sensational events are authors such as Robert C. Yeager, *Seasons of Shame: The New Violence in Sports* (New York, 1979). In contrast to Smith and Horrow, however, Yeager considers sports violence a moral problem to be solved by various un-

specified psychological-environmental changes. Horrow, "The Legal Perspective," p. 12.

26. Ronald Mottl and Rich Horrow, "The Legislative Perspective: The Sports Violence Act of 1980 and 1981," *Arena Review*, 5, no. 1 (February 1981), pp. 19–120.

27. *Sports Illustrated*, October 13, 1980, p. 50. An approach less comprehensive than Mulvoy's has been in effect in New Zealand rugby since early in 1979. Players sent from the field for rough play are supposed to be suspended for thirty days. The effects on the levels of violence have not, to our knowledge, been documented as yet. See J. M. Pearson, "Rugby—Focus on Violence," *British Journal of Physical Education* 2 (1979), pp. 337–339; John Underwood, "Viewpoint," *Sports Illustrated*, August 17, 1981.

28. C. B. MacPherson, *The Political Theory of Possessive Individualism: Hobbes to Locke* (New York, 1962).

X

Black Consciousness and Olympic Protest Movement, 1964–1980

Donald Spivey

Sport is fun and games, recreational activities, and athletic competition. It is also an important cultural, social, economic, and political force. Sport has long been a tool in the arena of international politics. In recent years, nations and peoples traditionally on the outside of international sport-politics have come into the fold, signaling a political awakening and a realization of the power of athletics as a propaganda weapon for the Third World. Black America and Africa utilized three of the recent Olympiads to promote their concerns. In so doing, they further illuminated the inequalities of the world we live in and the nature of international sport and character of the black protest movement.

The 1968 Olympic boycott movement stands as the cornerstone in the awakening of black America, Africa, and much of the so-called Third World to the power and utility of the international athletic contest as a political forum. The use of the Olympic boycott is not new. Egypt, Lebanon, and Iraq boycotted the 1956 Melbourne Games to protest the British-French-Israeli invasion of Egypt to allegedly maintain control over the Suez Canal. Mel Whitfield, black athlete and holder of three Olympic medals, advocated that blacks boycott the 1964 Olympics to be held in Tokyo, Japan. His reasoning reflected a rising consciousness:

I advocate that every Negro athlete eligible to participate in the Olympic Games in Japan next October boycott the Games if Negro Americans by that time have not been guaranteed full and equal rights as first-class citizens. . . . Even the people of foreign lands know that we are still not free in this country. In Africa, South America, and all the nations of Europe, they know that day-to-day civil rights struggles of the American Negro are but expressions of his earnest desire to break loose from the shackles that keep him from making his place in the sun. They know this, and they watch with discerning eyes to see what the outcome will be.

Whitfield challenged black athletes to act against racism. In his opinion, the black Americans' struggle would have repercussions throughout the world and serve as an example, particularly for the Third World nations. His was the first systematic call for black people in America to use the international sports forum to promote the cause of human rights both in the United States and throughout the world. Black America, however, was not ready to meet the challenge in 1964. It was more ready and able to do so in 1968.[1]

What black America and the Third World would eventually comprehend was what the powers of the West and East had long known—international sports provided a powerful platform for politics and propaganda, despite the denial of International Olympic Committee patriarch Avery Brundage. The Olympic Games and politics have always been familiar bedfellows. Having made tremendous strides in achieving independence, Third World nations began flexing their muscles in international sports in the 1960s. President Sukarno of Indonesia advocated that Third World countries establish their own world-class conference for amateur athletics. In 1963, the Games of the New Emerging Forces (GANEFO) was formed. Participating nations included Asian, African, and Latin American countries: Indonesia, the People's Republic of China, Cambodia, Guinea, Iraq, Mali, Pakistan, North Vietnam, and the United Arab Republic. In 1966, the Supreme Council for Sport in Africa (SCSA) was established, which represented thirty-two African nations. Its mandate was much the same as that of GANEFO: to coordinate and promote sports, but specifically to coordinate and promote sport throughout Africa, and even more specifically, to direct political action against South Africa and Rhodesia. GANEFO and SCSA were clear indications that the Third World now saw the advantage of united, international sport activism. The organizations were to stimulate athletic development within their countries but, most importantly, to utilize the arena of international athletics, especially the Olympic Games, as a political sounding board, a propaganda platform for Third World issues.[2]

In the late 1960s, black athletes in the United States were showing signs of a sport-politics consciousness. There were certainly enough issues to stimulate them: racism, discrimination, economic exploitation, the assassination of Dr. Martin Luther King, Jr., the murder trial of Black Panther leader Huey P. Newton, and the presidency of Richard M. Nixon, to name a few. The riots following the murder of Dr. King were poignant expressions of the deep-seated anger within the black communities of America. Protest sentiment was alive in every sinew of black America, including the sanctum of athletics. Black and sympathetic white athletes at the college and high school ranks boycotted the New York Athletic Club (NYAC) in 1968 because of its discriminatory policies against blacks and Jews; Manhattan College, New York University, St. John's, and City College of New York refused to compete in the NYAC track meet until the club changed its racial policies. Black students at Ohio State University protested against that institution's discriminatory policies in its academic and athletic programs. Similar protests were launched at Michigan State University, University of California at Berkeley, San Francisco State University, University of Kansas, University of Washington, Iowa State University, and others. The students demanded, among other things, that the athletic programs stop discriminating—that more black coaches and trainers be hired. Black collegiate athletes complained about a host of problems: about stacking, where a number of blacks are placed in competition for the same position; about racial stereotyping; about sports commentators biased in favor of white athletes; about the athletic associations' policing of their social activities (the most severely sanctioned social activity was interracial dating); about the policy of recruiting a limited number of blacks so as not to exceed the "quota." Eight black athletes of the University of Texas at El Paso's track team refused to participate in the school's annual track meet against Brigham Young University because of the Mormon doctrine that blacks were inferior and disciples of the devil.[3]

Black professional athletes were speaking out louder than ever before against racism. Several black athletes within the National Football League demanded that NFL Commissioner Pete Rozelle resign because of his insensitivity to racism within the NFL. Jim Brown, upon retiring from the Cleveland Browns, denounced the racial insensitivity and intolerance of Cleveland owner Art Modell and his coaching staff. Star halfback Leroy Kelley and five other black teammates on the Cleveland Browns seconded Jim Brown's complaints. Racial turmoil on the Atlanta Falcons prompted the NAACP to threaten suit against that club unless it changed its racial attitude regarding its black players. Bobby Mitchell, black star halfback with the Washington Redskins, spoke out against quotas limiting black players on NFL teams. Dallas Cowboys fullback Don Perkins of Albuquerque spoke out against the color line within and outside of the Dallas team. Perkins, who held a $50,000-a-year contract with the Cowboys, complained that none of the blacks on the team could get decent housing in Dallas. "Do you know my wife Virginia and I would be embarrassed to have someone visit our home in Dallas," he said. "The Negroes among the Cowboys can only find roach-infested houses. If I cannot find a decent house or apartment this year, I am going to camp on general manager Tex Schram's doorstep." Perkins added that he was caught "off guard" when he first went to the Cowboys from the University of New Mexico because there had been little discrimination at the university. "When we played a road game at UNM," Perkins said, "I always roomed with a white player. At Dallas it is Negro with Negro." Frank Robinson blasted major league baseball for not having a black manager. He also stood his ground against a barrage of racist hate mail and bitter criticisms from sportswriters for having held out during the spring for a substantial salary increase. Jackie Robinson, a life-long Republican, publicly criticized his party for its selection of Richard M. Nixon as the party's standard-bearer for the presidency. Robinson warned that Nixon's election would be a major step backward in the battle to abolish the color line. Tennis star Arthur Ashe summed up the feelings of many of the outspoken black professional athletes when he remarked that as a black person who had achieved some fame, he bore a greater responsibility to black people and to the struggle for equal rights. "I will be viewed as a black spokesman, I suppose," said Ashe. "I am not Rap Brown or Stokely Carmichael, but this country could use another three or four Browns and Carmichaels." [4]

The general thrust of the black activism of the period, however, was domestic rather than international. Black protest focused primarily on the inequities and injustices within American society. Despite America's shortcomings, moreover, the great majority of blacks still believed in the American system. The presidential administrations of John F. Kennedy and Lyndon Baines Johnson left blacks with a psychological and political sense of progress, especially with the passage of the Civil Rights Act and Voting Rights Act of 1964 and 1965, respectively. The *Chicago Defender*, the oldest black newspaper in the United States, expressed what many blacks felt: ''President Johnson had done much to bring the Black man into the mainstream of American society, and has raised the Negro's status nearer to the goal of full citizenship than any other chief executive since Lincoln.'' The aim of the civil rights movement was to reform the system, to improve the quality of life for black folk in America. Cleveland Mayor Carl B. Stokes, speaking to the graduating class of Wilberforce University in May 1968, declared that ''our great big nation has a wonderful and viable system of government, a tool for you to use—to shape, to bend, to mold, to improve.'' Stokes advocated ''non-violent militancy'' intended to improve America and not to destroy it. Equality and integration were the key concepts of the civil rights movement. Improving the home front was the goal. Regardless of Martin Luther King, Jr.'s, vigorous opposition to American involvement in Vietnam, and despite the disproportionately high percentage of blacks who would fight and die in Southeast Asia, the struggles in that part of the world, in Latin America, in the Middle East, and in Africa were at best secondary concerns to the overwhelming majority of black Americans.[5]

The African nations' proposed boycott of the 1968 Summer Olympic Games in Mexico City spurred political consciousness at the international level and sports activism. In 1966, African nations, through the Organization of African Unity and the Supreme Council for Sport in Africa, began sending signals that they were seriously contemplating boycotting the Olympics if South Africa was allowed to participate. A small number of black American athletes also took up the cry of boycott. Harry Edwards, an assistant professor at San Jose State University, organized the Olympic Project for Human Rights (OPHR). His aim was to politicize the black athlete and muster American public opinion in support of the boycott and an end to racism and oppression at home and abroad. In the official mission statement of the OPHR the point was made:

We shall work to establish a bond of communication between Black America and Black Africa, based upon our mutual descent and the problems growing out of the genocidal policies of certain white racist societies (i.e., the United States of America, the Union of South Africa, Southern Rhodesia, etc.).[6]

The movement to boycott the Olympiad accelerated when the International Olympic Committee (IOC) decided to admit South Africa to the games. African nations announced that they would definitely boycott the Olympics in Mexico City. In the United States, the OPHR gained momentum. The American Committee on Africa issued a statement signed by sixty athletes calling for a U.S. boycott of the 1968 Olympic Games unless South Africa was barred from participating. The signers were black and white amateur and professional athletes. Among these were Jim Bouton, a white pitcher for the New York Yankees, Rubin Amaro, a Mexican player for the Yankees, Hayward Dotson, a black basketball player for Columbia University, Steve Mokone, a South African soccer player who was attending the University of Rochester, and Kwaku Ohene-Frempong, a Ghanaian on Yale University's track team. Bill Russell, player-coach for the Boston Celtics, also supported the proposed Olympic boycott. "Athletes boycotting the Olympics have a point," Russell said. Curt Canning, captain of the Harvard University crew, and fellow white crew members announced formation of a group to support Professor Harry Edwards' Olympic Project for Human Rights, although they stopped short of endorsing the proposed boycott of the Summer Games.[7]

The efforts on the part of the African nations, black and white athletes in the United States, and many countries throughout the world forced the IOC to reverse its decision. On April 21, 1968, it rescinded the invitation to South Africa to participate in the XIX Olympiad in Mexico. In June, the Mexican organizing committee of the games decided that because of the recent resolution of the U.N. Security Council imposing sanctions on Rhodesia, it would deny admittance to any person traveling on a Rhodesian passport. Thus, Rhodesia was also barred from participating in the Mexico City games.[8]

The Soviet Union's position on South African participation was in harmony with that of the Africans and Third Worlders. The USSR endorsed the stand by the African nations at the outset. On the eve of the opening ceremonies for the Mexico City games, October 11, 1968, Russian minister Sergei Pavlov told a well-attended news conference that the Soviet Union reaffirmed its support of the African countries' demanding the expulsion of South Africa from international sports federations and organizations. "We will intensify our efforts to secure the exclusion of South Africa from all international participation," Pavlov said. His statement followed the announcement of Avery Brundage's reelection to another four-year term as president of the International Olympic Committee. Pavlov's remarks were meant to serve notice to South Africa, Avery Brundage, and others that any new effort to "legalize" South Africa would be met with immediate, sharp resistance.[9]

African nations, with victory in hand, would participate in the XIX Olympiad. The OPHR, however, was only partially satisfied. Its mandate had been twofold, and the issue of inequality in the United States remained unresolved. Edwards proposed that black American athletes go forward with the plan to boycott the games. The number of enthusiastic supporters of an American or black American boycott of the Olympics was drastically reduced when the issue over South Africa's participation was settled. Nevertheless, Harry Edwards, putting on virtually a one-man crusade, kept the boycott threat alive. As the start of the summer Olympiad grew nearer, Edwards made speeches and held conferences to stir up sentiment for a boycott. When not holding conferences or making speeches, he could be found working out of the back of his rented van near the Olympic Village, distributing literature urging would-be ticket buyers not to attend the games.

The setting at Mexico City and the athletes' response to it reflected the level of political consciousness among the Olympians and the efforts made to keep them uninformed. Athletes, as a group, have been accused of political insensitivity. The very nature of organized sports, with its militaristic posture and a player-coach relationship that is fundamentally a dictatorship, discourages political activism. If there was any level of political awareness among the Olympians, the situation in Mexico would have brought it to the surface. Political oppression and assassination were the order of the day in that country. Mexican student groups launched protests and demonstrations throughout much of 1968. Several demonstrators had been murdered a few weeks prior to the start of the games. In part, the protest was against the forthcoming Olympics. A growing number of Mexicans were angry about their nation's expenditure of $200 million in construction of the Olympic Village and other facilities while poverty, hunger, and illiteracy abounded in their country. Eight days before the games were to begin, a clash between 10,000 demonstrators and the Mexican military left 26 of the protestors dead and 100 wounded after the troops opened fire on them with automatic weapons. The threat of continued violence prompted the IOC to meet in emergency session to discuss the possibility of the games being canceled or moved elsewhere. They decided against taking any action after Mexican authorities assured the committee that peace and order would be maintained for the duration of the games. Despite the assurances, the demonstrations and the violence continued. Athletes arriving in Mexico City were quickly ushered off to the isolation of the luxurious Olympic Village, where they were under heavy guard and were not permitted to leave the compound. Outside communication was limited and local newspapers forbidden. The 8,000 Olympians seemed content enough with the arrangements and totally unaware of or uninterested in Mexico's problems. One athlete on the U.S. team allegedly remarked to a reporter, "I didn't even know any rioting was going on." [10]

Moreover, the proposed black American boycott of the games drew stiff resistance from the very beginning. The U.S. Olympic Committee (USOC) led the resistance. Former Olympic star and USOC member Jesse Owens headed the bandwagon in opposition to the proposed black boycott. Owens maintained that sports and politics were incompatible bedfellows. "This [boycott] is not the answer to the problem we are facing," Owens stated emphatically on arrival in Los Angeles to attend a fund-raising promotion for the Olympic team. "We have been able to bridge the gap of misunderstanding more in athletics than anywhere else." Stan Wright, assistant track coach of the Olympic team, who was black, lambasted the proposed black boycott of the games and predicted it would fail because

the Negro athlete in the United States has as much pride and responsibility in representing this country as any other American. I feel some athletes are being exploited because I question Edwards's motives in regard to the Olympic Games. I feel that he actually has personal objectives which are politically oriented.

Unprecedented measures were taken by the U.S. Olympic organization to guard against the possible negative consequences of the boycott movement. At the summer Olympic training facilities in South Lake Tahoe, California, an unusually large number of athletes were invited to the camp in the events that black athletes were strongest—namely, the sprints and hurdles. Reporter Steve Murdock suggested that this had been done as "a means of bolstering against a possible boycott." Interviews between athletes and reporters at the training facility were restricted after Lee Evans, one of the leaders of the Olympic Project for Human Rights, made statements in an interview supporting the boycott initiative. The television media did its share to downplay the demonstrations at the Mexico City games. Olympians Tommie Smith and John Carlos accused the American Broadcasting Company of minimizing the impact and significance of the protests at the games. When all else failed, the Olympic regulatory body was not above a smear campaign to discredit the more outspoken black athletes. At the very beginning of the Summer Olympiad, rumors were being circulated that some black athletes received illegal payment by two manufacturers of track shoes who wanted the athletes in question to wear their company's shoes during their events, thus promoting the company's athletic footwear. The evidence suggests that the United States Olympic Committee and the International Olympic Committee started the rumor. Although no proof was ever presented to substantiate the allegations against the athletes, the rumors nevertheless persisted. At the center of the controversy was USOC chairman Douglas Roby, who claimed that he had the evidence and would turn it over to the International Amateur Athletic Federation and to the United States Amateur Athletic Union, and said that it was up to them to follow through, if the evidence warranted it. At a businessmen's luncheon in Birmingham, Alabama, several weeks after the 1968 games, Roby, reflecting on the games, said, "Those fellows that gave us trouble down there were paid." [11]

Why were the efforts made to neutralize the black Olympic boycott movement? The answer is twofold. First, the Olympics is an international forum for nationalistic display. It is a tremendous opportunity to glorify a nation via the feats of its athletes. Victory at the games is a triumph for the political system, its people, and its way of life. Second, black athletes have been major contributors to America's success in the modern Olympiads. The United States made an excellent team showing in the 1968 games, beating the Russians in the unofficial point count of medals won. Much of that success was owed to America's black athletes, particularly to their predominance in track and field. "By the way, I'd like to note that the lion's share of awards in track and field was collected for the U.S. by their amazing Negro athletes," said Soviet high jumper Valery Brumel at the conclusion of the 1968 games.

U.S. officials well understood that they needed the services of the black athletes if they were going to come close to overtaking the Russians at the XIX Olympiad. What Avery Brundage said in 1959 rang true with even greater accuracy at Mexico City: "Before the war, we had won as many Olympic medals as all the rest of the world combined. Since then, if it weren't for our Negro athletes we would be out of the picture." Hence, the United States would make every effort to defuse the Olympic boycott movement and to keep its black athletes in line.[12]

Neither was the black boycott movement flawless on its own terms. From the beginning, the Olympic Project for Human Rights was practically a one-man show: Professor Harry Edwards. The warm-up boycott of the New York Athletic Club track meet in February 1968 at New York City's Madison Square Garden, orchestrated by Edwards, was only partially successful because of the divisiveness among the black athletes. The black protestors lashed out at the NYAC's discriminatory policies. Many black athletes stayed away, but at least nine crossed the picket line to compete in the meet. Jim Dennis of the Houston Striders was late for the sixty-yard dash after being delayed by traffic and by the pickets. "I broke my glasses when I got shoved on the way in," he said. "It wasn't a punch or anything and I'm not sure it was intentional." Bob Beamon participated in the meet, although he claimed that he did so in order to get a free trip home to New York. Frazetta Parham crossed the picket line, as did Lennox Miller. "I am not in favor of discrimination by the N.Y.A.C.," said Miller, "but I don't want to be dictated to by others." There was, to be sure, a great deal of heated rhetoric at the NYAC demonstration. Edwards intimated that blacks crossing the picket line to compete in the meet might get their heads busted, and H. Rap Brown suggested that the Garden be blown up.[13]

The black Olympic boycott movement had more rhetorical than organizational support. The Olympic Project for Human Rights had only a handful of active members, among them Tommie Smith, John Carlos, Lee Evans, and Harry Edwards. *Sports Illustrated* asserted that "most black athletes have been solidly against Smith and Evans and their plan to use the Olympics as a platform to dramatize their grievances at home." Black Olympians Mel Pender and Bob Beamon and their black women teammates were staunchly antiboycott. The OPHR made practically no effort to consider the opinions and gain the support of the black women athletes. Wyomia Tyus, holder of five world records in track and gold medal winner in 1964, remarked that the black male athletes never invited the black female athletes to attend their meetings. Jarvis Scott, a competitor in the 400-meter run, said that she supported the aims of the Olympic Project for Human Rights but not the boycott. Scott added that she and the other black women on the U.S. team "were most disappointed that our feelings were not brought out; while the men issued statements and held conferences, finding out what we felt was only a last minute thing." Even in the case of an Evans, a Carlos, or a Smith, it was difficult to believe that they, after years of training and sacrifice with the goal of attaining an Olympic gold medal, would boycott the games.[14]

The dominant objective of the Olympian and would-be Olympian was participation in the Olympics. Collegiate basketballer Merv Jackson was one of seventy-five college basketball players considered for participation in the Olympic trials in early 1968. His only thought: "It would be a great experience to play with the great players from around the country. I'm lucky to be playing in an Olympic year." Women's track star Wyomia Tyus said she had but one thing on her mind: Being ready for the Mexico City games. Traditionally, athletes able to win a spot on the Olympic team single-mindedly pursued that goal; the competition demanded it. They also tended to shy away from politics, personifying the Brundage adage that politics has no place in sports. Jesse Owens seconded the Brundage position. "I feel changes are being made for the better," Owens said, "and I also feel that the Olympics should not be used as a battle-ground for civil rights."[15]

As the start of the games grew nearer, the ranks of even possible boycott supporters grew thinner. The coaching staff and the press queried the black athletes and were told that they had no intentions of boycotting. When the press confronted Harry Edwards with this information, he made the best out of an otherwise dismal organizational failure. He said that what the athletes were doing was in keeping with an agreed-upon strategy to create an atmosphere of chaos for the U.S. Olympic Committee. 'If I were you," Edwards said, "I wouldn't believe everything we say. If you believe me now, that's beautiful, and if you don't that's still beautiful. You can choose to believe what you want to and disregard the rest. The boycott is still alive."[16]

It was not. The Olympic events proceeded on schedule and the black athletes competed. The proposed black boycott, in the final analysis, became nothing more than a few symbolic gestures. Some black

Olympians wore black socks during their heats. The major incident occurred when Tommie Smith and John Carlos, wearing black socks and one black glove each, gave a Black Power salute on the victors' stand after receiving their medals for taking first and third place in the 200-meter run. Theirs was a relatively mild demonstration, and giving the Black Power salute was a last-minute decision. Immediately after the incident, John Carlos said to reporters that the salute they gave on the stand—Smith with his right arm extended with black-gloved clenched fist and Carlos with his left arm extended with black-gloved clenched fist—symbolized a "U" for black unity. Another explanation as to why each wore only one glove may have been that they could only come up with one pair of black gloves owing to the last-minute nature of their demonstration. At any rate, their symbolic gesture was not intended as a revolutionary action or an act of defiance. Tommie Smith said, "As far as the black fists, it was very quiet. We wanted Black people to see, especially the young guys, to have something to be proud of, to identify themselves with." Yet their actions drew the wrath of the U.S. government and the official reprimand of the U.S. Olympic Committee, and the International Olympic Committee. Smith and Carlos were expelled from the games. Neither runner would find professional athletics welcoming him into the fold.[17]

The reaction of other black athletes at the XIX Olympiad was revealing yet predictable. They took, like the majority of humankind does, a centrist posture. The actions of human response run the gamut from radical to conservative, but most fall somewhere in the middle range. The majority of the black Olympians fell into this category. Black athletes at the Mexico City games failed to take unified action regarding the expulsion of Carlos and Smith. A few denounced the expulsion and a petition was circulated, but little else happened. Black Olympians sympathized with what happened to Smith and Carlos, and with the problems facing black America and the Third World. But, like Bob Beamon, Ralph Boston, Wyomia Tyus, and the majority of black America, they adopted a moderate position. Also, at the games, there was the antiprotest demonstration of George Foreman who, after winning the gold medal in boxing, paraded around the ring toting a miniature American flag. The political triad exemplified by the black athletes at the XIX Olympiad mirrored black American political consciousness: the activists, the sympathizers or silent majority, and the antiactivists.[18]

Fortunately or unfortunately, the 1968 Olympic boycott movement was more than the sum of its parts. The legacy of those games was a heightened awareness of the relationship between international sports and politics. The utilization of the Olympic Games as a forum for political statement carried into the XX Olympiad. Southern Africa was again a target as the 1972 Munich Olympics approached. There was the issue of the British-Rhodesian political settlement and the raging war against apartheid in South Africa. African political consciousness was flourishing. An intellectual movement was afoot in the motherland to end "Apedom," which was, as Okok Pbitek, a lecturer at Nairobi University, called it, "the aping the white man's ways." Pbitek, like many other African leaders, was a proponent of negritude. He objected to following the white man's lead and advocated a return to traditional African sensibilities and the utilization of any means necessary to achieve that goal.[19]

While Africa was marching forward, black America was under siege, facing a massive campaign of regression led by the Nixon White House. The clock seemed to be moving backward on every front of civil rights: antibusing, antivoting, antieconomic opportunity, antihuman rights throughout the world. This regression was exemplified by the police raid on the Black Panther headquarters in Chicago and the murder of Fred Hampton, the floundering membership of the NAACP and the lawsuits filed against the organization, and the incarceration of Angela Davis.

The sports scene for blacks in America was no better. Dwayne Thomas, the outspoken rebellious black running back for the Dallas Cowboys football team, was at odds with coach Tom Landry, owner Tex Schram, and the professional sports establishment in general. In February 1972, a group of Michigan State University black athletes which included, among others, Herb Washington and Billy Joe DuPre, launched protests against racial discrimination at MSU. In addition, they demanded that the Big Ten Conference appoint black athletic officials and more black varsity coaches and trainers. David Wolf's book, *Foul*, appeared in 1972. It explored the life story of black basketball player Connie Hawkins as a case study of how collegiate and professional sports cruelly exploited a black, former ghetto athlete. The Supreme Court decided against Curt Flood and his suit against the Reserve Clause in professional baseball; Willis Reed was jailed on a bad conduct rap; and Dwayne Thomas was conspicuously absent from the Dallas training camp in July. Members of the NAACP and other civil rights organizations banded together to picket the Liberty Bowl game in Memphis Memorial Stadium over the suspension of Eddie McAshan, the black quarterback of Georgia Tech. McAshan, a senior, was the first black quarterback to play at a predominantly white Southeastern school. He was suspended by coach Bill Fulchur for missing practice before Tech's regular season final game against Georgia. McAshan boycotted practice to protest the four years of racist harassment he had received at the hands of the all-white coaching staff. The Dallas Cowboys announced in August that they had traded Dwayne Thomas to the San Diego Chargers. Ripples were felt throughout the black community when Calvin Patterson, a black running back for Florida State University who was in serious grade trouble and unable to take any more of the pressure of big-time collegiate sports and the demands of academia, committed suicide. Finally, Dwayne Thomas was reported missing from the San Diego training camp.

Regardless of the setbacks on the domestic front, black America increasingly supported human rights and the struggles in the Third World. Several black and white church groups in the United States filed a petition in the United Nations against human rights violations in Southern Africa. Black American leaders kept a constant vigil over American foreign policy in Africa, Latin America, and the Middle East. The Congressional Black Caucus opposed the Azores Agreement between the United States and Portugal. Representative Charles Diggs, Jr., chairman of the House Subcommittee on Africa and a leading member of the opposition to U.S. foreign policy, criticized the Nixon administration's support of racist and oppressive regimes in Southern Africa and throughout the world. Other black organizations took a similar stand. The African-American National Conference on Africa met in Washington, D.C., in an attempt to galvanize interests in Africa into an instrument of discussion about relations between Africans and African Americans and U.S. policy in Africa. A poll conducted in June 1972 of 3,200 African Americans and Puerto Ricans in central Harlem, east Harlem, and Bedford Stuyvesant registered a 96 to 1 percent opposition to President Nixon's mining of North Vietnamese harbors and the stepped-up bombings. Former heavyweight boxing champion Muhammad Ali canceled his plans to fight in South Africa.[20]

When South Africa gave official notice in 1970 that it wanted to return to the Olympics, Africa and black America joined together in a resounding voice of disapproval. The South Africans argued that they had made tremendous progress in their country toward integrating sports. Rhodesia claimed to have done much the same. The *Wall Street Journal*, in an editorial titled "Sports and Politics," declared its support for Rhodesia's participation in the 1972 Summer Olympics in Munich. The editorial argued that Ian Smith had made great strides toward bringing his nation on a par with other nations throughout the world in protecting human rights. Furthermore, the *Journal* criticized the worldwide sports boycott against South Africa: "The only reason that athletes should be barred is if they break the rules. It is a mistake for an international athletic forum to capitulate to political pressures." Avery Brundage, the eighty-six-year-old president of the IOC, favored the readmission of South Africa and Rhodesia to the games. Commenting on Rhodesia Brundage stated: "Politics, it's all politics. Rhodesia has been extended an official invitation to compete in the Games. Rhodesia will participate." [21]

Black America, Africa, and their allies were steadfast. Vince Mathews and several other Olympians on the 1972 U.S. men's track team voiced their plan to walk out of the Olympics if Rhodesia was permitted to take part. A number of former Olympic athletes, black and white, declared their support of the proposed lockout of Rhodesia. Fifteen African nations plus Haiti, Cuba, and Yugoslavia gave notice to the IOC that if Rhodesia was allowed to participate in the Summer Games in Munich, they would not. In August 1972, the IOC announced that the invitation extended to Rhodesia to compete in the 1972 Olympic Games had been rescinded.

The 1972 Munich games proved to be one of the worst showings by a U.S. Olympic team since the revival of the modern Olympics. The question over Rhodesia had been won, but other occurrences diminished that achievement. The atmosphere of the 1972 games was tense and restrictive. Police were everywhere and the situation on the playing fields was foreboding. When Vince Mathews and Wayne Collet gave a black power salute upon leaving the victors' stand after receiving their medals for finishing first and second in the 400 meters, both were severely reprimanded and barred from competing in any further Olympic events. Beyond this, there was dissension among the blacks participating in the games. The failure of the black coach of the U.S. track team, Stan Wright, to get several of his athletes to the qualifying meet on time was a dismal display. The result was that Ray Robinson, a black athlete who many thought was the fastest human in the world in 1972, was disqualified for failing to show up for his qualifying heat. Wright never apologized to Robinson for his oversight and the chance he had lost the young athlete to run in the 100-meter dash. In a statement to the media, when asked if he would tour with the American track team in Ghana the following summer, Robinson said, "I will if coach Wright does not go on the tour." [22]

The XX Olympic Games were also the scene of a catastrophic intrusion of international politics—namely, the assassination of eleven Israeli athletes. The Palestinians who perpetrated the act hoped to focus world attention on the struggle in the Middle East, and to strike fear and terror in the hearts of Jews everywhere. What they did achieve was to galvanize public opinion against Palestinians and their cause, the Palestine Liberation Organization (PLO) and its leader Yassar Arafat, and the goals of their war against Israel. Why? First, and quite obviously, the murder of the Israeli athletes was unpalatable to public sensitivities. Second, the PLO had flagrantly misused and abused international sports. To be sure, the Olympic Games have always been a forum for international politicking, despite the insistence of sports purists to the contrary, and it has always been basically nonviolent. Protest yes, but revolutionary action no. It is an accepted norm for Russians and Americans to pulverize one another in the Olympic boxing ring. The fighters, however, do not quietly slip away to the locker room after the match and there engage in unofficiated, true warfare with guns and knives to the death. The Palestinians broke the basic premise of international sports competition, the implicit credo underlying the Olympics. The credo of the games is, as George Orwell, reflecting on the first modern Olympiad, said, "warfare minus the shooting." [23]

Moreover, the killing of the Israeli athletes made more difficult the unification of African, Arab, and other Third World efforts against Zionism and the nation-state of Israel. Third World nations had many conflicts with one another and a wide range of long-standing differences. Uganda's expulsion of some 50,000 Asians holding British passports on charges that they had sabotaged the Ugandan economy was one such example. In September 1972, in the midst of the Summer Games, Ghana announced that it had expelled all Lebanese and Syrian businessmen from its territories because, as one Ghanan official declared, 'they literally bled us white." The African and Arab nations were virtually united, however, in their condemnation of Israel and its economic and political ties with South Africa. African and Arab members of the United Nations were repeatedly proposing sanctions against South Africa, Rhodesia, and Israel. In America, the old coalitions between blacks and Jews seemed to be eroding. The Jewish Defense League reportedly threatened the life of Angela Davis. Black Jews who had immigrated to Israel were disallowed permanent-resident status and others were denied entrance altogether. B'nai B'rith and other noted Jewish organizations went on record in opposition to quota systems and subsequently endorsed the Bakke decision. Members of the Congressional Black Caucus and other black activists expressed concern over what they perceived as a substantial Jewish vote in support of the election and administration of President Richard M. Nixon. The death of the Israeli athletes placed anti-Jewish/Israeli sentiments in the United States and throughout much of the world on temporary hold. In the United States, Representative Ralph Metcalfe delivered a thunderous speech deploring the killing of the Israeli athletes. Bayard Rustin called for a strengthening of the black alliance with Jews and Israel. Every black Olympian at the XX Olympiad who uttered a word on the killing of the Israeli athletes vehemently denounced the assassinations as unwarranted acts of terrorism. Jesse Owens wept openly upon learning of the murders. Every African, Arab, and Third World nation participating in the games issued statements, at one point or another, condemning the killing of the Israeli athletes. An idea entertained earlier, very quietly, about possibly boycotting Israel's participation in future Olympiads was even more quietly dismissed.[24]

At face value, the 1976 Olympic Games did not seem to hold as great a potential for positive propagandizing on the part of the Third World nations. The Olympic sports boycott against South Africa and Rhodesia was holding. African nations, however, attempted to get what political mileage that they could from the XXI Olympiad and initiated a boycott against New Zealand's participation in the games on the grounds that the country had engaged in international sporting with South Africa. Dennis Brutus, the South African poet and visiting professor of literature at Northwestern University, had long been active in the struggle against apartheid sport. He praised the 1976 Olympic boycott movement, noting that New Zealand was involved in seventeen sporting exchanges with South Africa—not just rugby—and had remained insensitive to the pleas of African nations. Yet the reasons behind the

African nations' boycott of the 1976 games was not wholly focused on the issue of New Zealand's ties with South Africa. If every nation that had some dealing with South Africa was barred from competing in the Olympics, there would have been very few countries left to participate in the XXI Olympiad, including many of the African nations. What the African nations were doing, in fact, was political posturing via international sports. The African nations were, athletically speaking, unlikely to make a strong showing in the 1976 Olympics. Thus, the boycott action they took served the best propaganda purpose. This is not to say that South Africa was not a real concern, but it suggests that the African nations attained more effective political mileage by boycotting the games than participating in them.

Although other Third World nations pledged their support to the African nations' boycott of the Montreal Olympics, as did the Soviet Union, they really had no intention of doing so, at least for those nations who believed that they had more to gain from competing in the games than by boycotting them. Take, for example, the Russians and the Cubans, who pledged their support to the boycott but, in the end, competed in the games. The Russians routinely pledged their support to the Olympic protest movements by Third Worlders. They stopped short when it came to actually boycotting the games. The reason was quite simple: They had too much to lose. The Soviets won every Olympiad since they began participating in the games in 1952, with the exception of the 1968 Olympics. To boycott was for them to discard a tremendous propaganda opportunity. Cuba knew that it had a strong track team, and that their boxing squad had a superb chance of winning the Olympic boxing title in 1976.

The irony of the XXI Olympic Games was that when the Cuban boxing team competed for the championship, its major foe and eventual spoilers were the black American boxers. The several hundred million television viewers around the world witnessed, at a conscious level, a matchup of competing fighters. The reality was that the majority of the fighters in the finals were black Americans and Cubans. No sport is closer to actual physical war than boxing, where the main objective is to render your opponent helpless, hopefully by way of a knockout. When Teofillio Stevenson knocked John Tate senseless in the first round of their semifinal match, this was a victory, at one level, of Stevenson over Tate. When black Olympic boxers Sugar Ray Leonard, Leo Randolph, Howard Davis, and the Spinks brothers eliminated their opponents, this was, at one level, a victory for the individual fighters. At a more subliminal level at least, the battles were not merely fighter versus fighter—as it never is—but Cuban versus American, African versus African, Third Worlder versus Third Worlder. The irony for the black American boxer, given his peculiar nation-status, was that when he lost he lost, and when he won he lost.[25]

To better understand the dilemma of the black American Olympic athlete is to decode the power system that prevails over most of the world. Nowhere is the international power structure more clearly exposed than in international sports politics. The Carter-imposed boycott of the 1980 Summer Olympics reflected the bipolarism of the world we live in, the Cold War dichotomy, and the relevancy of international sports to the political arsenal. After the Russian intervention in Afghanistan, coupled with the Iranian seizure of the American embassy in Tehran and the taking of American hostages, President Jimmy Carter levied a grain embargo, SALT II talks were temporarily suspended, and draft registration was reinstated. Carter also took another course of action: He agitated for a boycott of the 1980 Summer Olympic Games, which were to be held in Moscow. Shortly after his announcement that he would seriously pursue a boycott of the games, the world, in a sense, showed its colors, dividing predictably into East versus West over support or rejection of the boycott. But within another few months, it became clear that the Russians had their traditional half of the pie, along with a substantial portion of Carter's piece. British Prime Minister Margaret Thatcher, for example, declared her support of the boycott but British athletes would be allowed to participate, unofficially, in the games. Two things had become quite obvious: that the United States, at least under Carter, was not the undisputed head of the Western world, and that allies and foes alike were suspicious that the politics he was attempting to play with the XXII Olympic Games were really an effort to reverse his faltering popularity in the polls.

Whatever his true motives, the role assigned to black America in Carter's boycott was revealing and reflective of his view of and political relationship with the black community. Carter's administration approach to the blacks was, in a word, token. He appointed some blacks to his administration and he often reminded the black community of this and of his appointment of several black judges. His administration was being criticized from all angles, however, including from black leaders such as the Urban League's Vernon Jordan and the NAACP's

Benjamin Hooks. The unemployment rate in the black community was twice that of white America. Nevertheless, when Carter asked for black support he received it, as he would in his losing bid for reelection. When he requested the support of black Olympic athletes to his boycott initiative, he got that too. There were moans and groans such as those from black Olympic gymnast Ron Galimore. But Galimore like his black and white counterparts would obey the dictates emanating from Washington. They had no choice.[26]

President Carter evidently drew certain conclusions about African people based on his experiences with American blacks. It is little wonder, then, that presidential spokesman Hodding Carter could issue a statement on January 25, 1980, that African nations would support the boycott of the Moscow games. He, like Jimmy Carter, seemed unaware of the Russians' more favorable image in Africa. When Hodding Carter was challenged to give a list of those African nations supporting the boycott, he said that "the list is unavailable at the moment." It was within this scenario of things that President Carter called upon "The Greatest," three-time heavyweight boxing champion Muhammad Ali, to serve as a special envoy, a sports ambassador to the African nations who was expected to garner African support for the boycott.[27]

Ali's mission was a complete failure. Most African leaders would not grant him an audience. Julius Nyerere, president of Tanzania, remarked that he loved and respected Ali as a boxer but that he would not discuss serious international politics with him. Those African officials who did speak with Ali offered their brother from across the Atlantic a political lesson. They reminded him of America's past relations with South Africa and the failure of the United States to support the African nations' boycott of the 1976 games. Ali was somewhat educable. By the time he returned to the United States he had arrived at a perceptive conclusion: "Maybe I was being used to do something that wasn't right."[28]

The dilemma for black America is how to do what is right in a world where everything is political and a belief in human rights at home and abroad may very well mean taking a stand in opposition to your own government. The politically conscious black Olympic athletes exemplified this perplexity of having to come to terms with being a representative of the most powerful country in the Western world and yet be a member of the African diaspora and a participant, on one side or the other, in the Third World's struggle. The solution is not easy. Political consciousness is the first step and we must not overlook an area as crucial as politicking in athletics. Sport is one of the biggest businesses in the world, a multibillion-dollar enterprise in the United States alone. The highest-paid individual in academia is not a college president, a Nobel Laureate scientist, or a renowned scholar; it is a college football coach in Texas. The largest television-viewing audience in history to watch a single broadcast was watching not a documentary special or an Academy Award–winning movie; they were watching the Super Bowl game. It was all there in the 1984 Olympic Games in Los Angeles, running the gamut from the Soviet boycott to crass commercialism and nationalistic slogans to the political nuances and the symbolic statements of the athletic competitions. It is incumbent upon all of us to broaden our political consciousness in order to decode the political messages embedded in sport.

NOTES

1. Clippings, Avery Brundage Collection, Box 287, University of Illinois Archives, Urbana-Champaign.

2. *New York Times*, 24 July 1967; Richard E. Lapchick, *The Politics of Race and International Sport* (Westport, Conn.: Greenwood Press, 1975), 73, 80–86; Richard Espy, *The Politics of the Olympic Games* (Los Angeles: University of California Press, 1980), 76, 81, 98, 157; William J. Baker and John M. Carroll, *Sports in Modern America* (St. Louis, Mo.: River City Press, 1981), 158–172.

3. Donald Spivey and Thomas A. Jones, "Intercollegiate Athletic Servitude: A Case Study of the Black Illini Student-Athletes, 1931–1967," *Social Science Quarterly* (March 1975), 939–947; *Chicago Defender*, 6 July–12 July 1968, 4, 27 July–2 August 1968, 6; Harry Edwards, *The Revolt of the Black Athlete* (New York: The Free Press, 1969), 91–93, 175–182; see Donald Spivey, "The Black Athlete in Big Time Intercollegiate Sports, 1941–1968," *Phylon* (June 1983), 116–125.

4. "Football's Big Problem," *Daily World* (New York), 24 July 1968, 8; *Daily World*, 31 July 1968, 8, 13 August 1968, 12; *Chicago Defender*, 20–26 July 1968, 10–11, 21 July–2 August 1968, 18.

5. *Chicago Defender*, 24–30 August 1968, 10, 11–17 May 1968, 31, 25, 31 May 1968, 12, 20–26 July 1968, 11, 25–31 May 1968, 2.

6. Edwards, *Revolt*, 93.

7. "Mixed Group Urges Nixing S. Africa," *Chicago Defender*, 13–19 April 1968, 20; *Chicago Defender*, 8–14 June 1968, 15, 27 July–2 August 1968, 19; *Daily World*, 20 August 1968, 12.

8. Minutes of the Meeting of the Executive Board of the International Olympic Committee, 21 April 1968, Avery Brundage Collection, Box 93.

9. *Daily World*, 12 October 1968, 12.

10. "Boycott of the 1968 Games," Avery Brundge Collection, Box 287; John Morin, "The Bloody Olympiad," *Daily World*, 5 October 1968, 12; *Daily World*, 4 October 1968, 12; International Athletes' Club to Avery Brundage, 18 April 1966, Brundage Collection, Box 176; *Chicago Daily News*, 2 February 1968, 24–26; Bob Ottum, "Grim Countdown to the Games," *Sports Illustrated*, 14 October 1968, 36–43.

11. *Chicago Defender*, 10–16 February 1968, 15, 27 April–3 May 1968, 15; *Daily World*, 21 August 1968, 12, 23 October 1968, 12, 24 October 1968, 12; Edwards, *Revolt*, 91–120; Udokwu to president of ICO, 19 October 1968, Brundage Collection, Box 176; Adrian Kissler to Avery Brundage, 3 July 1969, Brundage Collection, Box 287; *Chicago Defender*, 4–10 May 1968, 3–11; M. Kreissman to Avery Brundage, 22 October 1968, Brundage Collection, Box 287; *The Filipino Athlete* (1969), 4; *Daily Telegraph*, July 1970, 2; *South African Cape Herald*, 22, April 1967, 1–4; South African Non Racial Olympic Committee to Avery Brundage, 19 April 1967, Brundage Collection, Box 277; "The Last Living Amateur Is Still a King," *Sports Illustrated*, 22 May 1967, 70–73.

12. "Is America a Second-Class Track Power?" *Sports Illustrated*, 2 February 1959, 34–38; *Daily World*, 31 October 1968, 12; Harry Edwards, *Sociology of Sport* (Homewood, Ill.: Dorsey Press, 1973), 186–193, 273–316.

13. Pete Axthelm, "Boycott Now—Boycott Later?" *Sports Illustrated*, 26 February 1968, 24–26.

14. Ibid., 25; *Chicago Defender*, 1–7 June 1968, 15, 19–25 October 1968, 18; *Daily World*, 12 October 1968, 12.

15. *Chicago Defender*, 24 February–1 March 1968, 17, 4–10 May 1968, 18, 9–15 March 1968, 15; "After 32 Years, Owens Is Still Example for Youth," ibid., 11–17 May 1968, 31.

16. *Daily World*, 9 August 1968, 12, 3 September 1968, 12, 19 October 1968, 12.

17. *New York Times*, 6 October 1968; *Detroit Free Press*, 14 October 1972; Mike Jay, "Tommie Smith: After Four Years," *Daily World*, 14 October 1972, m–11.

18. La Bulgarie demande la réorganisation du C.I.O., *L' Equipe*, 4 August 1968, clipping in Brundage Collection, Box 187; *World Sports*, January 1969, 11; Comite Olympique Bulgare, Bulletin d'Informations, II (1971), 3–23; *Los Angeles Times*, 8 April 1970, 9; Gordon Allport, *The Nature of Prejudice*

(Cambridge, Mass.: Addison Wesley, 1950); George Spindler, *Personality and Social Change* (New York: McGraw Hill, 1966) and *Education and Culture* (New York: Holt, Rinehart and Winston, 1963); *Chicago Defender*, 19–25 October 1968, 18; August Meier and Elliott Rudwick, *Black Protest Thought in the Twentieth Century* (New York: Bobbs-Merrill Co., 1971), 77–87.

19. *Chicago Defender*, 26 January 1972, 8, 3 February 1972, 10; John Platter, "Black Africa—In Search of a New, Better Identity," *UPI*, 10 July 1972, Nairobi, Kenya.

20. *Chicago Defender*, 3 February 1972, 34, 23 February 1972, 28, 20 April 1972, 33; "Blues for Curt Flood," ibid., 19 July 1972, 32; ibid., 24 July 1972, 24, 31 July 1972, 24; *New York Times*, 2 August 1972; *Chicago Defender*, 31 August 1972, 32; *New York Times*, 19 July 1972.

21. *Wall Street Journal* (New York), "Sports and Politics," 9 August 1972; "South Africa Wants Back into Olympics," *Chicago Defender*, 2 February 1972, 28; ibid., 16, 28 August 1972, 8; Lapchick, *Politics*, 153–197.

22. "Robinson: 'Wright Refuses to Speak After Mistake,' " *Daily World*, 13 September 1972, 28.

23. Baker and Carroll, *Sports*, 159; for further discussion of the underlying philosophy of sports see Paul Weiss, *Sport: A Philosophical Inquiry* (Carbondale, Ill.: Southern Illinois University Press, 1979); *New York Times*, 16 January 1972, 16 February 1972, 22 August 1972; *Washington Post*, 16 February 1972.

24. Lloyd Hogan, "Olympic Games Missed the Boat," *Chicago Defender*, 12 September 1972, 24; ibid., 11 September 1972, 5, 24; *Daily World*, 6 June 1972, 6; *Chicago Defender*, 24 August 1972, 8, 6 September 1972, 24, 22 August 1972, 28; *London Times*, 22 August 1972.

25. *London Times*, 4 May 1976; *New York Times*, 23 May 1976, 12 July 1976; *Sports Illustrated*, 12 July 1976, 8, 26 July 1976, 17.

26. *New York Times*, 6 January 1980; *Chicago Defender*, 6 January 1980; *Daily World*, 13 January 1980, 24; "Japanese Oppose Boycott," ibid., 28 March 1980, 11; Thomas G. Paterson, *On Every Front: The Making of the Cold War* (New York: W. W. Norton, 1979), 2–68, 169–173, and passim; B. W. Hodder, *Africa Today* (New York: Africana Publishing, 1978); George Leonard, *The Ultimate Athlete* (New York: Avon Books, 1974); John W. Spanier, *American Foreign Policy Since World War II* (New York: Praeger, 1968); Kwame Nkrumah, *Neo-Colonialism: The Last Stage of Imperialism* (New York: International Publishing, 1965); Richard Lowenthal, *World Communism* (New York: Oxford University Press, 1964); *Moscow Tass in English* (1603 GMT, 7 January 1980); *Soviet Sport*, 13, 18, 24 January 1980; *Pravda*, 25, 28 July 1980.

27. *Daily World*, 7 February 1980, 24; for comparative perspective see "Muhammad Ali in Africa," *Sports Illustrated*, 1 June 1964, 20–24; and Ali

Mazrui, "Boxer Muhammad Ali and Soldier Idi Amin as International Political Symbols: The Bioeconomics of Sport and War," *Comparative Studies in Society and History*, 19, no. 22 (April 1977), 189–215.

28. *Daily World*, 25 January 1980, 16; *Chicago Defender*, 26 January 1980, 12; *New York Times*, 18 January 1980, 26.

Bibliographical Essay

There are a number of volumes that offer a good overview of American sport. Works I have found most useful are: William J. Baker and John M. Carroll, eds., *Sports in Modern America* (1981); John R. Betts, *America's Sporting Heritage* (1974); Frederick W. Cozens and Florence S. Stumpf, *Sports in American Life* (1953); John A. Krout, *Annals of American Sport* (1979); John A. Lucas and Ronald Smith, *Saga of American Sport* (1978); James A. Michener, *Sports in American Life* (1976); Benjamin G. Rader, *American Sports: From the Age of Folk Game to the Age of Spectators* (1982); Wiley Umphlett, *The Sporting Myth and the American Experience* (1975); and Earle F. Zeigler, *History of Physical Education and Sport* (1979).

The history and nature of play and leisure time are cogently addressed in: Foster Rhea Dulles, *America Learns to Play* (1940); Harry Edwards, *Sociology of Sport* (1973); Allen Guttman, *From Ritual to Record: The Nature of Modern Sports* (1978); Stephen Hardy, *How Boston Played, 1865–1915* (1982); John Huizinga, *Homo Ludens: A Study of the Play Element in Culture* (1955); Donald Mrozek, *Sports and Recreation in the West* (1978); and Dale Somers, *Rise of Sports in New Orleans, 1850–1900* (1972).

Quality topical studies have focused on the big four of sports: baseball, basketball, boxing, and football. Studies of most note are: in baseball: Robert Creamer, *Babe* (1974); Richard Goldstein, *Spartan Seasons: How Baseball Survived the Second World War* (1980); Donald Gropman, *Say It Ain't So, Joe! The Story of Shoeless Joe Jackson* (1979); Roger Kahn, *The Boys of Summer* (1971); Lee Lowenfish and Tony Lupien, *The Imperfect Diamond* (1980); Robert Peterson, *Only the Ball was White* (1970); Steven A. Riess, *Touching Base: Professional Baseball and American Culture in the Progressive Era* (1980);

Harold Seymour, *Baseball: The Early Years* (1960) and *Baseball: the Golden Age* (1971); Marshall Smelser, *The Life That Ruth Built* (1975); David Voigt, *American Baseball* (1970); in basketball: Neil Issacs, *All the Moves: A History of College Basketball* (1975); David Wolf, *Foul: The Connie Hawkins Story* (1972); in boxing: Anthony O. Edmonds, *Joe Louis* (1973); Al-Tony Gilmore, *Bad Nigger! The National Impact of Jack Johnson* (1975); Benny Green, *Shaw's Champions: G.B.S. and Prizefighting from Cashel Bryan to Gene Tunney* (1978); Randy Roberts, *Jack Dempsey: The Manassa Mauler* (1979); in football: William Cady, *The Big Game: College Sports and American Life* (1978); Harold Classen, *The History of Pro Football* (1963); Ivan N. Kaye, *Good Clean Violence: A History of College Football* (1973).

Blacks in sports are given reliable examination in: John Behee, *Hail to the Victors: Black Athletes at the University of Michigan* (1974); Edwin B. Henderson, *The Negro in Sport* (1949); Harry Edwards, *Revolt of the Black Athlete* (1969); Jack Orr, *The Black Athlete* (1969). Serious discussions of women in sports are had in: Gerber Felshin et al., *The American Women in Sport* (1974), and Stephanie L. Twin, ed., *Out of the Bleachers: Writings on Women and Sport* (1979). The history and politics of the world's greatest athletic event, the Olympic Games, are analyzed in: Richard Espy, *The Politics of the Olympic Games* (1979); Richard E. Lapchick, *The Politics of Race and International Sport: The Case of South Africa* (1975); John Lucas, *The Modern Olympic Games* (1980); Richard D. Mandell, *The Nazi Olympics* (1971) and *The First Modern Olympics* (1976).

The reader looking to stay abreast of the most current research in the field of sport history should turn to the wealth of essays in the *Journal of Sport History*. Some other essays that offer stimulating conceptualizations of sport and society from a historical perspective are: Harry Jebsen, "Sport: A Microcosm of Twentieth Century America," *American Quarterly* (1978); Peter Levine, "The Promise of Sport in Antebellum America," *Journal of American Culture* (1980); Benjamin Rader, "Modern Sports: In Search of Interpretations," *Journal of Social History* (1979); Steven A. Riess, "Sport and the American Dream," *Journal of Social History* (1980); Donald Spivey, "Sport, Protest, and Consciousness: The Black Athlete in Big-Time Intercollegiate Sports, 1941–1968," *Phylon* (1983); Jeffrey T. Sammons, "Boxing as a Reflection of Society," *Journal of Popular Culture* (1983); and Elliott J. Gorn, "The Social Significance of Fighting in the Southern Backcountry," *American Historical Review* (1985).

Index

Actives, 81
Addams, Jane, 202
Adelman, Melvin, 95
Afghanistan, 257
African-American National Conference on Africa, 252
African-Americans, 142, 145-146,
148, 150-152, 155-156, 159-160,
166, 168, 172, 181-182, 226,
239, 240-246, 250-258
Agues, 81
Alabama, 164, 247
Albany, New York, 98, 119
Alger, Horatio, 165
Ali, Muhammad, 145, 166-170;
boxing championship of, 170-172,
178-182; opposition to Vietnam
war, 172-173, 182; refuses military service, 172-175; regains
championship, 177-179; religious
views of, 169-170, 173, 178; as
special envoy to African nations,
258; stripped of heavyweight boxing championship, 171-173, 175,
252; Supreme Court clears of the

charge of refusing induction, 176-
177
Alley, George, 55
Amaro, Rubin, 244
Amateur Athletic Union, 102, 105-
106, 113, 118, 130-131, 136-137
Amateur sports, ix, 137, 209, 232,
244, 247. *See also* Sports, in
America
America, 177, 198, 220, 227, 252;
race relations in, 147-151, 153-
159, 163, 166, 168, 170-175,
177, 179-182, 240-244, 248, 252,
255, 258; race riots in, 147; racial
attitudes in, 146; values of, 226-
229, 233-234; violence in, 151,
225
American Association, 98
American Broadcasting Company,
175, 247
American Committee on Africa, 244
American Dream, 200
American Federation of Labor, 137,
158
American Historical Association, ix

American Jockey Club, 51-65; income of members, 57-58; members of, 54-56; occupations of members, 56-58; social mobility of members, 60-65
American League Against War and Fascism, 136
American Legion, 132-133, 173-174
American Medical Association, 210
American Physical Education Association, 209
American Youth Congress, 136
Amory, Cleveland, 62
Anderson, Marian, 159
Andrews, John, 11
Antebellum elites, 52
Antioch College, 86
Anti-Semitism, 164
Apedom, 251
Arabs, 254-255
Arafat, Yassar, 254
Archery, 211
Arkansas, 151
Arledge, Roone, 175
Army, Navy and Civilian Board of Control, 120-121
Army of the United States of America, 157, 165, 173
Arthur, Little. See Johnson, Jack
Aryans, 164
Ashe, Arthur, 242
Asia, 240
Asians, 254
Aspenwall, Tom, 84
Association for Humanistic Psychology, 193
Astor, John Jacob, 58
Athens, Greece, 194-195
Athletes, 42, 160, 194, 219, 221-224, 228-232, 239, 241-258; coaches of, 208-209, 214, 228, 241; politics of, 239-254; professional, 241-242, 244, 250-252;

violence of, 229-233. See also Sports, in America
Athletic clubs, 52, 101, 104-107, 109-119, 121, 123, 202-205, 208-209, 211-215, 219
Athletics. See Sports, in America
Atlanta, Georgia, 151
Atlanta Falcons, 242
Atlantic Athletic Association, 119
Atlantic Athletic Club, 98
Atlantics, 81
Austin, Sam, 106-107
Australia, 118
Austria, 135
Austrians, 131
Avonia Athletic Club, 106
Axis, 160
Axthelm, Pete, 176
Azores Agreement, 252

Backgammon, 9
Bacon's Rebellion, 4-5
Baer, Max, 161-163
Baker, John, 13
Bakke decision, 255
Balian Ice Cream Beauties, 206
Balinese cockfight, 6
Balough, Harry, 162
Baltimore, 151
Baltzell, E. Digby, 52, 63
Banners, 86
Barnard College, 208
Bartram, John, 8
Baseball, 78-89, 86-91, 122, 133, 136-140, 142, 148, 160, 203, 213, 227, 233-235, 242
Basketball, 137-138, 204, 206, 209, 213, 232, 244, 249
Beamon, Bob, 248, 250
Bearbaiting, 225
Bedford Stuyvesant, 252
Beecher, Catherine, 197
Beisser, Arnold R., 212

Belgium, 131
Bellefontaine, Ohio, 82
Belmont, August, 53
Bennett, Jamesbordon, Jr., 57
Betting. *See* Gambling
Beverley, Robert, 3, 8
Bibb, Henry, 39
Bible, 161-162
Bicycling, 90, 199, 203, 227
Biddle, Anthony J., 121, 123
Big Ten Conference. *See* Intercolle-
    giate sports
Billiards, 9
Bingham, Thomas, 107
Black, Julian, 160
Blackburn, Jack, 160
Black Muslims. *See* Nation of Islam
Black Panthers, 177, 241, 251
Black Power, 174, 250, 253
Blacks. *See* African-Americans
Blood sports, 225
Blue laws, 107
Blumen, Elsa Von, 90
B'nai B'rith, 255
Bondsmen. *See* Slavery; Slaves
Boston, 63, 152, 171
Boston, Ralph, 250
Boston Braves, 109
Boston Celtics, 214
Boucha, Henry, 232
Bouton, Jim, 244
Boxing, 95-129, 133, 137, 142,
    145-162, 169-174, 203, 254, 256-
    258
Boxing Board of Control, 121
Boys Clubs of America, 135
Braddock, James, 164
Brady, Diamond Jim, 109
Brady, William, 101
Brennan, Bill, 123
Breslin, Jimmy, 170
Brigham Young University, 241
Bristed, Charles Astor, 55

Bristed, John, 58
Britt, Jimmy, 108
Broadway Athletic Club, 103
Broadway Sporting Club, 113
Brooklyn, New York, 98
Brooklyn Dodgers, 107, 140
Brooklyn Society for the Prevention
    of Cruelty to Children, 113
Brooks, Charles F., 105
Brooks, Lillie Barrow, 161
Brown, Alexander, 101
Brown, H. Rap, 242, 248
Brown, Jim, 242
Brown, K. O., 110
Brown Bomber. *See* Louis, Joe
Brownsville, Ohio, 79
Brownsville, Texas, 151
Brumel, Valery, 247
Brundage, Avery, 240, 245, 248-
    249, 253
Brutus, Dennis, 255
Bryan, William Jennings, 149
Buckeyes of Findlay, 80
Buckley, Jim, 119
Buckley, William, 171
Buffalo, New York, 119
Bullocke, James, 11
Burgesses, House of, 3, 11
Burke, Walter, 133
Burnaby, Andrew, 7
Burns, Tommy, 148
Burton, Richard, 175
Buzzard Lope, 30
Byrd, William I, 9
Byrd, William II, 7-9

Cake walk, 32
California, 151, 171, 214
California, University of at Berke-
    ley, 241
Cambodia, 240
Camp, Walter, 228
Campanella, Roy, 140

Canadians, 145, 148
Canning, Curt, 244
Cannon, Jimmy, 170, 172, 177, 180
Capone, Al, 147
Cardgames, 5
Cards, 9
Carlos, John, 247-250
Carmichael, Stokely, 242
Carnegie Report, 208
Carnera, Primo, 160, 162
Carney, T. F., 98
Carpenter, George, 155
Carroll, Ted, 164
Carson, James, 38
Carter, Hodding, 258
Carter, Jimmy, 257-258
Carter, Robert, 7-8
Castro, Fidel, 165
Catholicism, 172
Catholics, 123, 135, 137
Caucasians, 146-152, 155-159, 163-164, 173-174, 177, 179-182
Cavett, Dick, 175
Cedarville, Ohio, 80
Central Park, 53
Chase, Canon W. S., 122
Chattanooga, Tennessee, 151
Cheyenne, 198
Chicago, 52, 102, 118, 134, 147, 151, 153-155, 173, 251
Chicago Defender, 243
Chicago Tribune, 152, 156, 174, 176-177
Chicago White Socks, 227
China, 240
Christian Century, 175
Christianity, 167, 170, 177, 229
Christmas holiday, 42
Churchill, Sir Winston, 52
Cincinnati, 152
Cincinnati Red Socks, 80-81
Circle Dance, 33
Civil Rights Act, 243

Civil rights movement, 129, 158, 166, 169, 174, 242-243, 248-253
Civil War, 25-26, 61-62, 78, 96, 147, 151, 156, 198
Clark, "Booby," 232
Clarke, Edward H., 201
Clay, Cassius. *See* Ali, Muhammad
Clayton, John, 10
Clergymen, 151
Cleveland, 134
Cleveland Browns, 242
Coaching, 245, 251, 253. *See also* Athletes
Cocke, Stephen, 14
Cockfighting 6, 9, 36
Codes Committee, 102
Cold War, 257-258
College athletics. *See* Intercollegiate sports
Collet, Wayne, 253
Collier's, 162, 202
Colorado, 151
Columbia University, 244
Comintern, 135
Communist International, Seventh World Congress of, 136
Communist Party of America, 129, 131, 135-142
Coney Island, 97, 100
Coney Island Athletic Club, 97-98, 101
Congressional Black Caucus, 252
Congress of Industrial Organizations, 130, 138-139, 158
Congress of the United States of America, 99, 152-155, 165
Connecticut, 155
Constitution Hall, 159
Cooke, R. S., 115
Corbett, James J., 98, 100-101, 104, 148, 150
Corneille, Marguerite, 104
Cosell, Howard, 175

Crain, Cal, 87
Croker, Richard, 99
Croquet, 91
Cross, Lave, 109
Cuba, 253, 256
Culpeper, Thomas Lord, 4
Curley, Jack, 117
Czechs, 131, 135

Dabney, Charles, 28
Dady, Michael J., 98
Daily Worker, 130, 137-141
Daley, Arthur, 176
Daley, Richard J., 173-174
Dallas, 206
Dallas Cowboys, 242, 251-252
Dancing, 204
Danes, 223-225
Darwinist theory, 226
Daughters of the American Revolu-
    tion, 159
Davis, Angela, 251, 255
Davis, Benjamin, 141
Davis, Howard, 256
Davis, Thomas, 11
Davis bill, 118
Dayton, Ohio, 152
Decoration Day, 82
DeGraff, Ohio, 86-87
Democrats, 98, 112, 120, 122
Dempsey, Jack, 121, 123, 146, 163,
    170, 172-173, 178
Denmark, 222-223
Dennis, Jim, 248
Department of Justice, 173
Department of Labor, 212
Detroit, 131-132, 162
Detroit Tigers, 114
Devery, Bill, 100-101, 104
Dice, 9
Didrickson, Babe, 206-207
Diggs, Charles, Jr., 252
Dill, William, 35

Dimaggio, Joe, 138-139
Dix, John A., 111
Dixon, George, 99
Doesserick, Charles, 119
Dooling, John T., 105
Dotson, Hayward, 244
Doubleday, Abner, 140
Douglass, Frederick, 40
Dundee, Johnny, 123
DuPre, Billy Joe, 251
Durand of Dauphine, 3-4, 7
Dwyer, Frank, 114, 117

Easter Baseball League, 108
Eastman, Monk, 99
Eaton, Ohio, 84
Ebbets Field, 113
Edgemere Country Club, 150
Edmonds, Shephard, 32
Edward J. Neil Memorial Award,
    165
Edwards, Harry, 231, 243-244, 245,
    248-250
Egypt, 239
Ehrenreich, Barbara, 196
Elites, 62
Empire Athletic Club, 96, 98
Encyclopaedia Brittanica, 123
England, 96, 104, 114, 222, 239,
    251, 254, 257
English, Deirdre, 196
Enlightenment, the, 222
Episcopalians, 102
Eppes, William, 14
Esquire, 175
Essayons, 79, 82
Ethnocentrism, 224
Europeans, 145, 220
Evans, Lee, 247-250
Exercising, 201-202

Fascism, 136, 159
Fairfield, Francis G., 53

Fairmount Athletic Club, 109-110, 119
Faney, John, 111
Fans. *See* Spectators
Farrell, Frank, 116
Federal Sportive Feminine Internationale, 205
Fedric, Francis, 39
Feldman, Charles, 102
Feminism, 129, 197, 199, 205, 209, 211, 212-215
Field Hockey, 203, 209
Field Hockey Association of the United States, 209, 213
Findlay, Ohio, 77, 85
Findlay Nine Spots, 89
Finland, 131, 222
Fishing, 33, 211
Fitzhugh, William, 6-7, 13
Fitzsimmons, William, 100-101, 148, 150
Fleischer, Nat, 153
Flood, Curt, 251
Florida State University, 252
Folklore, 79
Football, 102, 142, 199, 203, 214, 228-233, 241-242, 251-252
Forbes, Dave, 232
Forbes, Paul S., 53
Ford, Gerald, 178
Foreman, George, 177-178, 250
Fowle, Bentley, 197
Fowler, Gene, 122
France, 131, 195, 239
"Frank Merriwell," 229
Frawley, James J., 106, 111-112
Frawley Act, 106, 108, 111, 113, 116, 118-119
Frazier, Joe, 176-178
Freudian psychology, 157
Frick, Ford, 139
Fuchs, Emil, 116
Fulchur, Bill, 252

Galento, Tony, 159
Galimore, Ron, 258
Gallico, Paul, 163, 166, 210
Gallup Poll, 159, 165
Gambling, 9-10, 12-14, 36, 39, 122, 166
Games of the New Emerging Forces, 240
Gaming, 6, 10, 166
Gander pulling, 225
Gardner, John, 12
Gavin, William, 120
Gaynor, William, 98
Geertz, Clifford, 6
General Electric, 132
General Motors, 132
Genovese, Eugene D., 40-41
Gentlemen. *See* Virginia: gentry of
Georgia, 156, 176
Georgia Sea Island, 31
Georgia Tech, 252
Germantown, Ohio, 77, 84
Germany, 78, 135-136, 145, 159, 163-164, 251, 253
Ghana, 244, 254
Gibbons, Mike, 114
Gibbs, Leonard, 120
Gibbs bill, 120
Gibson, Billy, 119
Girl Scouts of America, 205
Gleason, Patrick G., 98
Glover, John, 35
Goebbels, Joseph, 163
Gold, Mike, 137
Goldbricking, 28
Golden Age of Sports, 124, 166
Golf, 201
Good Housekeeping, 211
Gould, Howard, 150
Graham, Mrs. Francis W., 122
Grangers, 81
Great Depression, 130, 138, 142, 158

Greece, 220, 222
Greeks, 194-195
Greenfield, Alf, 97
Grey, Zane, 79
Guinea, 240
Gymnastics, 203, 222, 258

Hackbart, Dale, 232
Haiti, 253
Hall, Basil, 27
Hamilton, Alexander, 56
Hamilton, James A., 56
Hammond, James H., 32
Hampton, Fred, 251
Harlem, 106, 135, 140, 141, 252
Harper's Bazar, 197
Harper's Weekly, 152
Hartly, John, 15
Hartwell, Josh, 230
Harvard Medical School, 201
Harvard University, 194, 244
Harvey, Charles, 119
Hawkins, Connie, 251
Hayden, William, 35
Hayes, Nicholas, 107
Haynie, John, 13
Hearst, Mrs. William Randolph, 162
Hecksher, John G., 95
Heenan, James, 96
Higgins, Frank, 106
Hilliard, Mrs. Issac, 28
Hitler, Adolf, 135, 160, 163, 164
Hoch, Paul, 231
Holidays, 40
Hollard, Tom, 27
Hollywood, 206
Hooks, Benjamin, 258
Hoover, Mrs. Herbert, 205
Hop Bitters, 82
Horseback riding, 211
Horsemen, 54-55
Horse racing, 10, 53, 63
Horseshoes, 91

Horton, George, 99
Horton Act, 99, 102, 103, 105, 110
House Armed Services Committee, 173
Household gambling, 9-10
House of Representatives of the United States, 219
House Subcommittee on Africa, 252
Houston, 173-174
Houston Striders, 248
Hughes, Charles Evans, 108
Humphrey, Joseph, 15
Humphries, Joe, 124
Hungarians, 132
Hunt, Davis, 195
Hunting, 33
Hurley bill, 119

Ice hockey, 224, 232
Id, 157
Idreat ideal, 223, 225
Illinois, 173
Illinois Athletic Commission, 173
Indentured servants, 4
Independence Day, 88
Indian tribes, 81
Indonesia, 240
Institute for the Study of Sport and Society, 215
Integration, 170
Intercollegiate sports, 209, 215, 228-230, 241, 244, 251
International Amateur Athletic Federation, 242
International Ladies Garment Workers Union, 138
International Olympic Committee, 240, 244-247, 250, 253
International Sporting Club, 121, 124
International Workers Olympics, 134
Iowa, 213
Iowa State University, 241

Iraq, 239, 240
Irish, 96, 107-109
Israel, 239, 254-255
Italians, 145
Italy, 159

Jackson, Merv, 249
Jackson, Nancy, 30
Jackson, Silas, 33
Jacktown, Ohio, 79
Jacobs, Mike, 162
Jaher, Frederic C., 61
Jamestown, Virginia, 3
Jazz Age, 156
Jeffries, Jim, 104, 147, 150
Jerome, Lawrence R., 54
Jerome, Leonard, 52
Jerome Park, 54
Jewish Defense League, 255
Jews, 131-132, 137, 241, 254-255
Jim Crow, 130, 139-140
Jockeys, 148
Johansson, Ingemar, 169
Johnson, Jack, 146, 148, 150-156,
    161, 163, 166, 169, 172, 174,
    178, 179-182
Johnson, Joseph H., 123
Johnson, Lyndon Baines, 243
Johnston, Jimmy, 113
Jones, Rev. Hugh, 10
Jordan, Vernon, 257
"Juba," 31
Julian, Martin, 101
Justice Department of the United
    States of America, 176

Kansas, University of, 241
Kazan, Elia, 175
Keating, Kenneth, 171
Kefauver Committee, 170
Kelley, Leroy, 242
Kelly, Paul, 99
Kempton, Murray, 171

Kennedy, James C., 98
Kennedy, John F., 147, 243
Kennedy, Robert, 147, 175
Kenner, Rodham, 15
Kentucky, 86
Kentucky Derby, 148
Kentucky House of Representatives,
    170
Kentucky State Senate, 173
Kerner, Otto, 173-174
King, Billie Jean, 213
King, Martin Luther, Jr., 149, 182,
    241-243
King Coronation Tournament, 114
Kirby, Gustavus, 108
Knickerbocker Athletic Club, 106
Knights of Columbus, 121
Korn, Henry, 180
Ku Klux Klan, 157

Labor Sports Union, 131-132, 134-
    137
Ladies' Home Journal, 204, 207
Lampard, Eric E., 51
Landry, Tom, 251
Lassman, Edward, 171
Latin America, 240, 243, 252
Lebanon, 239, 254
Lee, Mabel, 209
Leisure activities, 38. *See also*
    Sports, in America
Lenox Athletic Club, 101, 105
Leonard, Benny, 109, 123
Leonard, Sugar Ray, 256
Lewis, Dio, 197
Lewis, M. E., 101
Lewis bill, 102-103
Lewisohn, Jesse, 109
Lewiston, Maine, 171
Liberty Bowl, 252
Life, 175
Lima, Ohio, 82, 85
Lincoln, Abraham, 226

Lindbergh, Charles, 147
Lipsyte, Robert, 175-176, 231
Liston, Sonny, 169-170, 182
Literary Digest, 163
Little league, ix. *See also* Baseball
Locust Roots, 80
Loeb, William, 177
London, Jack, 148, 150, 152
Long, Billy, 116
Long Acre Athletic Club, 107
Look, 177
Lord, Franklin B., 116
Los Angeles, 169, 246, 259
Louis, Joe, 140, 146, 158-173, 177-182
Louisville, 152, 169
Luce, Henry, 175
Lynchings, 155, 159

McAshan, Eddie, 252
McCombs, Melvorne, 206-207
McCoy, Kid, 104
McCoy, Robert H., 149
McCue, Marty, 108, 119
McDonald, Young, 117
McFarland, Packey, 109, 114
McGary, Ethel, 210
McKane, John Y., 97-98
McKettrick, Dan, 117
Mackinaw, Michigan, 81
Mackinaw Base Ball Club, 81
McMahon, Jesse, 117
MacPherson, C. B., 234
Maddox, Lester, 175
Madison Square Garden, 96, 104-108, 112-116, 123-124, 176, 248
Maher, Peter, 100
Mahoney, Jeremiah, 137
Mailer, Norman, 175, 180
Maine, 152
Main Street Nine, 80
Major leagues. *See* Baseball
Malcolm X, 170, 182

Mali, 240
Manhattan Athletic Club, 97
Manhattan College, 241
Manhood, 146
Mann Act, 147, 153-154
Marble, Manton, 57
Marciano, Rocky, 169
Markus, Robert, 177
Marquis of Queensbury, 145
Marshall, William C., 114
Maryland, 155
Massachusetts, 155, 171
Mathews, Vince, 253
Mathewson, William F., 115
Memphis, Tennessee, 252
Metcalfe, Ralph, 255
Methodists, 32
Metropolitan Life, 132
Metropolitan Workers Soccer League, 132, 134
Mexico, 244-246
Miamisburg, Ohio, 77, 85, 87
Miami Valley, 77
Michener, James, 213
Michigan, 152, 213
Michigan, University of, 229
Michigan State University, 241, 251
Middle Ages, 201
Middle class, 227
Middle East, 243, 252, 254
Military Athletic League, 115
Miller, Lennox, 248
Millidgeville, Ohio, 82
Minnesota, 134
Minor, William J., 56
Mirror, 162
Miscegenation, 153, 155, 156-157
Miss America pageant, 207
Mississippi, 38
Missouri, 171
Mitchell, Bobby, 242
Mitchell, Charley, 97-98
Modell, Art, 242

Modocs, 81
Mormons, 241
Morrissey, John, 96
Morrow, Lance, 178
Moscow, 257. *See also* Soviet Union
Mosher, Clelia Duel, 205
Mottl, Ronald, 219, 232
Mottl bill, 232
Mount Victory, 86
Mulvoy, Mark, 232-233
Murdock, Steve, 247
Murphy, Charles Francis, 99, 109, 124
Murphy, Edward C., 98
Murphy, Frank, 164
Murray, Grace Peckham, 197

Nairobi University, 251
Napier, Robert, 11
Napoleonic Wars, 223
National Amateur Athletic Federation, 205, 208
National Association for the Advancement of Colored People, 172, 242, 251-252, 257
National Football League, 160, 231-232, 241-242
National Guard, 115
National Hockey League, 232
National Review, 174
National Sporting Club, 109
National Sports Club of London, 120
Nation of Islam, 170, 171, 173, 174, 176, 178
Navy Relief Fund, 165
Nazism, 159, 163-164
Negro. *See* African-Americans
Nevada, 152, 166
New Deal, 130, 140, 147, 158
New England, 62, 134

New Jersey, 119
New Left, 129, 130, 174
New Mexico, University of, 242
New Orleans, 151, 163
New Puritan Boxing Club, 98
New Right, 233
Newsweek, 175
Newton, Dick, 98-99
Newton, Huey P., 241
New York, 53, 59-62, 95-96, 101-107, 115, 119-120, 123, 129, 132-134, 139, 151, 155, 162-163, 169, 204, 248; clubs of, 63, 108; horse racing in, 63; population of, 57; reform in, 107; sportsmen of 54, 57; state senate of, 171-172; state supreme court of, 109, 175
New York, City College of, 114, 241
New York Athletic Club, 97, 108, 123, 241, 248
New York Athletic Commission, 173
New York Daily News, 166
New York Herald, 54, 148
New York Jets, 214
New York Mirror, 161
New York Morning Telegraph, 149
New York Post, 173
New York Sun, 99, 148
New York Times, 98, 110-111, 117-118, 149, 150, 174, 176, 214, 229
New York University, 241
New York World, 105
New York Yacht Club, 63
New York Yankees, 140, 244
New Zealand, 255-256
Nicholson, Francis, 4, 8
Nine-pins, 9
Nine Spots, 81
Nixon, Richard M., 241-242, 251-252, 255

North American Society for Sport History, ix
North Carolina, 35
Northup, Soloman, 31
North Vietnam, 240
North Vietnamese, 252
Northwestern University, 255
Nyerere, Julius, 258

Oakland, California, 151
Oberlin College, 215
Oblinger, Hugh, 90
Ohene-Frempong, Kwaku, 244
Ohio, 80, 155; small towns of, 80, 82-83, 84-87, 90; villages of, 79, 81
Ohio State University, 86, 241
Old Testament, 7
Olmsted, Frederick Law, 29
Olympic Games, 131, 134, 136-137, 160, 169, 194, 205, 239-259; in Berlin, 136; boycott of, 129, 136, 239, 243-253, 256-258; politics in, 239-255, 257-259; women in, 207-210
Olympic Project for Human Rights, 243, 244, 247, 248
Omaha, Nebraska, 149
Organization of African Unity, 243
Organization of American Historians, ix
O'Rourke, John H., 98
Orwell, George, 254
Outerbridge, Mary Ewing, 201
Owens, Jesse, 140, 160, 246, 249, 255

Paige, Satchell, 139
Pakistan, 240
Palace Athletic Club, 100
Palestine Liberation Organization, 254
Pan-American Exposition, 105

Panic of 1857, 53
Parham, Frazetta, 248
Pastime Athletic Club, 97
Pastimes, 81
Paterson, New Jersey, 149
Patten, Gilbert, 229
Patterson, Calvin, 252
Patterson, Floyd, 169, 170, 172
Pavlov, Sergei, 244-245
Pbitek, Okok, 251
Pegler, Westbrook, 163
Peloponnesian War, 221
Pender, Mel, 248
Pennsylvania, 155, 171
People's Voice, 140
Perenchio, Jerry, 176
Perkins, Don, 242
Pessen, Edward, 52, 60
Philadelphia, 63, 121, 151
Philadelphia Enquirer, 149
Physical education, 202-205, 208-210, 213, 215
Physical fitness, 226
Physicians, 196, 213
Pioneer Athletic Club, 119
Piqua, Ohio, 80
Piquet, 9
Pittsburgh, 134, 151-152
Pittsburgh Pirates, 140
Plain City, Ohio, 82
Plantation work, 39. *See also* Slavery
Plant-cutting riots, 5, 17
Plato, 195
Play, 78
Plimpton, George, 175
Plum Street Nine, 80
Police Athletic League, 200
Police Gazette, 99, 101-102, 105, 115
Pollack, Harry, 108
Polo Athletic Club, 106
Popular Front, 137, 139

Port Royal, South Carolina, 33
Portugal, 252
Powers, Patrick, 108, 116
Presbyterians, 80
Princeton University, 228
Prizefighting. *See* Boxing
Professional sports. *See* specific sport
Progressive Era, 147, 151
Protestants, 137, 227
Protestant work ethic, 45
Public School Athletic League, 133
Puerto Ricans, 252
Purdy, Samuel, 58
Puritans, 198
Put, 9
Putnam, Emily James, 195

Quarry, Jerry, 176
Quarter-horse racing, 5, 6, 14
Qui-nines, 81

Race relations. *See* America
Race riots, 168, 181, 241
Racism, 151, 153-155, 156, 160, 163-164, 170, 174, 177, 179, 240, 243, 248
Randolph, Leo, 256
Randolph, William, 14, 29
Raymond, Henry J., 53, 57
Reader's Guide to Periodical Literature, 207
Reagan, Ronald, 174
Real Estate Board of Trade, 123
Reconstruction, 147, 159
Reed, Willis, 251
Reno, Nevada, 150
Republicans, 105, 112, 117, 123, 242
Reserve Clause, 251
Reynolds, Quentin, 162
Rhodesia, 240, 244, 251-253, 255
Rickard, Tex, 124

Riding. *See* Horseback riding
Riess, Steven, 52
Riley, Con, 87
Ringers, 79
Ringling, John, 124
Ring Magazine, 162, 164
Ring shout, 32
Rivers, L. Mendel, 173
Robinson, Frank, 242
Robinson, Jackie, 140, 242, 253-254
Roby, Douglas, 247
Roddenberry, Seaborn A., 152
Rodney, Lester, 140
Roller derby, 213
Romans, 221
Roosevelt, Eleanor, 158, 165
Roosevelt, Franklin Delano, 158, 165
Roosevelt, Theodore, 102, 147-148, 152, 199, 219, 231, 233
Rough Rider, 219
Roxborough, John, 160-161
Rozelle, Pete, 241
Rugby, 228
Rumania, 224
Running, 90-91. *See also* Track
Russell, Bill, 244
Russians. *See* Soviet Union
Rustin, Bayard, 255
Rutgers University, 228
Ruth, Babe, 165
Ryan, Paddy, 97
Rynder, Isaiah, 96

St. Bartholomews Athletic Club, 106
St. John's University, 241
St. Louis, 151
St. Louis Post-Dispatch, 148
SALT II, 257
San Diego Chargers, 252
San Francisco, 95, 118, 151
San Francisco State University, 241
San Jose State University, 243

Saratoga Springs, 96
Sargent, Dudley Allen, 194, 198, 202
Sauer, George, 214
Sayers, Tom, 96
Scandinavia, 222
Schieren, Charles, 98
Schmeling, Max, 133, 160, 162, 164
Schram, Tex, 242, 251
Schulberg, Budd, 180
Scott, Jack, 215, 231
Scott, Jarvis, 249
Seabury, Samuel, 109
Seaside Athletic Club, 98
Selective Service System, 173, 176
Seltzler, Leo, 206
Semiprofessional sports. *See* Sports, in America
Sex roles, 193, 196-199, 201-214
Shamrocks, 81
Sharkey, Jack, 133
Sharkey, Tom, 100
Shecter, Leonard, 177
Sheed, Wilfrid, 177
Shooting, 211
Shortstop, 79
Show Corporation, 114
Skating, 196, 205
Slader, Mathew, 11
Slapsie Maxie's Curvacious Cuties, 206
Slaveholders, 27-28
Slavery, 8, 17, 25, 27, 34, 36, 38, 45, 196, 226
Slaves, 45, 131; activities of, 42; children of, 34; dancing of, 30, 31, 33; fishing of, 35; gambling of, 36, 39; games of, 39; gaming of, 33; hunting of, 34; pacified by sports, 43-44; quarters of, 35; wrestling of, 37
Slocum, 110

Smedes, Susan Dabney, 44
Smith, Al, 120, 123
Smith, John, 36
Smith, Red, 172
Smith, Tommie, 247-250
Soane, William, 11
Soccer, 134
Social clubs, 52. *See also* Athletic clubs
Socialism, 131, 136, 138
Socialization, 220
Social Security, 62
Softball, 205, 206
South Africa, 129, 240, 243-245, 251-256, 258
South America, 240
South Carolina, 29, 32, 35, 152, 155
South Dakota, 152
Southeast Asia, 243, 252
Southern plantations, 25-26, 32-33, 39, 41-42, 45; leisure time on, 44; work on, 45
Soviet Union, 139, 175, 178, 222, 224, 244-248, 254-259
Spalding, Albert Goodwill, 199, 227, 228
Spaniards, 132, 219
Spanish-American War, 228
Spanish Civil War, 137
Spartans, 195
Spaulding, Henry George, 33
Spectators, 129, 200, 213; violence of, 223, 224, 230, 233, 235
Spinks brothers, 256
Sport and Play, 135
Sports, in America, ix, 3, 25, 51, 77, 95, 129, 145, 193, 219, 239-241, 247, 251, 253; politics in, 95-129, 239-254, 257, 259; reform movement in, 95-129, 197-198, 203, 215, 233; violence in, 219, 222, 224-225, 229, 230-235

Sports for the People, 129, 235
Sports Illustrated, 175, 178, 213, 248
Sports Violence Act, 232
Sportswoman, 209-210
Spotswood, Alexander, 4
Springboro, Ohio, 81
Springfield, Illinois, 151
Springfield, Ohio, 81
Spring Valley, Ohio, 77, 82, 84
Spring Valley Boys, 82
Spring Valley Grays, 81
Stagg, Amos Alonzo, 229
Standard Oil, 132
Stanford University, 213
Star City Club, 81, 86
Stevenson, Teofillio, 256
Steward, John, 14
Stingley, Daryl, 232
Stokes, Carl B., 243
Stone, Gregory, 211
Stonewalls, 81
Stotesbury, Louis W., 115
Suez Canal, 239
Sukarno, President, 240
Sullivan, John L., 96, 145, 152, 178
Sullivan, Tim, 99, 102
Super Bowl game, 259
Supreme Council for Sport in Africa, 240, 243
Supreme Court of the United States of America, 168, 251
Sussman, Morton, 173
Sutherland, Bob, 98
Sutherland, Kenneth, 98
Sweden, 222-223
Swedes, 145
Swift, Jonathan, 147
Swimming, 206-207, 210
Switzerland, 131
Syracuse, New York, 129
Syria, 254

Tammany Hall, 96, 99, 101, 109, 120, 122
Tanzania, 258
Tate, John, 256
Tatum, Jack, 232
Tavern contests, 9
Taylor, Elizabeth, 175
Tennis, 201, 213
Terman, Lewis M., 211
Terrell, Ernie, 172
Texas, 152, 204
Texas, University of at El Paso, 241
Thatcher, Margaret, 257
Third Reich, 164
Third World, 179, 239-241, 244, 250, 252-256, 259
Thomas, Dwayne, 251-252
Tiffany, Charles L., 56
Tighe, James T., 97-98
Time, 163, 170, 172, 174, 177
Title IX, 213-214
Tobacco, 13
Tocqueville, Alexis de, 51
Today's Health, 210
Tokyo, Japan, 239
Tomjanovic, Rudy, 232
Track, 160, 203, 247-250, 253-254
Trade Union Athletic Association, 138
Triangle Shirtwaist Factory fire, 110
Troy, Ohio, 77, 79
Troy Baseball Club, 79
Trumball, John H., 141
Truth, Sojourner, 196
Tunney, Gene, 109, 133, 164, 173
Turfmen, 52, 56, 61
Twain, Mark, 226
Twentieth Century Athletic Club, 110
Twin Valley Club, 81
Twist, Kid, 99
Tyus, Wyomia, 249-250

Uganda, 254
Uncle Ben, 35
Uncle Tom, 160, 166, 172
Underwood, John, 233
Union Club, 61, 63-64
Unitarians, 33
United Arab Republic, 240
United Autoworkers Union, 138
United Nations, 252
United Nations Security Council,
    244
United Society of Christian En-
    deavor, 152
United States Amateur Athletic
    Union, 247
United States House of Representa-
    tives, 163
United States Olympic Committee,
    246-247, 249-250
Urbana, Ohio, 82
Urbanization, 78
Urban League, 257
Utah, 152
Uticas, 81

Vanderbilt, Gloria, 175
Vanderbilt, William K., 96
Vanderbilt, William K., Jr., 150
Van Deusen, John G., 165
Van Hook, John F., 34
Veterans, 171
Veterans of Foreign Wars, 173-174,
    177
Victorians, 202, 204, 227
Viet Cong, 173
Vietnam, 240
Vietnam War, 168, 182, 231, 233,
    243
Virginia, 151, 155, 163; cash crops
    of, 4, 9, 15; gentry of, 3-4, 6-11;
    gentry competitiveness of, 17;
    gentry gambling of, 5-6, 14-17;

gentry gaming of, 5, 9, 12, 15;
    slavery in, 5, 8
Volkes, Fred, 90
Voting Rights Act, 243

Wagering. See Gambling
Walker, Jimmy, 118, 121
Walker bill, 121-123
Wallack, J. Lester, 53
Wall Street, 53
Wall Street Journal, 253
Ward, Gene, 176
Ward, Richard, 14
Washington, D.C., 151, 159, 252,
    258
Washington, Herb, 251
Washington, Kermit, 232
Washington, University of, 241
Washington Redskins, 242
Wayman, Agnes R., 208
Weekly Jeffersonian, 84, 89
Weeks, Barton S., 108
Weight lifting, 214
Weismantel, John, 113
Weiss, Paul, 210
Wenck, Fred A., 114, 116
West Carollton, Ohio, 86
West Indians, 135
Westinghouse, 132
West Liberty, Ohio, 77, 82, 85
West Liberty Banner, 84, 89
West Liberty Club, 83
West Virginia, 151
Whist, 9
White, John, 116
White Citizens' Council, 174
White House, 164, 178, 251
Whites. See Caucasians
Whitfield, Mel, 239-240
Whitman, Charles S., 112, 116-117
Wilberforce University, 243
Wiling, Joe, 123

Wilkes' Spirit of the Times, 53
Willkie, Wendell, 165
Willard, Jesse, 156
Willbanks, Green, 43
Williamsburg, Virginia, 9
Williamson, Stryker, 98
Wills, Helen, 206
Wilmington, Delaware, 152
Wilmington, Ohio, 85
Wilson, Wash, 32
Wilson, Woodrow, 151
Wirth, Louis, 51
Wolf, David, 251
Wolfenstein, Martha, 206
Wolgast, Ad, 110
Women athletes, 194-195, 205-206, 208, 210-215
Women of the Christian Church, 85
Women's Christian Temperance Union, 122
Women Sports, 213
Women's Swimming Association of New York, 207, 210
Women's World Games, 207
Woodstock, Ohio, 85, 176
Working class, 131-132, 135-136, 142, 151, 196, 198, 212
World, 97

World Boxing Association, 171-173
World Labor Athletic Carnival, 137
World Series, 133, 139
World War I, 146, 156, 158, 165, 202-204
World War II, 147, 159, 165, 173, 179, 211-212
Wrestling, 37, 225-226
Wright, Richard, 141
Wright, Stan, 246, 253-254
Wurster, Fred, 100

Xenia, Ohio, 77, 85

Yale University, 114, 210, 228-229
Yankee Stadium, 162
YMCA, 121, 130, 132, 214
Yost, Fielding, 229
Young Americans, 80
Young Communist League, 130, 132, 134-135, 136, 138-139
Young Worker, 130, 132-133
Yugoslavia, 253

Zanesfield, Ohio, 84
Zeus, 194
Ziegfeld, Florenz, 109, 206
Zionism, 254-255

About the Contributors

MELVIN L. ADELMAN received his Ph.D. (history) from the University of Illinois at Urbana-Champaign. He has written several scholarly articles and has been a frequent contributor to the *Journal of Sport History*. He is currently Assistant Professor in the Department of Physical Education and Recreation at Ohio State University. He teaches a course in sport history.

CARL M. BECKER received his Ph.D. (history) from the University of Cincinnati. He is widely published in the field of Regional and Community History. Becker is currently Chairman and Professor of History at Wright State University, and teaches sport history.

T. H. BREEN received his Ph.D. (history) from Yale University. He is the author of several books and numerous articles and specializes in the History of Colonial America. Breen is currently Professor of History at Northwestern University.

RICHARD H. GRIGSBY is a graduate student in the Department of History at Wright State University.

FREDERIC COPLE JAHER received his Ph.D. (history) from Harvard University. He is one of the nation's foremost authorities on recent U.S. History and has authored and edited many books and has contributed widely to scholarly journals. He is currently Professor of History at the University of Illinois at Urbana-Champaign. He teaches a course in the history of sport.

PETER LEVINE received his Ph.D. (history) from Rutgers University. He has authored a book and has written many scholarly articles. He specializes in nineteenth-century American Social History and is currently Associate Professor of History at Michigan State University. He teaches a course in the history of sport.

MARK NAISON, Ph.D. (history) from Columbia University, is a specialist in Afro-American History. He is the author of a book and several learned articles. Naison is Chairman of the Board of Sports For The People, a sports and recreational advocacy group based in the South Bronx. He is currently Associate Professor of Afro-American and Urban Studies at Fordham University. He teaches a course in sport history.

STEVEN A. RIESS, Ph.D. (history) from the University of Chicago, is the author and editor of two books and has published many scholarly articles. He is editor of the *Journal of Sport History*. Riess specializes in the History of the Progressive Era and is currently Professor of History at Northeastern Illinois University. He teaches a course in sport history.

DONALD SPIVEY received his Ph.D. (history) from the University of California at Davis. He specializes in recent U.S. and Afro-American History and is the author of two books and many professional articles. Spivey is currently Associate Professor of History at the University of Connecticut. He teaches a course in the history of sport.

STEPHANIE L. TWIN received her Ph.D. (history) from Rutgers University. She is the author and editor of several books and has written a number of important scholarly pieces in the field of sport history.

PETER VINTEN-JOHANSEN received his Ph.D. (history) from Yale University. He is the author of several important articles and reviews and specializes in Modern European History. Vinten-Johansen is currently Associate Professor of History at Michigan State University.

DAVID K. WIGGINS received his Ph.D. (history of sport) from the University of Maryland. He has published several scholarly essays and is a contributor to the *Journal of Sport History*. He is currently Associate Professor in the Department of Health, Physical Education and Recreation at Kansas State University. He teaches a course in sport history.

WITHDRAWN
LIBRARY
MOUNT SAINT MARY'S COLLEGE
EMMITSBURG, MARYLAND

About the Editor

DONALD SPIVEY is Associate Professor of History at the University of Connecticut, Storrs. He is the author of *Schooling for the New Slavery: Black Industrial Education, 1868–1915* (Greenwood Press, 1978), and editor of *Union and the Black Musician*. His articles have been published in the *Journal of Negro History, Social Science Quarterly, History of Higher Education Annual, Chronicles of Oklahoma,* and *Phylon.*